*The*Election

Result:

May 1, 1997

Labour 419
Con. 165
Lib-Dem. 46
Others 29
───────
659

Majority 179 !

The **Election**

A Voters' Guide

Edited by
Martin Linton

FOURTH ESTATE • *London*

First published in Great Britain in 1997 by
Fourth Estate Limited
6 Salem Road
London W2 4BU

Martin Linton is a psephologist, a political reporter on the *Guardian*
and the prospective Labour candidate in the Battersea constituency.

1 3 5 7 9 10 8 6 4 2

A catalogue record for this book is available from the British Library.

ISBN 1-85702-513-X

Typeset by Type Technique, London W1
Printed in Great Britain by Clays Ltd, St Ives plc, Bungay, Suffolk

CONTENTS

PART TWO · POLICIES

THE STATISTICS

PART THREE   ELECTIONS

Research: Laurence Neville, Jane Mulholland, Stuart Millar and Stephen Lyle
Constituency profiles and lists: Julie Rowbotham and Bernardette Flynn

ACKNOWLEDGEMENTS

This guide was produced by the *Guardian* editorial department, the *Guardian* library and a number of outside researchers. The constituency profiles and lists were prepared by Julie Rowbotham, Bernardette Flynn and their colleagues in the *Guardian* library. Research was carried out by Laurence Neville, Jane Mulholland, Stuart Millar, Stephen Lyle, James McCarthy, Anupma Parihar, Mitchell Kaye and others. The notional results of the 1992 election on the new boundaries and the votes-into-seats table are based on the work of Colin Rallings and Michael Thrasher for the *Media Guide to the New Parliamentary Constituencies* published by the Local Government Chronicle Information Centre for BBC, ITN, PA News and Sky. The policies of the parties were prepared with the help of Andrew Cooper of the Conservative party, Margaret Mythen of the Labour party and Neil Stockley of the Liberal Democrats. Opinion poll figures are from ICM, MORI and Gallup. The proofs were read by Judith Attar.

INTRODUCTION

Hugo Young

The fifth general election in this Conservative era has had the longest build-up of any British election in modern times. The politics of the last twelve months, perhaps two years, has been almost entirely devoted to pre-electoral jockeying. From a governmental point of view, this was neither edifying nor effective. Sterility ruled, and cynicism burgeoned. But for the process of democracy, it has been useful. It shaped the ground for everyone to understand.

The campaign will surely contain surprises. The best of them were crafted months ago, with a countdown to the very day when the spin masters want them to break. Dirty tricks will abound, and the tabloid press will do its best to take over the agenda, with television following lamely behind. But the voters are better defended this time. They've had more chance to take a reading on what this election is all about. Not only are they more secure, it's likely that more than usual have already made up their minds.

The choice means a lot more than fashion, perhaps jaded by these interminable preliminaries, tends to say. The most prominent feature of the two-year run-up may have been Labour's repositioning as the party that rejected socialism, but the choice is still decipherable as one between left and right. In that choice, Labour and the Liberal Democrats stand in the same segment of the left, and for this purpose can be treated together. Tactical voting will matter in at least 50 seats. It may have a bigger impact than ever before – another consequence of the slow education of the people. The Lib Dems' performance could yet determine what sort of government emerges into the light of another five years. But, in the broad, this is a left-or-right decision. It is, in other words, the old choice in new clothing. It revolves around two great issues: the two phenomena, in fact, which are at the heart of most politics in time of peace. The nation. And the state.

The State

The left still believe in the role of the state. The state as enabler, as back-drop, as safety-net, as benign facilitator of the idea of community, has not been excluded from the revisionist discourse of Tony Blair. On the contrary, it is at the heart of what Blair believes Labour stands for. The state infuses most of the specifics the left are putting forward. What Gordon Brown has to say about unemployment speaks for an undiminished faith in state power, allied with private money. What Labour in general has to say about the health service and schools expresses an unashamed belief in the role of government, which in real millennial life will matter more than Labour's evasions over renationalising the railways.

The right, if they win again, will have a dramatically opposite tendency. Their incursions on government power may have been smaller than Margaret Thatcher wanted, but if they win, after being so widely predicted to lose, their anti-government tendencies will become much clearer. In the Tory party the debate about something called minimal government is already lively. If John Major gets back against all the odds, one may be sure the benches behind him will push further and faster in that direction than their manifesto dares propose.

This left-right choice seems to me quite real. It is not invented, and it transcends the cloudy softenings which both sides would like to apply to it. It has particular meaning on the vanguard issue of tax. Gordon Brown has spent years trying to strip Labour of its reputation as the party of tax-and-spend, and he sincerely means it. Labour will be exceedingly cautious about raising any form of tax except as a signal against the highest paid fraction. But Labour believes in the state and therefore, at the edge, is more tolerant of state spending than the Tories who have watched it rise so sharply under their stewardship. It is unimaginable that a Labour government will attack state power in the way a re-elected Conservative government will try to do.

The Nation

The right believe in nation with sharper zeal than the left. The left make obeisance to nation, and are much concerned to avoid being tagged as anti-British. But the left parties favour a different sort of structure for nation, and are infused by a different appreciation of what nation – the British nation – any longer needs to mean. This is most visible over Europe. Europe will enter the campaign, despite the plentiful evidence that the public is not primarily concerned about it. The Europe debate has become a debate about nation, and during the next few weeks Labour, though not the Lib Dems, are determined not to be outflanked by nationalist rhetoric. But in power it will be a different story. The left do not attach such importance to the emblems of national sovereignty as the right. Vote for the left, therefore, and you vote for a different attitude to sovereignty conflicts from that which has prevailed since 1992.

But nation reaches more deeply into the argument. It's the focus of the clearest divide between left and right: over constitutional reform. The left believe in, and will legislate for, a new shape of nation: a different second chamber, a half-separated Scotland and Wales, a new legal framework based on the European Convention on Human Rights. These, if they make it into law, portend radical change. They are rejected by almost all Conservatives: a blessed island of concord in the Tory civil war over Europe. They sincerely appal the Conservative leader, who thinks he won in 1992 by saying so. Because these changes would be permanent, not reversible – unlike, say, an economic crisis or a tax increase – they fire the Tory soul. They will get some people out of their chairs, and possibly out of their near-terminal disgust at some of the things the Tory Government in its 18 years has done.

That will be another matter in the public mind as we reach the climax. The simple matter of fair play will goad some, perhaps many, of the British towards the notion that the other chaps should have a chance, especially now that they appear so harmless, so unlikely to disturb a status quo which still, for all the pessimism at large, works well for the vast majority of the electorate. This pessimism is important. From the challengers' viewpoint, it's the most dangerous virus in the body politic. A belief in what governments can do is, at some level, the essential prerequisite for the success of the left, whose leader is passionately committed to that proposition himself. If people don't believe things can change for the better, why should they rouse themselves to vote for change at all?

Sheer longevity brings some answers to that. At the back, perhaps the front, of the voters' minds are bound to be memories of its consequences: the episodic corrupting of an uncorrupt politics, the systemic perversions revealed by the Scott Report, the mixture of fatigue and presumption that has manifestly overcome some of the ministers whose prime of life was spent in the seats of power. This, however, won't be the only thing worth voting about. Appearances sometimes to the contrary, there's a real decision to be made. The end of socialism is not the end of choice. Choice has been redefined, but it still matters greatly. Both the nation and the state, I believe, will have a different kind of future, depending on what the voters, after this long time of brooding, decide. ●

PART ONE

POLITICIANS

LEADERS

THE CVs

Name: John Roy Major

Personal Details

Born: 29 March 1943.
Parents: Thomas Major-Ball, owner of garden ornament works, former music hall impresario, one-time acrobat; and his second wife Gwendolin (née Coates), former chorus girl. One elder brother, Terry Major Ball, and an elder sister, Pat.
Childhood: Brought up in semi in Worcester Park, Surrey. Father sold company in 1955 to pay off debt and moved family into flat in Coldharbour Lane, Brixton, for four years.
Marital status: Married Norma Elizabeth Christina (née Johnson), 3 October 1970.
Children: James, 21, assistant manager at Marks and Spencer in Milton Keynes; Elizabeth, 25, a veterinary nurse.
Nickname: Comeback Kid.

Education

Schools: Cheam Common primary school. Won scholarship to Rutlish Boys' Grammar in Wimbledon. Left at 16.
Qualifications: Three O-levels.

Employment History

First job: Clerk at Price Forbes in City of London.
Start of career: Left desk job to become 'industrial sculptor' for Davids' Rural Industries. Unemployed for nine months in 1962, turned down for job as bus conductor after failing dexterity test. After spell with Electricity Board, joined District Bank, then moved to Standard Bank of West Africa, later to become Standard Chartered.
Mishap: Lost knee-cap and broke left leg in a car accident in Nigeria.

Political Career

Formative experience: Met Brixton's Labour MP Sir Marcus Lipton who showed him round Commons; joined Young Conservatives in 1960.

First position: Elected Tory councillor in Lambeth in 1968; became youngest housing committee chairman in Lambeth's history in 1969.

Greasy pole: Failed to win St Pancras North in 1974, but won Huntingdon for Tories in 1979; junior whip 1983; junior social security minister 1986; Minister of State for Social Security 1986; Chief Secretary to the Treasury 1987; Foreign Secretary 1989; Chancellor 1990; Prime Minister 1990.

Skills

Dogged fighter; diplomacy and interpersonal skills.

Weaknesses

Incoherent political views; grey public image.

Personal Interests

Reading; cricket; music, especially opera.

Name: Anthony Charles Lynton Blair

Personal Details

Born: 6 May 1953.

Parents: Upwardly mobile Edinburgh couple – Leo, a barrister and former secretary of the Scottish Young Communist League turned Conservative activist; and Hazel, a socially conscious housewife and mother. One elder brother, Bill, a QC, and a younger sister, Sarah, also a lawyer who works in legal publishing. Family shares a tradition of entertainment with John Major – his middle names, Charles Lynton, are a reminder of his music hall grandfather.

Childhood: Brought up in a modest bungalow in Edinburgh's Paisley Terrace and then in the precincts of Durham Cathedral after Leo secured a job as a law lecturer in the city. Father converted to Conservatism and supported the Thatcher revolution.

Formative experience: Developed strong religious beliefs aged 12 after father's stroke, which rapidly changed the financial position of the family.

Marital status: Married Cherie Booth in 1980, who retained her maiden name and took silk at Lincoln's Inn in 1995.

Children: Euan, Nicholas and Kathryn, all still at school.

Nicknames: Bambi until he took on the left, Stalin thereafter.

Education

Schools: The Choristers School in the grounds of Durham Cathedral – remembered for his 'impish smile'. Played cricket and rugby for the first teams. Stood as a Tory in a school mock election in 1966. Started to board at Fettes College in Edinburgh.

Qualifications: Studied for A levels at Fettes and won a place at St John's, Oxford, to read law.

Formative years: Suffered under a fagging regime at Fettes. Apparently uninterested in politics at Oxford, spending more time acting and being lead singer with a band called Ugly Rumours.

Employment History

First job: Worked as a barman and waiter in Paris for a year before going to Oxford.

Career move: Called to the Bar, 1976; joined the Chambers of Alexander Irvine QC where Cherie Booth was working.

Political Career

Formative experience: Irvine was a considerable influence on Blair's interest in politics. Only decided his future lay in politics after Thatcher's win in 1979 and a visit to Westminster with Tom Pendry, Labour MP for Stalybridge & Hyde.

First position: Elected MP for Sedgefield in 1983.

Greasy pole: Failed to gain nomination as a candidate for Hackney Borough Council. Came third in the Beaconsfield by-election in 1982. Became a frontbench spokesman on relations with the City in 1984.

Skills

Meticulous preparation for parliamentary questions; powerful oratory skills; determination and success at changing the Labour status quo.

Weaknesses

Perspective on 'grassroots' politics, which focuses on middle England rather than Labour itself, could threaten party stability after the election. Penchant for mentors – Mandelson, Irvine, Roy Jenkins, Peter Thompson, the Australian priest and Blair's spiritual guide to the election – may also provoke conflict.

Personal Interests

Committed Christian; squash, tennis and swimming.

Name: Jeremy John Dunham ('Paddy') Ashdown

Personal Details

Born: 27 February 1941.
Parents: John Ashdown, lieutenant-colonel in the Indian Army, and a lapsed Catholic from the south of Ireland; and Lois (née Hudson), a Northern Ireland Protestant.
Childhood: Born in New Delhi, India. Family returned in 1946 and bought a 1,000-pig farm in Ulster, which foundered in 1957.
Marital status: Married Mary Jane Donne (née Courtenay), 10 February 1961.
Children: Simon, 29, a rock musician; Katherine, 31.
Nicknames: Action Man, Paddy Climbdown, Paddy Pantsdown.

Education

Schools: Garth House prep school and Bedford School (where he was tagged 'Paddy').
Higher education: Hong Kong Language School 1967-70 – gained First Class Interpretership in Chinese.

Employment History

First job: Royal Marines captain 1959-71 on active service with commando units in Far East, Middle East and Belfast; commanded unit of Special Boat Service in Far East.
Career move: First Secretary to UK Mission (Foreign Office) to UN in Geneva 1971-76; moved to Westland Helicopters in Yeovil in 1976. Youth officer with Dorset County Council 1981-83.

Political Career

Formative experience: Eyes opened to excitement of ideas by two socialist teachers at Bedford School – Labour supporter until 'In Place of Strife' convinced him party was beholden to trade unions. Joined Liberal party in 1975.
First position: 'Made crazy, irresponsible, naive decision' to give up diplomatic career. Failed to win Yeovil in 1979, but succeeded in 1983.
Greasy pole: Liberal spokesman on Trade and Industry 1985-87; spokesman on Education and Science 1987-88; leader Social and Liberal Democrats 1988-89.

Skills

Skilled orator; constantly developing innovative ideas; charismatic; ability to fend off armed attackers.

Weaknesses
Slightly condescending manner; tendency to seize the moral high ground.

Personal Interests
Gardening, classical music, hill walking, wine making.

Most Glowing Tribute
'...the only party leader capable of killing Norman Tebbit with one blow while conversing in Mandarin.' Andrew Rawnsley, the *Guardian*.

MAJOR, BLAIR AND ASHDOWN

Michael White

When it finally comes, it is going to be a very rough general election campaign. One in which the nation's wholesome party leaders will not hesitate for long before letting their acolytes say or do whatever they judge to be necessary to attain the power that each believes to be his due. Yet some of the most enduring images of the past year are much less abrasive. There is the spectacle of John Major and Tony Blair, sombre and besuited, as they walked together through Dunblane in the wake of Thomas Hamilton's massacre. 'Tony and I,' the prime minister said, more than once, as if this was a commonplace occurrence outside the stylised formalities of Remembrance Sunday.

We know too that Paddy Ashdown sometimes rings the Labour leader's office to make sure that his rival in the coming fight for Tory marginals is not going to pursue the same line at prime minister's question time later in the day. One Tuesday last June Ashdown even took up cudgels in defence of Blair's wife against attack from Tory HQ. Old-fashioned gallantry notwithstanding, it is also certain that the civility is reciprocated. Prime Minister Blair would be quite content, eager even, to co-operate with the Liberal Democrat leader if the election numbers so dictated.

What does this tell us about those leaders? Or about the state of the nation's politics almost two decades after Margaret Thatcher's free-market radicals seized control of the creaking social democratic state Clem Attlee and his heirs struggled so mightily to create between 1945 and 1979? Cynics and reformers, nihilists and sophisticated post-modernists, none of them in short supply, will say that it shows that the main parties are all but hand-in-glove to share what remains of the spoils of a decayed political system. That, past ideological passions all exhausted, they are gripped by a feeble Thatcherised consensus in which the capacities of government to change anything are not thought very great.

Above all, that it doesn't matter which of them runs the country, because financiers like George Soros, supra-national politicians like Helmut Kohl, or the soaring GNP of South Asia – the second wave of Asian industrialisation – will really determine our collective European fate as the millennium approaches. 'One day they will only want to buy our wine and our cheese, and at prices they dictate,' as a gloomy German SPD official once put it. There is validity in every jibe, but not too much. Besides, they represent the counsels of despair. Australian leftists who say there may not be more than an inch of difference between their own parties – 'but it's an inch worth fighting for' – are making a more wholesome judgement. Even so romantic a political exile as John Redwood will probably offer the same defence of Major before the campaign is over. A more generous assessment might conclude that there is a compatibility of temperament between the three party leaders, all dutiful family men, born between 1941 and 1953, in varying degrees –

significantly varying – children of the great post-war surge in prosperity.

Just so, there is a compatibility in the policy programmes they will offer the electorate, very different from dispatch box battles barely a decade ago. You cannot imagine Thatcher and Foot going to Dunblane together, or Roy Jenkins ringing Neil Kinnock's office. Let alone an Owenite, ex-SDP apparatchik like Danny Finkelstein, however bright, being appointed research director of either main party. Yet he became Major's man. But those propositions do not amount to neo-Butskellism in policy terms, a revival of notions of so-called consensus in the 1950s when R.A. Butler and Hugh Gaitskell were supposed, or so the *Economist* quipped, to agree on everything. It was never much more than a posh joke, even then. Now as then, New Labour's instincts remain more interventionist, more proactive, more statist, however much its activism is clothed in the language of managed markets and of community, European Community included. They embrace the market, but they wish to steer it. 'Steering, not rowing,' as the American revisionists say.

As for the personalities, there again sharp differences and antagonisms remain. Since only the very naive or disingenuous believe that a politician's personality does not greatly affect his policies (Tony Benn himself is a perfect illustration of the very point he seeks to dismiss), a Blair premiership will make itself felt very quickly. As the Labour leader put it, not for the first time, in his devolution speech in Edinburgh in June 1996, 'I do not intend to lead this country like John Major has done. If there are arguments to have, I will have them. If there are decisions to be taken, I will take them. And I will take them in the interests of the country.' Does that sound vaguely familiar? You bet. There is a Thatcheresque self-certainty at the centre of Blair's public personality. That is not to say he does not have private doubts. Who would not when facing up to the prospect of becoming the youngest prime minister since Lord Liverpool, who succeeded the (uniquely) assassinated Spencer Percival in 1812? He was just 42.

As has been noted, the Labour leader likes to surround himself with gurus – Peter Thompson, his Oxford-and-Oz vicar, Derry Irvine, QC, his pupil-master, Gordon Brown, his erstwhile mentor, Peter Mandelson, his personal spin physician, Alastair Campbell, the sorcerer's turbulent apprentice. Thatcher too had a court. As her memoirs reveal she even had doubts, though she hid them well enough at the time. But at bottom Tony Blair despises John Major for the same reason Lady Thatcher has come to despise him. He thinks the prime minister is a trimmer, who bends with every passing breeze which comes to blow his Cabinet off course. 'The difference between us,' he told Major one question time, 'is that I will not buckle under pressure.' This is Blair as Conviction Politician: the Laddie's Not for Turning.

What about Major, what does he think? Looking across the dispatch box, he surely sees a middle-class, public school smoothie, all style and no substance. He sees the kind of condescension in his manner which so irritated the teenage Major, already a politics junkie, when he heard the local Labour MP, Colonel Marcus Lipton, in Brixton in the fifties. 'Feudal,' the thin-skinned future premier once called it. He hates being patronised – one reason why Paddy Ashdown annoys him even more than Blair – with holier-than-thou challenges about bombing Bosnia, about

Hong Kong passports or extra money for education – pledges everyone knows the Lib Dem leader will never be called upon to honour. There are days when Major almost spits back at him in frustration.

Another of these middle-class do-gooders, what do they know about the real knocks of life? he seems to be asking. What about moving from suburban Worcester Park to Brixton for example, or leaving school at 16 with 3 O-levels and elderly parents to care for? It is pointless to say that Ashdown's adolescence was troubled by financial insecurity (his father's farm failed) and that, at 18, he joined the Royal Marines, not the Brigade of Guards. Or that Tony Blair's father, Leo, rose through his own efforts, from illegitimacy and adoption in Govan, through the army and the law to professional success in Durham; a Thatcherite paradigm of self-improvement, who was struck down by a heart attack as he prepared to find a Tory, yes Tory, seat.

That is an important moment in defining the Tony Blair voters now know. His family background may be as insecure as that of the gnome-making Major-Balls – how that gets jeered at by people who've 'never taken a risk in their lives,' Major tells audiences. But Blair survived family misfortune to scramble on to post-war Britain's meritocratic ladder, much as Thatcher and Heath had done, albeit from greater initial disadvantage. So in a different way did Ashdown, from the Marines to the FCO, though he was actually unemployed and near penniless when first elected in Yeovil in 1983. What adversity has given both of them, apart from the natural self-confidence of the system's winners, is an awareness that it is also easy to be one of the system's losers.

In Blair's case, facing the prospect that his father might die, it also seems to have cemented his teenage faith: for the first time since Sir Alec Douglas-Home briefly held the highest office, an increasingly godless Britain faces the prospect of a prime minister to whom going to church is a central part of his life, rather than a photo-opportunity or God-as-Focus-Group – to be polled informally about those trickier decisions.

Whether or not it is true that young Major lost a bus conductor's job to a jolly West Indian woman who had better maths, the prime minister has none of his rivals' reserves of self-assurance. What differentiates him from his genial brother, Terry, the anorak chat-show star, is a mixture of unheroic political tradecraft and that vital, energising chip on the shoulder. Major believes he inherited a very difficult legacy from Thatcher in 1990 ('No, you ruined it by taking us into the ERM during your chancellorship,' they cry back), won an election he was supposed to have lost in 1992 and has kept an increasingly fractious party in office – also against the odds – with a dwindling majority ever since.

Once a whip, always a whip. No-one ever accused John Major of having a strategic vision, but he has the tactical wiles of a Harold Wilson: Major as Tactical Opportunist, keeping the show on the road where better men would long since have failed. The Brixton boy may not have been to Oxford, but he has street-smarts and that priceless political asset – being underestimated – that keeps him in the game. There are even smart Tories who believe that Major tilts one way, then the other, on tax or Europe, precisely to keep the party off balance. 'See, you can't manage without me,' is the subliminal message. A classic example was his meeting and lavish praise for Chris Patten during his Far East trip in the spring of 1996. The media lapped up the story. The right was cross. Yet – thanks to uncharacteristic lack of Victorian foresight – Patten is obliged to stay in the Governor's cobwebbed mansion until 1 July 1997, after polling day.

So Britain enters what may prove a watershed election. On one side, the Government offers more of the same, a modified version of the Anglo-Saxon model, the harsh and restless vision of free-market individualism in which we all stand a chance of becoming seriously richer or seriously poorer. We might do well, we might get shot. It will be risky, but, odds on, it will be fun. On the other side, Blair offers something closer to the European model which Germans call social solidarity (so does Ashdown in a more Thatcherised economic mode). More collectivist, more concerned with society's more vulnerable members, more determined to create jobs, preferably in the manufacturing sector, the impulse is not simply retrospective or sentimental, the post-modern equivalent of William Morris's hunger for the pre-industrial past. It wants to work globally, live locally. Unfortunately, the phrase is Stephen Dorrell's.

The contest, when it comes, will be fought between three upwardly mobile members of Britain's increasingly fluid middle class, each emblematic in their way, each representative of someone's aspiration – or someone else's horror of the same. The fact that the least professionally mobile option is the Tory, the one who has nonetheless managed to be prime minister for almost as long as that dysfunctional cross-party aristocrat, Winston Churchill, is, well, par for the course. Likewise the likelihood of our first public school Labour premier for half a century. In our post-imperial mode, anything goes – as long as it wears slippers. ●

THE ALTERNATIVE GOVERNMENT

Patrick Wintour

Tony Blair already has the 'Big Four' or 'Big Five' with whom he intends to run his government, assuming May 1997 does finally bring the Labour victory that has so far eluded three Labour leaders and the brightest communications minds on the British left. Informally, he has agreed a group of four Cabinet members who will act as his political inner cabinet. They will be Gordon Brown, Donald Dewar, Jack Straw and Robin Cook. Informally, the voice of Peter Mandelson, likely to be a Cabinet Minister within two years, and Alastair Campbell, the Downing Street press secretary, will also be highly influential.

So far only two Shadow Cabinet members have been promised their current portfolios in government. Gordon Brown will be Chancellor. He has thought long and hard in opposition as to how he wants to run the Treasury and relate to the Bank of England and he has established the personal contacts needed in the financial markets of America and Brussels. Brown has his rivals and detractors in the Shadow Cabinet, some of whom believe he is over-sensitive to criticism and over-cautious, mixed attributes for a Chancellor. His personal relations with Blair deteriorated after they both ran for the party leadership following the sudden death of John Smith. There have been tensions, too, between the Blair and Brown camps, as well as more notoriously between Mandelson and Brown, largely arising from the scars of the Blair-Brown leadership bids, for which some of the Brown camp blame Mandelson for encouraging Blair into action. Brown, however, holds Blair's absolute political confidence and the economic policy of the Labour Government will fundamentally be his. His performance in government will be one of the true tests of Labour nerve.

The other man certain to walk into the Cabinet in his current post is David Blunkett, the Shadow Education and Employment Secretary and now one of the spiritual blood-brothers of Blair. Ever since Blair became leader, relations between the two men have become close, partly because they share the same un-Labour approach to social issues, including encouraging communitarianism. The Labour leader has publicly promised Blunkett that he will be charged with pushing through higher standards in Britain's state schools, an agenda to which Blair has tried to stick despite the controversy over grant-maintained schools and his decision to send one of his children to a GM school. Blunkett, a figure from the left, has often had to take the flak for Blair and has behaved with impeccable loyalty. He will be rewarded.

There is a strong feeling that the utterly reliable and self-parodying gloomy talents of Donald Dewar might be wasted as Chief Whip, but the rows over the referendum requirements before the creation of a Scottish Parliament, and the inevitable complexities of pushing such legislation through the Commons, may now make it essential that he stays in the Commons cockpit to push the changes through.

Robin Cook, the party's policy supremo and Shadow Foreign Secretary, is already preparing himself for an unlikely life in the diplomatic service. Not one of nature's bipartisans, Cook originally wanted to stay in a domestic economic brief, believing Britain no longer had an empire to rule, but he has now travelled assiduously, building contacts, and it might seem perverse in the extreme if he was not given the brief in government. But Cook would also be a sceptical presence in the Cabinet, questioning the wisdom of early British entry into economic and monetary union. If this is seen as a problem, an alternative Foreign Secretary might be Donald Dewar.

Questions have been raised about the political grip of Jack Straw, the Shadow Home Secretary. But he was Blair's campaign manager, shows an admirable attention to detail and shares Blair's instinctive qualms about the constitutional agenda. Straw's critics claim he has not shown a sure touch on crime, showing too much taste for socially authoritarian gimmicks, such as curfews for teenagers, at the expense of a more balanced approach. In Michael Howard he has faced one of the deadliest debaters, occasionally failing badly, as in the big set-piece debate on Howard's handling of the prisons policy. This has all led to one scenario in which Straw might be Chief Whip and Cook a libertarian Home Secretary suited to the constitutional agenda.

In the Lords, the line-up is more certain. Blair will rely on Lord Richards, as Leader of the House, and Lord Irvine, one of his oldest friends, as Lord Chancellor. Further down the Commons pecking order, George Robertson, the current Shadow Scottish Secretary, cannot expect to be moved out of his present brief, especially given the pounding he has to take over referendums.

The jokers in the pack remain the Liberal Democrats. Speculation persists, with solid reason, that Blair might be willing to contemplate some kind of relationship with Ashdown's party even if he wins a small overall majority at the next election. New Labour thinking is that Blair has more policy in common with the front rank of the Liberal Democrats than he has with the far left of the Labour party. If Blair is also serious about running a two-term government, some of his allies argue he needs a long-term stable relationship with the Liberal Democrats. Ashdown has not formally laid down his terms of trade with Blair, apart from some clear movement on proportional representation for the election to the Commons, but in the past his allies have argued that there must be two or three Cabinet posts for Liberal Democrats, as well as some junior ministerial posts.

The experience of the Lib-Lab Pact of 1977-78 shows the pitfalls of trying to support an administration from outside government, something David Steel tried with discomfort. If indeed Ashdown wants a fully fledged role for his party in a Liberal Democrat government, including Cabinet posts, this complicates Blair's Cabinet dispositions. The German model suggests Ashdown would like the Foreign Secretaryship – unlikely given the sensitivity of the negotiations with Europe over the Inter-Governmental Conference. The other options are the Department of Environment, a natural berth for a green party like the Liberal Democrats, or indeed the Home Office, a sensitive position given the importance of the constitutional agenda. Either way, Blair would face hostility from within his own party if he did try to make such a favourable deal with Ashdown. Besides Ashdown, Menzies Campbell is the most obvious Liberal Democrat candidate for a Labour Cabinet, possibly in the Defence post.

But much remains to be resolved, not least a restoration of trust between Labour and the Liberal Democrats, given the sense of betrayal many Liberal Democrats feel about the handling of the referendum issue by the Labour inner sanctum. ●

HUNG SCENARIOS

Rebecca Smithers

On the eve of the 1992 election, the polls made it look almost certain that Britain would have its sixth hung Parliament of the century. In the event, they got it wrong. The Conservatives coasted to victory. But the closeness of the polls prompted a useful analysis of the various scenarios that might have arisen if no party had won an overall majority. The most likely were a Conservative-Unionist alliance or a Lab-Lib coalition, but other combinations were possible, including Conservative-Nationalist, Labour-Nationalist, Labour-SDLP, Lab-Lib-Nat or a grand non-Conservative coalition. Now, as the polls get closer in the run-up to the election, the idea of a hung Parliament begins to look at least conceivable again and the parties, although they would not admit it publicly, are giving some thought to what they should do with any of the possible hands the voters might deal them.

The final disintegration of John Major's majority on 12 December 1996, when Jeff Ennis won the Barnsley East by-election for Labour, has concentrated minds on how a minority government might work. The last hung Parliament in Britain was in 1977, when James Callaghan and David Steel fixed up the Lib-Lab pact. Although during the 18 months of the pact the Liberals did not formally join the Government, they were consulted on every important issue at that time. This helped Callaghan survive for three years as the leader of a minority government – partly because the larger minority parties had an interest in seeing him survive – until he lost a vote of confidence in March 1979. That situation has changed and in many ways Major's position has been more vulnerable because it is really only the Ulster Unionists whose support has been guaranteed – and even then at a price. Rebel Tories nearly sank the Government's flagship Family Law Bill by siding with Labour, and there were many occasions when other planks of legislation were only saved after much behind-the-scenes arm twisting.

Commentators point out that one overriding factor that makes the prospect of minority government increasingly likely after the election is the growing fragmentation of the parties. Jittery Tory nerves have not been boosted by a study commissioned by former deputy party chairman Lord Archer, which concluded that Sir James Goldsmith's anti-EU Referendum party could 'turn any foreseeable Conservative overall majority into a hung Parliament … and any Labour landslide into a rout'.

Yet elsewhere the political spectrum has been made infinitely more lively by the arrival of new parties whose representatives are scattered in admittedly small quantities in the House of Commons. While there were only three parties represented in the Commons between 1922 and 1931, the number of parties represented in the Commons has been increasing and was nine after the 1992 election – more than in many supposedly 'multi-party' countries with proportional representation. Despite the fragmented opposition, the importance of these parties cannot be underestimated. With John Major's Commons majority gradually disappearing in the final months of the Parliament, it was the 13 Unionists (nine Ulster Unionists, three Democratic Unionists and one United Kingdom Unionist) who effectively held the balance of power during the latter stages by cushioning the majority.

With the Unionists their closest allies in the Commons, the Tories have ruled out any deals with any other parties. Paddy Ashdown, for his part, has ruled out a coalition with the Conservatives. Labour and the Lib Dems, who have been bedfellows in the past, have a more difficult relationship these days. Tony Blair, accused of 'sitting on the fence' on the issue of electoral reform, has refused to give Paddy Ashdown the commitment he has sought through a pre-election pact, which would agree the scope and best method of implementing constitutional reform. But New Labour thinking is that if Blair is to be guaranteed the two-term Parliament he is seeking to carry out his package of wide-ranging reforms, then he will have to work on a long-term stable relationship with the Lib Dems which could even lead to some Lib Dem posts in a Labour government.

Despite much broad agreement on policy areas between the two parties – where the Lib Dems have moved on to traditional Labour territory such as social policy (including a minimum wage and backing the EU's Social Chapter) – there remain some fundamental sticking points. The Liberal Democrats appear to be more left-wing than Labour on issues such as tax – where the party is committed to raising the top income tax rate to 50 per cent – and transport, where it would renationalise Railtrack.

With John Major firmly against devolution in Scotland or Wales, there is clearly no prospect of any deals with either the Scottish Nationalist Party – which wants nothing less than complete independence for Scotland through a separate Parliament – or Plaid Cymru. And Tony Blair has upset those within his party as well as stirring up the anger of the two Nationalist parties by appearing to back-track on devolution by leaving it up to the electorate to decide through referendums.

With the number of seats in the new House of Commons up from 651 to 659, thanks to the Boundaries Commissioners, the arithmetic of hung Parliaments has changed. The magic number that a party needs for an overall majority is no longer 326 but 330. A party with 330 seats has a majority of one; with 331 seats it has a majority of three, with 332 five, and so on. The number of seats in Northern Ireland is up from 17 to 18 and the various Unionist parties are expected to take 14. Working on the assumption that the Unionists would stick with the Conservatives but Labour, the Lib Dems and the Nationalists would all vote against, the figure that the Tories need to achieve to keep Major in power is 316. Anything under 316 would almost certainly mean a Conservative defeat on the floor of the Commons. Labour will be aiming for an outright majority with 330 seats and preferably a double-figure majority with 335 to give it a cushion against the inevitable parliamentary complications such as backbench rebellions and protest votes, illnesses and whips' miscalculations. But it could probably count on the support of the four Nationalist MPs from Northern Ireland who are members of the Social Democratic and Labour party, a sister party of the Labour party through the Socialist International. Below 326 Labour will have to do a deal with the Liberal Democrats or possibly the mainland Nationalists, the SNP and Plaid Cymru. Indeed, since Labour is much better placed to secure the support of the minor parties other than the Unionists, it could form a minority government even though it is not the largest party.

So what actually happens after a general election when no party gets an overall majority? The outgoing prime minister is entitled to the first bite of the cherry. In February 1974 the Conservatives lost their majority and ended up with 297 seats – four seats fewer than Labour. Prime Minister Edward Heath held an impromptu Cabinet meeting and then went hot-foot to Buckingham Palace 'to report on the situation'. But Heath insisted on staying in office, where he remained for four days while he tried to put together a deal with the Liberals and Ulster Unionists. Eventually he resigned when his offers were spurned. Although he was strongly criticised for the way he spun out his resignation, he was perfectly entitled to do what he did.

If John Major got the most seats, but failed to secure an overall majority, then he could go to the palace and resign, at which point the Queen could invite Tony Blair to see what he could do. In theory, Major could advise the Queen to call fresh elections without recourse to Blair, but palace officials might think that a step too far… ●

SULTANS OF SWING

Simon Hoggart

The term 'spin doctor' is, of course, American. It describes people employed by politicians and their parties to put a favourable 'spin' on political events and speeches. Why 'doctor' and not 'spin lawyer' or 'spin washerperson' I do not know. The phrase is tossed around in the press and on television all the time these days, but most people aren't very clear about what these people (most are men, but an increasing number are women) actually do, or what the experience of being spun is like.

American and British spin doctors work in very different ways. Americans tend to be rude, overbearing and demanding. Their British equivalents are much worse. In America you encounter most of them during presidential election campaigns. At a big debate between the candidates there will be literally dozens waiting in the hall, and their most important work is carried out in the 20 minutes or so after the debate has finished. Their task is to persuade the assembled media (who may number hundreds or even thousands) that their man 'won' the debate. The most important spin doctors, the ones closest to the candidate himself, will brief the most important media: network political correspondents, the *New York Times*, the *Washington Post*, *Time*, *Newsweek* and so forth. If you represent the *Dogbreath South Dakota Tribune-Bugle*, you may be lucky to have two minutes with a spotty 19-year-old youth whose name is unknown to the candidate himself. If you are a foreigner, you'll be lucky to get anyone at all.

In Britain, before spin doctors were called spin doctors, they were known as press secretaries. They preferred murmurs to shouts. For example, Sir Tom McCaffrey was press secretary to Jim Callaghan when he was prime minister. Sir Tom would no more have yelled or sworn at someone than he would have consulted the intestines of eviscerated crows before briefing the parliamentary lobby. For instance, if your paper had written an article headlined 'Labour Plans Slaughter of the First-Born', and commencing: 'Prime minister Jim Callaghan has proposed a new bill to allow the execution of all first-born children as a means of economising on child benefit payments', Tom would come up to you later in the day and murmur something along the lines of: 'Prime minister a little puzzled by your piece this morning ... tells me he has no idea where it came from … wonders whether you might possibly have confused it with the scheme to slaughter diseased ducks in the High Wycombe area …' But he would never get cross.

All this changed with the arrival of Bernard (now Sir Bernard) Ingham, a former Labour candidate and *Guardian* reporter, who was the first real British spin doctor, in the sense that he saw his job as changing the news to suit his employer rather than merely trying to put the best gloss he could on events. He was the right man at the right time because Thatcher had a problem. Being Margaret Thatcher all day was a terrible strain. No-one could manage it. It would be like asking a Shakespearean actor to be Richard III not just for the course of the play but for 24 hours. So she employed Bernard to be Margaret Thatcher when she was too tired and too busy.

It was not always so. Once, when Bernard was press secretary to Tony Benn, I phoned him to ask why the then Energy Secretary had made a rather curious speech. The following (genuine) conversation took place, and you will quickly see why I have broken a promise made in the course of it:

Me: 'Why do you think Tony Benn said that?'

Bernard: 'I do know, and I'll tell you, but you have to promise never, ever, to say it was me.'

Me (by now quite excited about a potential scoop): 'Yes, of course I'll promise.'

Bernard: 'I've got a kid, you know, and a mortgage. If it ever gets out that I told you, I'll lose my job.'

Me: 'I promise I'll never breathe a word, not to anyone.'

Bernard: 'Right then, so I've got your word.'

Me: 'Yes, yes!'

Bernard: 'The reason is that the Secretary of State is stark, staring mad.'

Years later he went to work for Margaret Thatcher. Bernard was a classic example of the spin doctor in that he knew better than his own boss how his boss was thinking. This could lead to embarrassment and difficulty, as when he told lobby journalists that it didn't matter whether the pound sterling fell to parity with the dollar. Of course, in the ideal, Platonic Thatcherite world it wouldn't matter if the pound fell to five cents against the dollar: the market knows all, sees all, decrees all, and there is less point in trying to tamper with it than with the weather. Still, what Bernard hadn't taken into account was the fact that the market does not share this view of its own omniscience, and was inclined to believe that if the prime minister's press secretary was happy for the pound to decline, then perhaps they ought to bring it down on his behalf.

Bernard has no greater admirer than Alastair Campbell, who is Tony Blair's press secretary. Campbell used to be a political reporter, in the sense that he would write intensely admiring articles about the people he admired intensely. One was Neil Kinnock. He was also a considerable admirer of the late Robert Maxwell. There was a celebrated incident on the day in 1991 when Maxwell was first reported missing from his yacht. My colleague on the *Guardian*, Michael White, sauntered towards the *Daily Mirror* room in the Commons press gallery, mistakenly assuming that Maxwell's employees would share his view that he was dead, and would share his satisfaction at this event. On his short journey to the *Mirror* staff, he picked up a joke, which he (mistakenly) thought might amuse them, and asked: 'Have you heard the one about Cap'n Bob-bob-bob … ?' Instead of chuckling, Campbell hit him. White hit him back, drawing blood. Ringside judges would have had to award the bout to White, who is however generous to his opponent, pointing out that his own remark had been tasteless in the extreme and that many employees of the *Daily Mirror* must have been anxious about their future that day. However, I prefer to recall that Campbell was the man who hit a colleague for being rude about Robert Maxwell.

Modern spin doctors do not believe in the muttered reproof over a friendly drink. They prefer the bellowed assault down the phone. Editors are called as they prepare their children for the school run. Those who have written a front page article deemed unhelpful to the Labour cause (or more particularly, the leader's cause – the party is as full of rival factions as any mediaeval court) are liable to be telephoned at one in the morning and harangued, loudly. 'Call that journalism? That's effing crap, that's not journalism …' Campbell's practice on Blair's overseas visits is to receive by-lined accounts of the visit in the British newspapers, sent from London by fax. He will then hand these out to their authors, often with a word of praise or a shout of admonition. 'This is crap' or 'Crap headline, not a bad story', or to one Labour reporter (who his colleagues believe had merely rewritten a Labour party press release): 'Excellent!' On another occasion, Campbell was briefing a lobby correspondent about a speech Blair was about to make. The reporter expressed puzzlement about one paragraph. The silver-tongued amanuensis glowered at him and shouted: 'Just shut up, and write it down!' Campbell's close associate (and great rival) is Peter Mandelson, now the MP for Hartlepool. When Tony Blair had a great success in his first party conference speech, delivered in the autumn of 1994, Campbell and Mandelson began a competitive tantrum about who had contributed most to the text of the speech. Strangest of all, they held this tantrum in public, through the medium of Campbell's newspaper column.

If Mandelson likes you, he treats you with all the joyful loyalty of William Brown's dog Jumble. If he doesn't, he regards you with loathing and contempt. Being the recipient of his affection and admiration must be like being gummed by a toothless Rottweiler. Those who offend him are boycotted, though usually for a set period of time. Like community service, it is a relatively painless means of teaching people the error of their ways. One lobby correspondent deemed to have behaved badly was informed that he would be ignored for the next three weeks. At a party during the 1994 Labour conference I was in conversation with James Naughtie of the 'Today' programme and Barry Cox, a television executive who had helped to finance Blair's leadership campaign. These were clearly persons of some consequence in Mandelson's life, which is perhaps why I felt a frisson of admiration when he marched up to Naughtie, abruptly interrupted our conversation, and announced: 'I have a bone to pick with you' – while grabbing him by the lapels.

(Luckily Naughtie forgave him, and later that year invited him to a party at his home where he grabbed me by the lapels for some other error, real or imagined.) For a grey eminence, supposedly gliding through the shadows, flitting here and there, gently inserting a word in this person's ear, dropping a dribble of poison into another, Mandelson gets into the newspapers an awful lot. Hardly a weekend goes by without another three-page profile in one of the Saturday magazines, or a thundering denunciation in a Monday leading article. Should Mandelson murmur confidentially to a trusted correspondent that Gordon Brown's influence in the higher reaches of the Labour leadership is on the wane, then the very next day an excitable article will proclaim that the two men are at daggers drawn. They are a little like those couples in offices who are having an adulterous affair; they would like to think their secret is safe, yet rather enjoy the fact that every detail is followed with salacious satisfaction by the rest of the staff. In Labour politics, a good loathing is every bit as gratifying to the onlookers as sex would be in the real world outside.

And yet Mandelson does have a certain fascinating charm. Now a member of his party's frontbench, he makes only rare spoken interventions (words spoken in the Commons Chamber suffer from the drawback of being on the record) but may frequently be seen slumped on the green benches, legs slightly apart, arms across his chest, eyes hooded like a lizard after a good lunch. Now and again he consults a silent beeper, which has no doubt alerted him to a message by vibrating gently against his thigh. The implication is plain: the charade in front of me is of little moment. All truly important activity is taking place outside here, and I am in constant electronic touch with it.

At the 1995 Labour conference, Steve Bell and I were standing just below the platform, to one side. Bell remarked that he had not yet seen Mandelson. Was he present? I said I was certain that he was, but probably hiding behind the scenes. At that very moment a curtain to one side of the stage fluttered aside and out stepped Mandelson. Bell raised his camcorder to film him, and I expected this most secretive of spin doctors to spin round and disappear once more. But he didn't. Instead he smiled, and – the only word for it – sashayed towards us, pirouetting as he came, preening himself on his toes, smiling self-consciously for the cameras, for all the world as if he were being filmed by friends on a Costa Brava beach. It was a touching, even sweet moment, in the life of our leading Sultan of Spin.

Another difference between the spin doctors of today and the press secretaries of the past is the loss of irony. The old-fashioned spokesmen never tried to pretend that they were dealing with objective fact. Their tone implied a conspiratorial relationship with the press: we know that at least half of what we say is nonsense, you know it too, and we are only pretending to fool each other. Modern spin doctors, however, need to believe that everything they say is true. For this reason they tend to address journalists, even over a private drink, as if they were a public meeting. 'You'll have noticed the contemptible decision of the Tory government ...' they will say. Or 'Once again, our polls show there is massive public support for the stand Tony is taking ...' A spin doctor never gives up.

One of their most important skills is to be so determined, so persistent, and so incredibly boring that the journalist gives in for a quiet life. 'My man is making a fascinating new speech on new trends in National Insurance,' he tells you. 'Oh,' you reply, 'I'm afraid it's rather a busy night, what with several members of the royal family having been killed in a helicopter crash.' A few moments later he's back. 'I've been talking to the *Telegraph* and the *Indy*, and they are very excited about these new proposals on National Insurance. In fact, I'd not be a bit surprised if they didn't make them the lead story.' You reply that this seems highly unlikely, given the story about the dead royals. He makes a small concession: 'Well, maybe so, but it will be the second lead, for sure. I'm only telling you so that you don't look stupid when the first editions come out tonight.' By this stage you are ready to throw things. But he has still not given up. Half an hour later, he's back, rubbing his hands. 'The other lot are really getting upset about those National Insurance proposals! Reading between the lines of their hand-out, they seem to be saying our policy could lose them the next election! I just thought I'd mention it. It's the kind of thing your paper is keen on, and I know you need a good story …' In the end they may well be lucky. A small story of a few paragraphs appears, labelled 'New Insurance Row Storm'; the spin doctor's boss is happy, the spin doctor is delighted, and the readers bored out of their minds.

Spin doctors can be bullied back. On one occasion we in the _Guardian_ office at the Commons had been nagged interminably about the paper's decision to give prominence to a speech by John Major rather than one made the same night by Tony Blair. A succession of Labour spin doctors appeared, wheedling and moaning about the paper's choice, deploying a blend of sycophancy and sarcasm. Finally when one egregiously whingeing junior appeared, Michael White's patience snapped.

'I'll tell you why we didn't lead the paper on Blair's speech,' he said. 'We didn't lead it on Blair's speech because you and your colleagues trailed this story in _The Times_ yesterday, and what's more when he made the speech there was very little that was very new or interesting in it and may I remind you that for all his faults, John Major is still the prime minister of this country, unlike Tony Blair, even if he seems to give the impression sometimes that he has already got the job …' And more of the same.

The spin paramedic reeled back in confusion. 'I didn't realise you would take it seriously,' he stammered. 'I am not taking it seriously,' said White. 'If I had taken what you said seriously, you would have been pitched through that window ten minutes ago. Now get out!' But was he back the next day? Of course. Just as ambitious boxers have to roll with the blows, spin doctors have to whiplash with the spin. ●

WHO WOULD MAKE THE BEST PRIME MINISTER ?

Laurence Neville

Since March 1992, the Gallup poll has regularly been asking the question: who would make the best prime minister? There have only been two short breaks in the series – for Kinnock's resignation and John Smith's death. They show that John Major approached the last election with a huge personal lead over Neil Kinnock. But scarcely six months later Major was to become the most unpopular leader in polling history and Labour, now led by the reassuring presence of John Smith, had shot into the lead. Two factors had brought about this change in events: Smith, long the heir apparent, had been crowned king and set Labour on a steady path to economic credibility; and, most importantly, Major and Lamont's own strategy for economic success – membership of the ERM – was shot down in flames as speculators forced Britain out.

Over the ensuing months (and years) almost every issue played against Major as Eurosceptics held the Government to ransom over the Maastricht Treaty and Major's personal relaunches of the party, such as Back to Basics, foundered amidst a succession of Tory scandals. John Smith's death on 12 May 1994 could have dealt a serious blow to Labour. Instead the party emerged from its tragedy with an even stronger leader in Tony Blair, whose popularity soared to phenomenal levels after his election and has maintained that record since.

In an unprecedented decision to ward off the continual press speculation over his leadership and constant sniping from his backbenches, John Major resigned in June 1995. But his victory over John Redwood produced only a minor resurgence in his fortunes and his approval ratings have doggedly failed to rise above a fifth of the electorate. ●

Who would make the best prime minister?

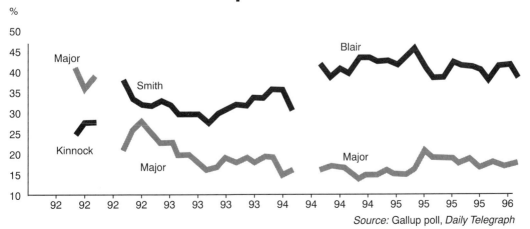

Source: Gallup poll, *Daily Telegraph*

MINISTERS, MPs AND CANDIDATES

Cabinet Changes since November 1990

Prime Minister
Nov 90-   John Major

First Secretary of State and Deputy Prime Minister
Jul 95-   Michael Heseltine

Chancellor of the Exchequer
Nov 90-May 93   Norman Lamont
May 93-   Kenneth Clarke

Chief Secretary to the Treasury
Nov 90-Apr 92   David Mellor
Apr 92-Jul 94   Michael Portillo
Jul 94-Jul 95   Jonathan Aitken
Jul 95-   William Waldegrave

Agriculture
Jul 89-May 93   John Gummer
May 93-Jul 94   Gillian Shephard
Jul 94-Jul 95   William Waldegrave
Jul 95-   Douglas Hogg

Defence
Jul 89-Apr 92   Tom King
Apr 92-Jul 95   Malcolm Rifkind
Jul 95-   Michael Portillo

Education and Science
Nov 90-Apr 92   Kenneth Clarke

Education
Apr 92-Jul 94   John Patten
Jul 94-Jul 95   Gillian Shephard

Education and Employment
Jul 95-   Gillian Shephard

Employment
Jan 90-Apr 92   Michael Howard
Apr 92-May 93   Gillian Shephard
May 93-Jul 94   David Hunt
Jul 94-Jul 95   Michael Portillo

Energy
Jul 89-Apr 92   John Wakeham

Environment
Nov 90-Apr 92   Michael Heseltine
Apr 92-May 93   Michael Howard
May 93-   John Gummer

Foreign Office
Oct 89-Jul 95   Douglas Hurd
Jul 95-   Malcolm Rifkind

Health
Nov 90-Apr 92   William Waldegrave
Apr 92-Jul 95   Virginia Bottomley
Jul 95-   Stephen Dorrell

Home Office
Nov 90-Apr 92   Kenneth Baker
Apr 92-May 93   Kenneth Clarke
May 93-   Michael Howard

National Heritage
Apr 92-Sep 92   David Mellor
Sep 92-Jul 94   Peter Brooke
Jul 94-Jul 95   Stephen Dorrell
Jul 95-   Virginia Bottomley

Northern Ireland Office
Jul 89-Apr 92   Peter Brooke
Apr 92-   Sir Patrick Mayhew

Scottish Office

| Nov 90-Jul 95 | Ian Lang |
| Jul 95- | Michael Forsyth |

Social Security

| Jul 89-Apr 92 | Tony Newton |
| Apr 92- | Peter Lilley |

Trade and Industry

Jul 90-Apr 92	Peter Lilley
Apr 92-Jul 95	Michael Heseltine
Jul 95-	Ian Lang

Transport

Nov 90-Apr 92	Malcolm Rifkind
Apr 92-Jul 94	John MacGregor
Jul 94-Jul 95	Brian Mawhinney
Jul 95	Sir George Young

Welsh Office

May 90-May 93	David Hunt
May 93-Jun 95	John Redwood
Jul 95-	William Hague

Chancellor of the Duchy of Lancaster

Nov 90-Apr 92	Chris Patten
Apr 92-Jul 94	William Waldegrave
Jul 94-Jul 95	David Hunt
Jul 95-	Roger Freeman

Minister without Portfolio

| Jul 94-Jul 95 | Jeremy Hanley |
| Jul 95- | Brian Mawhinney |

Leader of the House of Commons

| Nov 90-Apr 92 | John MacGregor |
| Apr 92- | Tony Newton |

Leader of the House of Lords

Nov 90-Apr 92	David Waddington
Apr 92-Jul 94	John Wakeham
Jul 94-	Lord Cecil of Essendon (Viscount Cranbourne)

Lord Chancellor

| Oct 87- | Lord Mackay of Clashfern |

Shadow Cabinet since July 1992

Leader of the Opposition

| Jul 92-May 94 | John Smith |
| Jul 94- | Tony Blair |

Deputy Leader of the Opposition

| Jul 92-Jul 94 | Margaret Beckett |
| Jul 94- | John Prescott |

Shadow Duchy of Lancaster

| Oct 95- | Derek Foster |

Shadow Chancellor

| Jul 92 | Gordon Brown |

Chief Secretary to the Treasury

Jul 92-Oct 94	Harriet Harman
Oct 94-Jul 96	Andrew Smith
Jul 96-	Alistair Darling

Agriculture

| Jul 92-Nov 92 | Ron Davies |
| Nov 92- | Gavin Strang |

Citizen's Charter and Women

| Jul 92-Oct 93 | Mo Mowlam |

Citizen's Charter and Science

| Oct 93-Oct 94 | Michael Meacher |

Citizen's Charter

| Oct 94- | Ann Taylor |

Defence

| Jul 92- | David Clark |

Disabled People's Rights

| Jul 92-Oct 94 | Barry Sheerman |
| Oct 94- | Tom Clarke |

Education

| Jul 92-Oct 94 | Ann Taylor |
| Oct 94-Oct 95 | David Blunkett |

Education and Employment

| Oct 95- | David Blunkett |

Employment

Jul 92-Oct 93	Frank Dobson
Oct 93-Jul 94	John Prescott
Jul 94-Oct 94	Ann Clwyd
Oct 94-Oct 95	Harriet Harman
Oct 95-	Michael Meacher

Environment
Jul 92-Oct 94   Jack Straw

Environment and London
Oct 94-   Frank Dobson

Environmental Protection
Jul 92-Oct 94   Chris Smith
Oct 94-Jul 96   Joan Ruddock
Jul 96-   Michael Meacher

Foreign Affairs
Jul 92-Oct 94   Jack Cunningham
Oct 94-   Robin Cook

Health
Jul 92-Oct 94   David Blunkett
Oct 94-Oct 95   Margaret Beckett
Oct 95-Jul 96   Harriet Harman
Jul 96-   Chris Smith

Home Affairs
Jul 92-Jul 94   Tony Blair
Oct 94-   Jack Straw

National Heritage
Jul 92-Sep 92   Bryan Gould
Nov 92-Oct 93   Ann Clwyd
Oct 93-Oct 94   Mo Mowlam
Oct 94-Oct 95   Chris Smith
Oct 95-   Jack Cunningham

Northern Ireland
Jul 87-Oct 94   Kevin McNamara
Oct 94-   Mo Mowlam

Overseas Development
Jul 92-Oct 93   Michael Meacher
Oct 93-Oct 94   Tom Clarke
Oct 94-Jul 96   Joan Lestor
Jul 96-   Clare Short

Scotland
Jul 92-Oct 93   Tom Clarke
Oct 93-   George Robertson

Social Security
Jul 92-Oct 95   Donald Dewar
Oct 95-Jul 96   Chris Smith
Jul 96-   Harriet Harman

Trade and Industry
Jul 92-Oct 94   Robin Cook
Oct 94-Oct 95   Jack Cunningham
Oct 95-   Margaret Beckett

Transport
Nov 88-Oct 93   John Prescott

Transport and London
Oct 93-Oct 94   Frank Dobson

Transport
Oct 94-Oct 95   Michael Meacher
Oct 95-Jul 96   Clare Short
Jul 96-   Andrew Smith

Wales
Jul 92-Nov 92   Ann Clwyd
Nov 92-   Ron Davies

Women's Issues
Oct 93-Oct 95   Clare Short
Oct 95-Jul 96   Tessa Jowell
Jul 96-   Janet Anderson

Shadow Leader of the House of Commons
Jul 92-Oct 94   Margaret Beckett
Oct 94-   Ann Taylor

Lord Chancellor's Dept
Jul 92-   Paul Boateng

Law Officer
Oct 83-   John Morris

REBELLIONS

Laurence Neville

John Major's ship of government has sailed on increasingly stormy waters since the last election. The number of rebellions since 1992 has been unprecedented. Though many centred on Britain's relationship with the European Union, the Government also experienced difficulty over domestic issues, notably VAT on fuel. The most consistent rebel has been Richard Shepherd, but the awkward squad has expanded to include some unusual names in the last five years. The divorce vote in April 1996, though technically unwhipped, was a nasty surprise for Major as ministers, including Michael Howard, lined up to vote against government legislation.

But while the Conservatives looked to be falling apart at the seams, Blair's well whipped New Labour has also failed to keep the troops in check. On the crucial 'middle England' issue of income tax, ten MPs defied the leadership's call for abstention on the basic rate cut to 24p, exposing the party to the charges of being unrepentant tax-and-spenders. Elsewhere, however, Labour has successfully exploited Conservative divisions through clever tabling of amendments designed to do maximum damage. The Social Chapter vote in July 1992 saw Tory Eurosceptics voting with Labour to support a policy they believe to be an abomination simply to inflict pain on the Government. ●

Issues on which rebellions occurred

Divorce: 25 April 1996: Divorce vote. Government defeated over length of 'cooling-off' period. Supporters of the amendment to extend the waiting time for divorce include Michael Howard and Stephen Dorrell.

EU: 1 March 1995: Labour vote on EU policy. Motion on government policy being against the national interest. Norman Lamont votes against the Government.

Finance: 28 November 1994: European Finance vote is turned into confidence motion by the Government. Nevertheless eight Tories vote against the Government and have the whip withdrawn.

Fisheries 1: 18 January 1995: Common Fisheries Policy. Nine Tories vote against the government motion praising the Common Fisheries Policy.

Fisheries 2: 19 December 1995: Common Fisheries Policy. Bill Cash and Michael Carttiss vote against the Government and 25 others abstain or are not in attendance.

Gays: 9 May 1996: Gay ban in the Military. Eight Tories vote against continuing the ban. Eight Labour MPs vote for retaining it.

Hospitals: 10 May 1995: London hospital closures. Former minister Peter Brooke defies the Government.

Maastricht 1: 4 November 1992: Maastricht. Vote on postponement of debate until after Edinburgh Summit.

Maastricht 2: 8 March 1993: Amendment 28 to Maastricht Bill. Required members of the Committee of the Regions to be drawn from elected local government representatives. Twenty-six Tories help to defeat the Government.

Maastricht 3: 20 May 1993: Third reading of the Maastricht Bill. Forty-one Tories vote no. Seventy-one Labour MPs refuse to abstain: 66 vote no, five vote yes.

Maastricht 4: 22 July 1993: Social Chapter vote is used by Euro rebels to voice opposition to the Maastricht Treaty. Twenty-three Tories defy the whip.

Nolan: 6 November 1995: Outside earnings. Twenty-three Tories back Labour amendment to force MPs to declare earnings from work 'in their capacity as MPs'.

Pit 1: 21 October 1992: Vote on pit closures. Six Tories vote against the Government.

Pit 2: 5 July 1993: Future of remaining coal pits. Labour motion demanding that the Government act to secure the future of the remaining pits. Six Tory MPs vote against the Government.

PTA: 2 April 1996: Prevention of Terrorism Act. Thirty Labour MPs vote against a guillotine motion on additional police powers under the PTA. Blair loyalists abstain.

Referendum: 11 June 1996: EU referendum. William Cash's bill to allow for a referendum on all aspects of Britain's membership of the EU.

Scott: 27 February 1996: Scott Report. Government wins by one vote as Peter Thurnham, who had resigned the whip, is joined by Quentin Davies and Richard Shepherd in the opposition lobby.

Tax: 5 December 1995: Income tax reduction. Ten Labour MPs defy Tony Blair's call for an abstention on income tax cuts.

VAT 1: 10 May 1993: VAT on fuel. Two Tories vote against VAT on fuel, five abstain.

VAT 2: 6 December 1994: VAT on fuel. Seven Tories vote against the Government on a Labour amendment to force a full-scale debate on the issue.

The rebels

Diane Abbott (Hackney N and Stoke Newington) Lab: Maas 3, PTA
Irene Adams (Paisley N) Lab: Maas 3
Peter Ainsworth (Surrey E) Con: Divorce
Jonathan Aitken (Thanet S) Con: Divorce, Referendum
Richard Alexander (Newark) Con: Pit 1,2, Referendum
Rupert Allason (Torbay) Con: Maas 3, Fish 1, Nolan
David Amess (Basildon) Con: Divorce
Michael Ancram (Devizes) Con: Divorce
Jacques Arnold (Gravesham) Con: Divorce, Referendum
Robert Atkins (South Ribble) Con: Divorce
Peter Atkinson (Hexham) Con: Divorce
John Austin-Walker (Woolwich) Lab: Maas 3
Kenneth Baker (Mole Valley) Con: Divorce, Referendum
Nicholas Baker (Dorset N) Con: Divorce
Matthew Banks (Southport) Con: Divorce
Robert Banks (Harrogate) Con: Divorce
Tony Banks (Newham NW) Lab: PTA
Harry Barnes (Derbyshire NE) Lab: Maas 3, PTA
Michael Bates (Langborough) Con: Divorce
Spencer Batiste (Elmet) Con: Divorce
Roy Beggs (Antrim E) UUP: Referendum
Henry Bellingham (Norfolk NW) Con: Divorce
Vivian Bendall (Ilford N) Con: Maas 3, Divorce, Referendum
Tony Benn (Chesterfield) Lab: Maas 3, Tax, PTA, Referendum
Andrew Bennett (Denton and Reddish) Lab: Maas 3, PTA
Roger Berry (Kingswood) Lab: Maas 3
John Biffen (Shropshire N) Con: Maas 1,2,3, Nolan, Referendum
Richard Body (Holland with Boston) Con: Maas 1,2,3,4, Fish 1, Referendum
Sir Nicholas Bonsor (Upminster) Con: Divorce
Hartley Booth (Finchley) Con: Divorce
Sir Anthony Bowden (Brighton Kempton) Con: Gay
John Bowis (Battersea) Con: Divorce
Jimmy Boyce (Rotherham) Lab: Maas 3
Sir Rhodes Boyson (Brent N) Con: Referendum
Julian Brazier (Canterbury) Con: Referendum
Graham Bright (Luton S) Con: Divorce
Peter Brooke (City of London & Westminster S) Con: Hospital, Divorce
Michael Brown (Brigg & Cleethorpes) Con: Divorce, Gay, Referendum
Ian Bruce (Dorset S) Con: Divorce
Nicholas Budgen (Wolverhampton SW) Con: Maas 1,2,3,4, Finance, Divorce, Referendum
Richard Burden (Birmingham Northfield) Lab: PTA

Simon Burns (Chelmsford) Con: Divorce
Alastair Burt (Bury N) Con: Divorce
John Butcher (Coventry SW) Con: Maas 1,3,4, Divorce, Referendum
Jim Callaghan (Heywood & Middleton) Lab: Maas 3
Ronnie Campbell (Blyth Valley) Lab: Maas 3, Tax, Referendum
Dennis Canavan (Falkirk W) Lab: Maas 3, PTA, Referendum
Jamie Cann (Ipswich) Lab: Maas 3
John Carlisle (Luton N) Con: Maas 1,2,3, Referendum
Sir Kenneth Carlisle (Lincoln) Con: Nolan, Divorce
Matthew Carrington (Fulham) Con: Gay
Michael Carttiss (Great Yarmouth) Con: Finance, VAT 2, Fish 2, Referendum
Bill Cash (Stafford) Con: Maas 1,2,3,4, Pit 2, Fish 2, Divorce, Referendum
Malcolm Chisholm (Edinburgh Leith) Lab: Maas 3
Winston Churchill (Davyhulme) Con: Pit 2, Referendum
Michael Clapham (Barnsley W & Penistone) Lab: Maas 3
James Clappison (Hertsmere) Con: Divorce
Dr Michael Clark (Rochford) Con: Pit 1, Maas 1, Divorce, Referendum
Ann Clwyd (Cynon Valley) Lab: PTA
Harry Cohen (Leyton) Lab: PTA
Michael Colvin (Romsey & Waterside) Con: Referendum
David Congdon (Croydon NE) Con: Divorce
Michael Connarty (Falkirk E) Lab: Maas 3
Derek Conway (Shrewsbury & Atcham) Con: Divorce
Anthony Coombes (Wyre Forest) Con: Divorce
Simon Coombs (Swindon) Con: Divorce
Robin Corbett (Birmingham, Erdington) Lab: PTA
Jeremy Corbyn (Islington N) Lab: Maas 3, Tax, PTA, Referendum
Jean Corston (Bristol E) Lab: Maas 3
James Cran (Beverley) Con: Maas 1,2,3,4
Bob Cryer (Bradford S) Lab: Maas 3
Edwina Currie (Derbyshire S) Con: Gay
David Curry (Skipton & Ripton) Con: Divorce
Ian Davidson (Glasgow Central) Lab: Maas 3
Denzil Davies (Llanelli) Lab: Tax, Referendum
Quentin Davies (Stamford & Spalding) Con: Scott, Divorce
David Davis (Boothferry) Con: Divorce
Terry Davis (Birmingham Hodge Hill) Lab: Maas 3, PTA
Stephen Day (Cheadle) Con: Nolan, Divorce, Referendum
Nirj Deva (Brentford & Isleworth) Con: Divorce
Don Dixon (Jarrow) Lab: Gay
Brian Donohoe (Cunninghame S) Lab: Maas 3
Stephen Dorrell (Loughborough) Con: Divorce
Lord James Douglas-Hamilton (Edinburgh W) Con: Divorce
Iain Duncan-Smith (Chingford) Con: Maas 1,3,4, Divorce, Referendum

Bob Dunn (Dartford) Con: Referendum
Gwyneth Dunwoody (Crewe & Nantwich) Lab: Maas 3
Hugh Dykes (Harrow E) Con: Nolan
William Etherington (Sunderland N) Lab: Maas 3
David Evans (Welwyn Hatfield) Con: Divorce, Referendum
Nigel Evans (Ribble Valley) Con: Divorce
Roger Evans (Monmouth) Con: Divorce
David Evennett (Erith & Crayford) Con: Divorce
David Faber (Westbury) Con: Divorce
Michael Fabricant (Mid-Staffordshire) Con: Nolan
Andrew Faulds (Warley E) Lab: Maas 3
Barry Field (Isle of Wight) Con: Divorce, Referendum
Frank Field (Birkenhead) Lab: Maas 3
Clifford Forsythe (S Antrim) UUP: Referendum
Dr Liam Fox (Woodspring) Con: Divorce
Douglas French (Gloucester) Con: Divorce
Peter Fry (Wellingborough) Con: Maas 3, Divorce, Referendum
Roger Gale (Thanet N) Con: Divorce, Referendum
Phil Gallie (Ayr) Con: Divorce, Referendum
Sir George Gardiner (Reigate) Con: Maas 2,3, Divorce, Referendum
Bruce George (Walsall S) Lab: Gay
Neil Gerrard (Walthamstow) Lab: Maas 3, PTA
Christopher Gill (Ludlow) Con: Maas 1,2,3,4, Finance, Fish 1, Divorce, Referendum
Dr Norman Godman (Greenock & Port Glasgow) Lab: Maas 3, PTA
Dr Charles Goodson-Wickes (Wimbledon) Con: Divorce
Mildred Gordon (Bow & Poplar) Lab: Maas 3
Teresa Gorman (Billericay) Con: Maas 1,2,3,4, Finance, Fish 1, Referendum
John Gorst (Hendon N) Con: Divorce, Referendum
Bryan Gould (Dagenham) Lab: Maas 3
Sir Anthony Grant (Cambridgeshire SW) Con: Divorce
Bernie Grant (Tottenham) Lab: PTA
Harry Greenway (Ealing N) Con: Maas 3, Divorce, Referendum
Peter Griffiths (Portsmouth N) Con: Nolan, Divorce, Referendum
William Hague (Richmond, Yorks) Con: Divorce
Peter Hain (Neath) Lab: Maas 3
Mike Hall (Warrington S) Lab: Maas 3
Sir Archibald Hamilton (Epsom & Ewell) Con: Divorce
Neil Hamilton (Tatton) Con: Divorce
Sir John Hannam (Exeter) Con: Divorce
Andrew Hargreaves (Birmingham, Hall Green) Con: Divorce
David Harris (St Ives) Con: Fish 1, Divorce
Nick Harvey (Devon N) Lib Dem: Maas 3, Referendum
Warren Hawksley (Halesowen) Con: Maas 2,3, Divorce, Referendum
Jerry Hayes (Harlow) Con: Gay

David Heathcoat-Amory (Wells) Con: Divorce
Charles Hendry (High Peaks) Con: Divorce
Sir Terence Higgins (Worthing) Con: Divorce
Kate Hoey (Vauxhall) Lab: Maas 3
John Horam (Orpington) Con: Divorce
Sir Peter Maudsley (Horsham) Con: Divorce
Michael Howard (Folkestone & Hythe) Con: Divorce
George Howarth (Knowsley N) Lab: Maas 3
David Howell (Guildford) Con: Divorce
Kevin Hughes (Doncaster N) Lab: Maas 3
Robert Hughes (Harrow W) Con: Divorce, Gay
Roy Hughes (Newport E) Lab: Maas 3
David Hunt (Wirral W) Con: Divorce
Andrew Hunter (Basingstoke) Con: Maas 2, Divorce, Referendum
Bernard Jenkin (Colchester N) Con: Maas 3, Divorce
Toby Jessel (Twickenham) Con: Maas 1,2,3,4, Divorce, Referendum
Sir Geoffrey Johnson Smith (Wealden) Con: Divorce
Lynne Jones (Birmingham Selly Oak) Lab: Maas 3, Tax, PTA
Robert Jones (Hertfordshire W) Con: Divorce
Michael Jopling (Westmorland & Lonsdale) Con: Divorce
Dame Elaine Kellett-Bowman (Lancaster) Con: Divorce
Robert Key (Salisbury) Con: Referendum
Tom King (Bridgwater) Con: Divorce
Timothy Kirkthorpe (Leeds NE) Con: Divorce
Roger Knapman (Stroud) Con: Maas 1,2,3, Divorce
Angela Knight (Erewash) Con: Divorce
Dame Jill Knight (Birmingham Edgbaston) Con: Divorce
Norman Lamont (Kingston-upon-Thames) Con: EU, Referendum
Sir Ivan Lawrence (Burton) Con: Maas 2,4, Divorce, Referendum
Barry Legg (Milton Keynes SW) Con: Maas 1,3,4, Nolan, Referendum
Edward Leigh (Gainsborough & Horncastle) Con: Maas 4, Divorce, Referendum
Mark Lennox-Boyd (Morecambe & Lunesdale) Con: Divorce, Referendum
Terry Lewis (Worsley) Lab: Maas 3, Tax, PTA, Gay
David Lidlington (Aylesbury) Con: Divorce
Peter Lilley (St Albans) Con: Divorce
Robert Litherland (Manchester C) Lab: Maas 3
Ken Livingstone (Brent E) Lab: Maas 3, PTA, Referendum
Michael Lord (Suffolk C) Con: Maas 1,2,3, Divorce, Referendum
Eddie Loyden (Liverpool Garston) Lab: Tax, PTA
Liz Lynne (Rochdale) Lib Dem: Referendum
John McAllion (Dundee E) Lab: Maas 3
Calum MacDonald (Western Isles) Lab: Maas 2
John MacGregor (Norfolk S) Con: Divorce
David Maclean (Penrith & the Border) Con: Divorce

Patrick McLaughlin (Derbyshire W) Con: Divorce
William McKelvey (Kilmarnock & Loudoun) Lab: Maas 3
Andrew MacKinlay (Thurrock) Lab: PTA
Kevin McNamara (Hull N) Lab: PTA
Sir Patrick McNair-Wilson (New Forest) Con: Referendum
John McWilliam (Blaydon) Lab: Maas 3
Max Madden (Bradford W) Lab: Maas 3, Tax, PTA, Referendum
David Madel (Bedfordshire SW) Con: Divorce
Alice Mahon (Halifax) Lab: PTA
Lady Olga Maitland (Sutton & Cheam) Con: Divorce
Gerald Malone (Winchester) Con: Divorce
Paul Marland (West Gloucestershire) Con: VAT 2, Referendum
Tony Marlow (Northampton N) Con: Maas 1,2,3,4, Finance, VAT 2, Fish 1,
    Divorce, Referendum
David Marshall (Leicester S) Lab: Maas 3
Jim Marshall (Leicester S) Lab: PTA
John Marshall (Hendon S) Con: Referendum
David Martin (Portsmouth S) Con: Nolan
Michael Mates (East Hampshire) Con: Divorce
Piers Merchant (Beckenham) Con: Divorce
Bill Michie (Sheffield Heeley) Lab: Maas 3, PTA
Iain Mills (Meriden) Con: Divorce, Referendum
Andrew Mitchell (Gelding) Con: Divorce
Austin Mitchell (Great Grimsby) Lab: Maas 3, Referendum
Sir Roger Moate (Faversham) Con: Maas 3
Sir James Molyneaux (Lagan Valley) UUP: Referendum
Sir Hector Monro (Dumfries) Con: Divorce
Sir Fergus Montgomery (Altrincham & Sale) Con: Divorce
John Morris (Aberavon) Lab: Gay
George Mudie (Leeds E) Lab: Maas 3
Michael Neubert (Romford) Con: Divorce
Patrick Nicholls (Teignbridge) Con: Divorce, Referendum
David Nicholson (Taunton) Con: Nolan, Referendum
Emma Nicholson (Devon W & Torridge) Con: Nolan
Bill Olner (Nuneaton) Lab: Maas 3
Sir Cranley Onslow (Woking) Con: Divorce
Richard Page (Hertfordshire SW) Con: Divorce
James Paice (Cambridgeshire SE) Con: Divorce
Robert Parry (Liverpool Riverside) Lab: Maas 3
John Patten (Oxford W & Abingdon) Con: Divorce
James Pawsey (Rugby & Kenilworth) Con: Maas 3, Divorce, Referendum
Elizabeth Peacock (Batley & Spen) Con: Pit 1,2, Divorce, Referendum
Colin Pickthall (Lancashire W) Lab: Maas 3, Tax
Greg Pope (Hydeburn) Lab: Maas 3

David Porter (Waveney) Con: Maas 1,3, Nolan, Divorce, Referendum
Ray Powell (Ogmore) Lab: Referendum
William Powell (Corby) Con: VAT 1, Divorce
Bridget Prentice (Lewisham E) Lab: Maas 3
Gordon Prentice (Pendle) Lab: Maas 3
Giles Radice (Durham N) Lab: Maas 3
Martin Redmond (Don Valley) Lab: Maas 3
John Redwood (Wokingham) Con: Divorce, Referendum
Timothy Renton (Sussex Mid) Con: Divorce
Jo Richardson (Barking) Lab: Maas 3
Graham Riddick (Colne Valley) Con: Divorce
Dr John Reid (Motherwell) Lab: Gay
Andrew Robathan (Blaby) Con: Maas 3, Divorce
Wyn Roberts (Conwy) Con: Divorce
John Robertson (East Lothian) Lab: Maas 3
Mark Robinson (Somerton & Frome) Con: Divorce
Marion Roe (Broxbourne) Con: Divorce, Referendum
William Ross (Londonderry E) UUP: Referendum
Andrew Rowe (Kent Mid) Con: Gay
Ted Rowlands (Merthyr Tydfil & Rhymney) Lab: Maas 3
Dame Angela Rumbold (Mitcham & Morden) Con: Divorce
Tom Sackville (Bolton W) Con: Divorce
Sir Tim Sainsbury (Hove) Con: Nolan
Brian Sedgemore (Hackney S & Shoreditch) Lab: Maas 3
Sir Nicholas Scott (Chelsea) Con: Divorce, Gay
David Shaw (Dover) Con: Divorce, Referendum
Sir Giles Shaw (Pudsey) Con: Divorce
Richard Shepherd (Aldridge-Brownhills) Con: Pit 1, Maas 1,2,3,4, Finance, VAT 2,
    Fish 1, Nolan, Scott, Divorce, Referendum
Sir Michael Shersby (Uxbridge) Con: Divorce
Peter Shore (Bethnal Green & Stepney) Lab: Maas 3
Alan Simpson (Nottingham S) Lab: Maas 3, Referendum
Roger Sims (Chislehurst) Con: Nolan
Sir Trevor Skeet (Beds N) Con: Maas 1,2,3,4, Divorce, Referendum
Dennis Skinner (Bolsover) Lab: Maas 3, Referendum
Llewellyn Smith (Blaenau Gwent) Lab: Maas 3, Referendum
Tim Smith (Beaconsfield) Con: Divorce
Rev Martin Smyth (Belfast S) UUP: Referendum
Peter Snape (West Bromwich) Lab: Gay
Nigel Spearing (Newham S) Lab: Referendum
John Spellar (Warley W) Lab: Gay
Sir James Spicer (Dorset W) Con: Divorce
Michael Spicer (Worcestershire S) Con: Maas 1,2,3,4, Referendum
Dr Robert Spink (Castle Point) Con: Divorce

Richard Spring (Bury St Edmunds) Con: Divorce
Iain Sproat (Harwich) Con: Divorce
Sir John Stanley (Tonbridge & Malling) Con: Nolan
Anthony Steen (South Hams) Con: Divorce, Referendum
Michael Stern (Bristol NW) Con: Divorce
George Stevenson (Stoke) Lab: Maas 3
Allan Stewart (Eastwood) Con: Nolan, Referendum
Gary Streeter (Plymouth Sutton) Con: Divorce
David Sumberg (Bury S) Con: VAT 2, Divorce, Referendum
Walter Sweeney (Vale of Glamorgan) Con: Maas 2,3,4, Nolan, Divorce, Referendum
Sir Peter Tapsell (Lindsey E) Con: Maas 1,2,3,4, Referendum
Sir Teddy Taylor (Southend E) Con: Maas 1,2,3,4, Finance, Fish 1, Referendum
Roy Thomason (Bromsgrove S) Con: Referendum
Patrick Thompson (Norwich N) Con: Nolan, Divorce
Sir Malcolm Thornton (Crosby) Con: Divorce
Peter Thurnham (Bolton NE) Con: Nolan, Scott
John Townsend (Bridlington) Con: Maas 3, Referendum
Richard Tracey (Surbiton) Con: Divorce, Referendum
David Tredinnick (Bosworth) Con: Nolan, Divorce
Michael Trend (Windsor & Maidenhead) Con: Divorce
Dennis Turner (Wolverhampton SE) Lab: Gay
Dr Ian Twinn (Edmonton) Con: Divorce, Referendum
Sir Gerard Vaughan (Reading E) Con: Divorce, Referendum
George Walden (Buckingham) Con: Divorce
Bill Walker (Tayside N) Con: Maas 1,2,3,4, Divorce, Referendum
Gary Waller (Keighley) Con: Nolan, Divorce
Charles Wardle (Bexhill) Con: Referendum
Nigel Waterson (Eastbourne) Con: Divorce
Mike Watson (Glasgow C) Lab: Maas 3
John Watts (Slough) Con: Divorce
John Whittingdale (Colchester S & Maldon) Con: Maas 3, Referendum
John Wilkinson (Ruislip) Con: Maas 1,2,3,4, Finance, Fish 1
Alan Williams (Swansea W) Lab: Maas 3
David Wilshire (Spelthorne) Con: Nolan
David Winnick (Walsall N) Lab: Maas 3
Ann Winterton (Congleton) Con: Pit 1,2, Maas 1,2,3,4, VAT 2, Divorce, Referendum
Nicholas Winterton (Macclesfield) Con: Pit 1,2, Maas 1,2,3, VAT 1,2,
    Divorce, Referendum
Audrey Wise (Preston) Lab: Maas 3
Timothy Wood (Stevenage) Con: Divorce
Timothy Yeo (Suffolk S) Con: Divorce

OUT WITH THE OLD

Ian Aitken

Harold Wilson, the supreme political statistician of the post-war era, always insisted that the most accurate guide to an election result wasn't what people told the opinion pollsters about their voting intentions but which party they said they expected to win; the side the majority plumped for was almost always victorious, he claimed. So perhaps there is a special significance in the somewhat larger than usual number of Members of Parliament who have announced that they won't be standing again this time. For the list reveals that the Conservatives among them outnumber Labour retirees by a factor of very nearly two to one. We can probably assume that quite a few of them don't expect to hold their own seats, while several others probably don't fancy the idea of several years in opposition without even the prospect of a knighthood, let alone a ministerial job, as a reward for loyalty.

By the same token, it is likely that some Labour MPs who would have preferred retirement to yet another four or five dreary years on the opposition benches have probably decided to stay on in the hope of getting the opportunity to do some of the things they have talked about for the past 17 years. These attitudes are significant, because no-one knows better than politicians that there is nothing quite so ex- as an ex-MP. Most of them have seen former colleagues hanging around the building, some looking for help in getting a job or a winnable constituency, others in search of reassurance that their opinions still matter.

The kindlier MPs will invite these unhappy figures for a drink in the Strangers' Bar, but at best they are regarded as a distraction, and at worst as intolerable pests. The hardest hit by this treatment are ex-ministers, who desperately miss their deferential civil servants, their ministerial motor cars and their red dispatch boxes. But they are closely followed by the sort of ex-backbencher whom parliamentary journalists know as the rentaquote mob. After being in constant demand by the news agencies and the BBC for off-the-cuff comments on everything from mad cow disease to the state of the royal family, these unfortunates suddenly find themselves in limbo, armed with a mobile telephone which is for ever silent.

There are several MPs already on the retirement list who fall into the rentaquote category, and they will certainly be joined by several more when the votes are counted on election night. But what makes the current list unusual is the number of former Cabinet or Cabinet-rank ministers who have decided to bow out without being pushed. Not surprisingly, most of them are Tories – nine, as against three from the Labour side. But the departure of the three Labour ex-ministers – they are Roy Hattersley, Peter Shore and Stan Orme – deprives Tony Blair of his last remaining source of experienced advice about running a government. It is true that, barring accidents, the next Parliament will still contain one formidable survivor from the last Labour Cabinet. But he is Tony Benn, who is not the sort of person to whom Blair would naturally turn for guidance.

On the Conservative side, the list of senior ex-ministers who are retiring includes no fewer than three former government chief whips – Michael Jopling, Tim Renton and Richard Ryder. Of the three, only Jopling can claim to be leaving Westminster with a relatively untarnished reputation as a whip. Renton, a Thatcher appointment, was the chief whip who failed so spectacularly to save his boss in the 1991 leadership contest. Ryder, John Major's choice as Renton's successor, attracted a tide of personal hostility for what were seen by backbenchers as his unusually robust disciplinary methods, not least during the passage of the Maastricht Treaty Bill. It was said of him at the time that he would have made a better secret police chief than a chief whip – a job in which his brand of icy intellectualism proved to be the exact opposite of the combination of low cunning and conviviality which it traditionally demands.

Of the other departing ex-ministers, several are genuine grandees of a sort which used to be the pride of the pre-Thatcher Conservative party. Douglas Hurd, the Old Etonian ex-Foreign Secretary, effortlessly heads the list as the grandees' grandee. But there is also Paul Channon, another Etonian, who inherited his Southend seat from his father, 'Chips' Channon, and simultaneously acquired lots of money from his mother, a Guinness. In theory, Paul's political career was more successful than his father's, since he achieved Cabinet office, while his father never got further than bag carrier to Rab Butler during the Munich years. But Chips seems likely to be remembered much longer than Paul, simply for his amazing diaries – even more riveting, in my opinion, than Alan Clark's.

Also departing are two relatively plebeian grandees in Kenneth Baker and John Biffen. The former will be remembered partly for the speed with which Margaret Thatcher whizzed him in and out of Whitehall departments like Environment, Education and the Home Office, where he demonstrated an uncanny ability to escape from successive jobs just before the ceiling fell in. He managed this trick without once allowing his Cheshire Cat grin to slip – a talent which once moved a colleague to remark: 'I have seen the future and it smirks.' His monument, however, will be his Dangerous Dogs Act, which seems likely to become the standing example of how legislation rushed through Parliament to please the tabloid press usually turns out to be a lemon.

After a long period of extreme loyalty, Kenneth Baker has recently begun to demonstrate a tendency towards embarrassing indiscretion. Biffen, on the other hand, was famously 'semi-detached' from the Thatcher Government even when he was a member of it. Since being sacked in 1987 he has set an admirable example of how to dissent from your own party with dignity, charm and good humour. Having joined the Cabinet as a committed free-marketeer, he quickly reached the conclusion that Thatcher's mood of permanent upheaval was causing serious damage, and he earned the distrust of his prime minister for describing himself as a 'consolidator' rather than a revolutionary. He and Peter Shore have together provided urgently needed intellectual weight to the Eurosceptic cause at a time when it has seemed – at least on the Conservative side – to be based increasingly on crude xenophobia.

Unlike some of his fellow retirees, 'Biffo's' ability to deflate the Euro-enthusiasts without causing personal offence will be sorely missed in a new Parliament which promises to be grievously short of those civilised qualities. No one would describe John Patten, another former Cabinet Minister on the retiring list, as a grandee. Nicknamed 'No Relation' because of his shared surname with the Governor of Hong Kong, his main claim to a footnote in the history books is that he was probably the education secretary whom teachers hated more than any other. He is widely credited with politicising the teaching profession, though that is perhaps an exaggeration. But at least one need not waste too much sympathy on these prospective political pensioners.

It is highly unlikely that any of the departing Conservative ex-ministers will find themselves in straitened circumstances. All can hope to pick up a quiverful of well paid directorships, even if few of them can expect to do quite as well as Douglas Hurd with his £250,000 retirement job as a part-time banker. Moreover, custom and practice dictate that they can claim a life peerage as a reward for their faithful service to the party and the nation. Most of them – with the possible exception of Biffen – seem likely to take it, if only to boost their prospect of landing those directorships.

The prospect of ennoblement is also available to the three Labour retirees, and it will be interesting to see which, if any, make use of it. But on the financial side, only Roy Hattersley seems certain of a substantial post-retirement income, thanks to his Stakhanovite qualities as a journalist and author. That, as they say, is the way the cookie crumbles – at least for the time being. For the probability is that having a former Tory Cabinet Minister on the company board will be a diminishing asset once the Conservatives are no longer in office.

On the other hand, having a Labour ex-minister on the board has never held much appeal for the City, whichever party is in office. But the departure of these ex-ministers will have more symbolic than practical impact on the day-to-day life of the Commons. Most of them have been infrequent attenders in the chamber, and even more infrequent contributors to the debates. However, the retirement of David Howell, a member of Thatcher's first Cabinet, will bring about a discernible change. Howell, as chair of the foreign affairs committee, has become something of an authority on overseas policy.

But when it comes to immediate and audible changes in the conduct of parliamentary business, the disappearance of two particular backbenchers, one Tory and one Labour, seems likely to have a much more immediate effect than that of any ex-minister, however grand. The Tory is Dame Elaine Kellett-Bowman, a woman who is the unchallenged possessor of the shrillest and most piercing voice at Westminster, and has never been shy about using it. The 80-year-old Sir Edward Heath, who is not retiring, sits in a seat immediately in front of her; he seems likely to be grateful for what promises to be a sharp fall in the decibel level after the election.

Her Labour opposite number is Andrew Faulds, the bearded thespian MP whose powerful bass-baritone voice was developed to its present pitch of perfection when he was once filmed in the part of William Morris bellowing his verse across a vast Greenland fjord. Successive Speakers have suspected that Mr Faulds still thinks he is bellowing across a Greenland fjord. His bogus points of order are painfully audible. In a sadder category is the departure of Julian Critchley, trundling his wheelchair towards the sunset. Sir Julian (for he finally landed the K which Thatcher long denied him) started his career as a considerable expert on defence policy. Alas, his hopes of advancement were blighted by a delightful inability to control his sense of the ridiculous. Critchley's loss, however, has been everyone else's gain. By the time a return of his childhood polio reduced him to immobility he had earned a reputation as Parliament's wittiest speaker and most irreverent essayist. Happily, the essays will continue, even if the speeches don't.

One final name jumps off the page for the present writer. I still vividly remember the maiden speech of Harold Walker, former Deputy Speaker and union-sponsored MP for Doncaster. It was delivered shortly after Labour's narrow but spectacular election victory in 1964, in the heady atmosphere created by Harold Wilson's commitment to the white heat of a technological revolution. The diminutive Walker, fresh from the shop floor of one of the factories which were likely to be in the front line of that revolution, had a sceptical message for his over-excited colleagues. He told them about a machine in his works which was over 100 years old but nevertheless played a key role in the factory's production process. Not surprisingly, it had a habit of breaking down from time to time. Whenever it did, a taxi was dispatched to the home of an octogenarian ex-employee who was the only man who knew how to mend it. That, said Walker, was the reality behind the white heat of the technological revolution.

Alas, he turned out to be all too correct. Walker's tragi-comic message is one which might with advantage be repeated to the flock of shining-eyed newcomers who will soon stream into Westminster, dedicated to doing better than their predecessors. Yet perhaps it would be kinder to let them find out in their own way how great are the limitations on even the most well-intentioned politicians. As Enoch Powell once said, all political careers inevitably end in failure. Some are just bigger failures than others. ●

Retiring MPs

Conservative

First Names	Last Name	Constituency Name
Michael	Alison	Selby
Thomas	Arnold	Hazel Grove
David	Ashby	Leicestershire North West
Jack	Aspinwall	Wansdyke
Kenneth	Baker	Mole Valley
Nicholas	Baker	Dorset North
Robert	Banks	Harrogate
John	Biffen	Shropshire North
John	Butcher	Coventry South West
John	Carlisle	Luton North
Kenneth	Carlisle	Lincoln
Paul	Channon	Southend West
Julian	Critchley	Aldershot
Anthony	Durant	Reading West
Tim	Eggar	Enfield North
Dudley	Fishburn	Kensington
Tristan	Garel-Jones	Watford
Anthony	Grant	Cambridgeshire South West
Michael	Grylls	Surrey North West
John	Hannam	Exeter
David	Harris	St Ives
Robert	Hicks	Cornwall South East
Terence	Higgins	Worthing
Peter	Hordern	Horsham
David	Howell	Guildford
Ralph	Howell	Norfolk North
John	Hunt	Ravensbourne
Douglas	Hurd	Witney
Michael	Jopling	Westmorland & Lonsdale
Elaine	Kellett-Bowman	Lancaster
Jill	Knight	Birmingham Edgbaston
David	Knox	Staffordshire Moorlands
Michael	Marshall	Arundel
Patrick	Mayhew	Tunbridge Wells
Patrick	McNair-Wilson	New Forest
David	Mitchell	Hampshire North West
Hector	Monro	Dumfries
Fergus	Montgomery	Altrincham & Sale
Richard	Needham	Wiltshire North
Steven	Norris	Epping Forest
Cranley	Onslow	Woking
John	Patten	Oxford West & Abingdon
Geoffrey	Pattie	Chertsey & Walton
Timothy	Renton	Sussex Mid
Wyn	Roberts	Conwy
Richard	Ryder	Norfolk Mid
Timothy	Sainsbury	Hove
Giles	Shaw	Pudsey
Roger	Sims	Chislehurst
Trevor	Skeet	Bedfordshire North
Keith	Speed	Ashford

James	Spicer	Dorset West
Roy	Thomason	Bromsgrove
Patrick	Thompson	Norwich North
Neville	Trotter	Tynemouth
Gerard	Vaughan	Reading East
George	Walden	Buckingham
John	Ward	Poole
Jerry	Wiggin	Weston-super-Mare
Mark	Wolfson	Sevenoaks

Labour

Roland	Boyes	Houghton & Washington
Jeremy	Bray	Motherwell South
James	Callaghan	Heywood & Middleton
Don	Dixon	Jarrow
James	Dunnachie	Glasgow Pollok
Kenneth	Eastham	Manchester Blackley
Andrew	Faulds	Warley East
John Denis	Fraser	Norwood
Mildred	Gordon	Bow & Poplar
Peter	Hardy	Wentworth
Roy	Hattersley	Birmingham Sparkbrook
Robert	Hughes	Aberdeen North
Greville	Janner	Leicester West
Joan	Lestor	Eccles
Robert	Litherland	Manchester Central
Edward	Loyden	Liverpool Garston
Max	Madden	Bradford West
Alfred	Morris	Manchester Wythenshawe
Gordon	Oakes	Halton
Stanley	Orme	Salford East
Robert	Parry	Liverpool Riverside
Peter	Shore	Bethnal Green & Stepney
Nigel	Spearing	Newham South
John	Thompson	Wansbeck
Harold	Walker	Doncaster Central
Gareth	Wardell	Gower
David	Young	Bolton South East

Liberal Democrat

David	Alton	Liverpool Mossley Hill
Alex	Carlile	Montgomery
Russell	Johnston	Inverness Nairn & Lochaber
Emma	Nicholson	Devon West & Torridge
David	Steel	Tweeddale, Ettrick & Lauderdale
Peter	Thurnham	Bolton North East

THE SCRAMBLE FOR NEW SEATS

Stuart Millar

No matter what happens at the polls, the actual election of the new Parliament will struggle to match the drama surrounding the selection of the candidates. Controversy and, in some cases, sheer farce have been the order of the day. For many Tories, the run-up to the election has involved a massive game of musical chairs where the prize is keeping a seat in the Commons. Faced with the prospect of boundary changes and what seemed like dire election prospects, Tory MPs and Cabinet Ministers decided to quit their seats in search of greener pastures elsewhere. Hardly able to contain their joy at this sign of pessimism in the government ranks, Labour dubbed it the 'chicken run'.

The trend began in the summer of 1995 with the revelation that five well-known Conservative MPs – three of them government ministers – were on the shortlist for the new safe seat of Mid-Sussex. The prize was finally won by Nicholas Soames, defence minister, who abandoned Crawley – estimated majority 3,000 after boundary changes – for the distinctly more comfortable prospect of a 17,000 majority.

What began as a run soon came to look more like a stampede. Even some MPs who would still retain a notional majority after boundary changes have decided their seats are not quite safe enough. Brian Mawhinney, the party chairman, earned the title 'Chairman Chicken' with his decision to find a more secure coop. His 5,300 majority in Peterborough would have improved slightly if he had stayed put – but it would be nothing like as comfortable as the estimated 18,000-vote margin he can now expect in the plum Tory seat of Cambridge North West. Mawhinney is not the only senior Cabinet member to join the chicken run. Stephen Dorrell, the Health Secretary, is quitting Loughborough, which has become marginal, for the new safe seat of Charnwood, while Sir George Young, the Transport Secretary, whose Ealing Acton is being replaced by a seat with a notional Labour majority of 3,500, is moving to North West Hampshire.

Peter Lilley, the Social Security Secretary, defeated the strutting Minister of State for Transport, John Watts, in the battle to represent Hitchin & Harpenden. Despite a notional majority of 9,000 after boundary changes in his St Albans seat, Lilley is erring on the side of caution. Watts will stand in Reading, moving from the neighbouring constituency of Slough, where his majority of 514 was made yet more precarious by the Boundary Commission. Even David Amess, the MP for Basildon, whose face is burned into the memories of voters everywhere as the first symbol of Tory victory in each of the last two general elections, is moving on. Although it may have seemed that his sole political purpose was to mention Basildon as often as possible in the Commons, especially when called upon to put a question to the prime minister, he is heading to the altogether safer seat of Southend West with a majority of over 11,000.

Other chicken runners include: Peter Bottomley, moving from Eltham to the new seat of Worthing West; Bill Cash, who has switched from Stafford to Stone; and Peter Luff, who goes from Worcester to Mid-Worcestershire. Perhaps the most desperate search for a new seat, however, has been that of Norman Lamont. His Kingston-upon-Thames constituency disappears at the election, forcing the former Chancellor to scour the country for a new home. Rumours placed him in Shropshire North, Vale of York, Epping Forest, Kensington & Chelsea, Tewkesbury, Weston-super-Mare, Southend West and Mole Valley, before he landed in Harrogate & Knaresborough in Yorkshire.

The chicken run and the decision by 40 Conservative MPs to stand down means an unprecedented number of vacant Tory seats, offering an opportunity for new boys and retreads – former MPs trying to get back into the Commons – to show their mettle.

The youngish Turks likely to make it onto the green benches are remarkably similar in age and background, almost all in their thirties and in senior management: Tim Loughton, 34, the director of an asset management company (East Worthing & Shoreham); Nick St Aubyn, 40, an investment banker (Guildford); Desmond Swayne, 38, a bank manager (New Forest West); David Prior, 41, a company chairman (North Norfolk); Owen Paterson, 39, managing director of British Leather (North Shropshire); Philip Hammond, 39, director of a business consultancy (Runnymeade & Weybridge); William Rogers, 36, an insurance broker (St Ives); David Cameron, the youngest at 29, head of corporate affairs at Carlton Communications. Another new boy, Ian Liddell-Grainger, 36, a property developer, will take on Torridge & West Devon, whose MP Emma Nicholson defected to the Lib Dems.

Retreads, too, have been remarkably successful in taking up the opportunity offered by the number of Tory vacancies. Ten candidates are attempting to get back into the House, compared with eight in 1992. Labour is running just five retreads. Unlike the last election, when the Conservatives fielded Sebastian Coe and Gyles Brandreth, they have no celebrity candidates this time round – unless you count Boris Johnson, the hell-raising Thatcherite columnist for the *Daily Telegraph*. But even learning Welsh is unlikely to help the blond bombshell overturn a notional Labour majority of 5,000 in Clwyd South. That means the only new Tory MP capable of kicking up a fuss will be Julian Lewis, the 45-year-old deputy director of the Conservative Research Department. Standing in New Forest East, Lewis is known neither for his subtle diplomacy nor his self-effacing political outlook.

Women-only shortlists

Labour has not escaped the selection process unscathed. The party's controversial policy of women-only shortlists came to a sticky end when two disaffected male members persuaded an industrial tribunal that it breached Britain's sex discrimination laws. On legal advice, Labour decided against challenging the ruling for fear that the 35 selections already made under the policy could be jeopardised. The

Conservatives were quick to jump on Labour's embarrassment. Michael Trend, the Tories' deputy chairman, tried to exploit the decision as another sign of Labour hypocrisy, insisting that all candidates selected by an illegal selection process cannot be legitimate.

Even before the ruling, the policy had caused resentment within the party, especially when the National Executive Committee felt forced to impose all-women shortlists on recalcitrant constituency parties. Tony Blair had always found the procedure distasteful, but he recognised the party needed to do something to address the gender imbalance in the Commons. With the scrapping of NEC rules requiring each constituency to include at least one woman on every shortlist, it was left with no legal means to enforce women candidates.

After the ruling John Prescott, the deputy leader, was charged with finding lawful means to exhort local parties to select women. The moves faced stiff opposition in places like Jarrow, Wansbeck and Washington, where favourite sons were waiting in the wings, but they met with a good deal of success. If Labour ends up with 50 additional women MPs in the new Parliament – which is entirely possible – 33 will have been selected in all-women shortlists, but another 17 will have been picked in winnable seats from mixed shortlists, 5 before the industrial tribunal ruling forced the party to abandon its policy and 11 since. This suggests there might have been a strong trend towards women candidates in the Labour Party anyway – as there was in the 1994 European elections when a third of the new Labour MEPs were women.

The number of women MPs in the new Parliament will depend very much on how well Labour does. From the present tally of 63 it will rise to 75 on a standstill result, to 93 if there is a 4 per cent swing against the Government in every seat and to 108 if there is an 8 per cent swing. Labour's current tally of 38 women will rise to 48 on a standstill result, to 58 on a 2 per cent swing, to 68 on a 4 per cent swing, to 81 on 6 per cent and to 87 on 8 per cent. But even at this level women will still account for one sixth of all MPs, well down the international league table from countries like Sweden and Finland where women account for about two fifths of all MPs.

Former and current council leaders account for many of those Labour women likely to make it into Parliament. Margaret Moran, 41, the candidate in Luton South, the ninth most marginal Tory seat, helped pioneer innovations such as citizens' juries and video boxes for community feedback as leader of Lewisham Council, while Sally Keeble, 44, froze poll tax three years running as leader of Southwark council. She is running in Northampton North, the 47th most vulnerable seat. They will be joined by Louise Ellman, the full-time leader of Lancashire County Council since 1981, who is replacing Bob Parry in Liverpool Riverside.

This election is an uncommonly family affair. It will give Parliament its first pair of identical twins, with Maria Eagle, 35, a solicitor specialising in housing and employment law, joining her sister Angela, MP for Wallasey, when she replaces Eddie Loyden in Liverpool Garston. Ann Keen, running in Tory marginal Brentford & Isleworth, is married to Alan, MP for Feltham & Heston. Her retread sister, Sylvia

Heal, was MP for Mid-Staffordshire from 1990 to 1992 and is the candidate for Halesowen this time around.

Other notable women include Barbara Follett, the founder of Emily's List UK (which campaigns for more female MPs) and Labour's image consultant, who is running in Stevenage. Follett, 53, and her novelist husband Ken, are Labour's most notorious champagne socialist supporters. Ruth Kelly, 28, a former *Guardian* economics correspondent, and now deputy head of the Bank of England's Inflation Report Division, is standing in Bolton West, while another journalist, Shona McIsaac, 36, who writes for women's magazines, is the candidate in Cleethorpes.

Lynda Clark, 47, the most senior woman in practice at the Scottish Bar, takes on Foreign Secretary Malcolm Rifkind in Edinburgh Pentlands. Lorna Fitzsimmons, 28, joins a long line of National Union of Students presidents, including Jack Straw, into Parliament. She is running in Rochdale, fourth on Labour's target list. Labour's male candidates follow a similar pattern to the women, with many coming from a local council background. They include: Bob Laxton, 51, the current leader of Derby City Council, standing in Derby North; Mark Todd, 41, former leader of Cambridge City Council, standing in South Derbyshire; Tony Wright, 41, leader of Great Yarmouth Council, standing in Great Yarmouth; Bob Blizzard, leader of Waveney Council, standing in Waveney; and Alan Whitehead, 45, former leader of Southampton City Council, standing in Southampton Test.

While Labour has no celebrities standing this time around, it is not short of interesting candidates. Clive Efford, 37, a London taxi driver, is standing in Eltham, the seat Peter Bottomley is vacating for a more secure majority. Gordon Marsden, 42, the editor of *History Today* magazine, and a contributor to several national newspapers, is running in Blackpool South. ●

BOUNDARY COMMISSION CHANGES: THE POLITICAL IMPACT

Laurence Neville

The parliamentary constituency boundary review, concluded during the summer of 1995, was expected to favour the Conservative party. Before the review began it was widely predicted that the Tories would gain up to 20 seats. Since the war, the drift away from inner-city Labour strongholds towards Conservative-supporting suburbia has become a feature of British life, increasing the average electorate of Tory seats and decreasing that of Labour. Boundary reviews, held roughly every 15 years, have sought to correct this drift, which favours Labour, and 1995 was expected to be no different. In the event the review narrowed, but did not eradicate, the gap between the average size of Labour and Conservative seats. The average electorate of Tory seats had drifted up to 71,509 and of Labour seats had declined to 62,176 at the last election. The review reduces the average Tory electorate to 68,457 and increases the average Labour electorate to 64,292. In other words, the fourth boundary review has reduced Labour's advantage but by no means eliminated it.

The Boundary Commission set a new target size of constituencies in England of 69,281 with lower targets for Wales and Scotland. It created eight new parliamentary seats – increasing the number of MPs from 651 to 659 – but also altered the boundaries of a further 450 constituencies. At the next election, over two-thirds of the electorate will be in a constituency which differs to some extent from that of 1992. Assuming identical voting patterns to the 1992 election, Colin Rallings' and Michael Thrasher's study of the impact of the constituency changes indicates a net gain of seven seats for the Tories. Labour would also benefit, gaining an additional two seats, while the Liberal Democrats would see their slender Commons representation reduced by two. In brief, they estimate that the boundary review gives the Tories a net gain of only five seats over Labour rather than the 20 that was widely predicted.

The overall figures disguise the considerable change within the regions caused by the review. The boundary review in Avon changed Bristol North West from a 1992 Tory seat to a Labour one. However, Kingswood – won by Labour in 1992 – will become a Conservative seat if voting is unchanged from the last general election. The greatest change is in the political profile of London, with the loss of ten seats, five on either side of the Thames. On 1992 results the Conservatives would lose seven of these with Labour losing the remaining three.

Manchester also poses problems for the Tories, as the Metropolitan County's reduction of two seats falls exclusively on the Conservatives. The Boundary Commission changes theoretically deprive Merseyside of its sole Liberal Democrat member. However, these predictions cannot take into account the increasing sophistication of the electorate and the growth of tactical voting. The Liberal Democrats are almost certain to do better than expected under the changes as their formidable campaigning machine targets areas with concentrated support such as the south-west. Labour research, based on local and general election results, forecasts that the Liberal Democrats could win as many as 15 extra seats on a swing of three per cent from the 1992 result. The Nationalist parties may also benefit from this trend.

The continuing discrepancy between the sizes of Labour and Conservative constituencies means that the electoral impact of even a small swing is startling. On a swing of 3.8 per cent, which would equalise the two parties' support, Labour would have 322 seats to the Conservatives' 289. Labour calculates that to remain in Downing Street John Major must hold a lead of at least four per cent over Labour at the election. To oust him Labour needs only a one per cent lead. However, the Boundary Commission has by no means won the general election for Tony Blair. Labour still requires a 4.3 per cent swing to win 57 seats and hold a majority in the House of Commons, according to Rallings and Thrasher. In 1992, the party needed only 4.1 per cent. Labour's own study of the changes estimates that 55 seats are needed to win a majority. To achieve a sufficient majority to enjoy a full term – at least 30 seats – Labour would need a massive swing of at least 7.5 per cent, the largest since 1945. Furthermore, in the unlikely event of a Tory landslide, the review has increased the number of Labour marginals and reduced the number of Conservative marginals.

So how did Labour do so well out of the boundary changes? The Conservatives gained seats in the review but the scale of their gains was limited by a well organised and determined Labour campaign run by the party's local government officer, David Gardner. Although it could never be more than a damage limitation exercise – as the changes were necessitated by established migration trends within Britain – Gardner's team performed valiantly at inquiries up and down the country over the course of the review. While local Conservative parties and Central Office squabbled over boundary changes, Labour presented a united front to the Commission. Dame Angela Rumbold, who ran the Tory campaign, conceded that discipline was a great advantage to Labour. The main problems for the Conservatives were complacency – after early reports had suggested 20 seats would be created in their favour – and a reduced number of electoral agents following redundancies to help pay off the debt from the 1992 election. Labour also effectively utilised community spokesmen such as vicars to argue the case for the continuation of town centre constituencies. The Commission was suitably impressed and altered their preliminary findings 37 times in favour of Labour. The Conservative campaign managed to alter findings only three times.

All the parties focused on how seats were to be divided within areas. The Conservatives wanted sandwiches. Labour wanted doughnuts. Doughnuts are places where parliamentary seats are organised around an urban core and an outer rural ring. Sandwiches are places where a town is split into North and South seats or East and West seats, with surrounding villages added to each seat to bring them up to the required size. Colchester, which was previously divided into North and South seats with adjoining villages in each seat, was successfully doughnutted in the review and now has a single city constituency. Chelmsford, on the other hand, has become a sandwich, with the town split between East and West. On the whole the Commission recognised the need for self-standing town constituencies and used the town centre as the basis of many new constituencies. The argument for doughnuts prevailed to the benefit of Labour.

The boundary changes will certainly have some impact on the election. They may even help Labour win the essential battleground of 'middle England'. Out of Labour's top 60 target seats, 39 are either new or changed constituencies. The review maintained the advantage Labour enjoys in having concentrated support in small constituencies. The unpredictability of tactical voting makes the precise effects of the changes impossible to assess. But if Tony Blair finds himself inside Downing Street after election day, at least a small portion of the credit must go to David Gardner, whose mastery of constituency electoral detail may well have delivered those few seats which make all the difference. ●

WILL THE POLLS GET IT WRONG AGAIN?

Nick Sparrow (Managing Director of ICM)

The failure of all the polls to predict the outcome of the 1992 election prompted detailed investigations, most notably by the Market Research Society, into the likely causes of the error. Among all the possible reasons for the failure, late swing explained around a quarter of the error. The use of out-of-date demographic controls (the method by which pollsters ensure samples are representative of all voters) also had some effect, but over half the error remained unexplained. The most likely cause was a 'spiral of silence' operating against the Conservatives.

The spiral of silence theory states that, if any group of voters perceive that there is a climate of opinion against the party of their natural choice, they will become inclined to silence. In opinion polling terms this means that they will either refuse to be interviewed altogether, or refuse to answer the voting-intention question ('won't say') or claim they 'don't know' whom they would vote for.

Evidence for a continuing anti-Conservative spiral of silence can be observed in all the major opinion polls. First, 60 per cent or so of people who take part in polls and say they 'don't know' whom they would support in an immediate election nevertheless admit to voting Conservative in 1992. Secondly, more people in poll samples claim to have voted Labour in 1992 than Conservative, indicating that it is harder to get former Conservative voters to participate in polls at all or, if they do, to reveal anything about their past or future intentions.

This theory helps explain many recent elections and shows that it does not always operate against the Conservatives. In 1983, when Labour wrote 'the longest suicide note in history' as its manifesto, the polls overestimated the Tories' electoral advantage. Such errors could easily be explained by a small group of Labour supporters hiding their true intentions because of what they saw as a wider anti-Labour climate of opinion.

Most pollsters agree that some Conservative supporters presently hide their probable actions by answering 'don't know' or 'won't say' to the voting-intention question. However, some see the discrepancy between declared past votes and the actual performance of the parties in the last election not as part of the spiral of silence at all but as resulting from two other distortions. First they point out that prior to 1992 large numbers of SDP/Liberal Alliance supporters forgot how they had voted, remembering instead a vote for Labour or the Conservatives. They also point to the tendency of recalled past votes to move in line with present intentions – in other words people who now intend to vote Labour 'remember' voting Labour in 1992 even when they didn't.

Panel research data suggests that while these tendencies persist they are not nearly enough to account for the under-representation of 1992 Conservative voters in recent polls. In panel surveys the same people are interviewed over time and are asked how they voted in 1992 on each occasion. In all, over 80 per cent of voters accurately recall their 1992 votes and of those that do not, less than half align their past votes with their present intentions. These effects only marginally increase the recall of voting Labour (by between two per cent and three per cent) at the expense of the Conservatives (who lose perhaps two per cent) at a time when intentions to vote Conservative are near an all-time low.

This panel data also shows that recall of voting Liberal lies within one point of voters' actual 1992 performance. Liberal Democrat supporters remain slightly more forgetful than other voters, but the net effect is cancelled out by a small group of mainly 1992 Conservative supporters who mis-remember voting Liberal.

The overall accuracy of the recall figures in the panel survey is matched in ICM's telephone polls, which interview fresh samples of people on each occasion. Both of these surveys record a Conservative victory just short of the actual winning margin. Quota polls continue to suggest Neil Kinnock won in 1992 by a margin of between five and seven per cent, well outside the range that could be explained by faulty recall. A large part of the discrepancy in declared past votes could be explained by some inadequacies in the operation of quota polls simply because they allow interviewers too much leeway on whom and where to interview. Whatever the reason, the direction of the error in recall is consistent with the spiral of silence theory.

The unadjusted poll figures are calculated in the same way as polls conducted prior to 1992, with more up-to-date demographic controls but with no correction for declared past votes and by simply excluding 'don't knows', refusers and those who say they will not vote. While there is general acceptance that some Conservative voters may, by some means, avoid giving a realistic voting intention when asked to do so in a poll, there is some disagreement on what measures to take to correct for the resulting distortion. This is, perhaps, not surprising because pollsters are dealing with missing data and the corrective measures inevitably involve some calculated guesswork.

ICM adjust poll data by weighting the declared past votes of respondents back to the actual performance of the parties in the 1992 general election. This adjustment has a relatively modest effect on the voting intention figures simply because they closely resemble the actual votes cast in 1992. More important in the process is the adjustment for 'don't knows'. Research in the 1992 election found that 60 per cent of those who said before the election they 'did not know' what they would vote actually turned out for the party they had supported in 1987. Therefore, ICM reallocate 60 per cent of the current 'don't knows' back to the party they voted for in 1992.

Other polling companies use variations on these techniques. Gallup weight their polls by matching the recall of past votes back to the actual results in 1992, but do not reallocate any of those who presently don't know who they would vote for. MORI reallocate all the 'don't knows' and refusers to the party they voted for in 1992, but do not weight the declared past votes of the sample as a whole back to the 1992 general election result. NOP weight the declared past votes not to the results of the last election but to the declared past votes of their random sample Omnibus survey, which puts the recalled 1992 result at 39 per cent Conservative and 39 per cent Labour. The 'don't knows' are reallocated to different parties on the basis of their answers to other questions. These include the party voters most closely identify with, and a question on which party has the best policies on the economy. ●

Guardian monthly poll figures

The *Guardian* has been publishing Marplan and then ICM poll figures since 1980, and they have appeared monthly since 1982. They have been calculated on the new adjusted basis since the 1992 election. Percentages shown indicate responses to the question 'How will you vote?' Like all poll figures, they relate to Great Britain only, not the United Kingdom. Likewise the election figures give the parties' share of the vote in Great Britain, not the United Kingdom.

	Con %	Lab %	Lib Dem %	Others %	Lead (Con over Lab) %
UNADJUSTED					
Apr 82	34	32	30	4	2
Jul 82	45	33	19	2	12
Aug 82	41	37	20	2	4
Oct 82	45	34	19	2	11
Nov 82	46	34	18	2	12
Dec 82	44	32	18	1	12
Jan 83	48	30	21	1	18
Feb 83	49	28	22	1	21
Mar 83	41	27	31	1	14
Apr 83	43	32	23	2	11
May 83	46	34	19	0	12
Jun 83	47	30	23	0	17
Election	**44**	**28**	**26**	**2**	**16**
Aug 83	45	30	24	1	15
Oct 83	42	37	20	1	5
Nov 83	42	35	22	1	7
Dec 83	41	37	21	1	4
Jan 84	42	38	19	0	4
Feb 84	39	40	20	0	−1
Mar 84	38	38	22	2	0
Apr 84	40	37	21	2	3
May 84	38	37	23	2	1
Jun 84	37	38	23	2	−1
Jul 84	34	39	26	1	−5
Aug 84	36	39	24	1	−3
Sep 84	39	38	21	2	1
Oct 84	38	36	24	2	2
Nov 84	42	33	24	1	9
Dec 84	41	32	26	1	9
Jan 85	41	33	25	1	8
Feb 85	38	36	25	1	2
Mar 85	36	36	27	1	0
Apr 85	33	38	28	1	−5
May 85	29	34	35	1	−5

	Con %	Lab %	Lib Dem %	Others %	Lead (Con over Lab) %
Jun 85	31	36	32	1	−5
Jul 85	31	34	33	2	−3
Aug 85	31	36	31	2	−5
Sep 85	31	32	36	1	−1
Oct 85	32	34	32	2	−2
Nov 85	34	35	28	2	−1
Dec 85	35	33	30	2	2
Jan 86	29	36	33	2	−7
Feb 86	27	36	35	3	−9
Mar 86	32	36	31	2	−4
Apr 86	32	35	30	3	−3
May 86	28	39	30	3	−11
Jun 86	33	39	26	2	−6
Jul 86	31	38	28	3	−7
Aug 86	32	38	27	3	−6
Sep 86	34	40	24	2	−6
Oct 86	36	39	24	2	−3
Nov 86	38	36	23	2	2
Dec 86	39	38	21	2	1
Jan 87	38	36	23	3	2
Feb 87	38	35	24	2	3
Mar 87	38	32	27	3	6
Apr 87	38	32	27	3	6
May 87	41	33	21	4	8
Election	**43**	**32**	**23**	**2**	**11**
Oct 87	45	39	13	3	6
Dec 87	47	37	13	3	10
Jan 88	42	40	17	2	2
Feb 88	43	43	14	1	0
Mar 88	45	41	12	2	4
Apr 88	43	42	12	2	1
May 88	44	42	11	3	2
Jun 88	47	42	9	2	5
Jul 88	45	43	9	3	2
Aug 88	45	41	11	3	4

	Con	Lab	Lib Dem	Others	Lead (Con over Lab)		Con	Lab	Lib Dem	Others	Lead (Con over Lab)
	%	%	%	%	%		%	%	%	%	%
Sep 88	42	44	12	2	−2	Nov 92	34	43	17	5	−9
Oct 88	44	40	13	4	4	Dec 92	33	45	16	6	−12
Nov 88	42	42	13	3	0	Jan 93	38	42	15	5	−4
Dec 88	45	39	12	4	6	Feb 93	37	45	13	5	−8
Jan 89	44	40	11	4	4	Mar 93	34	45	16	5	−11
Feb 89	42	39	14	4	3	Apr 93	34	46	15	5	−12
Mar 89	42	41	14	4	1	May 93	29	43	23	6	−14
Apr 89	44	40	13	4	4	Jun 93	27	43	25	5	−16
May 89	43	43	11	3	0	Jul 93	28	42	23	6	−14
Jun 89	38	42	11	9	−4	Aug 93	28	40	28	5	−12
Jul 89	38	42	10	11	−4	Sep 93	27	45	24	5	−12
Aug 89	37	45	9	9	−8	Oct 93	31	46	19	4	−15
Sep 89	38	46	6	10	−8	Nov 93	29	45	23	3	−16
Oct 89	39	49	6	7	−10	Dec 93	25	48	24	4	−23
Nov 89	36	49	9	6	−13	Jan 94	26	49	20	3	−24
Dec 89	37	49	8	6	−12	Feb 94	26	51	20	4	−25
Jan 90	38	47	8	7	−9	Mar 94	24	49	22	5	−25
Feb 90	36	51	8	5	−15	Apr 94	26	48	22	4	−22
Mar 90	31	52	9	8	−21	May 94	24	48	23	5	−24
Apr 90	32	56	6	6	−24	Jun 94	26	51	19	4	−25
May 90	32	50	13	6	−18	Jul 94	27	50	20	4	−23
Jun 90	35	54	51	6	−19	Aug 94	23	55	17	5	−32
Jul 90	35	51	8	5	−16	Sep 94	28	52	16	4	−24
Aug 90	38	49	9	4	−11	Oct 94	26	58	13	3	−32
Sep 90	37	50	8	6	−13	Nov 94	28	54	14	4	−26
Oct 90	36	49	9	7	−13	Dec 94	27	53	16	5	−27
Nov 90	33	49	13	5	−16	Jan 95	25	56	15	4	−31
Dec 90	45	43	9	3	2	Feb 95	24	58	14	4	−34
Jan 91	43	43	10	5	0	Mar 95	22	59	14	5	−37
Feb 91	44	42	9	5	2	Apr 95	20	58	17	5	−38
Mar 91	39	40	16	5	−1	May 95	23	56	17	4	−32
Apr 91	39	43	13	5	−4	Jun 95	20	59	18	4	−39
May 91	37	43	16	5	−6	Jul 95	26	57	14	3	−31
Jun 91	34	44	17	6	−10	Aug 95	26	56	14	4	−30
Jul 91	37	43	16	4	−6	Sep 95	26	55	16	4	−29
Aug 91	36	45	16	3	−9	Oct 95	23	57	15	6	−34
Sep 91	39	39	17	4	0	Nov 95	26	51	19	4	−25
Oct 91	41	43	12	4	−2	Dec 95	29	53	15	4	−24
Nov 91	41	43	13	4	−2	Jan 96	22	53	20	5	−31
Dec 91	39	42	14	4	−3	Feb 96	27	52	17	4	−25
Jan 92	42	41	12	4	1	Mar 96	26	51	20	4	−25
Feb 92	40	40	16	4	0	Apr 96	25	56	16	4	−31
Mar 92	39	42	15	4	−3	May 96	26	50	20	5	−24
Election	**43**	**35**	**18**	**4**	**8**	Jun 96	25	51	18	5	−26
May 92	46	36	14	6	10	Jul 96	25	50	20	5	−25
Jun 92	44	36	13	6	8	Aug 96	30	50	18	3	−20
Jul 92	45	39	12	4	6	Sep 96	28	51	15	5	−23
Aug 92	41	40	14	5	1	Oct 96	27	54	15	3	−27
Sep 92	38	38	19	5	0	Nov 96	33	48	15	4	−15
Oct 92	38	42	16	4	−4	Dec 96	27	53	16	4	−26
						Jan 97	29	50	17	4	−21

The **Election**

	Con	Lab	Lib Dem	Others	Lead (Con over Lab)		Con	Lab	Lib Dem	Others	Lead (Con over Lab)
	%	%	%	%	%		%	%	%	%	%
*ADJUSTED						Jun 94	30	44	20	6	−14
Election	**43**	**35**	**18**	**4**	**8**	Jul 94	31	44	21	4	−13
May 92	45	34	17	4	9	Aug 94	28	49	19	5	−21
Jun 92	45	36	16	4	9	Sep 94	33	45	18	4	−12
Jul 92	45	36	15	5	9	Oct 94	32	49	15	4	−17
Aug 92	41	36	17	5	5	Nov 94	31	49	16	3	−18
Sep 92	39	35	19	6	4	Dec 94	31	49	17	4	−18
Oct 92	38	38	19	5	0	Jan 95	30	48	18	4	−18
Nov 92	36	40	19	5	−4	Feb 95	31	49	17	4	−18
Dec 92	36	41	18	5	−5	Mar 95	27	52	17	4	−25
Jan 93	39	37	18	6	2	Apr 95	26	51	18	5	−25
Feb 93	37	39	18	5	−2	May 95	29	48	19	4	−19
Mar 93	36	41	18	5	−5	Jun 95	24	53	19	4	−29
Apr 93	34	39	21	5	−5	Jul 95	32	47	17	3	−15
May 93	32	38	24	6	−6	Aug 95	31	48	17	5	−17
Jun 93	31	38	26	6	−7	Sep 95	31	48	17	4	−17
Jul 93	32	37	25	6	−5	Oct 95	29	49	17	5	−20
Aug 93	30	36	27	6	−6	Nov 95	30	47	19	4	−17
Sep 93	29	40	26	5	−11	Dec 95	31	48	16	4	−17
Oct 93	36	39	20	4	−3	Jan 96	26	48	22	4	−22
Nov 93	34	38	24	4	−4	Feb 96	31	47	19	4	−16
Dec 93	31	42	23	4	−11	Mar 96	31	45	20	4	−14
Jan 94	31	43	21	5	−12	Apr 96	29	50	17	4	−21
Feb 94	30	44	21	5	−14	May 96	28	45	21	5	−17
Mar 94	29	44	22	5	−15	Jun 96	30	46	19	5	−16
Apr 94	30	42	22	5	−12	Jul 96	30	45	21	4	−15
May 94	29	44	24	4	−15	Aug 96	33	45	19	3	−12
						Sep 96	32	47	16	5	−15
*Con minus Lab						Oct 96	31	49	16	3	−18
						Nov 96	34	47	15	4	−13
						Dec 96	31	50	15	4	−19
						Jan 97	31	48	16	4	−17

Source: Marplan and ICM

PART TWO

POLICIES

CONSTITUTION

Richard Norton-Taylor and Laurence Neville

On 6 May 1992, John Major told the Commons in the debate on the Queen's Speech shortly after his general election success: 'I propose to make reforms at the heart of government. We will sweep away many of the cobwebs of secrecy which needlessly veil too much of government business.' Major kept to his cautiously phrased promise – up to a point. He published *Questions of Procedure for Ministers*, the code of behaviour and ethics which includes the obligation for ministers to be 'as open as possible with Parliament and the public', and not to mislead MPs. Major published the list of Cabinet committees and identified the new heads of the Security Service (MI5) and the Secret Intelligence Service (MI6).

In April 1994, the Conservative Government introduced a Code of Practice on Access to Government Information – its alternative to a Freedom of Information Act, a statutory 'right to know', which is supported by all other political parties. Although the code gives the Parliamentary Ombudsman the authority to take up complaints from the public against a refusal to disclose official information, the scheme does not have the force of law. The code also has a wide range of exemptions to disclosure, including information relating to 'defence, security and international relations', commercial confidences, immigration, and all policy advice and analysis by civil servants.

As part of what it called its 'open government initiative', the Major administration agreed to the publication of the minutes of the regular meetings between the Chancellor and the Governor of the Bank of England. It also opened up archives previously closed at the Public Record Office. They included papers relating to controversial criminal cases, the German occupation of the Channel Islands, and documents on the second world war activities of the security and intelligence agencies and the Special Operations Executive. However, the Conservative Government's main emphasis was not on the disclosure of Whitehall documents or the substance of policy-making. It concentrated more on schemes, notably the Citizen's Charter, designed to encourage the public to demand better services.

The Government's commitment to open government was seriously questioned by its handling of Sir Richard Scott's report into the arms-to-Iraq affair. Major asked Scott, a senior judge, to conduct an inquiry after the collapse of the Matrix Churchill arms-to-Iraq trial in November 1992. Scott published his 1,800-page report in February 1996. He concluded that ministers had repeatedly misled Parliament and that ministers had been told, wrongly, that they had to sign Public Interest Immunity certificates – so-called gagging orders – designed to suppress Whitehall documents.

Scott also found that ministers had failed to meet the obligations of ministerial accountability contained in *Questions of Procedure for Ministers*. He noted that the Government had redrafted the code by adding the qualification 'knowingly' to the duty of ministers not to mislead Parliament. He also criticised ministers for refusing to give Parliament information about arms sales.

The Government wanted to shut down all debate over Scott's recommendations. Labour and the Liberal Democrats, meanwhile, seized on his report as further proof of the need for a Freedom of Information Act. 'The very fact of its introduction will signal a new relationship between government and the people,' Tony Blair told the annual Freedom of Information Campaign awards presentation in March 1996. However, Peter Mandelson, Labour's frontbench spokesman on Whitehall, subsequently made it clear that a Labour administration would include a broad range of exemptions in a Freedom of Information Act, including civil service advice to ministers.

The 1994 Intelligence Services Act, which for the first time put MI6 and GCHQ on a statutory basis, also set up a parliamentary Intelligence and Security Committee. However, its powers are limited. Its members are appointed by the prime minister, it meets in private, and its reports are vetted by the prime minister before they are published. Meanwhile, the 1996 Security Service Act for the first time gives MI5 broad powers to tackle 'serious crime' in co-operation with the police and Customs. Previously MI5's functions had been restricted to protecting national security by fighting terrorism, espionage, and subversion. Jack Straw and Alun Michael, Labour's frontbench law and order spokesmen, supported the measure. It was left to Alan Beith, the Liberal Democrat home affairs spokesman, to warn of the potential threat to civil liberties. During debates on the bill, he expressed concern about MI5's lack of accountability and the uncertain relationship between its agents and the police.

Labour has had difficulties of its own over constitutional matters. While Major scorned their plans for reform of the House of Lords as 'a sort of teenage madness' Blair had added little to his promise to abolish the voting rights of hereditary peers. Although this reform is envisaged as the first part of a wider change there is considerable doubt over the level of commitment to further reform should hereditary peers be disenfranchised. The issue of the greatest hereditary institution of them all, the monarchy, has not been broached by Labour. The Shadow Home Secretary Jack Straw has, however, ruled out packing the Lords to guarantee a Labour majority over constitutional issues. The Liberal Democrats – as ever less constrained in their policy-making – advocate complete abolition of the Lords and replacement with a proportionally elected second chamber with delaying powers.

The accusation that public interest in constitutional reform is confined to the 'chattering classes' is one the Tories will run with. The high standard of debate and accumulated knowledge of the Lords, including two Nobel Prize winners, combined with the maxim of 'if it ain't broke …' will be the main Conservative defence over challenges to the authority of the Lords. But the sheer unfairness of the second house – they vote against Major about ten times a year and voted against the last Labour government about 70 times a year – makes opposition to any reform problematic. In addition the membership of this exclusive club is far from representative. Out of 1,192 members only 83 are women while 755 owe their position to their forebears' favours to royalty.

Major believes the constitutional agenda belongs to the Conservatives. That is not to say the Conservatives have an agenda other than the maintenance of the status quo, but Major believes the issue can only benefit the Tories at the polls. He may be right. Even if he cannot convince the electorate that constitutional reform is only of interest to the Islington elite, he may be able to scare voters away from it. Despite polls showing a narrow margin of support for the Labour shopping list of reforms – changes to the Lords, possible electoral reform, and the rest – constitutional change is difficult to get right. A Conservative rallying call to defend all that made Britain great may become a powerful one if there is sufficient doubt in the minds of the voters.

Labour also favours a stepped approach to a Bill of Rights, beginning with the incorporation of the European Convention of Human Rights into domestic law. A state-of-the-nation poll commissioned by the Rowntree Reform Trust in 1995 indicated widespread public support for a Bill of Rights with 79 per cent in favour. The most popular right to be incorporated in a Bill of Rights was the right to hospital treatment in reasonable time.

The status of unelected quangos would not undergo wholesale change under Labour but a number of the most controversial, including the Prisons Agency, would be brought back under ministerial control. Accountability of these bodies, which now control £40 billion, two-thirds as much money as local government receives from Whitehall, would be tackled. However, a purge of quango members, whose appointments are notoriously partisan, has been ruled out as the natural turnover of quango members is high enough to create an impact within the first year of an alternative government.

The confirmation of Labour's commitment to a referendum on electoral reform at the conference in 1995 came as something of a surprise. Tony Blair's well-known scepticism on the issue appears to be weakening, although it remains to be seen if the lure of removing power from the centre will remain as strong once the power is Labour's. ●

Main events since 1992

9 November 1992: Matrix-Churchill arms-to-Iraq trial abandoned. Government sets up Scott Inquiry.

March 1993: John Smith pledges a future Labour government to introduce a Bill of Rights.

19 May 1993: Labour's National Executive receives report of Plant Commission. John Smith accepts its recommendations except for House of Commons, where he promises a referendum.

5 October 1993: Labour Conference votes 45-42 in favour of a referendum on electoral reform, but also votes in favour of first-past-the-post system by 45-35.

29 June 1994: Prince Charles says in a television interview that he wants to be a 'defender of faith' and admits having an affair.

October 1995: Labour reaffirms commitment to referendum on electoral reform.

6 November 1995: MPs vote 322 to 271 to require MPs to declare earnings.

30 November 1995: Labour and Lib Dems agree through cross-party Scottish Convention to set up Scottish Parliament elected by additional-member system.

15 February 1996: Scott Report published on arms to Iraq.

18 March 1996: Tony Blair hints that he is willing to consider a shift away from first-past-the-post voting for the Commons.

Legislation

Intelligence Services Act 1994
- placed MI5 and MI6 on statutory footing
- set up system of ministerial warrants for surveillance
- created parliamentary committee with limited oversight of security service

Standing Orders 1995
- banned paid advocacy by MPs
- required declaration of earnings
- appointed Parliamentary Commissioner for Standards

Security Service Act 1996
- allowed MI5 to assist police in fight against crime

Policies

Bill of Rights
Con: Elected representatives safeguard our freedom. Unelected judges should not be given the power to overturn Acts of Parliament.
Lab: Incorporate the European Convention on Human Rights (ECHR) into British law as a first step towards a domestic Bill of Rights.
Lib Dem: Entrench a new Bill of Rights within a written constitution, upheld by a Supreme Court. The ECHR to be incorporated as a first step.

Electoral Reform
Con: Britain's first-past-the-post system produces strong and stable government. Alternative systems increase the power of minority parties and lead to political chaos.
Lab: Committed to holding a referendum on voting systems for the House of Commons.
Lib Dem: Guarantee to introduce a fair voting system for local, national and European elections using the Single Transferable Vote system.

Freedom of Information
Con: Have published membership of Cabinet Committees and given parents, patients and users detailed information about the performance of public services.

Lab: Pass a Freedom of Information Act establishing a general right of access to official information held by national, regional and local government and public bodies.

Lib Dem: Establish a public right of access to government and other official information including factual information and policy advice.

House of Lords

Con: The House of Lords works: it brings independent thought to Parliament, provides a forum for first-class debate and acts as an effective revising chamber.

Lab: Abolish the voting rights of hereditary peers as the first step towards reforming the House of Lords.

Lib Dem: Transform the House of Lords into a directly elected Senate, representing the nations and regions of the UK.

Party Funding

Con: Follow Select Committee's code of practice. Donors do not influence party decision-making; Labour's trade union donors do.

Lab: Ban donations from foreign nationals living outside the UK and declare donations over £5,000.

Lib Dem: Introduce state funding for parties, spending limits and a requirement to publish donations.

Quangos

Con: Continue to increase accountability by setting targets and publishing reports – and to wind up quangos when their usefulness ends.

Lab: Have proposed a comprehensive register of all quango members and called for greater democratic scrutiny of public services at national, regional and local levels.

Lib Dem: Disband unnecessary non-elected bodies and establish democratic rules for the rest.

Women MPs

Con: The party is meritocratic. Does not discriminate against men in a politically correct attempt to patronise women.

Lab: Committed to the proper representation of women in Parliament.

Lib Dem: It is expected that on a candidate shortlist of three one must be of a different sex.

Polls

CONSTITUTIONAL REFORM

Should there be	% Yes	% No
a limit on national spending by parties?	81	14
a Freedom of Information Act?	77	9
a Bill of Rights?	72	11
fixed-date elections?	56	23
proportional representation?	50	23
compulsory voting?	49	42
an elected second chamber in place of Lords?	40	29
public money to finance party campaigns?	39	53

Source: Rowntree Trust / MORI State of the Nation 1995

Which of these comes closest to your view?	%
I strongly support the monarchy as it is	36
I'm not especially keen on the monarchy, but it's better than the alternatives	34
I'd like to keep the monarchy while the Queen is alive, then end it	20
I think we should end the monarchy now	8

Source: ICM January 1995

Most-quoted statistics

In 1992 the Tories won the general election with less than 42 per cent of the vote. Only one government since the second world war has won a majority of votes cast.
Liberal Democrat policy guide

There are nearly 7,000 non-elected public bodies (quangos), responsible for spending some £60 billion, around one-third of all government expenditure.
Liberal Democrat Policy Guide

Under the Tories there are more quango appointees than local councillors and they control £60 billion of our money.
Labour Election Guide

In 1988, the votes of Tory hereditary peers introduced the poll tax – which cost £14 billion to implement, modify and then abandon.
Labour Election Guide

Women make up 52 per cent of the population, but under the Tories fewer than one in ten MPs.
Labour Election Guide

There are currently 62 women MPs out of 651, or 9.5 per cent.

Quotable quotes

'To depend on the Liberals is to dance with the devil.'
Alan Watson, *Labour Conference delegate, on plans for a referendum on electoral reform, 5 October 1995*

'I find it outrageous that we should acquiesce in that democratic scandal because every ten or 15 years our turn in the sun might come around.'
Robin Cook, *on the first-past-the-post system*

'Well, it's our old friend being economical, isn't it?' 'With the truth?' 'With the actualité.'
Alan Clark, *being questioned at the Matrix-Churchill trial*

'I do not regard changing the way we are governed as an afterthought, a detailed fragment of our programme. I regard it as an essential part of new Britain, of us becoming a young, confident country again.'
Tony Blair

'The first right of a citizen in any mature democracy should be the right to information.'
Tony Blair

Asked whether the Conservatives might benefit from a period in opposition: 'That's crazy. If you went into opposition, you might not get back for many years. They might change the voting system.'
Margaret Thatcher

CONSTITUTION: THE REGIONS

Martin Wainwright

Millions of pounds' worth of business was being done in marquees on the country house lawn – miles from London and redolent of local rather than central power – but the woman from the Government's regional office was not getting carried away. Although her lunch table was full of significant guests, well aware of the office's role in attracting Single Regeneration Budget and similar cash from Whitehall, she had no illusions about who was really pulling the strings. 'For goodness' sake, don't call us the "regional government office",' she said. '*They* don't like that. They feel it gives the wrong idea.' They, of course, are the Sir Humphreys in London – and behind them the Rt Hon Jim Hackers – who do not share the romantic and recently fashionable view that the eight offices are a secret launchpad for real devolution.

Regional policy is one of the prime suspects as a duff firework in the election – fizzing here and spurting there, but in the end failing to burst into exhilarating life. Like proportional representation, it loses its appeal the closer any party gets to power. Other than saintliness, whatever could motivate the holders of centralised clout to give some back to the edges? A heavyweight town hall player in the north-east, where regional enthusiasm is the strongest in the country, swears he was in the same room as a prominent Labour MP and heard him say: 'We're not winning power in order to hand it back to duffers in the north-east.' Labour's deputy leader, John Prescott, has made some headway since the summer of 1996 on pushing a more positive line; but the man in charge of the shadow regional brief, Jack Straw, does not have the glad heart of a true believer.

The Conservatives, however, have by far the least enthusiasm for anything which might sap at the London-based and -directed administration of an island physically smaller than some American states. Although choice and variety are important to the appeal of many of their policies, centrally-decided rules provide the context. A grant-maintained school is portrayed as proof of choice in education, but its staff (and even those in supposedly 'independent' schools) must march to the National Curriculum drum. One of the few generally-agreed attractions of the privatised utilities was their local identification – Northumbrian Water, for instance, drawing its endless Geordie supplies from mighty Kielder Dam. But the centralised market and its takeovers have taken priority over that.

In the areas where regional enthusiasm is strongest, too, the Conservatives are like Lewis Carroll's Snark: simply not there. William Hague has the lonely distinction of being the only Cabinet Minister with a seat in one of the four northern government regions of England (half the national total). And he is the Secretary of State for Wales. Willie Whitelaw, in his mellow retirement in Cumbria, must wonder what happened to the party's tradition of keeping some of its heaviest cannons beyond Birmingham. The local authority elections of 1996 saw the blue tiles picked from the mosaic further and further south; and recent local government conferences have seemed extraordinarily radical gatherings for John Major's Britain – until you realise that there simply are *no* Conservative councillors in the room.

The party has weathered far too many reversals to be downhearted, however, and it believes – with the backing of opinion polls – that strengthening local government has a fundamental electoral flaw. 'Not more bureaucracy, not *another* tier of government, not more jobs for the boys' is a damaging argument on doorsteps, backed by the lamentable financial history of almost every attempt to alter the structure of local government. Even the Conservatives' own, most recent attempt to streamline things in the regions, by creating new unitary authorities and abolishing unhappy novelties like Avon and Humberside, ran into the Law of Change Always Costing More. Any love won by abolishing Cleveland county, another uneasy 1970s invention, in April 1996 was lost as the price of redundancies and setting up new, smaller councils rose from the Government's predicted maximum of £18 million to £32 million (and rising: the new unitary authorities like Middlesbrough and Hartlepool want borrowing powers of £40 million to help pay for the change).

This sort of bill has made Tony Blair extremely cautious about commitment to anything as expensive as democracy in the regions. Labour's regional chambers are the product of midnight oil discussions on the cheapest way to add some local accountability to the government regional offices. Not just opinion polls, but the actual abysmal level of polling in local elections has not been lost on the party's policy-makers. Labour's very strong presence in the regions – Blair, Prescott and just about everyone else in the party hierarchy represent constituencies miles from London – is also a useful card in avoiding any substantial devolution of real power. The Conservatives have made good psychological use for nearly two decades of moving very important, high profile government offices out of London (health, tax and parts of education) without actually giving local people any say in how they are run. Similarly, the presence of a prime minister in County Durham and his deputy in Hull would mean more to many Joe Punters than the right to vote for a regional assemblyman/woman at Darlington.

As befits those furthest from power, the Liberal Democrats are much the most enthusiastic about devolving democracy, holding that the whole operation is meaningless if voting for regional assemblies is not involved. Carried along by years of success at 'community politics', their package envisages a similar energisation of people at a level higher than the district or county; it also accepts the logic of 'no representation without taxation': an elected assembly is meaningless without the power to raise money for its plans. Even to some supporters, such hopes of returning to the hugely effective days of local government proudly running trams, parks and public health on a rich rating/tax base are a romantic pipedream.

But the enormously significant new factor of the European Union has great potential here. The official interest of all British parties in regionalism, whether through devolved government offices or elected assemblies, owes much to the fact that Europe is used to regions and has a lavish budget – or rather budgets – specially for them. Labour and the Liberal Democrats have scored effectively on this, with regional players like Lancashire's Louise Ellman swift to set up bureaux in Brussels or Strasbourg to attract funds into their areas. The faith of flagging regionalists has been transformed by the way that highly centralised European countries like France have accepted stronger, elected regional councils as part of the EU framework.

This, however, brings in a much more dramatic and powerful election spectre than regionalism: the great issue of Europe, Sir James Goldsmith, referendums and John Major's island, 'battered by history but determined to survive intact'. The determined progress of the EU has forced all parties to look again at that old political conundrum: devolution for Scotland and Wales. The question might seem more important than mere English regionalism, with historic nations involved; but the issues are the same and familiar from circular debates going back to Harold Macmillan's days. For government regional offices, read the considerably grander

Scottish and Welsh Offices as the limit of Conservative concessions. For Labour's English chambers, read (in theory) a Parliament for Scotland and an assembly for Wales which (in practice) will lead to the mother of all debates about what should happen in detail and how soon.

The Liberal Democrats stick, as they always have, to full-scale local power, and the Nationalists would top it with embassies and flags. But there is a feeling common to all parties that if this election was a cereal packet competition, with issues to be ranked in order of burning importance, very few electors would put their cross, or saltire, by regionalism/devolution as Priority Number One. ●

Main events since 1992

2 June 1992: John Major rules out significant changes in the government of Scotland by ruling out an assembly.

13 December 1992: Ministers promise improvement to the government of Scotland after 25,000 people demonstrate in Edinburgh for home rule.

9 March 1993: Government White Paper 'A Partnership for Good' proposes upgrading of Scottish Grand Committee and is denounced by Opposition as 'political theatre'.

13 March 1995: Arthur Bell, chairman of the Scottish Tory Reform Group, voices grassroots misgivings about the Government's opposition to devolution.

12 May 1995: Malcolm Rifkind, then Defence Secretary, causes a storm when he tells Channel Four News that he agrees with the principle of devolution for Scotland.

9 September 1995: John Major, as part of his 'meet the people' tour of Britain, dismisses devolution proposals as 'loopy' and fit only for the dustbin.

21 October 1995: Labour, Liberal Democrats, trade unions, church and community organisations in the Scottish Constitutional Convention agree blueprint for devolution.

27 November 1995: Fifteen leading companies employing more than 9,000 workers threaten to quit Scotland if devolved Parliament is set up.

30 November 1995: Scottish Secretary Michael Forsyth announces plans to give Scottish MPs wide-ranging new powers over legislation affecting Scotland; Labour and Liberal Democrats unveil blueprint for a devolved Scottish Parliament; and SNP announces proposals for an independent Parliament.

27 June 1996: Labour changes policy on devolution and announces that referendums would be held before Scottish or Welsh devolution took place.

Policies

Scotland and Wales

Con: Scotland's best interests as a nation lie in strengthening, rather than weakening, its relationship with the rest of the United Kingdom.

Lab: Referendums in Scotland and Wales to pave the way for a Scottish Parliament and a Welsh assembly in the first year of office.

Lib Dem: Introduce Home Rule for Scotland and an elected Senedd for Wales.

London and the Regions

Con: Any new level of government would increase bureaucracy and reduce local inefficiency.

Lab: Committed to an elected strategic authority for London and to English regional chambers, or directly elected assemblies where there is consent.

Lib Dem: Create an elected strategic authority and devolve power to the regions and communities of Britain.

Poll

Do you want devolution of power to regional assemblies or parliaments in	%
all regions of Britain?	15
regions that want them?	16
Scotland and Wales only?	12
Scotland only?	6
Total any devolution	**49**
No devolution at all	**28**
Don't know	22

Source: ICM January 1995

Most-quoted statistics

In Scotland, five government ministers, whose party has been rejected by 87 per cent of the Scottish people, control a Scottish Office budget of £14 billion.
Labour Election Guide

Welsh Office ministers can be directly questioned about their actions for just 40 minutes once every four to six weeks while Parliament is sitting.
Labour Election Guide

A Labour assembly would mean a tartan tax of three pence in the pound, making Scotland the highest taxed part of the United Kingdom.
Conservative Research Department

Between 1979 and 1991, the Scottish economy grew by an average of 1.7 per cent a year, compared with less than one per cent between 1974 and 1979.

Conservative Research Department, Scotland: Strength through Diversity in the United Kingdom

Scottish manufacturing exports reached their highest ever level in 1991, rising by three per cent in value terms to £8.8 billion.
Strength through Diversity in the United Kingdom

The civilian workforce in Scotland has increased by 169,000 since June 1983.
Conservative Research Department

Quotable quotes

'I hope the whole of Scotland will recognise your smugness in assuming that, because you happen to have a bit of a lead in the polls at the present time, you have a mandate to make the Scottish people pay more in income tax than any other part of the UK.'
Michael Forsyth, *to Shadow Scottish Secretary George Robertson, 1 May 1996*

'It is a useless talking shop that will waste money and add nothing to good government in Wales.'
John Redwood, *then Welsh Secretary, on Labour's proposed Welsh Assembly, 13 May 1995*

'With these plans Labour is treating Wales with the same contempt as the Tories.'
Dafydd Wigley, *president of Plaid Cymru, 13 May 1995*

'William Hague's appointment is a contemptuous insult to the people of Wales.'
Ron Davies, *Shadow Welsh Secretary, on the new Welsh Secretary, 11 July 1995*

'The English won't stomach it. It is fundamentally flawed and wrong.'
Tam Dalyell, *Labour MP for Linlithgow, on Scottish devolution, 17 January 1995*

'Transferring power to a Welsh assembly would break the link between Wales and Westminster and result in the break-up of the United Kingdom.'
Llew Smith, *Labour MP for Blaenau Gwent, 17 January 1995*

'I am a professional marketing man and I reckon you can't continue to tell people they are wrong if their views are different from yours. You cannot win from that position.'
Scottish Tory Reform Group chairman **Arthur Bell**, *on the party's anti-devolution stance, 13 January 1995*

DEFENCE

David Fairhall

The paradox of defence as an election issue is that the Opposition is reluctant to let it become one. Defence makes the Labour leadership feel vulnerable. It has a dangerous potential for internal party division, particularly on nuclear matters, rather as Europe does for the Conservatives. An adult subject of obvious importance – if only because it involves the third-largest departmental budget after social security and health – but one best not discussed in front of the party conference.

Fortunately for Tony Blair, events have conspired to make this a much more comfortable election, from a military perspective, than the last. The hard work of running down the armed forces and their supporting industries since the end of the cold war is largely complete. The annual defence budget may not be quite in line with the average of our major European allies when measured as a percentage of GDP – the goal to which Labour used to aspire – but it has fallen a couple of points since the 1980s. In absolute terms, Britain now spends less on defence than either France or Germany.

As for the sensitive question of the nuclear deterrent, the defeat of last year's regular conference motion to scrap the Trident missile submarine force was an acknowledgement of industrial reality. Whereas in 1992 it would still have been possible to save several hundred millions by cancelling the fourth boat (a decision Labour would have been loath to contemplate, however, because of its impact on jobs in isolated Barrow-in-Furness), the entire £12 billion is now either spent or committed.

Conservative defence policy over the past five years has been about managing a process of rapid change. Scaling the armed forces down, pulling them back from cold war garrisons in Germany, trying to shed some of their bureaucratic infrastructure, injecting an element of commercial competition, and reshaping them to face the demands of 'peacekeeping' operations worldwide. And as the reforms came through they were immediately put to the test in Bosnia.

Taken on the Government's own terms, the record is a good one. The three services have emerged with a clearer idea of their future role than they had in 1992, with a range of modern equipment either available or in prospect – a decent tank, an attack helicopter, Eurofighter, stand-off missiles and new amphibious naval forces. Military expenditure has stabilised about a third lower, in real terms, than its peak in the mid-1980s. The failures lie mainly in areas Conservative policy has deliberately not addressed – above all the depressing failure of British arms manufacturing industries to reduce their dependence on export trade that sooner or later drags them down into the murky world uncovered by the Scott Inquiry. There has been something of a peace dividend since the Berlin Wall came down, but precious little sign of swords turning into ploughshares. Nor has the Government generally played more than a neutral, conservative role in adapting Nato to new European alignments or pursuing disarmament initiatives opened up by the end of the cold war. Support for a comprehensive nuclear test ban was typically grudging – just following Washington's directions.

The first move of an incoming Labour government – almost inevitable but not something the armed forces welcome – would be to conduct a six-month 'defence review'. This is a device much maligned by the Conservatives, but twice used by them in recent years under different names: 'Options for Change' to decide the scale of armed forces rundown, and more recently *Front Line First*, a defence costs study to cut £1.5 billion out of the budget over three years by pruning military infrastructure.

Labour's defence review would not be likely to produce dramatic changes. At most it would shift the emphasis in certain areas, for example in offering wholehearted support for a nuclear test ban and seeking the prohibition of all anti-personnel land-mines. On the fundamentals – maintaining nuclear deterrence, support for Nato and the United Nations, the level of expenditure – the review would probably strike much the same balance as recent Conservative administrations, albeit for somewhat different reasons. For instance, Labour's latest policy document specifically states that the review 'is not a device by which to make cuts in defence spending'. Given the reductions that have already been made, the Shadow Defence Secretary Dr David Clark says he would probably be satisfied with the target of 2.7 per cent of GDP set for 1998-99 by the latest defence estimates, which they compare with a current average of 2.3 per cent among Britain's European Nato allies.

The same policy document says, 'We will retain the British nuclear deterrent, Trident, and when satisfied with verified progress towards our goal of global elimination of nuclear weapons, we will ensure British nuclear weapons are included in such negotiations.' Little change there, although Labour's promise that the Trident force will carry no more nuclear warheads than the old Polaris boats – a pledge it shares with the Liberal Democrats – implies a downward shift in total firepower. Key decisions to phase out air-launched nuclear weapons by 1998, and not replace them, have already been taken.

The purpose of the review would be to establish priorities and define military commitments to which resources would then be matched. In theory, therefore, military expenditure might increase. But a Labour administration is more likely to balance this equation by reducing commitments, so as to reduce the 'massive overstretch' from which Clark believes all three services are currently suffering.

The difficult areas for Labour are those which might attract the jibe that it is 'soft on defence' and those where its concern to preserve jobs works against the need to reduce unnecessary expenditure. For instance, the cuts in naval shore support which resulted in the rundown of nuclear refitting at Rosyth and the end of warship building on the Tyne, would have been far more painful politically for Labour than they were for the Tories. Arms exports are another problem area. Clark says his party sees nothing intrinsically wrong with the arms trade. Everyone is entitled to defend themselves. But he believes the trade needs more stringent controls and there would in any case be no question of a Labour administration selling weapons that could be used for internal repression.

One time bomb a Labour review must somehow defuse is the question of homosexuals in the armed forces. Tony Blair's declaration that servicemen and women should not be penalised for their sexual orientation, as opposed to sexual activity, suggests that Labour would settle for something like the American 'don't ask, don't tell' policy.

In some ways the Liberal Democrat policy on defence is what Labour might espouse if the latter was less inhibited by historical baggage and electoral calculation. The Lib Dems are in favour of retaining all four Trident submarines, holding expenditure at its 1994 level in real terms, expanding Nato and strengthening the United Nations. But the party's defence spokesman Menzies Campbell is prepared to develop these ideas in specific ways that would make Labour nervous.

In certain circumstances, for example, his party would seek higher defence spending – 'We have an open mind on that.' While both parties want to make the UN more effective, the Lib Dems' plans to assign rapid reaction forces and open a UN staff college sound more ambitious than Labour's talk of 'earmarking' troops and providing better military advice. Where Labour speaks generally of the need to strengthen the 'European pillar of Nato' by developing the Western European Union, Menzies Campbell is positively searching for 'pragmatic, ground-up' integration as exemplified by the Anglo-Dutch amphibious forces or the Anglo-French air group. For example, his party would favour co-ordinating the British and French nuclear deterrent forces. As a long-term objective, it can foresee the absorption of the WEU into the European Union. ●

Main events since 1992

19 November 1992: Britain makes first substantial commitment – 2,500 troops – to UN relief operations in Bosnia.

February 1993: MoD reprieves four regiments threatened by ongoing 'Options for Change' defence review, designed to cut military expenditure and scale down armed forces.

July 1993: Navy bears the brunt of second tranche of 'Options for Change' cuts.

December 1993: MoD launches 'Front Line First' defence cuts study to reduce defence budget by a further £1.5 billion over three years.

July 1994: Fresh defence cuts announced. 18,750 jobs to go including 20 jobs of the rank of major-general and above, a reduction since 1990 of a third. Recruitment Centres to close.

20 December 1995: Nato-led forces including 13,000 British troops go into Bosnia to implement Dayton peace accord.

Legislation
Army Act 1992
● abolished the Ulster Defence Regiment.

Policies

Key Theme
Con: The drive to achieve value for money to continue, with resources concentrated on the front line.
Lab: Conduct a strategic defence review to reassess Britain's essential security objectives and defence needs.
Lib Dem: European co-operation to be increased. Defence spending to be maintained in real terms and increased if European security is threatened.

Land-mines
Con: An active campaign for a worldwide ban on anti-personnel mines to be pursued. Export of mines to be prohibited.
Lab: Ban the import, export, manufacture and use of anti-personnel landmines. Impose an immediate moratorium on their use.
Lib Dem: Immediate ban on the use, production and export of land-mines.

Trident
Con: Commission a four-boat Trident fleet with a new sub-strategic capability.
Lab: Retain Trident and ensure that British nuclear weapons are included in negotiations on the elimination of nuclear weapons.
Lib Dem: Retain Trident for the time being but with no more warheads than on Polaris.

Poll

Which party has the best policies on defence?

as %	1992 Mar	1993 Sep	1994 May	1995 Jul	1996 Mar
Con	48	32	29	30	30
Lab	21	19	28	19	19
Lib Dem	7	12	12	5	7

Source: MORI

Most-quoted statistics

Nato countries' defence expenditure

As % of GDP (market price)		Per capita (US$)	
Greece	4.6	UK	1,048
US	3.9	Norway	863
Turkey	3.9	France	820
UK	3.1	Denmark	600
France	3.1	UK	586
Norway	2.9	Netherlands	527
Portugal	2.7	Germany	509
Netherlands	2.1	Greece	481
Italy	1.9	Belgium	455
Denmark	1.8	Luxembourg	365
Belgium	1.7	Italy	349
Germany	1.7	Canada	310
Canada	1.6	Portugal	285
Spain	1.5	Spain	216
Luxembourg	0.9	Turkey	97

Reduction in armed services' manpower

	1992-93	1998-99 (planned)
Royal Navy	61,089	46,000
Army	148,531	114,000
Royal Air Force	83,219	56,000
Total service personnel	**292,839**	**216,400**

Government spending

£ million	90-91	91-92	92-93	93-94	94-95	95-96	96-97	97-98	98-99
Current terms	21,709	22,913	22,910	22,757	22,562	21,210	21,420	21,910	22,620
1994-95 prices	25,200	25,000	24,000	23,200	22,600	20,600	20,300	20,300	20,400

Source: Financial Statement and Budget Report 1996-97
All figures from 1995 are estimates. Figures for 1994-95 are rounded.

Quotable quotes

'While everybody recognised that it was bound to lead to bad news for some, there was wide acceptance that there was room to improve efficiency and make savings in the support areas without damaging operational capability.'
Front Line First, Conservative policy document, 1993

'The classless in Downing Street and the clueless in the MoD are doing nothing to stop a tide of redundancies engulfing the defence sector.'
Jack Dromey, *TGWU National Secretary, 12 November 1992*

'This is one more sign that the Labour party is now a modern, left-of-centre party, totally in tune with the interests of the British people. This vote shows a new maturity in the party's attitude to defence.'
Tony Blair, *on the Labour Conference vote against unilateral nuclear disarmament, October 1995*

'I would not be prepared, and neither would the party, to have Britain left without a deterrent that is credible and deliverable.'
Paddy Ashdown, *March 1992*

'A catalogue of incompetence and error has jeopardised Britain's capacity to defend itself.' *National Audit Office, 31 October 1995*

EDUCATION

Donald Macleod

MPs were startled when Education Secretary Kenneth Clarke declared that the state of schools was nothing to do with him. 'They are not my schools. I do not employ a teacher or appoint a head teacher. I won't take responsibility for things that are utterly beyond my control,' he told the Commons Select Committee on Education to the sound of jaws dropping. Clarke's outburst reflected a growing frustration among ministers that despite sweeping legislation, including the 1988 Education Act which specified a National Curriculum for England and Wales in great detail, they seemed unable to lay their hands on the levers of change in the classroom. The Conservative Government attempted to tackle the problem in two ways – by prising schools away from local education authorities whom they regarded with suspicion even when they were Tory-controlled and by a renewed emphasis on testing children.

The two strands of their approach met in the philosophy of parental choice. Parents were encouraged to vote for their children's schools to become grant-maintained – opting out of local authority control – and they were also to be given tables of examination and test results to help them choose the best schools. Schools which failed to get good results would have to change their ways or be closed while the best would flourish. Both supporters and opponents of grant-maintained schools assumed that schools were waiting for the result of the 1992 election before committing themselves and the Conservative victory would turn the trickle into a flood. Promoted enthusiastically by the new Education Secretary, John Patten, the number of parental ballots soared with 555 schools voting to opt out in 1992-93. At the Tory Conference in 1993, Patten famously declared he would 'eat my hat garnished' if a majority of secondary schools were not grant-maintained by the next election.

The flood, however, dried up. During the course of the next year 'no' votes outnumbered 'yes' ones in secondary schools by 55 to 52 and although more than 100 primaries opted out, the grant-maintained bandwagon ran out of momentum. In the academic year 1995-96, 32 schools voted to opt out and 31 voted against. Dwindling financial incentives played a part. The first schools to become grant-maintained benefited considerably both in revenue and capital projects but the differential became steadily less.

Opting out was built on the concept of parental choice and ministers realised too late they had underestimated the conservatism of parents. For some time they pinned their hopes on a radical overhaul of local authorities to shake up the present structure enough to make grant-maintained status and the York-based Funding Agency for Schools the safe option, but in the event the changes agreed by the Banham Commission hardly registered on the Richter scale of public awareness. In Scotland the local government map was redrawn, but opting out had been strangled at birth as an English imposition.

If the grant-maintained sector is to expand, a future Conservative government would have to legislate to remove, say, all secondaries from local authority control. It would be a mistake, however, to think the grant-maintained initiative sank with little trace. Firstly, the threat of opting out helped drive a revolution in funding and control in which schools were given their own budgets and greater autonomy – Local Management of Schools (LMS) in the jargon. Accepted now by Labour and the Liberal Democrats in town and county halls, local management was the carrot used to keep schools from opting out. Secondly, the issue proved an embarrassment to Labour since Tony Blair decided to send his son to a grant-maintained school, compounded when Harriet Harman, his health spokeswoman, opted for a GM grammar school. Rather than simply bring GM schools back into the local authority fold as the Liberal Democrats advocate, Labour offered GM schools a rather nebulous 'foundation status' with some privileges but no financial advantage.

Patten and his successor Gillian Shephard encouraged comprehensive schools to select an increasing proportion of their pupils by academic ability or aptitude in sport or music. John Major wanted to push this aspect of choice to embrace a grammar school in every town. Labour is opposed to selection but not against using aptitude tests to balance schools' intake and the party leadership has distanced itself from the old comprehensive ideal by urging schools to specialise. Labour toned down its rhetoric on independent schools but is pledged to phase out the Assisted Places Scheme, which subsidises school fees for low-income families.

After a ramshackle start, exam league tables have become established, though the effect on schools' and parents' behaviour is disputed. Shephard bowed to right-wing pressure to introduce primary school league tables based on tests at age 11. The National Curriculum with its tests, it soon became clear, was overcrowded and bureaucratic and teachers' frustration eventually boiled over in a stunningly effective boycott of the 1993 tests that humiliated John Patten. To restore peace in the classroom he called in Sir Ron Dearing, former chairman of the Post Office, to sort out the mess – a precedent the Government has followed on two more occasions. The National Curriculum was pruned, tests were made more manageable and Sir Ron's consultative approach ushered in a new era, confirmed by the arrival of Gillian Shephard at the department. She asked Sir Ron to try to sort out the confused state of vocational education and A-levels and then to look at the funding of higher education.

Nursery education, increasingly seen as the key to improving education standards, became a guinea-pig for the Conservatives' most ambitious experiment in parental choice – vouchers. In four pilot authorities parents of four-year-olds were issued with vouchers worth £1,100 to spend at local authority or private nursery schools or playgroups. Opposition parties condemned the scheme as a bureaucratic nightmare which failed to create extra places but the Tories said they would press ahead with a national scheme. Vouchers will go out in February 1997.

Inspection of all schools every four years by the Office for Standards in Education, which incorporated the old HM Inspectorate, demonstrated that the Government wanted to get tough on standards, and under a high-profile Chief Inspector, Chris Woodhead, it has become politically controversial. But the effect on parent voters has been to increase anxiety and destroy some of the feel-good factor they felt in schools.

In the universities the Government was too successful. The vision that a third of young people should go into higher education by the end of the century was almost reached by 1993 when the Treasury took fright and slammed the brakes on expansion. Consolidation did not extend to funding per student, which continued to fall until the university vice-chancellors threatened to impose top-up fees. If funding for a mass higher education system was not to come from the public purse, students would have to pay. Labour took a cautious step towards a graduate tax on the Australian model, but limited to living costs. The Government, unwilling to court middle-class unpopularity by charging students tuition fees, made its now habitual response: a call to Sir Ron Dearing for his third inquiry. ●

Main events since 1992

4 February 1994: Michael Portillo courts controversy by alleging that foreign students bought their A-levels.

22 July 1994: Gillian Shephard replaces John Patten.

20 January 1995: Government-funded Adult Literacy and Basic Skills Unit finds that people in their twenties have lower literacy and numeracy standards than those ten and 20 years older.

15 April 1996: Nursery vouchers start in four 'phase one' education authorities, Westminster, Wandsworth, Norfolk, Kensington & Chelsea.

8 May 1996: Ofsted report on the London boroughs of Islington, Southwark and Tower Hamlets finds eight out of ten 11-year-olds are behind in reading and four out of ten are two years behind. Gillian Shephard responds by attacking 'trendy' teaching methods.

21 May 1996: Labour announces the replacement of student grants, parental contributions and student loans with a 20-year loan package to be repayable through the National Insurance system.

February 1997: Parents of all four-year-olds to receive first £1,100 nursery vouchers.

Legislation

Further and Higher Education Act 1992
- 450 further education colleges and 113 sixth form colleges moved out of local authority control
- polytechnics and larger HE colleges allowed to call themselves universities

Education Act 1993
- introduced easier 'opting out'
- introduced Funding Agency for Schools – quango to fund grant-maintained sector
- introduced national inspection system under Office for Standards in Education with powers over failing schools

Policies

Education Funding
Con: Since 1979, in real terms, there has been a 47 per cent rise in funding and a 50 per cent rise in expenditure per pupil.
Lab: Reprioritise existing education budget. Scrap Assisted Places Scheme and use funds to lower class sizes for five- to seven-year-olds.
Lib Dem: Invest extra £2 billion in education. Ask people to pay an extra penny on their income tax, if necessary.

Grant-maintained Schools
Con: Encourage every school to opt for GM status. Allow GM schools to select up to 50 per cent of their pupils without central approval.
Lab: GM schools to become 'foundation schools' without financial privileges. Work of Funding Agency for Schools to be devolved to LEAs.

Lib Dem: Abolish GM status and bring all state schools under the 'light-touch' planning guidance of LEAs.

Selection
Con: Aim for a grammar school in every town – relax regulations governing selection.
Lab: Admissions to be based on fair criteria which remove artificial blocks on parental preference and offer the right of independent appeal – oppose any return to 11-plus.
Lib Dem: Local education authorities to assess the impact of grammar schools on local education and determine selection policy accordingly.

Nursery Education
Con: Voucher scheme to be extended to all three-year-olds after four-year-old provision established. Set target of pre-school place for all four-year-olds whose parents want one.
Lab: Scrap vouchers. Free nursery place to be guaranteed for every four-year-old, to be extended later to three-year-olds.
Lib Dem: Oppose nursery voucher scheme. Spend £900 million a year to provide early-years education for every three- and four-year-old whose parents want it.

Independent Schools
Con: Double the Assisted Places Scheme, widening eligibility to include children as young as five.
Lab: Phase out Assisted Places Scheme and use £110 million savings on extra teachers to cut class sizes to a maximum of 30 pupils for all five-, six- and seven-year-olds.
Lib Dem: The Assisted Places Scheme to be abolished, but LEAs to be allowed to support pupils in independent schools.

Higher Education Funding
Con: Have established national inquiry into future shape of higher education under Sir Ron Dearing.
Lab: Grants to be replaced with a loan payable over 20 years through the National Insurance system. Tuition fees to remain government-funded.
Lib Dem: Propose a learning bank to provide a secure and flexible funding framework geared to providing the needs for a lifelong learning society.

Discipline
Con: School heads to be given more flexibility; periods of exclusion to be extended from 15 to 45 days.
Lab: Teachers to be given power to exclude disruptive or violent pupils for up to a term, and those pupils to be placed in pupil referral units.
Lib Dem: Introduce a flexible system, possibly including the reinstatement of indefinite exclusion. Wider use of specially established units for disruptive pupils.

Standards

Con: Standards can be raised through the National Curriculum, regular testing and performance tables.

Lab: Introduce baseline assessment. Focus on literacy and numeracy in the early years. Set targets for all schools, linked to national targets.

Lib Dem: Replace standard assessment tests with records of achievement. Establish 'slimmed down' minimum curriculum entitlement. Provide clear information to parents on progress.

Polls

Which party has the best policies on education?

as %	1992 Mar	1993 Sep	1994 May	1995 Jul	1996 Mar
Con	23	21	20	15	19
Lab	41	32	40	46	44
Lib Dem	19	15	15	8	11

Source: MORI

Grant-maintained schools should be

	%
left as they are	18
returned to local council control	23
allowed to remain separate so long as council-run schools are guaranteed the same level of funding	51
Don't know	9

Source: ICM September 1995

Most-quoted statistics

UK education system ranked 35th in World Competitiveness Report.
Labour Conference, 1995

Grant-maintained schools account for 5.6 per cent of all schools yet they account for 14.1 per cent of the total capital spending on schools, or 2.7 times more than LEA schools.
Labour policy document, Diversity and Excellence

One in five 21-year-olds have trouble with maths. One in seven with writing.
Tony Blair, *Labour Conference, 1995*

Number of pupils getting three good GCSE passes in Britain is half that of France and Germany. Only one-third of UK pupils gets two A-level passes. France 48 per cent. Germany 68 per cent.
Tony Blair, *Labour Conference, 1995*

One in three primary children is in a class of over thirty.
David Blunkett, *Labour Conference, 1995*

£500 million cut from schools.
David Blunkett

Eighty per cent of South Koreans will have the equivalent of three A-levels by the year 2000, while the British Government plans to have only 50 per cent.
Labour

Out of 24 countries the UK came 23rd in terms of 18-year-olds in full-time education. The only country below it was Turkey.
Labour

The 7 per cent of children who go to independent schools obtain 50 per cent of all A grades at A-level.
Labour

Government spending

Education and employment

as £ million	90-91	91-92	92-93	93-94	94-95	95-96	96-97	97-98	98-99
Current terms	8,963	9,298	10,053	12,845	13,573	14,190	14,040	14,510	14,520
1995-96 prices	10,400	10,100	10,500	13,100	13,600	13,800	13,300	13,400	13,100

All figures from 1995-96 are estimates.
1995-96 figures are rounded.
Source: Financial Statement and Budget Report 1996-97

Quotable quotes

'Duff schools are debauching their communities.'
John Patten, *then Education Secretary, 28 September 1993*

'Mrs Shephard has replaced chaos with complacency.'
David Blunkett, *3 October 1995*

'We should refuse to go back to selection but refuse to make do with conformity.'
Tony Blair, *29 January 1996*

'I predict the majority will go the whole hog by the mid-1990s.'
Stuart Sexton, *Director of the Education Unit at the Institute of Economic Affairs, on opting out,* Independent, *23 February 1989*

'There are no easy conference words to persuade anyone that we are not going through a U-turn on whether students should make a contribution.'
Don Foster, *Liberal Democrat education spokesman, 20 February 1996*

'I don't object to the Liberal Democrats being known as the party which is willing to put a penny on income tax.'
Paddy Ashdown, *17 October 1995*

'Insufficient resources now threaten the provision of education in the state school sector, including grant-maintained schools.'
Civil Service memorandum to Cabinet, 14 September 1995

'I am having no truck with middle-class left-wing parents who preach one thing and send their children to another school outside the area.'
David Blunkett, *Shadow Education and Employment Secretary, 21 November 1994*

'I would prefer the school that I have sent my child to not to be selective, but we must deal with the circumstances as they are now.'
Harriet Harman, *24 January 1996*

EMPLOYMENT

Seumas Milne

If unemployment and the role of trade unions were the labour market issues which threaded through the past four general elections, this time the focus is more likely to be on the spread of job insecurity and the argument over whether there should be a floor of minimum standards in the workplace. It is a measure both of the transformation wrought by the Conservatives' own policies and the ruthlessness with which Tony Blair has marginalised the unions inside the Labour party that the trade union question stands little chance of making a significant impact on the campaign – however much government ministers might try to crank up the hardy union-bashing perennials of the past. With union membership half what it was in 1979 and the number of working days lost through strikes down to a puny 415,000 in 1995 – only modestly above the previous year's twentieth-century low and a very long way from the 29 million in Margaret Thatcher's first year in office – it would take a remarkable Tory campaign to frighten floating voters with the spectre of organised labour. Unions are, in any case, now more popular with the public than at any time in their history.

As for unemployment, despite the massaged official jobless total still hovering around the two million mark, the Conservatives can be expected to crow about their job creation record, while both the main opposition parties will shy away from the previously much trumpeted goal of full employment. Instead, Labour will highlight the heightened sense of insecurity felt throughout the workforce during the 1990s, a key component of the so-called 'feel-bad' factor that dogged John Major's post-1992 government. Despite attempts by Conservative ministers to argue that insecurity is a state of mind rather than fact, the statistics almost all point in the other direction.

More than ten million employees have been unemployed since 1990; the toll of annual redundancies actually rose as unemployment fell after mid-1993; the increase in the number of short-term contract workers and involuntary part-timers is accelerating; benefits for the jobless have been cut back and average pay after a period on the dole has fallen; average male job tenure has declined sharply; and the proportion of the workforce which has been long enough in full-time work to qualify for basic employment rights has slumped from 56 to 36 per cent over the past two decades. But Labour may find it difficult to exploit the spread of job insecurity under the Conservatives. Although Tony Blair and Gordon Brown favour 'social partnership' against the 'hire-and-fire' employment culture they say John Major has encouraged, they also regard greater flexibility and job mobility as an inevitable – even welcome – consequence of economic globalisation.

The response of both New Labour and the Liberal Democrats is to equip workers to survive the employment roller-coaster with better training. Hence Labour's two flagship training policies: levying a windfall tax on the privatised utilities to fund a young unemployed training and employment programme – backed up by the threat of benefit loss – and an 'individual learning account' scheme for workers to develop their skills. The Liberal Democrats go further and advocate the compulsory training levy Labour ditched for fear of being damned for adding to the 'burdens on business'.

The Conservatives will stand on their record of job creation and brand Labour as the harbingers of job-destroying labour market regulation in the Tory-fostered 'enterprise centre of Europe'. With Britain first in and first out of recession in the early 1990s, the Government can point to the lowest official jobless rate of the major European Union states. The Conservatives put Britain's falling unemployment and relatively high proportion of adults in work down to the country's 'lightly regulated' and flexible labour market. The opposition parties can counter that between 1980 and 1994 employment grew far more rapidly in France and Germany; that British jobless figures have dropped partly because fewer people are seeking work; and that the entire increase in employment of 300,000 between the autumn of 1993 and summer of 1996 was, according to the Government's own labour force survey, accounted for by part-time jobs.

John Major and his party will in turn hammer away at the notion that Labour's commitment to employee 'stakeholding', a legal minimum wage, signing the

European Union's Social Chapter and a package of minimum standards at work would cost Britain jobs by the bucketful and become an incubus weighing down on struggling small businesses. How this will play with the most discontented and most overworked labour force in the EU – particularly when the wildly over-hyped Social Chapter has so far produced only three months' unpaid parental leave and consultative works councils for the largest companies – remains to be seen.

But Tony Blair is taking no chances and has stripped down Labour's programme of employee rights to a bare minimum. Setting the rate for a minimum wage has been left until after the election of a Labour government. Among Labour commitments abandoned during 1996 were a compulsory training levy on firms; John Smith's pledge to give all employees, part-time or full-time, the right to unfair-dismissal protection on the first day in a job – instead of after two years, as at present; outlawing of bogus self-employment and 'zero-hours contracts', which oblige employees to be on continuous call with no guarantee of work; the right to reinstatement of strikers sacked during lawful stoppages; and a relaxation of the current tight restrictions on industrial action and strike ballots.

In several areas, such as unfair-dismissal protection, these changes have left the Liberal Democrats occupying Labour's own traditional territory. But Labour notably remains committed to legislating for a statutory right to trade union recognition where a majority of employees want it – something the Conservatives may find difficult to vilify. ●

Main events since 1992

3 April 1995: Research by the London School of Economics reveals the proportion of the working population in full-time employment has fallen by about 35 per cent over the last 20 years.

7 September 1995: Labour pledges that those over 50 will get legal protection from age discrimination if it wins the next election.

8 March 1996: Leaked letter written by President of the Board of Trade, Ian Lang, reveals plans to bar access to industrial tribunals to between 5 million and 10 million workers.

8 March 1996: All-party employment committee gives the Government a green light to introduce more pilot workfare schemes.

14 March 1996: Unemployment rises for the first time in two and a half years.

16 May 1996: The Government proclaims Britain's unemployment as the lowest in any major European country after the number of people out of work and claiming benefit falls to a five-year low.

16 May 1996: Labour proposes £1.5 billion scheme to take 600,000 young unemployed off benefit and into work.

Legislation

Employment Act 1989
- introduced a pre-hearing review of cases going to industrial tribunals and a £150 deposit to prevent groundless applications
- removed restrictions on the work of women and children; exempted employers with fewer than 20 staff from including disciplinary procedures in employment contracts
- restricted time off for union representatives; required employees to have two years' service before being given written reasons for dismissal; abolished redundancy rebates; and abolished the Training Commission

Employment Act 1990
- constrained the closed shop by making it unlawful not to employ non-union members
- made all secondary action other than picketing unlawful
- stipulated that ballots on industrial action must include regular casual workers
- introduced more stringent measures requiring unions to repudiate unofficial action and allowing for the selective dismissal of staff taking unofficial action

Policies

Job Creation
Con: Using legislation to ensure that the unemployed do more to get back to work. Financial penalties imposed for those not making a substantial effort.
Lab: Every under-25 out of work for over six months to be offered a job in the private sector, work in the voluntary sector, full-time education or a place on a task force.
Lib Dem: The long-term unemployed to have benefits paid as a voucher to an employer, who would provide them with work and training.

Minimum Wage
Con: A minimum wage would discourage wealth creation and increase unemployment.
Lab: A low pay commission to recommend the level of a national minimum wage, to be introduced as soon as is practicable after the general election.
Lib Dem: Introduce a regionally varied minimum hourly rate of pay.

Trade Unions
Con: Continue legislation to ensure harmonious industrial relations and flexibility of labour market.
Lab: Ensure that everyone is entitled to join a trade union. Employees should have the right to have their union recognised where there is a majority amongst the workforce.
Lib Dem: Employees must have the right to join, or not to join, the union of their choice.

GCHQ

Con: No plans to end ban on trade union membership at GCHQ.
Lab: Restore trade union rights at GCHQ.
Lib Dem: Employees at GCHQ to have the right to join a trade union.

Poll

Which party has the best policies on unemployment?

as %	1992 Mar	1993 Sep	1994 May	1995 Jul	1996 Mar
Con	20	11	12	12	15
Lab	46	43	51	50	48
Lib Dem	10	11	11	5	5

Source: MORI

Most-quoted statistics

Nearly nine million people, one in three men and one in five women, have experienced at least one spell of unemployment since 1992.
Michael Meacher, *Shadow Employment Secretary, 17 March 1996*

Strikes – and working days lost as a result of industrial action in 1994 – were the lowest since records began over a hundred years ago.

Unemployment has remained ... more than double the level of the last Labour Government on the Tories' massaged statistics.
Labour

Today there are 300,000 people in Britain who earn less than £1.50 an hour and over one million who earn less than £2.50 an hour.
A New Economic Future for Britain, *Labour policy document, 1995*

At the moment unemployment costs us £22 billion a year in benefit and lost tax revenue.

Quotable quotes

'The extent of job insecurity is going to be a central feature of the general election.'
Tony Blair, *3 March 1996*

'We will introduce a national minimum wage to prevent the competitive undercutting of pay and conditions that so disfigures and damages so many industries.'
Michael Meacher, *Shadow Employment Secretary, 17 March 1996*

'A minimum wage set at £3.50 an hour would destroy an estimated quarter of a million jobs.'
Conservative policy document on social security, 9 January 1995

'Job security will mean fewer jobs for life but more jobs in a lifetime.'
Michael Portillo, *then Employment Secretary, 23 February 1995*

'You cannot build world-class companies by making workers second-class citizens.'
Bill Morris, *General Secretary, Transport and General Workers Union*

'An insecure workforce with no commitment to or from the firms in which they work will not deliver the productivity and competitiveness Britain needs.'
A New Economic Future for Britain, *Labour, 1995*

'We should stop seeing the unemployed as a part of the problem and see them as part of the solution. It's only by retraining and re-employing the army of the unemployed that we can get the economy moving again.'
Tony Blair

ENVIRONMENT: GREEN ISSUES

Paul Brown

In the political collision between market forces and the effort to protect the natural world, the environment has always come off second best, not just in the last five years but in the last 50. Politicians of all parties, most notably Margaret Thatcher, sensed the danger in the 1980s over public concern about the environment and its clash with the prevailing political wind. She staved it off by being adept at green rhetoric, a pattern subsequently followed by all politicians. However, when such high-flown notions as sustainable development came into conflict with 'the great car economy' there was no doubt about which would emerge the winner under her regime and her successor's. This has continued to be immensely frustrating for the green movement and the Green party. Politicians of the three main parties have all apparently endorsed many of their environmental policies and accept at least some of their demands. Yet as time has passed they have not seemed likely to address or capable of addressing the fundamental issues involved.

Certainly, John Gummer, the then Environment Secretary, who seemed to have been personally convinced by the arguments, failed to deliver when there was a clash with other departments like Transport and particularly Trade and Industry. His more right-wing colleagues brushed aside his green policies if they interfered with the purity of the market as they saw it. Even in setting up the Environment Agency, the main success for Gummer in the last five years, market forces intruded. The agency was instructed to show that costs must be justified by benefits before taking action to improve the environment, thereby potentially shackling the agency from its inception, but this issue has yet to be properly tested. Only differential taxes on green petrol and land-fill taxes seemed to escape the ideological axe.

The Labour party, with its traditional trade union belief that protecting the environment means loss of jobs, has also seemed stuck in the same mould for the last decade. Many were surprised by Tony Blair's long-awaited first speech on the environment in February 1996, which was very positive. Observers were impressed by his grasp of the issues and that he endorsed the document *In Trust for Tomorrow* which had been written by the former environment spokesman Chris Smith, the first Labour frontbencher to show he really understood what the greens were on about. This document had been gathering dust since the death of John Smith, but Blair had clearly read it and added promises of 50,000 jobs from energy-saving schemes. He also produced a much tougher target on reducing the emissions of gases which cause global warming than either Labour or Conservatives had previously considered. More cynical greens were not convinced, saying the speech sounded like more greenwash and would not challenge existing Labour party endorsement of free market economics. They muttered darkly that some of his frontbench colleagues needed extensive re-education.

The Liberal Democrats, and notably Paddy Ashdown before he became leader, have always had a much greener tinge than their main rivals and their policy documents reflect this. Critics say it's easy to be radical when there is no chance of being elected, but many of the policies endorsed ten years ago by the Liberal Democrats are now accepted by everyone else, even if they are not yet delivered.

Environment improvements in the last decade have been driven by a series of directives from the European Commission, often to the irritation of the Government. These have led to multi-billion-pound investments in new sewage treatment and a steady improvement in the state of rivers and beaches. Having been forced into the expenditure, the Government has made a virtue out of necessity and claimed all the credit for itself. The EC has also done much to improve air quality with a series of Europe-wide initiatives on cutting sulphur dioxide emissions to reduce the impact of acid rain and cleaning up vehicle exhausts. The Government's own science in this area made clear that even more needed to be done to cut the number of early deaths, but publication of air quality objectives was delayed again and again as government ministers clashed over the economic consequences.

Many serious domestic issues cannot be addressed by Europe, principally transport, where a policy vacuum has existed for some time. The frustration of many people with both the Government and the failure of the public inquiry system to take the environment into account has shown itself in a series of demonstrations against road schemes. The determined attempts to stop the M3 extension through Twyford Down, the M11 in London, and most recently the Newbury by-pass have drawn attention to the transport issue in dramatic fashion. A whole network of new groups has sprung up in the last five years which are often prepared to draw on a pool of activists to take direct action to promote their causes.

A number of organisations exist which regard themselves as outside the normal political process. They take direct action because they have given up on mainstream politics, which they regard as irrelevant to ordinary people. They campaign on environmental issues and occupy construction sites or offices and shops to draw attention to environmental wrongs, which might be anything from illegal timber imports to action against Shell oil operations in Nigeria. The Labour, Liberal Democrat and Green parties have all made a pitch to appeal to these disenchanted people. They are regarded as representing the active minority of a large section of young people who are in serious danger of dropping out of the political system altogether, because they claim no-one represents their views.

The Green party faded as a national electoral force, even before this Parliament began, because of its own internal feuding. It was also because every other party claimed to have endorsed the green agenda. It has picked up again recently and is a force in some local areas, winning some seats in the May 1996 elections. It continues to bring environmental issues before the public, which sharpens the mind of political parties. It describes the heavyweight political organisations as 'the grey parties'.

Public concern about the environment and therefore politicians' interest in it has varied remarkably in the last ten years and appears to be directly related to economic trends. The recession and fears over job security eclipsed environmental concern. Despite this, the environment still figures quite high in polls when people are asked what will affect the way they vote. Early in 1996 MORI said that 31 per cent of voters said party policies on the environment would affect the way they voted, only seven points behind the economy. Past experience shows that when it comes to the run-up to the election, the environment disappears off the politicians' agenda and tax cuts dominate the sound-bite culture, although time may alter that. Many problems associated with the environment, like BSE, air pollution, water shortages and lack of transport policy may seem to voters to be more to do with government incompetence than the green agenda.

For environmental groups, many of which individually have a far higher membership than all the political parties put together, the lack of political campaigning on these issues is very frustrating. Thirty-two of them, including Oxfam and the World Wide Fund for Nature, have joined together to form an organisation called Real World to try to alter this in the run-up to the general election and beyond. Time will tell whether this approach works. ●

Main events since 1992

June 1992: Rio Earth Summit. Over 150 countries commit themselves to promote sustainable development. Agree targets on emissions, biodiversity, world trade and climate change.

May 1993: John Selwyn Gummer succeeds Michael Howard as Secretary of State for Environment.

March 1994: John Gummer announces new planning guidelines to prevent out-of-town shopping developments and protect stagnating town centres.

1 August 1995: Government pleads with motorists to leave their cars at home as pollution rises to danger levels.

1 October 1995: Government launches £6 million television advertising campaign featuring a family of dinosaurs to promote domestic energy conservation.

25 October 1995: The Department of Environment is forced to reveal the membership of committees which determine pollution limits for industry and are dominated by industry representatives.

12 March 1996: Government publishes *Indicators of Sustainable Development for the UK*, a measure of trends in environmental performance, which shows people consuming more energy and using up irreplaceable resources.

1 April 1996: The Environment Agency, chaired by Lord de Ramsey, comes into effect. It takes over responsibility for regulating polluters, waste-dumpers and the nuclear industry, managing rivers and protecting against coastal and river flooding, as well as being the Government's key environment adviser.

2 July 1996: An official DoE Report predicts climate change in Britain over the next 30 years, with southern England experiencing weather similar to the Champagne region of France and Yorkshire replacing Kent as the Garden of England.

Legislation

Environment Act 1995
- established environment agencies for England and Wales and Scotland
- created ten new national park authorities
- introduced regulations forcing industry to cut unnecessary packaging
- introduced environmental regulations to take account of costs as well as benefits

Wildlife Bill 1996
- private members' initiative supported by the Government – will probably be enacted before the end of this Parliament
- extended protection for sites of special scientific interest

Policies

Energy tax
Con: European Commission proposals for an EU-wide carbon or energy tax are not needed to meet environmental targets and are to be rejected.
Lab: Opposed to EU's proposal for a carbon-energy tax because of the impact on the low-paid, but supports the principle that taxes should promote protection of the environment.
Lib Dem: Introduce a UK carbon tax, and with the money raised reduce other taxes.

Carbon Dioxide Emissions
Con: Carbon dioxide emissions are now expected to be some 4 to 8 per cent below 1990 levels by 2000.
Lab: Aim to reduce UK carbon dioxide emissions by 20 per cent by 2010.
Lib Dem: Aim to reduce CO_2 emissions by 2 per cent every year.

Sulphur Dioxide Emissions
Con: Reduce emissions of sulphur dioxide by 80 per cent by 2010 compared with 1980 levels.
Lab: Reduce emissions by 90 per cent within ten years.
Lib Dem: Introduce tradable emissions licences to reduce SO_2 emissions by 70 per cent in five years.

Air Quality
Con: The Environment Act 1995 gives local authorities new powers to tackle air pollution more effectively.
Lab: Set air quality targets for all areas and give local authorities power to enforce targets.
Lib Dem: Introduce market-based mechanisms and air quality targets to reduce pollution.

Renewable Energy
Con: Stimulate the development of new and renewable energy sources, with a target of 1500 megawatts of generating capacity for UK as a whole.
Lab: Set target of ten per cent of electricity generation from renewable resources by 2010, and 20 per cent by 2025.
Lib Dem: Set target of 20 per cent of generating capacity in 15 years and 30 per cent in 30 years.

Nuclear Power
Con: Privatisation of British Energy will bring benefits to consumers, taxpayers and the nuclear industry itself.
Lab: No new nuclear power stations.
Lib Dem: No new nuclear power stations and eventually phase out all nuclear power stations.

Animal Welfare
Con: Have secured European agreement to new rules for animals in transit. Seeking to add a protocol to Treaty of Rome on animal welfare.
Lab: Bring in free vote on legislation to ban hunting with hounds. Introduce compulsory dog registration. Ban fur farming. Redefine farm animals as 'sentient beings'.
Lib Dem: Establish Animal Protection Commission to advise local and national government, investigate abuses and enforce the law. Bring in free vote on hunting with hounds.

Food and Farming

Con: Remain the party of the countryside, tackling a wide range of issues in Rural White Paper, including reform of the Common Agricultural Policy.

Lab: Establish independent Food Standards Agency. Expand organic food scheme within the Common Agricultural Policy.

Lib Dem: Introduce new independent Food Commission to be responsible for food quality, and countryside management contracts to ensure quality and safety of food.

Poll

Which party has the best policies on protecting the natural environment?

as %	1992 Mar	1993 Sep	1994 May	1995 Jul	1996 Mar
Con	10	11	11	10	11
Lab	14	13	20	21	20
Lib Dem	8	23	20	15	21
None	21	35	29	41	35

Source: MORI

Most-quoted statistics

Emissions of carbon dioxide increased by 50 per cent during the 1980s.
In Trust for Tomorrow, *Labour's policy document*

Around 20 per cent of Britain's beaches regularly fail EU quality standards.
In Trust for Tomorrow

Emissions of greenhouse gases declined by around 15 per cent between 1970 and 1993, well on target to meet global targets – mainly due to the switch from coal to gas electricity generation.
Department of Environment, 12 March 1996

Energy consumption by the manufacturing sector has fallen by 40 per cent.
Department of Environment, 12 March 1996

The market for environmental goods and services is worth £140 billion in the run-up to the millennium.
John Major, *8 July 1991*

Over two-thirds of the population of the UK use recycled or ozone-friendly goods and there are over 800,000 members of the RSPB.
Tony Blair, *27 February 1996*

Since 1930, the world population has more than doubled to 5.8 billion.
Tony Blair, *27 February 1996*

Up to four-fifths of the money spent on energy by the poorest families is wasted because of poor home insulation and inefficient domestic appliances.
Agenda for Sustainability, *Liberal Democrats policy document*

Traffic congestion costs the British economy an estimated £12 billion a year, and the total cost for environmental degradation costs around £14 billion a year.
Agenda for Sustainability

More than 32 million prescriptions for asthma were made in 1994 in England alone.
Liberal Democrats

Nuclear power stations account for 27 per cent of total electricity generation. Renewable sources account for two per cent.

Government spending

as £ million	90-91	91-92	92-93	93-94	94-95	95-96	96-97	97-98	98-99
Current prices	1,777	1,927	2,223	2,562	2,475	2,370	2,400	2,270	2,050
1994-95 prices	2,100	2,100	2,300	2,600	2,500	2,300	2,300	2,100	1,900

All figures from 1995-96 are estimates.
Figures for 1994-95 are rounded.
Source: Financial Statement and Budget Report 1996-97

Quotable quotes

'The environment is no longer an optional, add-on, peel-off extra. It is no longer the easy option – the option which it's easier not to take.'
John Major, *8 July 1991*

'We must be getting close to some kind of embarrassment point – Mr Major came out with this great spiel about sustainable development, yet … it doesn't sit too well with transport policies.'
Sir Geoffrey Pattie, *Tory MP for Chertsey & Walton and former government minister, 23 February 1994*

'If we want a Britain we will be proud to hand on to our children and grandchildren, it must be one in which the environment – in all its manifestations – is protected and enhanced.'
Tony Blair, *speaking to the Royal Society, 27 February 1996*

'For too long Labour has neglected the environment as a socialist issue. We could and should have done more to raise the profile of what ought to be one of our issues.'
Chris Smith, *then Labour frontbench environment spokesman, 5 August 1994*

ENVIRONMENT: HOUSING

James Meikle

Tony Blair presents the Labour party as the defender of home owners as well as of social housing tenants, a bold move that annoys Conservatives, who acted for so long as if they patented the idea. He has even threatened legal regulation of mortgage lenders on the same lines as other financial services and called for the market to develop more flexible packages on repayment including 'holidays' for the financially strapped.

Labour and Liberal Democrats have over the last five years increasingly exposed Tory 'failure' to support home ownership, listing in evidence countless statistics over arrears and repossessions and cuts in help available to mortgage payers through income support and in mortgage income tax relief. This avenue of attack is a reflection of at least one resounding Conservative triumph since they assumed power in 1979. The early fifties share of ownership – a third of all homes in England and Wales – appeared to have peaked at 56 per cent, as council housing too had at about a third, while private renting had slumped from 90 per cent in 1914 to little over ten per cent. Margaret Thatcher, however, introduced the right to buy for social tenants too, and so helped cement the domination of the home owner – another 4 million households entered the sector, which now accounts for nearly 70 per cent of all domestic properties. This is a share unlikely to fall significantly, even if its remarkable growth may also now have been stunted by the nineties economic recession.

Forecasts of up to 4.4 million new households needing accommodation over 20 years assume most needs will be met in the private sector, even if long battles can be expected over finding space for the new homes whether in cities, suburbs or rural areas. This concern with home owning, where interests appear ever more closely linked to the health of the economy and the ever less certain nature of employment, has helped disguise other changes in the housing picture. Some estimates suggests that 'bricks and mortar' investment in social housing, including the private funds secured by housing associations, is now under £4 billion a year – less than a third of the £15 billion real-terms equivalent of 1975, before the last Labour Government began the process of cuts.

Critics of government policy highlight a backlog of repairs and maintenance – and a 'hidden' need for social homes. The number of newly built homes in this sector – nearly all through the housing associations – is about 50,000 a year, a third of the total an early fifties Conservative government once funded in the childhood of the Welfare State. The 1996 Budget inflicted such savage cuts in the Housing Corporation budget that even this is now expected to fall to 30,000 by the end of the decade. In spring 1995, the all-party Commons Environmental Committee of backbench MPs expressed reservations about the Government's apparent satisfaction with its estimate for new social lettings – 60,000 a year, taking into account stock transfers from councils and some re-use of empty accommodation. This was the Department of Environment's lowest projection of need, while the MPs would have preferred ministers to target their attention nearer the 100,000-a-year upper estimates. The difference derives from the Tory hierarchy's determination to leave social housing only to take up the slack left by the home ownership and private rented sector. It believes private financial investment will be the key to improving social housing as well as other sectors.

Labour is increasingly shifting towards outside sources of finance too, including local housing companies, but it has promised local authorities will be able to phase in some of the receipts from council house sales to fund building both by themselves and housing associations. The cuts in bricks and mortar spending on social housing, and subsidies on rent, coincided with an explosion in personal subsidies, mainly through the housing benefit system. Even at the end of the last Tory administration in 1992, the benefit bill was £7.26 billion. By April 1996, it was nearly £11 billion, and some of that, anything up to a fifth by MPs' estimates, was being frittered away in fraud. The Government has acted to limit this expense, without shifting the resources back into building and renovations, where it believes private funds will help close the investment gap.

Critics argue that the measures – such as caps on benefit levels paid and on the payment of new claims in arrears – will disadvantage those most in need of help and accentuate discrimination against some claimants. They also fear that changes in local authorities' legal duties to the homeless and increasing reliance on the private rented sector to temporarily house those on waiting lists will bring more disruption to already disturbed families. But Conservatives' actions have not always matched their rhetoric. While stressing the importance of defending family values through housing policy, ministers did not remove single mothers from priority housing categories as some suggested might happen. They have had successes in social housing as well as in private housing. Although their attention to helping the street homeless once seemed prompted by a fear of upset tourists passing sleeping bundles in the Strand, the programmes that followed were widely welcomed by charities and political critics alike.

Tory political attacks on alleged uniformity of municipal management and design of housing estates have coincided with rises in public expectations of 'consumer' involvement of tenants, even if there is still a long way to go both in local authorities, where four-fifths of social tenants remain, and in housing associations. The Conservative insistence that it has preserved the 'safety net' for those in most need and some regeneration spending on flagship schemes has also shifted attention from growing disquiet among all political parties that some, often edge-of-town, social housing estates may become 'sinks' where unemployed or low-income tenants struggle in a deepening spiral of physical and spiritual decline.

The Tories will pledge more of the same this election, with home ownership still a keystone of wider social policy. They acknowledge real difficulties in recent years but economic growth, low interest and low inflation are their chosen routes to improvement. It remains to be seen whether their faith in the small private landlords, given new quicker powers of eviction, delivers growth in their share of the market at the further expense of social housing.

New cautious Labour has already insisted it will take at least ten years – two terms of government – to meet the policy challenges of engineering a recovery in the housing market without risking a return to the boom/bust economics of the 1980s, achieving an expanded social housing programme of good-quality homes, offering greater choice of tenure (along with closer regulation of standards in the private rented sector), ending homelessness and ensuring balanced communities.

The Liberal Democrat package, some of which mirrors Labour, for instance on the phasing of capital receipts and raising of extra capital on the open financial market, includes a reversal of many of the Government's benefit changes. It also promises a mortgage benefit to help home owners who lose their jobs, but risks upsetting others used to state aid in buying their homes by completely phasing out mortgage income tax relief 'when the housing market permits'. ●

Main events since 1992

26 October 1993: Prince of Wales criticises modern housing and holds the Scottish tenement up as a model for regeneration.

February 1994: Housing market shows first glimmer of hope as new orders for private housing rise by 45 per cent.

April 1994: Number of empty homes has risen by 30 per cent over the previous decade. 864,000 homes unoccupied.

18 March 1996: DoE announces that the entire housing stock of the MoD – 60,000 homes – is to be privatised.

Legislation

Housing Act 1988
● introduced a system of Housing Action Trusts which could take over estate management where tenants voted for this to happen. After refurbishment the stock would be transferred to the private voluntary sector. Minimum period for shorthold tenancy cut to six months

Housing (Scotland) Act 1988
● established body called Scottish Homes with housing powers including ability to acquire public sector homes occupied by secure tenants.
● introduced local authority grants to enable tenants to secure housing other than public sector housing

Leasehold Reform, Housing and Urban Development Act 1993
● aimed to offer greater protection to leaseholders against landlords

Policies

Home Ownership
Con: The right to buy is being extended to tenants of new housing association properties.
Lab: Encourage flexible tenure schemes so people can move from renting to home ownership or switch back to renting when their circumstances change.
Lib Dem: Improve the scope and level of housing benefit, and introduce a parallel benefit for home owners, to be paid for by phasing out mortgage interest tax relief.

Social Housing
Con: Local authorities should not have to construct or purchase housing. Housing associations can attract private investment and build more homes.
Lab: Phase the release of local authority receipts to enable councils to build new homes. Encourage partnerships between councils, tenants and the private sector.
Lib Dem: Allow councils to invest in new homes and carry out repairs, using money raised from council house sales.

Homelessness
Con: Local authorities to be under obligation to secure accommodation for a minimum of 24 months for any household which is unintentionally homeless.
Lab: Keep local authority duty to provide permanent housing to homeless families, the elderly and people with disabilities.
Lib Dem: Give local authorities power to bring into use any property left empty without reasonable cause for more than 12 months.

Polls

Which party has the best policies on housing?

as %	1992 Mar	1993 Sep	1994 May	1995 Jul	1996 Mar
Con	23	13	13	10	12
Lab	45	43	53	48	51
Lib Dem	8	11	10	4	5

Source: MORI

In your view, who is most to blame for negative equity?	%
Estate agents and councils that sold the houses	6
People who bought the houses	11
Banks and building societies that lent them money	13
The Government	62
Don't know	12

To the extent the Government is at fault, which politician is most to blame?	%
Lady Thatcher	54
Nigel Lawson	13
John Major	7
Someone else	5
Don't know	23

Source: ICM June 1995

Most-quoted statistics

1,000 homes are being repossessed every week. A third of a million homes have been repossessed in the last five years.
Liberal Democrat election guide

13.7 million households in England own their own homes (68 per cent), almost 4 million people have become home owners since 1979; and over 1.25 million tenants have exercised the right to buy their home.
Conservative Research Department, 1996

Under this Government repossessions have increased from 60 a week to more than 1,000 a week.

68 per cent of households own their own homes – up from 57 per cent in 1979.

Over the next 20 years demand from an extra 4.4 million households means that 176,000 homes will have to be built every year. At present 160,000 homes are being built and the market is unprepared to build more.

Each day 300 people move from towns and cities to rural areas.

Government spending

as £ million	90-91	91-92	92-93	93-94	94-95	95-96	96-97	97-98	98-99
Current prices	6,725	7,422	8,156	7,733	7,173	6,700	5,840	5,660	6,050
1994-95 prices	7,800	8,100	8,600	7,900	7,200	6,500	5,500	5,200	5,500

All figures from 1995-96 are estimates.
Figures for 1994-95 are rounded.
Source: Financial Statement and Budget Report 1996-97

Quotable quotes

'Home ownership is what 80 per cent of the people want … we want to give yet more people the opportunity to buy.'
John Gummer, *27 June 1995*

'We have to be clear who should be in charge of housing. It is not the Government, not councils, not housing associations but the people themselves.'
Tony Blair, *30 January 1996*

'The spectacle of 1,000 home owners being put out of their homes every week inevitably acts as a damper to other families' hopes.'
Nick Raynsford, *Labour housing spokesman, 3 January 1996*

'The answer is … effective action to deal with those tenants who consistently refuse to behave reasonably and make life a misery for those around them.'
Tony Blair, *23 March 1995*

ENVIRONMENT: LOCAL GOVERNMENT

James Meikle

Pessimists see the last five years as another period of declining power and influence as the shifts in regeneration, education, training and housing functions from councils to quangos or other non-elected bodies introduced by previous Tory administrations began to gather force. The council tax bedded down as the replacement for the short-lived poll tax, but levels began to rise as the Government shifted more of the burden for raising cash to local authorities by cutting central grants. Ministers retained their centralising grip by capping overall municipal spending and effectively determining the main services that should get any real increases in funding that might be allowed.

The media were blamed by some for portraying local government elections simply as tests of public opinion on John Major's team – and by May 1996, the Conservatives controlled barely a dozen of the 480 county, district and unitary councils in England, Wales and Scotland. But Labour's May 1996 council campaign was largely based on a 'you can't trust the Tories' approach', denouncing alleged broken promises on a range of national issues from income tax to mad cow disease, although they also found time to attack ministers for 'fiddling' grants to local authorities and flagship Tory councils, especially Westminster, which was shortly to be accused by the district auditor of gerrymandering.

The Tories said Labour local government – high taxes, inefficiency, political correctness and excessive bureaucracy – was symptomatic of Labour in national government. Yet Labour's high command's determination to launch investigations into alleged misbehaviour and even to call for suspension of councillors in areas such as Monklands in Scotland, Walsall in the Midlands and Hackney, north London, contrasted with Conservative reluctance to condemn Dame Shirley Porter's regime in Westminster until the full process of law had been exhausted.

The Liberal Democrats had a run of success at local elections, even though opponents accused them of the dirtiest streetfighting. They had their setbacks – the neighbourhood committee system in Tower Hamlets, east London, proved a disaster and the borough went back to Labour. But they seized once true-blue areas such as Hastings and Tunbridge Wells. Paddy Ashdown's long-running promise of 1p on income tax to fund extra education spending, if necessary, may have helped. Municipal contests also allowed the Liberal Democrats numerous opportunities to stake their claims for proportional representation, as their party strengthened its grip as the second major power in town and county halls.

Local government was reorganised again following the Tory 1974 shake-up and subsequent partial recantation that saw Margaret Thatcher abolish strongholds of municipal socialism, the metropolitan counties, the Greater London Council and the Inner London Education Authority. The two-tier systems in Scotland and Wales were wiped out in one go by law, while a more gradual review of the English shires saw a mixed economy with metropolitan and rural unitary authorities existing alongside county and district councils, where the former retained services such as education and social services and the latter stayed responsible for housing, refuse collection and other services.

The Conservatives were disappointed more unitaries did not emerge in England, but both Labour and Liberal Democrats may also set a new review in motion if they achieve power. The pressure for both more formal regional representation and devolution of some powers to the often forgotten parish, community and town councils seems certain to lead to more questions about whether the remaining county/district council bureaucracy in the middle can survive.

Optimists see the prospect of a third great age of municipal government – replacing Victorian paternalists and the post-war professionals, the planners, teachers and social workers, who were finally vilified in the Thatcher era, with new managers, partners and 'facilitators', who do not mind who controls services but mastermind their quality and are given legitimacy by new democratic methods. Councils began experimenting with postal surveys, citizens' juries, right-to-reply-style video-boxes for local voters and 'question times' at council meetings. Decentralisation of services down from town hall to local area offices continued apace, a trend rather more successful than decentralising political control.

The idea of directly elected mayors, a notion once espoused by Deputy Prime Minister Michael Heseltine, became Labour property as Tony Blair adopted it, particularly for London, but others in his party, both in Parliament and in local government, were not so keen. Some felt the assumption of such political clout instead of the ceremonial and council-chairing functions of the present mayoralty would create civic leaders who might undermine the position of local MPs. Others said a revolution would be needed too in the political and bureaucratic administration that relies on political groups electing their own leaders and, where necessary, on hung authorities doing deals with other parties. In big cities the mayor's office and powers would cut across those of several local authorities.

There were concerns among local politicians of all parties that the Government's distribution of regeneration funds concentrated too much on a beauty contest approach between glamorous projects that sometimes distorted longer-term housing, employment or training needs while the Government insisted the extra competition, and pressure to work and seek matching funds from the private sector, had sharpened priorities.

The 'challenge funding' approach spread to mainstream parts of local government capital finance as well, although the wider Private Finance Initiative, applied right across the public sector, made little municipal headway. There were fears too about the impact of the National Lottery on town hall decision-making. There would be pressure on councillors and planners to back myriad projects which had grants distributed from the proceeds of the nation's weekly gamble, but would councils be left to pick up the tab years down the line when half-empty, expensive to run, arts centres and concert halls began to feel the financial pinch?

Labour, once reluctant even to highlight its local government record, a legacy of the eighties 'loony left' onslaughts, began to parade its 'partnership' successes with private enterprise and other public bodies – the Manchester Metro and the McAlpine Stadium, Huddersfield, part of the Kirklees authority, among the most obvious. Labour-led Coventry was the first to hand over management of its city centre to an American-style private company, an experiment supported by the Government. Such examples proved that councils were still key players in economic and social regeneration, argued Labour. Optimists see other welcome changes in municipal culture. John Major's once-derided Citizen's Charter programme was followed by many authorities keen to demonstrate more customer-focused attitudes and practices. Conservatives boasted that compulsory tendering of services had focused minds on cost and quality, making councils concentrate on meeting needs rather than directly running all services.

Labour argued that compulsion was not the answer, and indeed that it put cheapness above quality, as well as damaging the pay and conditions of workers. But as the election approaches, the party is putting together a package that will provide a national framework of standards for all municipal services, in much the way that the Office for Standards in Education and its inspection service was meant to for schools. The party insists, however, that any such scheme would have to fully involve local authorities and not become the centralising, political force that many saw Ofsted becoming. Dispelling the old image of municipal socialism is a key strategy for Labour, which promises to end the capping system, while keeping a reserve power to rein back 'extreme' high spenders. 'Hit squads' to run councils that have failed to buck up their poor performances are also proposed, as Blair's lieutenants blame the Government for interfering in council affairs while doing nothing to remedy spectacular failures among a few councils of all political persuasions. ●

Main events since 1992

5 May 1995: Conservatives lose more than 2,000 seats in local elections.

21 December 1995: Monklands District Council cleared of nepotism and political and religious bias in job appointments.

29 March 1996: Avon, Cleveland and Humberside are abolished along with scores of district councils. Unitary authorities, including Bristol, Bath, York and Glasgow, take over education and social services.

4 May 1996: Conservatives lose a further 573 seats in local elections.

10 May 1996: Dame Shirley Porter and other members of Westminster Council are surcharged £31.7 million by the district auditor for gerrymandering.

Legislation

Local Government (Scotland) Act 1994
Local Government (Wales) Act 1994

- created new unitary councils in place of two-tier system

Policies

Capping

Con: Capping has prevented excessive council tax increases; however, some extra flexibility to be allowed in 1997.
Lab: Remove capping to increase the power and responsibility of councils. Secretary of State for Environment to have reserve powers in exceptional circumstances.
Lib Dem: Remove capping to encourage local initiative and local accountability.

Responsibility

Con: Councils have a vital role to play and have been given new responsibilities in community care and the environment.
Lab: Councils to have an overall duty to promote the social, economic and environmental well-being of the communities they serve.
Lib Dem: Local and regional authorities to assume the main responsibility for the regeneration of their economies.

Compulsory Competitive Tendering

Con: Competition delivers value for money and often improves quality.
Lab: End CCT. Tendering decisions to be left to local authorities; increased emphasis to be placed on value for money over cost.
Lib Dem: Compulsory competitive tendering is unnecessary. Abolish it.

Local Democracy

Con: Councils have a vital role as leaders of their local communities. Regional assemblies would hamper decision-making at a local level.

Lab: Councils to be encouraged to adopt new institutional structures to enhance their responsiveness to local needs. Possibility of elected mayors.
Lib Dem: Fair electoral systems to be introduced for all elections. Power to be devolved to community or parish council level where appropriate.

Most-quoted statistics

Local government employs 12 per cent of the national workforce, spends £60 billion a year running services and owns one in six of the nation's homes.

The number of houses built by local councils has fallen from 66,000 in 1979 to 1,235 because Government has cut back funding.
Labour Conference, 1995

Government-appointed or self-appointed bodies now spend over £30 billion which was previously controlled by elected local authorities.
Labour Conference, 1995

The locally raised share of local council funds has fallen from 50 per cent in the early 1980s to less than 20 per cent now.
Labour Conference, 1995

Government spending

as £ million	90-91	91-92	92-93	93-94	94-95	95-96	96-97	97-98	98-99
Current prices	20,522	28,356	31,175	29,378	29,913	30,320	31,320	31,380	31,530
1994-95 prices	23,800	30,900	32,700	29,900	29,900	29,500	29,700	29,000	28,500

All figures from 1995 are estimates.
Figures for 1994-95 are rounded.
Source: Financial Statement and Budget Report 1996-97

Quotable quotes

'Millions of Tory voters sat on their hands yesterday … the general election is a different ball game.'
John Major*, after the humiliation of the 1996 local elections*

'We are being sacrificed to the New Labour Party. I am not going to go easily.'
'Citizen Dave' Church*, Labour leader of Walsall Council, suspended from the party and accused of running a separate group within the party*

EUROPE AND FOREIGN AFFAIRS

John Palmer and Ian Black

At first sight the explosive character of the European issue in British politics is difficult to understand. True, membership of the European Community (now the European Union) has always been a subject of controversy – more within political parties than between them. But the intensity of the current debate, notably in the Conservative party, has come to overshadow almost every other question and now seems to touch on Britain's sense of basic national identity. One reason for this is that the process of European integration has moved beyond the economic 'common market' agenda which dominated the debate at the time of the UK's entry into the European Community in 1973. That phase ended to all intents and purposes with the Single European Act of 1985 (reluctantly accepted by the then Conservative Government led by Margaret Thatcher) and the subsequent introduction of the single European market two years later.

The questions at the heart of the European debate since then have been far more directly political and constitutional. It is true that the impetus for European monetary union – and the eventual creation of a single European currency – has been and still is largely economic, but its impact is necessarily highly political. The transfer of decision-making power from the national to the European Union level implied in moving to a single currency has had major domestic political repercussions. In a sense, with the introduction of the single market, many pro-European Conservatives felt their agenda for closer European co-operation had been completed. On the other hand, the adoption by the EU of an increasing range of policies covering issues from higher environmental protection standards to new minimum social rights – including workers' rights – appealed far more to Labour than to the Conservatives.

The internal debate over Europe has often, but wrongly, been described in terms of a conflict between European federalists and anti-federalists. This is misleading on two levels. By many in Britain – in all political parties – federalism is seen as a euphemism for a 'centralised European superstate'. But in all other EU countries federalism means a delicate system of power-sharing between local, regional, national and European Union institutions, with 'decisions taken as close to the people as possible'. This may, indeed, also account for the remarkable shift in 'pro-federalist' attitudes to Europe in Scotland and Wales – especially among Nationalist voters. But the converse is that the divisions over European policy are not interacting with the separate but related debate over devolution – and in a way which some Conservatives fear is calling into question the very character of the UK state. In practice, full-scale Euro-federalism – however defined – will not be the outcome of the special inter-governmental conference which has been charged with reviewing the operation of the Maastricht Treaty.

The Conservative Government does appear, however, to be in a very small minority in resisting any serious reform of the EU institutions (including greater majority voting and more powers for the European Parliament) in the inter-governmental conference. For that reason the other 14 EU countries may delay any final agreement on a new treaty until after the general election. The assumption is that a Labour government – already pledged to joining the EU Social Chapter and accepting greater majority voting – would prove a more flexible negotiating partner, especially if Labour established a broad 'understanding' with the Liberal Democrats.

It remains to be seen whether and to what extent the Tory divisions on Europe reassert themselves in the Labour party. Labour does have concerns about the move to a single currency, although these may appear less threatening as the monetary union timetable approaches the 1999 deadline. Labour, however, still shares Conservative opposition to any serious changes in the way decisions are taken in Brussels about foreign policy and both internal and external security as well as defence. But as far as Britain's EU partners are concerned, almost any other UK government would be a welcome relief after more than a decade of bitter strife with the Thatcher and Major administrations in London.

Beyond Europe, where there are few immediately obvious differences between the two main parties, Labour is pushing its internationalist credentials in a way designed to highlight Conservative insularity. In one key change, the Overseas Development Administration – subordinate to the Foreign Office under the Conservatives – is to be transformed into a Department of International Development headed by a Cabinet Minister.

Labour wants a new focus on the world's 1.1 billion poorest people because 'Britain and other developed countries have a clear ethical responsibility to help combat such poverty,' says the party's foreign policy document. Tackling poverty and promoting sustainable development is a matter of self-interest because they will also promote greater global stability, it argues. But help for the former Communist regimes of Eastern Europe should not take precedence over aid to the poorest countries in sub-Saharan Africa: the Tories have been criticised for prioritising wealthier countries – the scandal over the Pergau dam in Malaysia is the best-known example – for reasons that have more to do with commercial and political advantage than poverty eradication. Labour reaffirms Britain's commitment to the UN target of spending 0.7 per cent of GNP on development aid and pledges to 'reverse the decline in UK aid spending', but it gives no hostages to fortune by offering either figures or timetable. Under the Conservatives the British figure has sunk to an all-time low of 0.29 per cent.

Labour will also work for reform of the United Nations and increase pressure for an early resolution of its chronic funding crisis – which could mean strains in relations with the United States, the biggest debtor. With Bosnia and Somalia in mind it wants 'clear and achievable mandates' for any future UN-led or UN-authorised missions and better military advice for the Secretary-General.

In a break with the Conservative habit of recent years Labour wants a revitalisation of the link between Britain and the Commonwealth, arguing that a unique trans-regional network that includes several dynamic economies is being ignored or at best treated as a wearisome obligation. It hopes to use the 1997 Commonwealth summit in Edinburgh to press for a Commonwealth economic declaration on trade and sustainable development. Labour has consistently criticised the Tories for being too soft on repression, especially in Nigeria.

Labour plans to look carefully at the question of arms exports and general aid and trade links with regimes which have questionable records on human rights – an issue highlighted by the row over the attempted deportation of the Saudi Islamic dissident, Muhammad al-Masari. On the Middle East, Labour has supported a Palestinian state more openly and consistently than the Tories. On the spending front, Labour promises strong support for the BBC World Service and the British Council, both badly hit by Treasury cuts, but again there are no figures. And in a move that has already attracted controversy it is to look at the appointment of businessmen to head British embassies in countries which offer 'strategic market opportunities'.

Robin Cook, Shadow Foreign Secretary, sees the West's engagement with a changing China as one of the greatest challenges ahead for the new century. He is concerned by the future of Hong Kong, to be handed back to China on 30 June 1997, possibly only weeks after a Labour government has taken power. Labour had no say in the long process of negotiation that led to the 1984 Joint Declaration by Britain and China, nor in the limited democratic reforms made by Chris Patten since he became the colony's last governor in 1992. But if in power, Labour is likely to face sharp criticism when the Chinese march in.

New Labour sees Britain as a 'medium power' that is more likely to prosper in alliance than in isolation and should avoid the pretension that it is a global power that can go it alone. In that context Robin Cook upbraided the former Conservative Foreign Secretary, Douglas Hurd, who liked to talk about Britain 'punching above its weight'. 'I am not at all sure,' Mr Cook told the Britain in the World Conference in 1995, 'that such a pugilistic metaphor encourages the frame of mind most conducive to success in forming alliances.' ●

Main events since 1992

16 September 1992: Black Wednesday. Britain leaves Exchange Rate Mechanism.

1 January 1993: Entry into force of the Maastricht Treaty on European Union.

8 December 1995: Madrid European Union summit confirms 1999 as start of final move to monetary union and a single European currency.

19 January 1996: Government announces it will issue a White Paper on further European integration.

7 March 1996: Former Chancellor, Nigel Lawson, attacks Conservative party plans on the single currency to the delight of backbench Eurosceptics.

29 March 1996: Inter-governmental conference on European integration in Maastricht.

29 March 1996: Turin European Union summit begins inter-governmental conference to review the Maastricht Treaty.

2 April 1996: Government promises to hold a referendum if a future Tory government decides to join a European single currency.

10 April 1996: Millionaire businessman, Sir James Goldsmith, threatens to run pro-referendum candidates against sitting MPs in the next general election.

24 April 1996: Sixty-six Tory MPs back private member's bill which would give Parliament powers to overrule the European Court of Justice. The bill is defeated.

Legislation

European Communities (Amendment) Act 1993
- changed UK legislation to comply with the single European Act, agreed at Luxembourg summit in December 1985 and signed in February 1986. The Act rewrote the definition of 'the Treaties' and 'the Common Treaties' in line with plans for the next stage of European harmonisation

British Nationality (Hong Kong) Act 1990
- provided for the acquisition of British citizenship by up to 50,000 selected Hong Kong residents, their spouses and children

Policies

Single Currency
Con: A manifesto commitment to hold a referendum on any decision to join a single currency.
Lab: Committed to a referendum on entry into a single currency.
Lib Dem: Commited to a referendum.

Common Agricultural Policy
Con: Member states will have to tackle the reform of the CAP and of structural funds which cannot possibly be extended to the new members in their present forms.
Lab: Supports fundamental reform of the CAP to cut waste and fraud, putting that money to use to benefit the wider rural community.
Lib Dem: Replace the CAP with a common rural policy.

Social Chapter
Con: The 'opt-out' of the Social Chapter ensures that British labour law is not subjected to a new raft of regulations.
Lab: Sign the Social Chapter, giving British workers the same rights as workers on the Continent.
Lib Dem: Oppose the UK's Social Chapter and economic and monetary union 'opt-outs'.

Overseas Aid
Con: Maintain our commitment to a substantial, high-quality aid programme; promote trade and reduce the levels of Third World debt.
Lab: Start to reverse the decline in UK aid spending. Resources to be switched to programmes that have the greatest impact on the poorest countries.
Lib Dem: Increase UK development assistance to meet the UN target of 0.7 per cent of GNP.

Polls

Which party has the best policy on Europe?

as %	1992 Mar	1993 Sep	1994 May	1995 Jul	1996 Mar
Con	35	21	23	21	20
Lab	25	19	29	27	25
Lib Dem	9	14	14	7	10

Source: MORI

Should there be a referendum on whether we should join a single European currency?

as %	All	Con	Lab	Lib Dem
Yes	71	65	74	72
No	24	31	22	24
Balance	+47	+34	+52	+48

Source: ICM September 1995

How would you vote in a referendum on the single currency?

as %	1994* Dec	1995* Feb	1995* Apr	1995† Jun	1996‡ May
Yes	28	34	35	34	29
No	72	66	65	66	64

* ICM
† Europinion barometer
‡ ICM: Do you approve or disapprove of Britain joining in?

Most-quoted statistics

Last year the British taxpayers paid £8.9 billion into the Brussels coffers and got £4.8 billion back.
Daily Mail, *9 May 1996*

Aid has been halved from 1.6 to 0.8 per cent as a proportion of government spending and is only 0.3 per cent of gross domestic product, less than half the United Nations target of 0.7 per cent.

Government spending

Overseas development

as £ million	90-91	91-92	92-93	93-94	94-95	95-96	96-97	97-98	98-99
Current prices	1,737	1,994	2,140	2,234	2,234	2,369	2,290	2,370	2,420
1994-95 prices	2,000	2,200	2,200	2,300	2,400	2,300	2,200	2,200	2,200

All figures from 1995-96 are estimates.
Figures for 1994-95 are rounded.
Source: Financial Statement and Budget Report 1996-97

Quotable quotes

'If I thought [a single currency] would damage the nation state, I would choose the nation state.'
John Major, *3 April 1995*

'No British government can join a single currency without the consent of the British people.'
Robin Cook, *Shadow Foreign Secretary, 13 March 1996*

'If I'd signed the Social Chapter, I could never have looked the unemployed in the eye again.'
John Major, *19 January 1996*

'Every single other Conservative party in Europe is in favour of the Social Chapter, as is every other Conservative government.'
Tony Blair, *19 January 1996*

'The day of artificially constructed megastates has gone: so the Euro-federalists are now desperately scurrying to build one.'
Margaret Thatcher

'Government policy must not be put at the mercy of millionaires who play with British politics as a hobby or as a boost to newspaper sales.'
Douglas Hurd, *former Foreign Secretary, 27 April 1996*

'There is a sense in the electorate in Europe and in the UK, whether one looks at the question of Bosnia, ERM, fishing or a host of other matters, that the Maastricht Treaty has failed the people.'
Bill Cash, *Tory Eurosceptic*

'Around the world three letters send a chill down the spine of the enemy – SAS. And those letters spell out one clear message: don't mess with Britain.'
Michael Portillo, *Defence Secretary, 10 October 1995*

'I'm never wildly enthusiastic about phrases … You know – 'semi-detached', 'heart of Europe'. But what the British public expect is for us to actually identify what will affect prosperity in Britain.'
Malcolm Rifkind*, Foreign Secretary, 12 May 1996*

'I have no doubt whatsoever that whenever I come to London in future I will be able to appreciate your wonderful artistic traditions, the banter of the London cabby, the smell of fresh-mown grass and warm beer on the village cricket green.'
Jacques Santer*, President of the European Commission, 5 May 1996*

HEALTH

David Brindle

On one count, the NHS internal market has proved a success for the Conservatives. Damaging winter crises in hospitals, brought on by shortages of beds and staff, have become far less of a political liability – if not yet a thing of the past. By devolving the responsibility for commissioning health care to health authorities and fundholding GPs, ministers have managed to make the NHS pace itself much more evenly over the financial year. The dividend has been an end to upheaval on the scale seen in winter 1987-88, when then Prime Minister Margaret Thatcher was prompted to order the policy review that led to the internal market.

But although the internal market has cleverly devolved the responsibility for tricky decisions on issues like health care rationing, and although local health managers may then get the immediate blame in cases like that of 'Child B' Jaymee Bowen, there remains an underlying grievance that such cases are somehow the Government's fault. The Tories have some reason to feel resentful about this. They have honoured their 1992 election pledge to award above-inflation increases in NHS funding, year on year, even if the 1995-96 rise of 1.1 per cent in real terms barely covered the growing costs of the ageing population and advances in medical technology – generally reckoned each to require at least 0.5 per cent more annually.

Hospital waiting times – but not lists – have been brought down by the controversial strategy of pouring money into a drive to treat all patients waiting the longest, irrespective of the seriousness of their illness. As a result, whereas in 1990 more than 130,000 people in England had been waiting more than a year for treatment, and 80,000 two years, two-year waits have been virtually eliminated since 1992-93 and a one-year wait is now the maximum in many parts of the country. The downside of this, doctors say, is that patients with grave and potentially disabling conditions can now be kept waiting longer while surgeons deal with more trivial cases which happen to have been in the queue for more than 12 months. There are, moreover, still one million people on English hospital waiting lists, despite anecdotal evidence of doctors being reluctant to add more names and risk breaching waiting-time targets.

These targets are part of the Patient's Charter, which has done much else to make hospital and community health service trusts a generally popular innovation. Self-governing trust status, introduced as an option in 1991 but as good as universal by 1996, has undoubtedly given health units a sharper identity and greater pride: public areas have been smartened up, non-clinical services greatly improved and corporate spirit reinvigorated. Trusts, or something very like them, are here to stay.

Stephen Dorrell, appointed Health Secretary in 1995, has meanwhile moved effectively to address areas of weakness which became increasingly telling under Virginia Bottomley, his predecessor. Applying the focus and urgency of the waiting-times drive, he has moved to tackle (though by no means solved) problems in delivery of emergency hospital services and of care in the community for mentally ill people. He has also ended the Bottomley practice of reeling off endless series of statistics to try to prove the success of Tory health policies.

There does, however, remain much for Labour and the Liberal Democrats to go at: trusts and health authorities are crying out to be 'democratised'; fundholding is costly and, according to the Audit Commission, so far generally ineffective; bureaucracy everywhere has been swollen by the market system; and strategic planning of health care – including, critically, the long-sought shift to a primary-care-led NHS – has been rendered almost impossible by the market's fragmentation.

The Tories have been seeking to prepare the ground for a revolution in primary care by offering GPs a new contract. But this fails to appreciate that such a revolution will be delivered only by the primary care team as a whole, including nurses, therapists and pharmacists, and that trusts will fight tooth-and-claw to protect their business unless some strategic planning body is there to take it away from them. Both Labour and the Lib Dems would retain the separation of the purchasing and providing of health care, while portraying themselves as ending the market. Both would keep a system of GP purchasing of health care, while saying they were abolishing fundholding. Both would keep local pay flexibility for NHS workers, while saying they were restoring the national terms and conditions abolished by the Tories.

Whichever party forms the next government, there will be little immediate change in the way the NHS goes about its business. There may be little in the longer term, too. One thing all the parties accept is that the service has had so much structural change in the past 25 years that it has proved debilitating. Labour maintains it would release resources to put back into patient care by cutting bureaucracy: the market, it says, has cost £1.4 billion without a penny of it going into patient care. The Lib Dems go along with this, but acknowledge also that the service would require greater government investment. Overseas observers, indeed, continue to be astonished that the NHS runs on as little as 5.7 per cent of GDP – well below the average for health care spending in the industrialised world.

Notwithstanding any relatively small increase in tax funding for the service, though, the next government will face tough choices. Is dentistry to be brought back into the NHS family, or finally cut adrift in the private health care waters where it has been allowed to sail? Is continuing care of the elderly and long-term sick to be rehabilitated as an NHS service, or shall we all need private insurance to cover us for the eventuality? Most fundamental of all, how is the NHS to spend its £40 billion a year? Whether you call it 'priority-setting' or plain rationing, hard and often heart-breaking decisions will increasingly be necessary about which of an ever-growing range of treatments and drugs will be paid for on the service – and which patients benefit.

None of the parties will want to discuss such matters on the hustings. The policy battle will be fought on simpler slogans about red tape, fat-cat hospital managers and nurses' pay. But many NHS workers, and that means almost one million voters, know full well what is really at stake. ●

Main events since 1992

17 December 1992: Death of Jonathan Zito from attack by psychiatric patient intensifies debate on care in the community.

19 September 1995: Inquiry by former NHS Chief Executive Sir Duncan Nichol reports that higher taxes cannot meet demand resulting from increasing elderly population, rising expectations and escalating technology costs.

September 1995: Berkshire Health Authority sets rationing trend when it announces it is banning or cutting down on non-essential operations to save £7 million.

October 1995: Rationing policy brought to the fore by Jaymee Bowen, known as Child B, who is refused treatment for leukaemia.

1996: Death of Nicholas Geldard highlights lack of Intensive Care bed space.

16 May 1996: British Medical Association warns that hospitals across the country are facing financial meltdown and patient care is being put at risk.

21 May 1996: Jaymee Bowen dies after her leukaemia relapses.

Legislation

National Health Service and Community Care Act 1990
- hospitals given the right to become self-governing trusts (outside health authority jurisdiction)
- GP fundholding introduced
- local authorities given responsibility for enhanced care in the community

Policies

NHS Internal Market
Con: Division between commissioning and provision of health care now accepted. Institutional stability now needed so mechanism can fully mature.
Lab: Abolish the market and replace annual contracts with longer-term agreements. A clear separation between the planning and delivery of health care remains.
Lib Dem: Develop distinct roles of commissioners and providers, but rethink the role of the market in NHS decisions.

GP Fundholding
Con: Provide for the development of fundholding in ways that can be adapted to suit local circumstances.
Lab: Replace fundholding with GP commissioning in which GPs and health authorities work in partnership to get the best for patients.
Lib Dem: Extend the principles of GP fundholding, removing the current two-tier service.

Nurses' Pay
Con: A clear commitment to local pay in the NHS.
Lab: Favour local flexibility to meet local need, but only on the basis of a satisfactory national framework for pay and conditions.
Lib Dem: Support national negotiations guided by appropriate pay review bodies.

Private Finance
Con: The NHS and the independent sector to co-operate more closely whenever NHS patients stand to benefit.
Lab: Private finance must be in partnership with public finance and not a substitute for it.
Lib Dem: Care can be commissioned from outside the NHS if it represents the best value for money. The NHS should continue to be funded from general taxation.

Regional Health Authorities
Con: Devolve more decision-making to the local level. Administrative costs to be reduced by the elimination of an unnecessary tier of management.
Lab: Has strongly opposed the Government's move to replace regional health authorities with outposts of the civil service.
Lib Dem: Believe that there should be a regional tier within the NHS and oppose abolition of regional health authorities.

Health Care Rationing
Con: Process of prioritisation represents sensible allocation of NHS resources. Health spending to rise 1 per cent above inflation.
Lab: Committed to the maintenance of a comprehensive National Health Service. Cancer patients to be treated promptly.
Lib Dem: Waiting lists are not a responsible way to set priorities. The public must be involved in setting priorities for the NHS.

NHS Charges

Con: Those who can afford to do so should contribute towards the cost of their medicines through prescription charges.
Lab: Undertake a full review of charges.
Lib Dem: Abolish eye and dental check-up charges and freeze prescription charges – to be paid for by increasing tobacco taxes.

Care in the Community

Con: Reforms give elderly and vulnerable people more choice and better support, plus services better tailored to their needs.
Lab: Moratorium on further psychiatric bed closures until community services are developed. Propose a new Mental Health bill.
Lib Dem: Users should be given effective rights to influence decision-making and carers given proper recognition through enhanced carers' benefit and respite care.

Long-term Care

Con: Have increased the amount of capital that people can keep before having to pay for long-term care.
Lab: Establish national eligibility criteria, a long-term care charter and a framework for local charging policies.
Lib Dem: Medical care must remain free of charge for those in long-term care. Charges for care to be capped by the Social Services Inspectorate.

Smoking

Con: The need to encourage a reduction in the use of tobacco forms an important part of health promotion strategy.
Lab: Work to reduce preventable deaths from smoking – a significant measure to be the banning of tobacco advertising.
Lib Dem: Tobacco advertising to be banned and tobacco taxes increased to fund measures to promote better health.

Dentistry

Lab: Revive NHS dentistry and develop a strategy for the maintenance of oral health.
Lib Dem: Reinstate free dental check-ups for all and maintain a comprehensive NHS dental service for children.

Public Health

Con: Promotion of good health and prevention of illness will lead to longer, healthier lives.
Lab: Minister for public health to co-ordinate across government departments to improve the nation's health.
Lib Dem: Health Education Commission should be free of government interference. All government departments to report regularly on progress in health promotion.

Poll

Which party has the best policy on health care?

as %	1992 Mar	1993 Sep	1994 May	1995 Jul	1996 Mar
Con	26	13	12	10	13
Lab	49	48	55	56	55
Lib Dem	11	12	12	4	6

Source: MORI

Most-quoted statistics

Spending on the NHS in the UK stands at nearly £41 billion in 1995-96 – representing £697 for every man, woman and child.
Conservative Research Department, September 1995

Between 1983 and 1993, the number of hospital doctors and dentists rose by 8,000, and the number of qualified nurses and midwives by 18,000.
Conservative Research Department, September 1995

A child born today can expect to live two years longer than a child born in 1979.
Conservative Research Department, September 1995

There are 37,000 fewer nurses since 1990 and 15,000 more managers. As a result of the internal market, administration costs have risen from six per cent of the budget to 12 per cent.
Tony Blair, *3 October 1995*

In a survey of 582 randomly selected hospital consultants, nearly half said that the standard of care had declined in the last five years.
Renewing the NHS, *Labour policy document*

The pay bill for top NHS managers has increased by £450 million while £100 million is spent administering the fundholding scheme.
Renewing the NHS

At present, only 15 per cent of UK hospital in-patient medical procedures have proven beneficial outcomes.
Building on the Best of the NHS, *Liberal Democrat policy document*

Half the country's psychiatric beds were closed in the 1980s at a saving of £2 billion.

Since the Health Service reforms the cost of administration has risen from 6 per cent to 12 per cent of total costs. In the United States it takes up 22 per cent.

Under this Government prescription charges have risen from 20p to £5.25.

Government spending

as £ million	90-91	91-92	92-93	93-94	94-95	95-96	96-97	97-98	98-99
Current prices	22,461	25,544	28,213	29,773	31,582	32,930	33,750	34,180	34,970
1994-95 prices	26,000	27,900	29,000	30,300	31,600	32,000	32,000	31,600	31,600

All figures from 1995 are estimates.
Figures for 1994-95 are rounded.
Source: Financial Statement and Budget Report 1996-97

Quotable quotes

'Not so much an internal market as an infernal bazaar'.
Dr Sandy Macara, *Chairman of the BMA, on the Government's NHS reforms, 4 June 1995*

'The best result for the next 12 months would be zero media coverage of the National Health Service.'
John Maples, *Tory Deputy Chairman, in an internal memorandum, 30 September 1994*

'It's absolutely no good throwing money at the NHS at one end if we are creating more diseases at the other.'
Jenny Tonge, *chair of Liberal Democrat working group on health*

'Government must take the lead, and a Labour government would do that. We would get public and private finance working together in … capital projects in health and education.'
Tony Blair, *4 October 1994*

'Market-testing represents creeping privatisation, as does the Private Finance Initiative.'
Margaret Beckett, *then Shadow Health Secretary, 19 April 1995*

'The public in the end need to understand that there is so much effective but high-cost and sometimes distressing treatment now available that we can't have it all.'
Professor Maurice Lessof, *chair of Royal College of Physicians working party on setting priorities in the NHS, 22 May 1996*

'The accounting rules in the NHS are seriously flawed. If you bring in more patients you are effectively penalising your department.'
Christopher Adams, *consultant neurosurgeon at the Radcliffe Infirmary, Oxford, 16 May 1996*

HOME AFFAIRS: CRIME AND PRISONS

Alan Travis

It was never all Michael Howard's fault. The script had been written long before his entrance on the stage, but the most abused Home Secretary for 30 years did come to personify the Conservatives' greatest U-turn on law and order policy for a generation. John Major had indicated his desire to put law and order back at the centre of the political debate soon after the 1992 general election, when he made a speech saying that when it came to crime 'society needs to understand a little less and condemn a little more'. It was a message which, in the wake of the horrific murder of the Merseyside toddler Jamie Bulger by two other children, appeared to have a deep resonance as the fear of crime rose sharply on the back of official crime figures recording rises of more than ten per cent a year.

On the day after James Bulger's funeral the then Home Secretary, Kenneth Clarke, announced the creation of a new national network of private 'secure training centres' to deal with the hard core of 12 to 14-year-old persistent offenders. These private child jails were to form the centrepiece of the 1994 Criminal Justice and Public Order Act. Although Ken Clarke was Home Secretary for only 12 months, many of the Government's law and order 'reforms' since 1992 were based, albeit loosely, on ideas of the Nottingham lawyer's. It was Clarke who first bowed to pressure from the *Daily Mail* and parts of the judiciary to reverse some of the key parts of Douglas Hurd's liberal 1991 Criminal Justice Act, which had been based on the principle that 'prison is an expensive way of making bad people worse'. The destruction of the 1991 Act marked a fundamental change in the game. It put an end to a 30-year consensus in which it was traditionally the job of a Conservative Home Secretary to be booed at the Tory Conference for refusing to pander to its most atavistic instincts.

Over the next three years Michael Howard employed no such restraint. It seems surprising now, but at first he appeared more consensus-minded than 'bruiser' Clarke. He scaled back the Sheehy reforms which had sparked an unprecedented 20,000-strong Wembley protest rally by police officers and switched his own position on capital punishment, making plain he was not to be a hanging Home Secretary. But that was as far as it went. At his first party conference in the job Howard was cheered to the rafters when he unveiled his '27-point' law and order package that was to prove the most coercive anti-crime programme for a decade. It included his now famous 'prison works' declaration and sparked the first of many clashes with the senior judiciary, with Lord Woolf attacking it as the 'short-sighted, easy option' for tackling rising crime.

The '27 points' were supposed to have contained the Government's response to the Royal Commission on Criminal Justice which had recommended wholesale reforms to prevent high-profile miscarriages of justice, such as the Birmingham Six. Michael

Howard ignored most of its preferred nostrums and instead proposed limiting the historic 'right to silence'. The legislation putting the law and order package and the police reforms into effect was repeatedly mauled in the House of Lords as his conference triumph began to turn sour. Former Conservative Home Secretaries, even the venerated Lord Whitelaw, joined in Howard's 'humiliation by instalments'.

Despite the storms, it seemed to be working: crime figures started to record small reductions as the police adopted a more 'targeted' approach to known criminals. The summer of 1994 saw the Home Secretary working on what he thought would be another Tory party crowd pleaser, the introduction of identity cards. The crime figures showed another 5.5 per cent fall. But a month before he was due to deliver his second instalment in October 1995 an armed IRA breakout at Whitemoor Maximum Security Prison and the discovery of a kilogram of Semtex within its perimeter fence fell as a major blow. His attempts to introduce civilian street patrols were restricted by the police to 'walking with a purpose' and half the Tory Party Conference greeted his ID cards plan as 'rubbish' because he wouldn't make it compulsory. It was capped by the escape of three extremely dangerous life prisoners from a second maximum security prison – this time Parkhurst.

Howard's reputation never recovered. Despite the get-tough 'prison works' break with the past and the falling crime figures, the Conservatives actually lagged behind Labour in the polls on their heartland issue of law and order. It did not get much better. Howard pressed on with a 'never apologise, never explain' policy and continued to announce crackdown after crackdown with more and more emphasis on US-style authoritarian options such as boot camps, electronic tagging and even the reintroduction of a British version of the Alabama chain gang. A fierce battle with the Director-General of the Prison Service, Derek Lewis, over who should take responsibility for the Parkhurst debacle ended with Lewis's sacking. It marked the start of a six-month campaign by Lewis which stripped bare Howard's interference in even the smallest details of prison life.

Instead of retreating, the Home Secretary decided to turn up the heat. He pronounced a 2.4 per cent reduction in the crime figures in 1995 as the most sustained fall in crime for 40 years and decided to introduce a sentencing package which would take the British criminal justice system into the American world of mandatory minimum sentences, automatic life sentences for repeat offenders and rocketing prison populations. It only served to infuriate his now widespread critics. The retiring Lord Chief Justice, Lord Taylor, declared: 'Quite simply it amounts to a denial of justice' – a view which began to be shared by the Tory establishment. In the first half of 1996, the crime figures started to rise again and Howard sealed his reputation as the worst Home Secretary since Henry Brooke in the early 1960s.

The Government's desperation to find law and order nostrums was in part fuelled by the astonishing opinion poll lead that Labour built up on the issue in the wake of Tony Blair's dramatic revision of his party's policy when he was Shadow Home Secretary. The introduction of his now famous 'tough on crime, tough on the causes of crime' catchphrase played to *Crimewatch* fans and replaced the 'old Labour' sole civil liberties test on crime policy with a 'Will it cut crime?' test. The result sent the

Tories into a tail-spin. Although the new policy came under constant attack within the party from civil libertarians, Blair cleverly kept up the pressure on Clarke and Howard, always stressing the question of 'Will it work?', while appearing to conduct a 'Who's the toughest?' auction on law and order. While Howard stressed the need to lock up more and more young teenagers, Blair stressed how few criminals were being caught in the first place and pursued a successful battle to get the victims of violent crime properly compensated.

Although Labour abstained on the 1994 Criminal Justice and Public Order Act, but voted against individual measures during its committee stage, the strategy paid dividends with a spectacular collapse of the Tory lead on law and order. The replacement of Blair by Jack Straw as Shadow Home Secretary saw a continuation of a similar policy but with a rather sharper debate with civil libertarians inside and outside Labour. He dropped the party's historic opposition to the Prevention of Terrorism Act. The clash with the libertarians was crystallised by Straw's speech in which he called for the streets to be reclaimed for the law-abiding citizen from the aggressive begging of 'winos, addicts and squeegee merchants'. He clashed with libertarians again when he supported a clause in the 1996 Police Bill giving chief constables, rather than judges, the right to approve police surveillance through bugging devices. But in early 1997 he changed his mind and supported judicial scrutiny. ●

Main events since 1992

6 October 1994: Michael Howard tells police conference of proposals to reform the right to silence.

10 October 1994: Home Office puts forward proposals for national ID card scheme.

16 December 1994: European Commission on Human Rights decides that Home Secretary should have no say in when to release young murderers.

6 February 1995: Proposals for US-style 'boot camps' for young offenders announced by the Home Office.

16 October 1995: Learmont Report on the escape from Parkhurst High Security Prison accuses the prison service of 'a chapter of errors at every level and a naivety that defies belief'. Calls for Home Secretary's resignation. Derek Lewis, head of the prison service, is sacked.

17 October 1995: Prison inmate numbers reach record level of 52,000. A rise of 10,000 in two years since Michael Howard became Home Secretary.

3 April 1996: 'Protecting the Public' Home Office White Paper published. Main proposals include minimum sentences for repeat burglars and drug dealers and automatic life sentences for third-time sex offenders.

3 May 1996: Home Secretary's decision that juveniles who murdered Liverpool toddler James Bulger should serve minimum of 15 years in prison is declared unlawful by High Court.

Legislation

Criminal Justice and Public Order Act 1994
- allowed 12 to 14-year-olds to be sent to private secure training centres
- increased maximum sentences for 15 to 17-year-olds
- ended unconditional right to silence
- gave police new powers against raves, New Age travellers and mass protests

Police and Magistrates' Court Act 1994
- ended local authority majority control of police authorities

Firearms (Amendment) Act 1996
- banned ownership of handguns over .22 calibre
- restricted .22 handguns to gun clubs

Policies

Criminal Justice
Con: The Criminal Justice Act is the centrepiece of the strategy to ensure that the criminal justice system protects the law-abiding public, not offenders.
Lab: Develop measures to provide a fast, fair and firm criminal justice system. These include reforming the Crown Prosecution Service in order to tackle declining conviction rates.
Lib Dem: Improve the effectiveness and fairness of the criminal justice system and promote greater awareness of the needs of victims.

Crime Prevention
Con: Recognise the importance of a partnership approach – encouraging local people, businesses and councils to work together with the police.
Lab: Place a duty on every local authority to consider the impact on crime of decisions it takes on planning, design and urban environment.
Lib Dem: Introduce community-based response to crime prevention, based on strong partnerships between people, councils and police. Put an extra 3,000 bobbies on the beat.

Prisons
Con: Further prisons to be built. All to be designed, constructed, financed and run by the private sector.
Lab: Has made clear its intention to take privatised prisons back into the public sector as soon as contractually possible.
Lib Dem: Prison is the least effective and most expensive way of deterring crime. Opposed to further prison building.

Identity Cards
Lab: The £600 million cost would be better spent on extra police.
Lib Dem: The limited benefits of identity cards are outweighed by their expense, infringement of civil liberties and potential for increasing tension.

Sentencing
Con: Punishment handed out must reflect the seriousness of the crime.
Lab: New arrangements to ensure consistency and progression in sentencing. Halve time taken to bring young offenders to justice.
Lib Dem: Sentences have not been long enough in some cases. There should be alternatives to custody for younger offenders, including hard work and education.

Polls

Which party has the best policies for dealing with crime/law and order?

as %	1992 Mar	1993 Mar	1993 Sep	1994 Mar	1994 Oct	1995 Jul	1996 Feb	1996 Mar
Con	40	19	23	21	15	23	23	28
Lab	26	23	21	27	29	29	24	30
Lib Dem	8	4	11	6	4	4	5	6

Source: ICM/MORI

Do you favour mandatory identity cards?

	%
Yes	74
No	22

Source: ICM September 1995

Most-quoted statistics

In 1993 crime fell by one per cent, in 1994 by five per cent and in 1995 by 2.4 per cent. Recorded crime has fallen for three years in a row only twice before this century.
Conservative Research Department, 15 April 1996

Since 1979 recorded crime levels have more than doubled. Since 1979, recorded crime figures show that violence against the person has increased by 131 per cent, robbery by 379 per cent, burglary by 129 per cent and vehicle crime by 134 per cent.
Safer Communities, Safer Britain, *Labour policy document, 1995*

The number of criminals actually being convicted has been plummeting for sixteen years.
Liberal Democrat policy guide, 1996

Reported crimes had risen from 2.5 million to 5 million cases by 1994.
Alex Carlile, *Liberal Democrat home affairs spokesman, 27 February 1996*

Crime has fallen by ten per cent in the last two years, but it is up 101 per cent over the last 15.
Labour

One crime in 50 ends in conviction.

The clear-up rate has fallen from 34 per cent in 1984 to 26 per cent.

Government spending

as £ million	90-91	91-92	92-93	93-94	94-95	95-96	96-97	97-98	98-99
Current prices	4,845	5,525	5,830	5,972	6,258	6,600	6,520	6,640	6,760
1994-95 prices	5,600	6,000	6,100	6,300	6,400	6,200	6,100	6,100	6,100

All figures from 1995-96 are estimates.
Figures for 1994-95 are rounded.
Source: Financial Statement and Budget Report 1996-97

Quotable quotes

'Many people feel that the law is letting them down. Too many criminals are raising two fingers at justice.'
John Major, *1994*

'It's true. The fact is they have consistently opposed the changes we have made. There are villains behind bars today who would be walking free if Labour had their way.'
Michael Howard, *29 January 1996*

'Since 1979, burglary has increased by 160 per cent, theft from vehicles by nearly 200 per cent and violent crime by 400 per cent. That's the real Tory record.'
John Prescott, *29 January 1996*

'We have literally to reclaim the streets for the law-abiding citizen from the aggressive begging of winos, addicts and squeegee merchants; make street life everywhere an innocent pleasure again.'
Jack Straw, *4 October 1996*

'As usual on law and order, it is this Government which is showing the way while Labour trail feebly in our wake.'
Michael Howard, *19 June 1995*

'The privatisation of the prison service is morally repugnant.'
Jack Straw, *7 March 1995*

'And the Prime Minister shakes his head and wrings his hands at the rising crime rate. The Conservative Government has only one answer to the problem of crime – build more prisons.'
John Smith, *4 March 1994*

'Each individual should be treated on his or her merits … Any politician, particularly a Home Secretary, strays into this territory at some risk. Quite rightly the judiciary is highly sensitive to any suggestion that its sentencing practice should be dictated to by the Government.'
Douglas Hurd, *1989*

'I've got a simple answer. If you don't want the time then don't do the crime.'
Michael Howard, *21 March 1996*

'It is one thing to be governed by the rule of law. It is quite another to be governed by a despotic, albeit no doubt benevolent, government.'
Lord Donaldson, *former Master of the Rolls, 1 December 1995*

'Such measures as the strengthening of law and enforcement agencies and criminal justice systems are worthwhile, but we must simultaneously look at the real roots of the disease.'
HRH Queen Elizabeth II, *23 February 1994*

'There isn't the slightest doubt the Government has taken a totally superficial approach to the crime problem.'
David Owen, *Chief Constable of North Wales, 20 February 1994*

'Existing policies treat symptoms not causes. We won't reduce crime just by asking others to take responsibility, if we don't also accept responsibility ourselves.'

'What the [prison] service most needs at this juncture is continuity, consistency and genuine ministerial support. It is a matter of great regret that you have not chosen to give it that support.'
Sacked Director-General of the Prison Service ***Derek Lewis***, *in a letter to Michael Howard, 17 October 1995*

'Prison works. It ensures that we are protected from murderers, muggers and rapists – and it makes many who are tempted to commit crime think twice.'
Michael Howard, *Conservative Party Conference, 6 October 1993*

HOME AFFAIRS: RACE AND IMMIGRATION

Alan Travis

As Andrew Lansley, the then Director of the Conservative Research Department, memorably noted halfway through the last Parliament: 'Immigration, an issue which we raised successfully at the 1992 general election and again during the 1994 European elections, played particularly well in the tabloids and has more potential to hurt.' It was an admission which was repeatedly seized upon by both Labour and Liberal Democrat MPs to explain the political motivation of the highly controversial 1996 Asylum and Immigration Act, which did much to shape the debate in this area. In fact the roots of the new laws, which amounted to a significant tightening of the asylum rules, lay as much in Europe as in Conservative party electoral tactics.

In some ways Michael Howard, whose own father, Bernard Hecht, had come to Britain as a Romanian Jewish immigrant fleeing the pogroms, was more sensitive than most Home Secretaries to the impact of a volatile immigration debate on race relations. Unlike with his criminal justice policies, Howard generally sought to maintain the consensus on community relations. In the face of growing concerns over violent racial attacks, the law was strengthened to introduce new measures to deal with persistent harassment and intimidation, even if the Government was not prepared to concede to Labour demands that there should be a specific criminal offence of racially motivated violence. The debate ensured that racial attacks were treated more seriously by the police, who began to develop specialist squads. However, the murder of a black London schoolboy, Stephen Lawrence, and the subsequent failure of a private Old Bailey prosecution for murder brought by his parents against a gang of white youths, proved a shameful episode.

Official census surveys showed that increasingly the 3.5 million ethnic minority population, particularly the black and Irish communities, was becoming more integrated into British society, albeit at higher levels of unemployment and facing greater pockets of poverty. There was, however, little evidence that African-American-style ghettos were developing in British cities. The Commission for Racial Equality continued to break new ground with exposures of racism within the Household Regiments in the army and winning compensation cases for Irish people who had suffered discrimination at work. But the repeated warnings by the CRE chairman, Herman Ouseley, that the Conservatives would play the 'race card' in the run-up to the general election proved only too accurate.

As Michael Howard told the 1995 Conservative Party Conference: 'I am proud of this country's record on race relations. But good race relations and firm immigration control go hand in hand. One thing should be understood. Nothing we do to control immigration will be racist. Anyone lawfully in this country will have nothing to fear. And let me make one thing absolutely clear. Our immigration policy will be decided here in Britain. And not in Brussels. We will never surrender control of our frontiers.'

His denial of the European influence in both immigration and race relations proved to be short-lived. Although not directly under the influence of Brussels, the issue of Europe for one faction of the Tory party became a way of waving an English nationalist flag which provoked xenophobic attacks which damaged community relations. The influence of Europe was also important in framing many of the key aspects of the 1996 Asylum and Immigration Act. It was preceded by the introduction of European-style 'internal border' checks, encouraging schools, hospitals and social security officials to check with the Home Office if they suspected illegal immigrants were trying to use public services.

A barrage of 'bogus immigrant' stories appeared repeatedly in the tabloids, setting the scene for the legislative clamp-down that was to follow. Two Home Office research studies which concluded that Britain was under-using the skills of most refugees who generally came from highly educated urban elites were published only after long delays. The introduction of new internal checks was swiftly followed by the announcement of the withdrawal of welfare support from asylum seekers who failed to make their refugee claims as soon as they landed in Britain. The new legislation contained many of the features of immigration control to be found in the rest of the European Union, including the introduction of a 'white list' of countries from which asylum claims would be presumed to be unfounded. It also introduced a system of fining companies who were found to have employed illegal immigrants and brought in new penalties against those who organised illegal immigrant rings.

The appeal rights of rejected asylum seekers were also severely curtailed. This latter move was heavily criticised by the United Nations High Commissioner on Refugees. An independent inquiry, chaired by a retired Appeal Court judge, found that the Government's measures were essentially discriminatory and warned they would do great damage to race relations. It warned that the Government's objectives of reducing the backlog of refugee applications and combating bogus immigrants would not be achieved. A revolt in the House of Lords, led by Baroness Williams of Crosby and supported by the Churches and the Duke of Norfolk, secured a concession ensuring that individual torture victims would be exempted from the new 'fast-track' decision-making processes.

Labour fought the Asylum Bill in Parliament. Although no clear-cut commitment to its repeal was ever made, the party is pledged to 'review all immigration and asylum law'. The Refugee Council claimed that more than 8,000 asylum seekers were left without official support as a result of the changes – some of them facing severe hardship. ●

Main events since 1992

14 March 1995: Home Secretary confirms that he is to introduce new measures to curb illegal immigration including a 'white list' of countries from which it will be presumed asylum applications are unfounded.

June 1995: Riots erupt in Bradford after police arrest two Asian youths.

25 September 1995: Home Secretary rules out relaxation of immigration controls for people from Hong Kong.

20 November 1995: Proposals for employers to carry out identity checks on new employees revealed by Home Office and condemned by industry.

23 November 1995: Home Secretary Michael Howard publishes letter to refugee groups listing 35 countries, including Nigeria and Algeria, from where some asylum claims will be processed under a fast-track pilot scheme.

November 1995: Writer and activist Ken Saro-Wiwa is executed by the Nigerian military regime. His death leads to renewed calls for Nigerians to be granted asylum in Britain. All but one of 2,032 applications for asylum had been turned down.

2 December 1995: Paddy Ashdown is attacked by racists in Yeovil after launching an investigation into racial harassment in his constituency.

14 December 1995: Proposals to cut benefits for asylum seekers to be implemented in January 1996 are postponed.

14 December 1995: Brixton riots break out after a number of deaths in police custody.

May 1996: Debate rages after Christopher Brand's book *The g Factor* is withdrawn by his publishers. Brand admits 'scientific racism' in his claim that white people are more intelligent than black people.

Legislation

Immigration Act 1988
- removed concession, previously given to men who had settled here before 1973, that allowed their wives and children allowed to enter without marriage tests or financial and accommodation tests

British Nationality (Hong Kong) Act 1990
- extended British citizenship to 225,000 Hong Kong residents

Asylum Bill 1991
- aimed to reduce the number of asylum seekers admitted to Britain
- new grounds for refusal were added to the bill, including failure to apply immediately on arrival and failure to seek refuge either in a safer part of home territory or in a neighbouring country

Revised Asylum and Immigration Act 1996
- established a 'white list' of eight countries from where no refugees will be accepted

Policies

Asylum

Con: Welcome genuine refugees, but emphasise preventing abuse of the system.
Lab: Believes each asylum or immigration case must be considered on its own merits and that there should be a reasonable opportunity to appeal. Restore benefits during appeal.
Lib Dem: Oppose the Asylum and Immigration Bill as it could increase racial discrimination. Asylum policy should be based upon the UN Convention on Refugees.

Immigration

Con: Legislation to be introduced with more effective asylum procedures. The new legislation to strengthen the enforcement of immigration control.
Lab: Committed to firm but just immigration policies which tackle unfairness and delay and uphold British obligations under international law.
Lib Dem: Britain needs a coherent immigration strategy which notes labour requirements and upholds the rights of the individual and family union.

Polls

How prejudiced are you against people of other races?

as %	1987	1991	1995
Very prejudiced	4	2	3
A little prejudiced	34	29	16
Not at all prejudiced	60	68	77

Source: ICM March 1995/SCPR

How prejudiced are people in your street?

as %	1995
Very prejudiced	6
A little prejudiced	22
Not at all prejudiced	40
Don't know	32

Source: ICM March 1995/SCPR

Most-quoted statistics

13,000 asylum seekers with 4,000 dependants, most of them children, will be caught by the Immigration and Asylum Bill.
Refugee Council, 5 December 1995

2,800 asylum seekers were deported last year after their applications had been rejected – an increase of more than 35 per cent over 1994.

Estimates of the number of illegal immigrants resident in Britain vary from 20,000 to one million. In 1994 5,032 illegal immigrants were deported.

Quotable quotes

'There is no question of giving 3 million people in Hong Kong the right to live in this country.'
Michael Howard*, Home Secretary, 24 May 1995*

'Immigration, an issue which we raised successfully in 1992 and again in the 1994 Euro elections campaign, played particularly well in the tabloids and has more potential to hurt.'
Andrew Lansley*, former Director of Research at Conservative Central Office, October 1995*

'Many of us here are the grandchildren, great-grandchildren, of immigrants. I'm one. You, Michael Howard, are another. That's why it is so disgraceful of you and the Tory party to play the race card.'
Jack Straw*, Shadow Foreign Secretary, 5 October 1995*

'Companies are already asked to be unpaid tax inspectors. Now they are being asked to be immigration officers as well.'
Richard Brown*, spokesman for the Association of British Chambers of Commerce*

'We have a longer history of laws affecting race relations than almost any other country in the European Union. More comprehensive legislation and better race relations.'
Michael Howard*, 25 November 1995*

'For far too long, this country has been seen as an attractive destination for bogus asylum-seekers and illegal immigrants.'
Michael Howard*, May 1995*

'It is no wonder, when they see on their television screens the life that exists in Europe and the USA, that if they can get on a banana boat or a 747 they will come by any way – legally or illegally.'
Winston Churchill *MP, 29 April 1995*

NATIONAL HERITAGE

Dan Glaister and Andrew Culf

A proven senior politician running a single department with responsibility for all aspects of the nation's cultural life, from fine art to football, a seat at the Cabinet table and an annual budget of almost £1 billion. It sounded too good to be true. It was. The arts honeymoon lasted only a few months following the creation of the Department of National Heritage in 1992. The fall of David Mellor, in whose image the DNH was created, was accompanied by a reversion to business as usual. The arts assumed their familiar low profile on the political agenda. Ministers were handed the arts portfolio on their way down the political ladder, or during a career lull, with little regard for their interest in the arts. Even the arrival of huge sums of money courtesy of the National Lottery failed to inject a sense of urgency or importance into the daily political management of the arts. Peter Brooke, Stephen Dorrell and Virginia Bottomley all took the culture brief with little enthusiasm. The policies that flowed from their department reflected it.

Prior to the unveiling of its arts manifesto, the Labour party had done little to dispel the gloom. The appointment of Jack Cunningham to the heritage brief has the distinct air of a consolation prize. Edged from the heights of Trade and Industry, Cunningham is not known for his love of the arts. The Labour party's policy document on the arts was originally due to be delivered in September 1995. That document, however, was scrapped after Tony Blair's visit to Australia. Inspired by Paul Keating's 101-page policy document for cultural regeneration, 'Creative Nation', Blair ordered his shadow heritage team to start again and report the following summer. Unfortunately, Keating lost the Australian election, so the Labour team are trumpeting their policy as one that goes beyond Keating, taking his ideas and projecting four or five years ahead.

The basis of Labour's plans is a DNH that looks at all actions by government departments that have a bearing on the cultural life of the country. It is described as a holistic approach that will set Britain apart from other countries, taking Mitterrand's cultural project as a lead, combining it with bits of Keating, and grafting the lot on to local conditions. The emphasis will be on individuals and promoting Britain's excellence as a creative, innovative society. Fine-sounding words, but the devil's in the detail. For the film industry, the Irish experience in providing financial incentives is cited as an example to follow, while a chief architectural officer will be appointed to oversee government building. There is also an emphasis on cultural training geared towards the needs of the cultural industries: a nod to the demands of the drama students?

The main heritage battleground has turned out to be the National Lottery. John Major promised when it was launched in November 1994 that it would revolutionise life in Britain. Speaking to the accompaniment of a desultory dawn firework display at the Tower of London, he said, 'The country as a whole is going to be richer because of the lottery. It is in every sense the people's lottery.' But apart from becoming a national talking point to rival the weather and a £1-million-a-week goldmine in profits for operator Camelot, it also became a political football between the parties.

The all-party Heritage Select Committee, which carried out a detailed inquiry into the lottery's first 18 months, provided an upbeat analysis: 'The National Lottery could be better ... but, just for once, let us praise something which has been done well and has gone right.' The Conservatives have trumpeted the success of the lottery, quickly established as the most efficiently run in the world, raising the most for good causes. But Labour and the Liberal Democrats are both pledged to substantial reforms, primarily because of their dissatisfaction with what they see as Camelot's excessive profits.

Joe Ashton, the Labour MP for Bassetlaw, memorably compared Camelot's role to shovelling bank notes into a furniture van. 'The Government have created a licence to pinch money,' he said. Labour has said it will honour Camelot's seven-year licence but then wants to shift the lottery into a not-for-profit organisation or cap profits. The party also wants to increase the number of good causes receiving grants from five to eight and separate the roles of the director-general of the lottery regulator Oflot. At present he both chooses the operator and regulates its activities. While the Liberal Democrats also propose a review of Camelot's profits, the party has latched on to concerns raised by the Churches about the lottery's role in encouraging gambling. It would ban scratchcards and limit jackpot pay-outs.

Privacy was another hot potato. Virginia Bottomley belatedly backed the Government away from the Draconian kind of restrictions on the press advocated by Sir David Calcutt and ruled out privacy legislation. Tory backbenchers, embarrassed by a succession of sleazy tabloid stories about wayward ministers, were angered by the decision to pursue self-regulation under a beefed up Press Complaints Commission. Labour has been more hawkish on the question of a privacy law, but would insist on the counter-balance of a Freedom of Information Act.

On broadcasting, the differences between the main parties have been subtle: the extension of the BBC's charter for another ten years and the drive towards the introduction of digital television received broad support. The 1996 Broadcasting Act proved less controversial than its predecessor; the significant amendment to safeguard terrestrial television coverage of Britain's sporting 'crown jewels' won cross-party backing. Labour, rather than the Conservatives, has made the running on the charge towards the much heralded information superhighway, allowing British Telecom's entry into the cable entertainment business in return for the establishment of a nationwide network linking schools, hospitals and libraries.

But it was in the politically sensitive area of cross-media ownership that positions became most confused: a Conservative government laid down a 20 per cent circulation threshold restricting newspaper groups from diversifying into television, while Labour united with right-wing Tory rebels to scrap the limits altogether. This topsy-turvy affair was partly fuelled by partisan allegiances: the 20 per cent ceiling ensured the Labour-supporting Mirror Group titles would be unable to expand further into ITV. It also limited Rupert Murdoch's News International, but the company was more sanguine about the restriction because of its dominant position in the pay-TV market.

The most important element of Labour's arts policy may indeed prove to be the human element: the choice of politician to run the department. There are several capable figures associated with the party – Melvyn Bragg, anyone? – but few suitably dynamic politicians leap to mind within the parliamentary party. At least the party is free of the days of 'Luvvies for Labour' and Billy Bragg's tuneless Red Wedge. Instead, New Labour has drafted in Mick Hucknall of Simply Red, an ageing bid for the youth vote.

The Conservative party aims to continue running Heritage in broadly the same way as it has done since the creation of the DNH. In the memorable words of one department insider, 'It is not part of our culture to have a cultural policy.' A policy paper is expected to propose fine-tuning the existing regulations governing the use of lottery money for arts and Heritage projects to allow organisations scope to appeal for crucial revenue funding, as opposed to capital funding. Nevertheless, with cuts to the Arts Council budget, film, museums and galleries, the Conservative party will have to address the criticism that the National Lottery is becoming an alternative to government funding for the arts. ●

Main events since 1992

2 August 1994: The law governing the ownership of radio companies redefined by the High Court when it allows Emap to take control of its eighth company.

22 August 1994: Future of Press Complaints Commission chairman Lord McGregor thrown into doubt after he becomes embroiled in controversy over nuisance phone calls made to a friend of the Princess of Wales.

29 August 1994: Former National Heritage Secretary David Mellor criticises Baroness Thatcher for allowing Rupert Murdoch to secure a dominant position in the British newspaper and TV market.

19 September 1994: Lord Hollick, managing director of MAI, which owns Meridian and Anglia TV, calls for tighter controls on cross-media ownership to defend democracy.

5 October 1994: Association of British Editors survey reveals that majority of MPs would back tougher controls on journalists.

21 October 1994: Office of Fair Trading decides to take no action over the newspaper price war, ruling that consumers had benefited from the turmoil.

28 October 1994: MEPs serve notice that they can no longer tolerate the European Commission turning a blind eye to the growing concentration of media power in the hands of Rupert Murdoch, Silvio Berlusconi and other magnates.

Late October 1994: Chris Smith succeeds Mo Mowlam as Shadow National Heritage Secretary. He is later promoted to Social Security, to be replaced by Dr Jack Cunningham.

7 November 1994: David Mellor accuses the tabloid press of tactics worthy of the former East German security police.

19 November 1994: Britain's first National Lottery is televised on BBC1.

21 November 1994: Lord Wakeham, former Conservative Cabinet Minister, is confirmed as new chairman of Press Complaints Commission.

27 November 1994: Tony Blair appoints a commission to draw up plans for an information superhighway capable of entering every home, school, hospital and library in Britain.

Late November 1994: Government refuses to ban satellite stations from gaining exclusive TV coverage of top sporting events. Stephen Dorrell says sporting rights holders must decide how their events are televised.

11 January 1995: Labour MP Chris Mullin unsuccessfully brings in a parliamentary bill to 'regulate ownership of the media'.

18 January 1995: Conservative MP Michael Fabricant alleges that BBC correspondents have squandered licence fee money to ship grand pianos from South Africa to Europe and to run up five-figure phone bills to sex lines. The remarks are protected by parliamentary privilege.

8 February 1995: Michael Grade, Chief Executive of Channel Four, condemns the decision by the Independent Television Commission that the station must give £57.3 million of its 1994 profits to ITV companies after the Government refuses to allow changes in C4's funding formula.

9 February 1995: Government's White Paper, 'The Future of the BBC', is debated by MPs. Published in July, the White Paper announces the plan to renew the BBC's charter for a ten-year period.

17 February 1995: Stephen Dorrell, National Heritage Secretary, hints that Whitehall prefers self-regulation to privacy legislation and statutory controls.

27 April 1995: Purchase of Churchill papers for £13.25 million with first Heritage lottery grant causes controversy.

23 May 1995: Leading civil liberties lawyer, Geoffrey Robertson QC, calls for the creation of a new privacy law, describing the Press Complaints Commission as a 'fraud and confidence trick' and a 'secret and highly political quango'.

5 July 1995: Virginia Bottomley becomes National Heritage Secretary, swapping jobs with Stephen Dorrell, who moves to Health.

17 July 1995: Government retreats from legislation to curb intrusive behaviour by newspapers in heavily watered-down White Paper which is greeted in the Commons by jeers from backbench Tories.

9 February 1996: Merger of MAI and United News (owner of the *Express*).

22 April 1996: Associated Newspapers (owner of the *Daily Mail* and *Evening Standard*) buy a fifth of ITN.

Legislation

Sexual Offences (Amendment) Act 1992
- banned media from publishing a rape complainant's name, address or picture, if likely to lead to her identification

Lottery Act 1993
- provided for changes in gambling law to allow National Lottery to be established

Broadcasting Act 1996
- introduced a barrier to prevent newspaper companies with over 20 per cent of the market entering terrestrial television

Policies

Lottery
Con: The National Lottery is the most efficient and raises more money for good causes than any lottery in the world.
Lab: The lottery to be run by a non-profit organisation at the end of Camelot's contract. No cap on prizes.
Lib Dem: A maximum prize limit to be introduced. Scratchcards to be ended and Camelot's contract and profit margins to be reviewed.

Media Ownership
Con: Current market-share limits to public television ownership, 15 per cent for television companies and 20 per cent for newspaper groups, to remain.
Lab: Regards 20 per cent market-share rule as arbitrary and wants to see a stronger role for the Monopolies and Mergers Commission.
Lib Dem: The current 20 per cent threshold to be maintained, although the political motivation behind the policy makes it an imperfect limit.

Information Superhighway
Con: Continue to work to enforce intellectual property rights across frontiers in the global information age and push for liberalisation of the telecommunication networks.
Lab: Set a timetable for BT and others to enter competition with the cable companies.
Lib Dem: Committed to universal access to a broad-band network by 2000.

Privacy

Con: Have not ruled out legislation and would consider it if there was a collapse in press standards.

Lab: Voluntary regulation of the press is preferable; the Press Complaints Commission needs to be tougher and more independent.

Lib Dem: Create a civil offence of intrusion by the media and establish an Independent Media Tribunal with judicial powers to investigate breaches.

Poll

The National Lottery

%	Yes	No
Should it give more money to charity?	87	11
Should it be non-profit-making?	75	21
Should jackpots be limited to £10 million?	70	28
Should individual prizes be limited to £1 million?	63	35
Should it be scrapped completely?	12	86

Most-quoted statistics

Nearly £2.5 billion of consumer spending was diverted to the lottery in its first year.

71 per cent of the population participates in the lottery.

Government spending

as £ million	90-91	91-92	92-93	93-94	94-95	95-96	96-97	97-98	98-99
Current prices	778	883	1,004	976	984	1 020	960	940	940
1994-95 prices	900	1,000	1,100	1,000	1,000	1,000	900	900	800

All figures from 1995-96 are estimates.
Figures for 1994-95 are rounded.
Source: Financial Statement and Budget Report 1996-97

Quotable quotes

'The people outside London, playing the lottery, are subsidising the arts in London.'
Joe Ashton MP, Observer, _29 October 1995_

'I simply don't remember.'
Stephen Dorrell, _then National Heritage Secretary, on being asked what was the last film he saw,_ The Times, _12 February 1995_

'A profit of £77.5 million for the operator of a state-protected monopoly is nothing short of obscene.'
Robert Maclennan, _Liberal Democrat National Heritage spokesman, 4 June 1996_

NORTHERN IRELAND

David Sharrock

Northern Ireland is arguably the one area of policy for which John Major can with some justification claim his share of success. From the later stages of 1993 until this general election he has devoted more time and effort to solving its problems than any prime minister since Gladstone, putting his signature to two important Anglo-Irish documents.

British government commitment and policy towards Northern Ireland has waxed and waned down the years of this century. From the establishment of the six-county state in 1921 and the Partition of Ireland until the modern Troubles erupted in 1969, Downing Street's attitude was one of studied ignorance. In the mid-1960s Harold Wilson was certainly aware of its sectarian nature and discriminatory practices, but Westminster MPs were forbidden to raise Northern Ireland issues. Once the violence took hold and the troops were sent in to restore order in 'John Bull's political slum', Ulster could no longer be ignored.

Since the Troubles began, British policy has passed through two distinct phases. The first saw attempts to reform the existing structure and make Stormont work. Three NI premiers tried to restore order, but the 'internal' solution quickly foundered and Edward Heath suspended the Parliament in March 1972. For the first time in 51 years Northern Ireland was ruled wholly from London, with its own Secretary of State, similar to Scotland and Wales, and legislation brought forward by Orders in Council which could not be amended on the floor of the Commons. It is a system which has prevailed ever since, creating a democratic deficit which neither Unionist nor Nationalist has ever welcomed.

In the second phase, Britain began to acknowledge a role for the Government of the Irish Republic. While it began tentatively, it has inexorably gathered pace as London and Dublin gradually saw the mutual benefits of sharing the burden of responsibility. It is, however, a development which has been and is still fiercely resisted by the Unionists. First there was the Sunningdale Agreement and the attempt to establish a power-sharing executive between moderate Unionists and Nationalists. But it was the body's all-Ireland dimension – the Council of Ireland – which brought Loyalists out on to the streets in their thousands, paralysing the province. Direct rule was resumed.

Since then, a series of conventions – six separate initiatives – all ended in failure. Then in 1985, Margaret Thatcher astonished Unionists by signing the Anglo-Irish Agreement with Garrett Fitzgerald, giving the Irish Republic for the first time a direct input into the affairs of Northern Ireland. Thatcher has since claimed that to have been a mistake, having seen the AIA's merits as lying in the promised cross-border security co-operation in the fight against terrorism. Consequently, Anglo-Irish relations struck a series of rocky patches during the late 1980s and early 1990s. With the failure of the 1992 negotiations between Northern Ireland's constitutional parties – the Unionists blaming the SDLP leader John Hume for withdrawing – and the annual death toll beginning to climb once more, largely thanks to the improving deadliness of the Loyalist paramilitaries, the situation looked impossibly bleak.

So the sudden appearance of the 'peace process' seemingly out of nowhere, first with the *Observer* revelation that British contacts had been ongoing with the IRA since 1990, shook the political establishment. Major appeared enthusiastic about seizing the opportunity, and after intense negotiations with his Irish counterpart Albert Reynolds, the two governments signed the Downing Street Declaration in December 1993. This Declaration stated that Britain had no 'selfish strategic or economic interest' in Northern Ireland and placed the principle of consent of the majority of Northern Ireland people to any constitutional or political change centre-stage. Dublin believed that an IRA ceasefire was inevitable, with Reynolds boasting that he had stripped away any excuses the Provisional IRA and Sinn Fein clung to for justifying the campaign of violence. London did not believe that a ceasefire would emerge, but was proven wrong in the late summer of 1994. With the commencement of the Combined Loyalist Military Command ceasefire six weeks later, an uneasy peace settled in. But even from the outset the seeds of its undoing were there to be seen, if anybody wished to look. The refusal of the IRA to clarify whether or not the ceasefire was tactical or permanent led Major to his 'working assumption' that it was indeed intended to last for good. But proof of this was required from the IRA in the form of a handover of its weaponry in order to allow Sinn Fein full entry into the political process.

With Ulster and Democratic Unionists refusing to parley with Sinn Fein until the IRA had disarmed or disbanded, the Republican movement's politicans grew steadily more frustrated with the snail's pace set by London towards their objective of round-table negotiations. At the same time, Major slowly but surely retreated from his original objective of dismantling the massive weaponry arsenals held by the IRA. Security sources repeatedly advised that, in their view, it was more important to decommission the mindset of those prepared to use weapons than the armaments themselves.

As the months passed, and the House of Commons arithmetic began to add up against him, Major became increasingly dependent upon the support of the Unionist MPs. He had already managed to weather one serious crisis with the agreement and publication of the British and Irish Governments' Framework Documents, which they 'strongly commended' to all the parties as a basis for a political settlement. While Major was quick to point out that these were simply suggestions for the parties to consider, Unionist suspicions went into orbit.

The Frameworks were strongly Nationalist in rhetoric and outlook, proposing 'dynamic' cross-border institutions with executive powers and hinting at an imposition of the structures unless Unionists accepted them. The leadership of the Republican movement were privately delighted with the Framework, possibly interpreting it as a first instalment towards British withdrawal, via joint sovereignty. Gerry Adams said it had an 'all-Ireland ethos'. Some Unionists have since 'rationalised' Major's backing of the Framework as the price that had to be paid by

Downing Street in early 1995 in order to maintain the IRA ceasefire. What is clear is that while the Ulster Unionist leader David Trimble is prepared to go some way towards accommodating the aspirations of Northern Ireland Nationalists with improved links with the South, this would only be acceptable as part of a larger package in which the relationship between Britain and Ireland is strengthened.

As the ceasefire wore on problems closer to home distracted Major; he was no longer capable of keeping a keen eye on the developing situation. The mistakes began to creep in, chief of which, in the eyes of Nationalist Ireland, was the release of Paratrooper Lee Clegg who had been jailed for the murder of a joyrider in West Belfast. This came at a time when prison conditions for Republicans in England were actually deteriorating and there seemed no prospect of the 'imaginative' steps which had been promised before the IRA called its ceasefire.

The decommissioning saga finally proved to be the downfall of the IRA ceasefire. Canary Wharf was bombed in February 1996, killing two men and causing massive damage. From that point onwards it was inevitably harder to restore confidence in the peace process, since the Government's and Unionists' worst fears had been realised: the IRA ceasefire had been shown to be a tactic rather than a genuine change of heart. On the other side, however, many Nationalists argued that in fact it was John Major's fault for squandering 17 months of peace and attempting to get an IRA surrender by means other than on the security front.

On 10 June all-party talks finally began – a date that had been agreed only days after Canary Wharf, signalling all too dangerously that violence is the only language that counts. Sinn Fein wasn't there, owing to the IRA's refusal to reinstate the ceasefire, and chose to stage a noisy protest at Stormont instead. Ten days earlier the party had scored its biggest ever electoral success, in an election opposed by Nationalists, by polling 15.4 per cent of the vote. Sinn Fein was now in a position to seriously challenge the SDLP as the voice of Northern Ireland Nationalists.

In spite of the commencement of talks, lasting peace and stability appeared no nearer in the summer of 1996 and Nationalists were eagerly awaiting Major's downfall in a general election. His earlier successes in negotiating the Downing Street Declaration and achieving, for the first time, an all-Ireland consensus on the key principle that the consent of Northern Ireland's Unionist population was a prerequisite to political and constitutional change were all but forgotten. As with Gladstone, so with Major: the Irish question had apparently defeated him. ●

Main events since 1992

September 1993: Agreement reached after secret talks between Sinn Fein President Gerry Adams and John Hume, leader of the SDLP.

October 1993: Shankhill and Greysteel massacres by IRA and Ulster Freedom Force claim 17 lives.

15 December 1993: John Major and the Taoiseach, Albert Reynolds, publish the Downing Street Declaration, recognising the validity of Republican ambitions but enshrining the principle of consent for the people of Northern Ireland. It asserts that the British Government has 'no selfish strategic or economic interest in Northern Ireland'.

24 July 1994: Sinn Fein rejects Downing Street Declaration.

31 August 1994: IRA declares ceasefire, but refuses to specify whether it is permanent, leading to protracted arguments over disposal of paramilitary weaponry.

13 October 1994: Loyalist ceasefire declared.

October 1994: Troops leave the streets of Londonderry for the first time in 25 years.

25 January 1996: Mitchell Commission concludes that decommissioning of terrorist weapons should run in tandem with peace talks. An 'elective body' would aid the peace process. Principles include the use of exclusively peaceful means to resolve political issues, disarmament, agreement to abide by the outcome of all-party negotiations and an end to punishment beatings.

9 February 1996: The IRA ceasefire comes to an end with the death of two in the Canary Wharf bombing.

18 February 1996: IRA bomb detonates before reaching its intended target and kills bomber in London.

25 April 1996: Failed IRA attempt to destroy Hammersmith Bridge in London.

21 May 1996: Gerry Adams says he is prepared to sign up to the Mitchell principles, but fails to reinstate a ceasefire and tries to distinguish Sinn Fein from the IRA.

30 May 1996: Sinn Fein scores its highest ever electoral share in elections to Northern Ireland Forum, demands an unconditional place without calling a ceasefire at all-party talks on 10 June, but refuses to take its 17 seats.

May 1996: Continued disagreement between the British and Irish Governments over the decommissioning of paramilitary weapons.

Legislation

Prevention of Terrorism Act 1989
- renewed 14 March 1996; Labour abstained after opposing the Act since 1983; renewal was approved by 222 votes to 26

Prevention of Terrorism (Additional Provisions) Act 1996
- emergency powers to search individuals, property and vehicles passed by 236 to 18 on 2 April 1996

Northern Ireland (Entry to Negotiations) Act 1996
- introduced Northern Ireland elections for a Forum to debate the next stage of the peace process at the end of April 1996

Policies

Key Theme

Con: No change in the current constitutional status of Northern Ireland as part of the UK, save with the consent of a majority of the people of Northern Ireland clearly expressed.

Lab: No change in the constitutional status of NI without the consent of the majority of its people.

Lib Dem: Decommissioning must be addressed in parallel negotiations as envisaged by the Mitchell Report. Maintain strictly non-sectarian policy. Prepared to support any agreement reached by the main parties.

Poll

Which party has the best policy on Northern Ireland?

as %	1992 Mar	1995 Jul	1996 Mar
Con	24	36	29
Lab	16	14	16
Lib Dem	5	3	3

Source: MORI

Most-quoted statistics

Almost 3,200 people have been killed since the Troubles began.

In the last 25 years almost 200,000 people, 15 per cent of the population, have left Northern Ireland for more stable countries.

The European Commission has put £240 million towards a peace programme aimed at binding grassroots Catholic and Protestant organisations into joint management of locally inspired regeneration schemes. At least 15 per cent of the fund will be devoted to forging closer Northern Ireland–Republic of Ireland links.

Northern Ireland receives a £3.5 billion subsidy from the British taxpayer.

The state accounts for 35 per cent of those in employment in Northern Ireland.

Government spending

as % million	90-91	91-92	92-93	93-94	94-95	95-96	96-97	97-98	98-99
Current prices	5,525	6,018	6,580	7,085	7,408	7,820	8,010	8,210	8,270
1994-95 prices	6,400	6,600	6,900	7,200	7,400	7,600	7,600	7,600	7,500

Excludes cyclical social security
All figures from 1995 are estimates.
Figures for 1994-95 are rounded.
Source: Financial Statement and Budget Report 1996-97

Quotable quotes

'We are not the IRA.'
Gerry Adams *arguing that Sinn Fein should be admitted to the June 1996 talks on the basis of its electoral strength*

'The IRA ceasefire must be "credible, clear-cut and certain" for Sinn Fein to be admitted to all-party talks.'
John Major

'It's the last time that we will have a roll-call of the Unionist people to completely and totally repudiate and reject the interference of Dublin and to stop the terrible slide that has taken place towards Dublin rule in this province.'
Ian Paisley, *leader of the Democratic Unionist party, defining the purpose of the June 1996 elections*

'Unionists cannot and will not negotiate with a gun pointed at their heads.'
David Trimble, *leader of the Ulster Unionists*

SOCIAL SECURITY

David Brindle

One of the key battlegrounds of this election will be the future of the Welfare State. Since 1992, politicians of all parties have increasingly called into question its growing costs and its suitability for twenty-first-century Britain. And the focus of debate has been social security. At an annual cost of £90 billion, it accounts for more than a third of central government spending and costs every working person £15 every working day. Assumptions which at previous elections would have been regarded as beyond argument are now under fierce scrutiny: Should every youngster get child benefit? Does society owe the middle classes a pension? Will the state pay for long-term care of the elderly and disabled?

Peter Lilley, Social Security Secretary, claims responsibility for starting the political and public debates about such issues. In a lecture in 1993, he warned that benefits spending was forecast to rise 3.3 per cent faster than inflation each year until the end of the century. It was clear, he asserted, that such an underlying position was unsustainable. This declaration paved the way for a series of what Lilley called reforms, and others called cuts, which within little more than 18 months enabled him to revise his figure of future real growth in benefits spending to 1.3 per cent a year to 1997-98, and 2.1 per cent thereafter. Total expenditure in 2000-01 would, he said, be £8 billion less than he had forecast.

Some critics accused the minister of exaggerating the prospective costs in 1993 in order to smooth the way for his reforms/cuts in long-term sickness, unemployment and housing benefits. For good measure, the state pension age for women was also raised. But Lilley was anyway in error in claiming to be setting the pace alone in this policy area: Labour, in fact, had acted six months ahead of him. It is the distance travelled by Labour since the last election that is the most striking thing about current thinking on social security. Then, Labour was committed to two enormously costly promises: to increase state pensions and child benefit, the funding implications of which were so huge that they left scarcely any room for anything else. Now, the party is offering no such carrots and is, indeed, proposing to deploy the stick against benefit recipients in ways which would have been seen as unthinkable five years ago.

Labour leader Tony Blair is famously said to have told Chris Smith, Shadow Social Security Secretary, to think the unthinkable about benefits. But it was the late John Smith, Blair's predecessor, who had in 1992 set up the party's commission on social justice to examine, *inter alia*, how the social security system could be overhauled better to match limited public resources to people's needs. The commission reported in 1994, proposing that the system be re-orientated to offer 'a hand-up rather than a hand-out'. That thinking, and that sound bite, have survived. But many of the commission's detailed recommendations have been jettisoned by Labour as its policy-making process became shaped by Chris Smith's fresh approach and constrained by the firmly tied purse-strings of his colleagues in the shadow Treasury team.

Labour goes into the election committed neither to restore the link between benefits and earnings, abolished in 1980, nor to introduce the commission's idea of a guaranteed minimum pension. It is not promising – as the commission proposed – to scrap the six-month Jobseeker's Allowance and revert to 12 months' entitlement to unemployment benefit. Indeed, the party has sparked alarm in some quarters by suggesting a pilot scheme of 'flexible' benefits, under which individuals could by agreement take their entire six-month entitlement in one go and use it to finance a training or business scheme.

Smith insists that Labour is not abandoning its mission to the needy, nor its commitment to the founding Beveridge principles of the Welfare State, but he has caused unease among some of the party's traditional supporters by talking of a growing role for private insurance within a Welfare State 'framework'. Labour has also declared that it would not increase spending on social security. It believes there are substantial savings to be made in administration (while criticising the Tories' goal of 25 per cent cuts in three years) and by reducing benefit fraud. The two main parties' enthusiasm for talking up the extent of fraud has alarmed welfare rights groups and brought a warning from the Liberal Democrats of a witch-hunt against claimants, the overwhelming majority of whom are genuine.

One issue on which Labour and the Tories do still differ sharply is the growth of poverty in Britain since 1979. Argument over this has provided a revealing sideshow to the broader debate about the Welfare State, with Lilley conceding only that there has been 'greater mobility up and down a wider span of earnings' and the Government as a whole refusing to take any measures as part of the 1996 United Nations year for the eradication of poverty. The traditional indicators suggest a near-tripling of numbers living in poverty between 1979 and 1993, from 5 million to 14 million. They also show that the poorest tenth of the population suffered a 17 per cent cut in real income over that period, while average income rose 38 per cent and those of the richest tenth increased 62 per cent.

Lilley has produced new earnings data, however, showing that the poorest tenth of workers in 1978 did relatively better than average over the next 15 years. He has also questioned how people can be considered poor if they have a car, fridge-freezer and video recorder. Eradicating poverty, he says, is a matter for the Third World. Labour has promised to 'write poverty back into the script' of government, but has also said it would seek consensus agreement on a new definition of it. Certainly, there is likely to be a lot more consensus on social security over the next few years, whichever party is in power.

One area of certain change will be a continuing shift of emphasis to in-work benefits. The Tories have swallowed hard and accepted that many people need to be given money to make it worthwhile for them to work: almost 600,000 families are now on family credit benefit, twice the number in 1990, and the principle has recently been extended on a pilot basis to people without children. Labour is proposing additionally to offer loans to people on family credit, or newly employed, but it faces a dilemma in not wanting to subsidise low-paying employers. Without an effective minimum wage, this could be treacherous territory.

The other area where the landscape will change, irrespective of the election outcome, is the role of private insurance. Withdrawal of state help with mortgage payments during unemployment, and with long-term care in old age, has already opened the Welfare State door to the private sector. More of the same lies in store. The leading insurance companies have been asked by the Tories to come up with further ideas. Labour, too, has been talking to the key players. One way or another, the private sector's influence will undoubtedly grow. As Labour's Chris Smith has said: 'The principle must surely be that the state acts as the guarantor of all provision, the regulator of all provision – and the administrator of some.' ●

Main events since 1992

30 November 1993: Budget: women's pension age raised from 60 to 65 from 2020. Unemployment benefit replaced by Jobseeker's Allowance. Invalidity benefit replaced by taxable incapacity benefit.

November 1994: Social Security Secretary Peter Lilley announces £600 million package in the wake of the budget, aimed at improving incentives to work.

15 April 1996: Peter Lilley considers limiting child benefit to one child in an attempt to stem costs.

7 May 1996: Conservatives and Labour announce radical shake-ups in the Welfare State, foreshadowing a new and looser compact between the individual and government.

4 June 1996: Labour Shadow Cabinet discusses the merits of removing child benefit for 16 to 18-year-olds to fund a scheme to encourage youngsters to stay on at school.

Legislation

Social Security Act 1988
- altered eligibility for income support and pattern of benefit contributions
- withdrew benefit from unemployed school leavers who do not join YTS
- put cold-weather payments on a statutory basis
- tightened the law on payment of attendance allowance after a court ruling which the Government said interpreted it as being more generous than the legislation had intended

Child Support Act 1991
- enforced maintenance payments for children and traced errant fathers
- linked with establishment of Child Support Agency, starting work in 1993, to track down fathers defaulting on payments
- established that mothers refusing 'unreasonably' to identify fathers may face reductions in benefit

Jobseeker's Act 1995
- integrated and replaced unemployment benefit and income support for un-employed people with a new Jobseeker's Allowance
- halved period for which benefit is paid after employment from twelve to six months and excluded allowances for dependants
- established that unemployed people who have not paid National Insurance contributions may qualify for means-tested benefit – payment conditional on jobseeker's agreement between the claimant and the Employment Service
- introduced 'sanctions on the work-shy'
- enabled some unemployed and lone parents on benefits for six months or more to claim housing benefit for four weeks after returning to work

Carers (Recognition and Services) Act 1995
- private members' bill gave carers the right to have their own needs assessed by local authorities
- enabled local authorities to provide support and services

Child Support Act 1995
- provided for major changes in the Child Support Act 1991
- new regulations altered assessment formula by setting ceiling on assessments of 30 per cent of net income
- allowances made for property transfers before April 1993 and for work travel costs for those living more than 15 miles from workplace

- new regulations enabled absent parent to deduct all reasonable costs of housing his or her new partner or stepchildren from the assessment
- enabled Child Support Agency or appeals tribunal to depart from amount assessed to take account of exceptional circumstances or past property settlements
- deferred indefinitely the CSA's taking on of non-benefit cases where parents have a maintenance agreement

Disability Discrimination Act 1994

- replaced quota system for employment of disabled people with new right to non-discrimination and made it unlawful for service provider to discriminate against a disabled person
- established National Disability Council to advise the Government on the elimination of discrimination against disabled people

Policies

Unemployment
Con: The Jobseeker's Allowance will improve incentives to work and concentrate the attention of unemployed benefit claimants on the need to look for work.
Lab: Establish new mission for DSS with personalised service provided by one-stop shops.
Lib Dem: Establish a fair and effective system of tax and benefits, which opens up opportunities and encourages enterprise and independence.

Child Support Agency
Con: Introduced Child Support Act 1995, providing for major changes in the assessment formula by setting a ceiling on assessments of 30 per cent of net income.
Lab: Wants fundamental reform of the CSA so that children benefit from maintenance payments and both parents are treated fairly.
Lib Dem: Repeal the Child Support Act. Child maintenance should be settled under a unified family court system, with a right to appeal.

Young People
Con: Raise standards in schools, colleges and universities; create high-class vocational training including modern apprenticeships; reduce incentives to benefit dependency.
Lab: Create new opportunities for work and training for young unemployed people and expect them to fulfil their responsibilities by taking up those opportunities.
Lib Dem: Restore benefit entitlements to students and 16- and 17-year-olds, and restore full income support for under-25s.

Child Benefit
Con: Have honoured 1992 manifesto commitment to increase child benefit in line with prices.
Lab: Fully committed to universal child benefit. Reviewing post-16 non-universal child benefit.

Lib Dem: Child benefit to be retained for all children under 18.

State Pension
Con: The basic state pension to remain the foundation for retirement. £1.2 billion a year has been directed at vulnerable pensioners since 1988, above normal upratings.
Lab: Committed to and looking at ways of ensuring that additional help gets to pensioners on low incomes.
Lib Dem: Retain a basic universal state pension with a top-up for those most in need and abolish the contributory principle.

SERPS and Private Pensions
Con: Continue to encourage people to provide for themselves, while promoting group personal pensions.
Lab: Improve personal pension provision by ensuring that people's hard-earned savings are not eaten away in excessive charges and commissions.
Lib Dem: Replace SERPS with an obligatory occupational pension plan.

Age of Retirement
Con: Retirement age to be equalised at 65 by 2020.
Lab: Favours a flexible decade of retirement at no net cost to the exchequer.
Lib Dem: Introduce a flexible decade of retirement between 60 and 70 for men and women, so people can decide for themselves when to leave work.

Disabled People
Con: Have introduced legislation to tackle discrimination.
Lab: Aim to maximise opportunities for disabled people and improve the workings of the Disability Working Allowance.
Lib Dem: Introduce comprehensive disability discrimination legislation, properly enforced by a human rights commission.

Most-quoted statistics

Social security costs £86 billion every year – equivalent to £15 for every working person every working day; set to go on growing at more than three per cent a year above inflation.
Peter Lilley, Social Security Secretary, Mais Lecture, 1993

Benefits for elderly people more than trebled in real terms since 1979 to £37 billion in 1993-94; benefits for long-term sick and disabled people have risen by around 45 per cent since 1979 to £17 billion in 1993-94; benefits for families with children doubled since 1979 to over £14 billion in 1993-94.
Reshaping Our Social Security System, *Conservative Party Research Department, 1995*

Spending on housing benefit has more than trebled since 1979 to £10 billion in 1994-95.
Conservative Party Research Department, 1995

In the 1994 budget the Government increased the personal income tax allowance for pensioners by £430 – four times the rate of inflation – taking 190,000 pensioners out of income tax altogether.
Conservative Party Research Department, 1995

Labour's pension plans will require an average of an extra £27 a week in compulsory contributions.
Conservative Central Office, 8 April 1996

Over two million pensioners now have an income at or below the level of income support.
Labour election guide

The number of people wholly dependent on means-tested benefits has doubled, from one in 12 of the population to one in six.
Labour election guide

A typical family is still paying £670 more tax than in 1992 as a result of the 22 Tory tax increases, but benefit should you become unemployed or ill has been cut.
Labour election guide

The Jobseeker's Allowance will halve non-means-tested unemployment benefit.
Liberal Democrat policy guide

As a direct result of Conservative policies, 156,000 young people are now homeless.
Liberal Democrat policy guide

The UK has such inadequate childcare facilities that 50 per cent of single parents go out to work compared to nearer 90 per cent in northern Europe.
A New Economic Future for Britain, *Labour policy document*

Government spending

as £ million	90-91	91-92	92-93	93-94	94-95	95-96	96-97	97-98	98-99
Current prices	48,932	55,219	61,839	67,862	70,405	73,730	76,810	79,600	82,250
1994-95 prices	56,700	60,300	64,800	69,100	70,400	71,800	72,800	73,600	74,300

All figures from 1995 are estimates.
Figures for 1994-95 are rounded.
Financial Statement and Budget Report 1996-97

Quotable quotes

'As life expectancy increases, it becomes progressively more important to ensure that sufficient provision is made to enable retired people to enjoy a comfortable and fulfilling retirement. The principal responsibility for making that provision must rest with the individual citizen.'
Stephen Dorrell, *Health Secretary, 8 May 1995.*

'Surely it is time to get away from the sterile battle lines of public and private and, instead, to look at how the two can work together in the best interests of the citizen.'
Chris Smith, *Shadow Social Security Secretary, 7 May 1996*

'If we couldn't even have done this, voters might have started to wonder if we were going to do anything at all.'
Senior Labour MP on plans to replace the Jobseeker's Allowance with a 12-month unemployment benefit, 5 May 1996

'The distress and material losses which were experienced by a number of children were clearly damaging rather than beneficial to their welfare.'
Losing Support, *report commissioned by NSPCC and four other children's charities.*

'Conditions among the poorest people in Britain are desperate and getting worse.'
Peter Townsend, *president of the Child Poverty Action Group, 10 May 1995*

'The danger is that the party will use the [Social Justice] Commission to delay firming up its policies until the last minute.'
Labour Co-ordinating Committee discussion paper, October 1994

'Far from helping people back to work, the Tories have created a welfare system which encourages dependency and traps people in unemployment.'
A New Economic Future for Britain, *Labour policy document, 1995*

TRANSPORT

Keith Harper

Britain is gradually strangling itself to death because its transport system, particularly in London and the south-east and increasingly in the larger conurbations, is seizing up. Road rage has become the disorder of the day, and the irate driver out of sheer frustration tends to blame the motorist in front if there is a traffic jam, without accepting that the heavily overcrowded roads network is constantly failing. The politicians continue to offer platitudes and dire warnings of what is to come. If the Department of Transport, the refuge of ministers who are either on their way up or down and out, is to be believed, Britain will be facing total gridlock in the first decade of the twenty-first century. It should make a motorist fearful of using the car, save for the most urgent need, but will it?

In spite of government forecasts that road traffic will increase by 30 per cent over the next ten years, and between 75 and 90 per cent over the next 30 years, the love affair between motorist and car shows no sign of diminishing. It will always be the most convenient way to travel. Since the last election, until the arrival of Dr Brian Mawhinney at the Department of Transport, the debate had been road-led. Mawhinney may have been an unpleasant boss to many of his civil servants at the DoT, but at least he turned transport into an issue. During his comparatively brief tenure at the department, he instituted a debate, the first since Barbara Castle tried 25 years ago. But he left to become Conservative party chairman, and the debate stopped. Attempts by his successor, Sir George Young, to keep it going were confined to generalities, but being a keen cyclist, Sir George successfully helped to promote this transport Cinderella.

Dr Mawhinney, however, did something very important. His last calling card was to dump Sir George with a difficult problem. He quietly approved the Newbury by-pass project, thereby opening up yet another well organised public protest against an important road project. The past few years have been studded with glittering examples: the M11 in Essex, and the M74 in Scotland, which led to the resignation of a junior Scottish minister for punching a protester. They all kept transport as a dominant feature of public concern, which has still not been properly understood by the politicians. For a brief moment, Mawhinney bravely appeared as if he was prepared to confront the issue. But his rapid withdrawal and the onset of a general election conspired to force the Government into deferring unpopular decisions and cutting the roads programme by 20 per cent. The pent-up anger over the Newbury by-pass, which Mawhinney unwittingly released, clearly demonstrated that the transport debate was being pursued from outside, not by the Government. Time and again the Government was invited, by bodies ranging from leading institutions to industry and the unions, to initiate the debate but balked.

Except, that is, over rail, which it tackled head on, and which has dominated transport in the past five years. It was supposed to be 'the privatisation too far'. Tory backbenchers, particularly those in the south-east marginals, blanched at the idea. But in the end, the Government was left with no option but to go full tilt for privatisation. After considerable pressure from its rank and filers led to an ignominious climbdown by Michael Heseltine on Post Office privatisation in 1994, it was left with a hole in its parliamentary programme which had to be filled. The break-up of the railway industry was the most complicated of the Government's privatisations. British Rail was sliced into 100 separate parts instead of being sold off and preserved as a single entity, an argument forcibly put forward by its former chairman, Sir Bob Reid.

At the heart of the privatisation were Railtrack, the industry's signalling and track authority, and from British Rail's carcass, 25 parts of the railway leased out to private operators. The Government prevented BR from bidding for the private franchises, which have been going to bus companies like Stagecoach and National Express, to management buy-outs, and one to a French multinational specialising in waste collection and sewage disposal. Railtrack's value, around £6 billion when it was parted from BR, rapidly diminished as opposition to its sell-off mounted. It eventually went for £1.9 billion. But the Government made sure that the flotation was temptingly pitched to potential investors. Profits of 25 per cent on shares were guaranteed in the short term. The exercise had the desired impact. Within 24 hours of buying them, ten per cent of shareholders cynically got rid of their shares to make their quick buck.

Rail privatisation exposed many problems for the Government, which it had to plug on the hoof. Fare increases under the privatised operators were capped to no higher than inflation until beyond the year 2000, through-ticketing was protected and a belated attempt was made to co-ordinate timetabling. On the positive side, final approval was given to the Channel Tunnel rail link, a substantial project involving both private and public-sector finance. It will not be completed until 2002, but will cut the journey time from London to Paris by 30 minutes from three hours. The project will bring benefits to the rest of the railway system, opening up the prospect of faster journey times from other parts of Britain to the rest of Europe.

Since the last election, organisations like the CBI have joined the debate to press the Government to accept that a national transport plan is central to modern economic and social life. The UK is the world's fifth largest importer and exporter and the world's sixth most popular tourist destination. High-quality domestic and international transport links can help transform a potential weakness into a strength. Getting the public on side has been the most important argument put forward by many leading institutions.

The public often makes contradictory demands on transport. People wish to improve their local environment, but they also wish to have freedom to travel. They have a rising expectation for goods and services, but often oppose transport projects aimed at meeting these expectations. People can usually see immediate detrimental impacts, but often do not appreciate the wider effects. The growing impact of pollution on the health of the population in our biggest cities contributed to the wider involvement of the public in the latter period of this administration.

Greater freedom and flexibility for local authorities to be given a say has been important, but difficult to achieve in the absence of any broad strategy guidance. If this had happened in the case of the Newbury by-pass, the outcome might not have been different, but local people, both in support of and opposed to the project, would have felt they had been reasonably consulted. The Newbury issue suggested that future funding for such projects is likely to be limited in the face of opposition from protest groups. As their methods became more sophisticated and capable of holding up completion dates, they impressed upon the politicians that the Government would have to ensure that road systems were managed soundly so as to maximise the use of existing capacity. Pressure groups said this required policies which could be applied to all transport systems. It means, for example, effective management of the highway network, including pricing. Future investment will have to rely more on private capital, but achievement requires certainty about how much the motorist is prepared to pay, and hence about returns on capital.

Whoever is returned to power after the next election will have to concede that politicians cannot ignore the tree protesters or the asthma sufferers. A new government will have the opportunity to make far more radical proposals on transport use than ever before. The car cannot be knocked from its pedestal, but its use can be better directed. ●

Main events since 1992

6 May 1994: Channel Tunnel opened.

5 November 1994: Rail privatisation enacted.

1 April 1995: Railtrack takes control of track and privatisation of service providers begins.

November 1995: £19 billion cut from motorway and trunk road building programme in the budget.

2 March 1996: Department of Transport predictions show prospective gridlock for central London, the entire M25 and large sections of the M1, M2, M3, M4, M5, M6, M40, M62 and M67 by 2005.

Early 1996: Environmental protesters hold up construction work on the Newbury by-pass at a cost of up to £12 million in policing.

Legislation

Railways Act 1995
● broke up British Rail for sale

Policies

Motoring

Con: No turning against the motorist. Cars give freedom, choice and opportunity.

Lab: Shift tax from car ownership to car usage. Review company car taxation and improve public transport.

Lib Dem: A ten per cent reduction in road traffic is necessary. Switch car taxation from ownership to usage and redirect tax relief towards public transport.

Rail

Con: Privatisation of the rail network is the only way to enhance consumer choice, raise standards of service and lower fares.

Lab: Introduce a structured programme to return railways to integrated national system; a tough regulatory framework and commitment to extension of ownership of Railtrack.

Lib Dem: Committed to repurchasing a 51 per cent stake in Railtrack. A new National Railway Authority to take over the responsibilities of Railtrack.

Polls

Which party has the best policy on public transport?

as %	1992 Mar	1993 Sep	1994 May	1995 Jul	1996 Mar
Con	19	10	12	8	10
Lab	34	37	46	45	42
Lib Dem	6	10	11	5	6

Source: MORI

City centres should be

as %	Yes	No
open to traffic	20	73
closed to private cars but open to buses and taxis	57	38
closed to all traffic	24	70

Source: ICM August 1995

Most-quoted statistics

The number of vehicles on the roads may top 42.8 million by 2025, up from 25.2 million in 1994.

The average speed in central London is 8.7 mph.

6.9 per cent of journeys are for less than half a mile, up from 3.8 per cent in the mid-1970s.

RAC survey, November 1995

Air pollution in urban areas, created largely by road transport, has an annual impact of £3.9 billion on health.
Department of Transport

There are 225,000 miles of British roads. Motorways make up less than 1 per cent but carry 15 per cent of the traffic.

Government spending

as £ million	90-91	91-92	92-93	93-94	94-95	95-96	96-97	97-98	98-99
Current prices	4,692	5,391	6,604	6,001	5,937	4,620	4,180	4,660	4,410
1994-95 prices	5,400	5,900	6,900	6,100	5,900	4,500	4,000	4,300	4,000

All figures from 1995-96 are estimates.
Figures for 1994-95 are rounded.
Source: Financial Statement and Budget Report 1996-97

Quotable quotes

'You don't have to put up with dreadful human beings sitting alongside you.'
Steve Norris, *then minister with responsibility for public transport in London, on the advantages of the private car over public transport*

'There is a funny vocabulary whereby we talk about investment in the roads industry but subsidy for the rail industry.'
Sir Crispin Tickell, *environmental adviser to John Major*

'Driving is as much to do with sexuality as mobility. Ask any phallocentric male, for whom the bicycle does nothing.'
Sir Jonathan Porritt, *environmentalist*

'There are those who long for the "Big Idea" that would ban cars or force people onto public transport. But that is not how change is achieved.'
John Gummer, *Environment Secretary, 18 January 1996*

TREASURY: ECONOMIC POLICY

Larry Elliott

With one caveat, the economy has performed exceptionally well since 1992. Inflation has been the lowest for a generation, unemployment has fallen and the trade gap has narrowed. The caveat, however, is crucial. It is that voters, when judging the economic record of John Major's administration over the past four years, should ignore the events of 16 September 1992. And that, it has proved, is akin to asking Mrs Lincoln what she thought of the play.

Devaluations have a symbolic, almost totemic importance in British politics. Governments that suffer them are always grievously, and usually mortally, wounded. Harold Wilson never really recovered from the devaluation in November 1967. The defining moment for the economy came at around 7.45pm on Black Wednesday when the then Chancellor, Norman Lamont, emerged blinking into the flashbulbs outside the Treasury. Battered by a day of relentless selling of sterling on the foreign exchange markets, the Chancellor announced that Britain was leaving the Exchange Rate Mechanism (ERM).

For the economy, this was a godsend. Sterling had been pegged to the German mark at DM2.95 in October 1990, at a time when Britain was sliding into recession and Germany was starting to suffer the inflationary consequences of reunification. The Bundesbank, sore at being outmanoeuvred by Helmut Kohl over the terms of German monetary union, responded with a policy of tight interest rates designed to bear down on inflation. For other European nations, particularly Britain, this was a problem. The UK recession of 1990-92 had led to record numbers of bankruptcies and home repossessions. Unemployment, having fallen below 1,600,000 in early 1990, was heading back towards three million by the summer of 1992.

Britain needed lower base rates in the summer of 1992, but the ERM commitment meant it could not have them. The markets, seeing a disparity between the needs of the domestic economy and the dictates of defending sterling's ERM parity, began to push. The Government responded in the way that British governments have always responded in the past. Ministers said that not only was there no question of devaluation, but devaluation was fool's gold, a quack doctor's remedy. By doing so, of course, they staked their reputation on preventing a devaluation, upping the political stakes in the event of an enforced U-turn.

This was what happened on 16 September, just six days after Major had insisted in Glasgow that the 'no-devaluation' line would be held come what might. The Bank of England emptied its vaults of reserves in an attempt to prevent the pound falling through the bottom of its ERM band; bank base rates were raised from ten to 12 per cent in the morning, and when that failed to stem the tide a further rise to 15 per cent was announced for the following day. At that stage, everyone knew the game was up. Base rates of 15 per cent would have sounded the death knell for the economy, and for large chunks of the financial system as well. Sterling was allowed to float, the interest rate rises were rescinded and base rates began to fall to more sensible levels.

The six months after Black Wednesday saw a recovery strategy put in place. Within weeks, the Treasury announced a new monetary framework to replace the ERM, including an inflation target, a monthly meeting between the Chancellor and the Governor to discuss interest rates, and an independent quarterly report of the inflation outlook from the Bank of England. At the same time, monetary policy was eased, with base rates falling in regular one-percentage-point steps to 6 per cent by January 1993, and the pound more than ten per cent cheaper against a basket of world currencies. The economy's response was rapid and flatly contradicted the dire warnings of ministers in the summer of 1992. Unemployment started to fall within three months of Black Wednesday and there was no sign of higher import prices triggering an explosion in wages.

Indeed, it was almost a textbook case of how to make a devaluation work. Consumer confidence had been shattered by the lurch from Lawson boom to Lamont bust and job insecurity was rampant. Workers were more concerned about keeping their jobs than pressing for pay rises. This downbeat mood was reinforced by the third leg of the post-Black Wednesday economic strategy – the tightening of fiscal policy. The budget of March 1993 had to contend with two competing forces – the need to reduce the ballooning Public Sector Borrowing Requirement without jeopardising the fledgling recovery. The Treasury's answer was to announce one of the biggest peacetime increases in taxation, but to delay the start of its implementation for a year.

Again, it was hard to argue with the economics of what was to prove Norman Lamont's swansong. The mixture of loose monetary policy and tight fiscal policy was designed to bear down on consumer spending, thereby diverting resources into manufacturing and exports. Again, the politics were the problem. John Major owed his success at the April 1992 election in no small measure to the idea that Labour would put up taxes and the Conservatives would not. Yet, less than 12 months later, Lamont was announcing an array of tax increases, including the most controversial levy of all, VAT on domestic fuel and power.

So it was that, as the economy strengthened, support for the Government waned. In 1994 Britain enjoyed something of an *annus mirabilis*: the economy grew by four per cent, unemployment fell by 280,000, inflation averaged 2.4 per cent, the balance of payments deficit fell from £11 billion to £2.1 billion. Yet the public mood remained sour as the phased tax increases were brought in and base rates raised as a pre-emptive strike against inflation. Since 1994, economic performance has been less impressive. Both the Treasury and the Bank of England have been baffled by the failure of investment to respond to high profitability and the benign macro-economic environment. And, with the election looming, the Government started to get twitchy about weaker growth. Lamont's successor, Kenneth Clarke, fought and won a high-profile battle with the Governor of the Bank of England, Eddie George, over interest rates, first refusing to raise them, then cutting them to 5.75 per cent by mid-1996. But despite the disagreement, both the Treasury and the Bank like the new monetary framework, which now includes the release of the minutes of the Chancellor-Governor meetings.

The Conservatives will fight the next election on their record since Black Wednesday and hope that the electorate fails to recollect that it did everything in its power to resist the policies that have delivered growth and falling unemployment. Ministers have already air-brushed devaluation out of the reckoning in their assessments of the economy's performance, arguing that Britain is now reaping the benefits of the supply-side changes – labour market deregulation, curbs on trade unions and the education reforms of the past 17 years.

Neither of the other two main parties will challenge the need for macro-economic stability – low inflation and tough control of the public finances. The Liberal Democrats have pledged to put a penny on income tax to increase spending on education, would make the Bank of England fully independent, and support the idea of a single currency. Like the Conservatives, Labour has been somewhat hobbled by its support for the ERM. Gordon Brown, the Shadow Chancellor, saw his popularity within the party plummet after Black Wednesday and this may have cost him the leadership in 1994. However, Brown now believes that as a result of his cautious approach, Labour can no longer be dubbed the party of devaluation and high taxation. The Opposition will be more cautious than the Lib Dems on a single currency and the Bank of England, but has pledged to introduce a national minimum wage and will focus on the need to boost Britain's skills, increase investment and tackle long-term and youth unemployment.

The prospects for the economy in 1997 are good, even though the public finances remain a serious problem. Growth is expected to pick up, inflation will remain low and unemployment should dip below two million. Labour views these developments with mixed emotions. On the one hand, for the first time ever it could arrive in office without the economy being in a state of crisis. On the other, it fears that when polling day arrives, voters will have forgotten Black Wednesday and welcomed back a long-lost friend: the feel-good factor. ●

Main events since 1992

16 September 1992: Black Wednesday – Britain forced out of Exchange Rate Mechanism.

October 1992: Second consecutive quarterly GDP rise signals end of recession.

April 1993: Inflation falls to 1.3 per cent – lowest since 1964.

27 May 1993: Norman Lamont sacked as Chancellor.

30 November 1993: Kenneth Clarke delivers first integrated autumn budget.

1 May 1994: Michael Portillo says Britain should 'never' join single currency.

27 May 1996: UK slides from 15th to 19th in *World Competitiveness Yearbook*.

Policies

Fiscal Policy
Con: Maintain sound public finances, reduce proportion of national income taken by the state to below 40 per cent and cut taxes when prudent to do so.
Lab: Meet the Golden Rule of public finance – over the course of the economic cycle to borrow only for investment purposes.
Lib Dem: Ensure that over the course of the economic cycle borrowing is used only to finance capital items.

Inflation
Con: An underlying rate of inflation below 2.5 per cent to be maintained in the next parliament.
Lab: Pursue an inflation target within a medium-term framework to raise the trend rate of economic growth, and eschew short-term tax-spend-and-borrow solutions.
Lib Dem: Introduce new 50 per cent rate for incomes over £100,000 and expand the 0 per cent band to take 750,000 low earners out of tax altogether.

Monetary Policy
Con: Look at a whole range of data when assessing monetary conditions: prices, monetary and financial developments and data on activity.
Lab: Fiscal and monetary policy must work hand in hand.
Lib Dem: The attainment and maintenance of price stability is the most useful contribution monetary policy can make towards an investment-friendly economic climate.

Bank of England
Con: Maintain an open monetary policy framework with explicit inflation target and publication of minutes of meetings between the Chancellor and Governor.
Lab: Establish a new Monetary Policy Committee at the Bank of England, overseen by a more representative Court.
Lib Dem: Establish an operationally independent UK reserve bank.

Public Sector Borrowing
Con: The plans that have been put in place will eliminate the Public Sector Borrowing Requirement by the end of the decade.
Lab: Maintain the ratio of government debt to GDP stable at an appropriate and prudent level, and over the cycle borrow only to invest.
Lib Dem: Separate capital from current spending in public expenditure.

Public Spending
Con: Bring public spending below 40 per cent of national income.
Lab: No target, but committed to save before spending.
Lib Dem: No specific target but borrowing levels to be no higher than the Conservative Government's.

Polls

Regardless of which party you support, which party do you think is most likely to produce successful economic policies?

as %	1990 Sep	1991 Sep	1992 Sep	1993 Sep	1994 Sep*	1995 Sep*	1996 May*
Conservative	40	41	35	24	22	18	22
Labour	28	24	26	39	36	33	31
Liberal Democrat	4	11	8	20	8	5	8
Other parties	2	3	4	4	4	2	1
Don't know	25	21	26	21	29	42	38

* Question: Which party has the best policies for dealing with the economy?

Source: ICM

Most-quoted statistics

Real take-home pay for the average family has risen by about 40 per cent – over £80 a week in today's money – since 1979. Under Labour it rose by less than one per cent in five years – a mere £1.50 in today's money.
Conservative Research Department

Under the Tories Britain has experienced the two deepest recessions since the war.
Labour

Growth at 1.6 per cent since 1979 is the slowest of the G7 . . . and slower than in any other 15 years in Britain since the second world war.
Labour

Britain has lower productivity than any of our main competitors.
Labour

Britain is 22nd out of 24 OECD countries in the share of national income devoted to investment.
Labour

Investment per worker in manufacturing is more than 30 per cent less than in Germany and the USA and only a quarter that of Japan.
Labour

Britain is investing 17 per cent less today in manufacturing industry than we did in 1979.
Labour

Quotable quotes

'Rising unemployment and the recession have been the price we've had to pay to get inflation down. But that is a price well worth paying.'
Norman Lamont, *16 May 1991*

'Je ne regrette rien.'
Norman Lamont, *12 May 1993*

'I'm not an expert on the economy.'
Norman Lamont, *8 September 1992*

'Ideally a Chief Secretary to the Treasury should be flinty-eyed, stony-hearted and odious. I believe that I fit the bill.'
Michael Portillo, *15 July 1993*

'The Conservatives talk tough on inflation, but they have actually delivered boom and bust because they have no strategy for strengthening the supply side.'
A New Economic Future, *Labour policy document, 1995*

TREASURY: TAXATION

Richard Thomas

Taxation is the issue which strikes most fear into Labour hearts. Senior frontbenchers are convinced the 1992 election was lost to the Saatchi 'tax bombshell' campaign, which zeroed in on John Smith's carefully constructed shadow budget. The lesson of 1992 was that voters notice cuts and hikes in taxes on their income much more than VAT on their weekly shop or off-setting increases in benefits or improved services provision. Polls show an overwhelming majority of people prepared to pay more taxes for better health and education, but polling booths do strange things to altruism. And while most of us are certain that the rich should pay more tax, virtually none of us describe ourselves as rich.

The Conservatives have known these political facts of life since 1979, when they set about trimming income tax by pushing up hidden taxes – VAT, excise duty, petrol levies. For each £1 you spent on the high street in 1979, the Treasury took an extra eight per cent. Today the Government tacks on 17.5 per cent. Until 1992, the Tory strategy of shifting from direct to indirect tax was politically effective. From a complex system of income tax with nine bands ranging from 25 pence to 83 pence in 1979 the Conservatives have delivered just two tiers, 24 per cent and 40 per cent. And contrary to popular perception, the tax system has become more progressive. The rise in earnings at the top, combined with lower wages and increased joblessness at the bottom, means that the top one per cent of taxpayers now contribute 15 per cent of the total – up from 11 per cent when Margaret Thatcher came to power. Meanwhile the bottom half contribute 15 per cent of revenue, down from 20 per cent in 1979.

Since 1992, the Tory record on tax has been tarnished, however, perhaps fatally. In 1994 the gradual shift from taxes on income to taxes on consumption – VAT now contributes 16 per cent of total government income, against just nine per cent in 1979 – was almost derailed by a backlash against imposing a tax on domestic fuel use. A Conservative backbench rebellion ensured the defeat of the second-stage increase of VAT on fuel, which would have pushed the rate up from eight per cent to 17.5 per cent. Opposition to the rise was based on mounting evidence that poor households, who spend a high proportion of their income on fuel, would be harder hit than richer families.

The heated debate about VAT on fuel came close to exposing the fact that Conservative taxes were just as high as Labour's, but disguised in price tags and allowances. Since the last election there have been a number of invisible or semi-visible tax rises. On top of the 8 per cent VAT on fuel, National Insurance has been raised from 9 per cent to 10 per cent; airport and insurance tax introduced; mortage interest relief cut; car, cigarette, alcohol and fuel duties pushed up faster than inflation; tax-free allowances were frozen two years running.

The bizarre politics of taxation were amply demonstrated by the negligible reaction to the one penny NI rise, which has virtually the same impact on most workers' take-home pay as an extra penny on income tax – a move which would undoubtedly have caused a political storm. But Kenneth Clarke handed Labour a rod when he admitted in 1994 – to the delight of the Opposition – that the tax rises since the 1992 election had increased the overall burden by the 'equivalent of 7 pence in the pound'.

Since those dark days the Government has re-established something of its tax-cutting image. In the 1995 budget the Chancellor trimmed the basic rate of tax from 25 pence to 24 pence – which he has described as an 'important step towards the ultimate goal of a 20 pence standard rate'. At the same time, Clarke pushed up the limit on tax-free inheritance, from £154,000 to £200,000. These are the buttons the Government really wants to push: first, cutting the truly visible rate – the standard one – while leaving others (such as National Insurance) at their new, higher rate. Secondly, trimming taxes on wealth accumulation and entrepreneurialism.

John Major wants a 'cascade of wealth down the generations', and has committed the Conservatives to abolishing entirely both Inheritance Tax and Capital Gains Tax (CGT). But the Treasury is reluctant to scrap some useful earners for the Exchequer – between them the two taxes raise £2.5 billion – and is concerned that small businessmen would avoid tax by paying themselves in shares rather than wages.

These twin themes, slashing the basic rate and helping the middle class reap the rewards of their savings, will form the central plank of the Conservative tax message. These will be combined with attempts by Central Office to cost the vaguest of Labour commitments (and they will be vague) in order to put figures on possible tax rises by a Blair government.

Labour's strategy is therefore designed to neutralise the tax issue. The ideal result for Shadow Chancellor Gordon Brown would be a news blackout on tax. Given the unlikelihood of this eventuality – a Labour backbencher merely has to mention tax to generate a dozen tabloid headlines – Brown has drawn up a two-pronged attack. First, Labour will highlight Conservative 'broken promises' on tax in an effort to dilute the already fading image of the Conservatives as a low-tax party. Secondly, Brown has attempted simultaneously to erode the 'Labour equals high tax' equation by promising no rise in basic or higher rate and a new starting rate of 10 pence.

The only other areas where Labour is prepared to breathe many words are either one-off levies, such as the windfall tax on utilities, or obscurely technical – such as a possible two-tier rate of CGT to encourage investors to hold shares for longer. Meanwhile, the Liberal Democrats are seizing on the stand-off between the main two parties to portray themselves as the guardians of responsible fiscal policy, refusing to contemplate tax cuts with public spending still above £20 billion. The Lib Dems have retained their policy of putting a penny on the standard rate of income tax to boost education spending, which was widely seen as popular last time around, although in part at least because many voters thought the penny for education meant, literally, a penny.

The single area which unites the three parties is environmental taxation. In his 1995 budget, Kenneth Clarke introduced a levy on landfill waste which will raise £450 million from next year. Both opposition parties are committed to green taxes, which could be used to cut employer National Insurance contributions, in an attempt to generate more jobs. But politicians are ultimately most interested in their own jobs and the sensitivity of the tax issue means the election campaign is likely to consist of a war of words rather than concrete policies. The question will be distilled into a qualitative one: whom do you trust with your taxes? The answer will probably determine who forms the next government. ●

Main events since 1992

17 March 1993: Norman Lamont announces plans to introduce 8 per cent VAT on fuel in 1994 rising to 17.5 per cent in 1995.

13 January 1994: *Times* tax survey shows families on up to four times the average national earnings will pay more tax in 1994 than 1979.

16 March 1994: *Guardian* ICM poll shows Labour in 34-18 lead over Tories as the party with 'the best policies on taxation'.

25 November 1994: Paddy Ashdown says Lib Dems would push top rate to 43 pence.

6 December 1994: Government defeated in Commons by 319 to 311 in vote on second-stage VAT rise on fuel from 8 to 17.5 per cent.

Budgets

Lamont's last budget, March 1993
- personal tax allowances frozen
- low 20p income tax band extended from £2,000 to £2,500
- 20p on cigarettes, 6p on wine, 2p on beer, nothing on spirits
- 3p on petrol and car tax up from £110 to £125

Clarke's first budget, November 1993
- National Insurance up from 9p to 10p in the £
- VAT on fuel at eight per cent
- personal tax allowances frozen
- mortgage tax relief reduced from 25 to 20 per cent
- low 20p income tax band extended from £2,500 to £3,000
- 14p on petrol, 11p on cigarettes, 2p on wine, nothing on beer or spirits
- airport tax introduced
- insurance tax introduced at 3 per cent on buildings and household premiums
- car tax up from £125 to £130

Clarke's second budget, November 1994
- VAT on fuel up to 17.5 per cent (defeated in Commons)
- mortgage tax relief reduced from 20 to 15 per cent
- car tax up from £130 to £135
- 10p on cigarettes, 3p on petrol, nothing on alcohol

Clarke's mini-budget, December 1994
- extra 1p on petrol
- 1p on beer
- 5p on wine
- 20p on cigarettes
- 26p on spirits

Clarke's third budget, November 1995
- basic rate of income tax cut from 25p to 24p
- 15p on cigarettes, 27p off spirits, nothing on beer or wine
- 4p on petrol, car tax up from £135 to £140
- 6 per cent off pools duty and 1 per cent off betting duty
- starting point for Inheritance Tax raised from £154,000 to £200,000

Clarke's fourth budget, November 1996
- basic rate of income tax cut from 24p to 23p
- 15p on cigarettes, 26p off spirits, nothing on beer and wine
- 3p on petrol, car tax up from £140 to £145
- prescription charges up 15 per cent to £5.65

Policies

Income Tax

Con: Make progress towards objective of a 20p basic rate of income tax when it is prudent to do so.

Lab: Has set the long-term objective of a lower starting tax rate, 15p or preferably 10p in the pound. No rise in basic or top rate.

Lib Dem: Abolish National Insurance contributions and create an integrated tax on income.

Taxes on Capital

Con: Cut – and eventually abolish – both inheritance and capital gains tax, so boosting investment, saving and enterprise.

Lab: Abolishing Inheritance and Capital Gains Tax will benefit only a few. Instead, introduce a new starting rate to benefit the many.

Lib Dem: Replace Inheritance Tax with an accessions tax (charged to recipient). Tax gifts as income.

Other Tax Policies

Con: Boost Britain's competitiveness by continuing to cut taxes, when prudent to do so.

Lab: Introduce a windfall profits tax on utilities. Cut VAT on fuel to 5 per cent.

Lib Dem: Put 1p on income tax to fund education.

Polls

Which party has the best policy on taxation?

as %	1992 Mar	1993 Sep	1994 May	1995 Jul	1996 Mar	1996 Mar*
Con	38	23	21	20	26	27
Lab	33	28	37	39	33	45
Lib Dem	13	14	15	6	8	8

*Source: MORI/*Gallup*

I would pay more taxes for better public services

as %	Yes	No	Balance
All	56	32	+24
Con	48	39	+9
Lab	61	29	+32
Lib Dem	69	19	+50
Social class AB	68	20	+48
Social class C2	47	36	+11

Source: MORI, March 1996

Should the basic rate be cut from 25 to 20p in the pound even if it means spending less on public services?

as %	All	Con	Lab	Lib Dem
Yes, cut to 20p	27	28	26	20
No	68	66	69	77
Balance	−41	−38	−43	−57

Source: ICM September 1995

Is the overall level of taxation higher than when the Tories came to power in 1979?

as %	All	Con	Lab	Lib Dem
Higher	64	47	75	64
Lower	14	19	10	21
Balance	+50	+28	+65	+44
The same	10	16	5	6

Source: ICM September 1995

Most-quoted statistics

The basic rate of income tax has been reduced from 33 to 23 per cent. A new lower rate of 20p has been introduced.
Conservative Research Department

The main rate of corporation tax has been reduced from 52 to 33 per cent.
Conservative Research Department

The top one per cent of income earners have received tax cuts under this Government worth £300,000 each.
Labour

Only families earnings £64,000 a year or more are paying less tax now than they were in 1979.
Labour

The poorest tenth of the population pay 20 per cent of their income in Value Added Tax. The richest tenth pay only 8 per cent.
Labour

Quotable quotes

'There are, no doubt, teams of researchers under the watchful gaze of Brian Mawhinney scouring through the pre-manifesto lectures from Labour's Treasury team, searching for the tax bombshell which will unsettle Tony Blair and Gordon Brown.'

'The cumulative effect of Tory tax increases over the past 16 years amounts to £735 billion.'
Hugh Bayley, *Labour MP*

Taxation

	Which party was in power?	Who was Chancellor of the Exchequer?	What was starting rate of tax?	What was the basic rate?	What was the top rate?	What was employee's national insurance contribution?	What was combined rate of tax and national insurance?	At what % of average pay did single people start paying tax?	At what % of average pay did married people start?	What was the basic rate of VAT?	What was the pension worth as a share of average earnings?	What was the NHS prescription charge?
1973	Conservative	Barber		30	75	flat rate	n/a	26	47	10	20	£ 0.20
1974	Labour	Healey		33	83	flat rate	n/a	23	45	10	22	£ 0.20
1975	Labour	Healey		35	83	5.50	40.5	20	38	8	22	£ 0.20
1976	Labour	Healey		35	83	5.75	40.75	19	40	8	23	£ 0.20
1977	Labour	Healey		34	83	5.75	39.75	23	43	8	24	£ 0.20
1978	Labour	Healey	25	33	83	6.5	39.5	20	36	8	23	£ 0.20
1979	Conservative	Howe	25	30	60	6.5	36.5	21	32	15	23	£ 0.45
1980	Conservative	Howe		30	60	6.75	36.75	20	31	15	23	£ 1.00
1981	Conservative	Howe		30	60	7.75	37.75	18	28	15	22	£ 1.00
1982	Conservative	Howe		30	60	8.75	38.75	19	30	15	23	£ 1.30
1983	Conservative	Howe		30	60	9	39	20	31	15	22	£ 1.40
1984	Conservative	Lawson		30	60	9	39	21	33	15	21	£ 1.60
1985	Conservative	Lawson		30	60	9	39	21	34	15	21	£ 2.00
1986	Conservative	Lawson		29	60	9	38	21	33	15	21	£ 2.20
1987	Conservative	Lawson		27	60	9	36	20	31	15	20	£ 2.40
1988	Conservative	Lawson		25	40	9	34	20	31	15	19	£ 2.60
1989	Conservative	Lawson		25	40	9	34	19	30	15	18	£ 2.80
1990	Conservative	Major		25	40	9	34	19	30	15	18	£ 3.05
1991	Conservative	Lamont		25	40	9	34	19	29	17.5	18	£ 3.40
1992	Conservative	Lamont	20	25	40	9	34	19	29	17.5	18	£ 3.75
1993	Conservative	Lamont	20	25	40	9	34	18	28	17.5	18	£ 4.25
1994	Conservative	Clarke	20	25	40	10	35	18	27	17.5	18	£ 4.75
1995	Conservative	Clarke	20	25	40	10	35	18	24	17.5	18	£ 5.25
1996	Conservative	Clarke	20	24	40	10	34	18	25	17.5	18	£ 5.50
1997	Conservative	Clarke	20	23	40	10	33	19	25	17.5	n/a	£ 5.65

THE STATISTICS

THE ART OF THE STAT DOCTOR

Stephen Lyle

May 1996 was an extraordinary month for Britain. In the space of just three days, the country went from a position of inexorable decline to being among the world's leading nations in terms of both productivity and competitiveness – at least it did if you believe in statistics. The party stat doctors were at it again, lauding the achievements of their own party whilst attacking the record of their opposition – quoting reports, official figures and the results of surveys in an attempt to convince the electorate to back them the next time the polls come around.

That no parliamentary or television debate is complete without ministers profusely quoting numbers and percentages is testament to the important role statistics play in politics' modern adversarial age. Shadow Home Secretary Jack Straw described their use as 'the key to the partisan battle of the hearts and minds of the electorate'. Of course Straw's party is not alone in recognising the persuasive power of the statistic. As well as New Labour, the Tories and the Liberal Democrats have on board experts in the analysis and subsequent manipulation of the most important social and economic indicators.

The tactics deployed by the party stat doctors are simple, but remarkably effective. They work because people have a fear, but at the same time a respect, for numbers and all things scientific. What occurred in May 1996 was an example of the most straightforward and often used tactic in the numbers game – simply using the data set that is most suitable. May 1996 saw first the Institute for Management Development publish their *World Competitiveness Yearbook* and then just days later the World Economic Forum release their *Global Competitiveness Report*. Because the reports used different criteria to judge countries' living standards and potential for growth, they presented different conclusions. The stat doctors made sure they used the one that best suited their party. So it follows that the Conservative party will seldom refer to yearly unemployment figures in a debate, but instead rely upon quarterly figures which will hopefully show the monthly falls they use as their defence. Better too for the

Government to quote hospital waiting times than draw attention to the growing length of waiting lists.

Of course, the solution to such disputes would be to ensure that all parties used just the one set of statistics. The Office for National Statistics established in 1995, the successor to the Central Statistical Office and Office for Population Censuses and Surveys, was set up with this in mind. The Office is now the sole home and co-ordinator of all *official* statistical information to be used by the parties. Yet still the manipulating goes on: the stat doctors are not so easily beaten and have simply responded by deploying their other principal *modus operandi.* It is in their manipulation of the same sets of data that the stat doctors really come into their own. Official statistics on inflation and most notably unemployment (the most manipulated data set of them all) have seen the doctors hone their skills down to a fine art.

'The key to misleading people is leaving out information but not telling a lie,' explains Colm O'Muircheartaigh, senior lecturer in statistics at the London School of Economics. 'All the stat doctors do is use a different starting point for their comparisons. The great thing about statistics for politicians is that if you pick your spot you can make them look like anything you want.'

Unemployment is one good example. Faced with a table showing rates of unemployment since 1970, government statisticians would most likely choose the early 1990s as a starting point, ignoring other years. Then they could say that unemployment has fallen by nearly 600,000 since 1992 and by around 40 per cent since 1993. The Opposition, however, would start right back in 1979 when the Tories were elected, and point out that the rate of unemployment has doubled since this date, that since 1979 unemployment has reached its highest post-war rates under Tory Governments and that the average rate of unemployment under the last Labour Government was less than half that of the Tories. Vastly different tales from the same data simply by starting analysis at a different year.

Using statistics in this way inevitably leads to fierce clashes between the parties and allegations of foul play. In September 1995, Labour accused the Tories of lying to the electorate over falls in the crime rate. Tory stat doctors hailed crime figures published that month as the lowest in four years; they said the fall was the largest ever over a two-year period and the longest uninterrupted fall since quarterly figures for crime were collected and published. Labour countered by going back to the years 1951 and 1954, when crime fell by 17 per cent. As usual the numbers came packaged in the form of a political attack: 'It shows you can't trust the Tories on crime,' Jack Straw said.

Few other tools of everyday battle in British politics allow for this kind of attack and counter-attack and as a result few other weapons of political warfare are used as frequently as statistics. In essence, politicians view stats like a trip to the fairground: there is something in them for everyone. ●

FIGURES IN DEPTH

Inflation 1960–95

Year	Retail price index	Annual inflation rate %	Average rate %	Prices up % since 1979	Prices up % since 1992	Value of 1979 pound
1960	12.5	1.0				
1961	12.9	3.5				
1962	13.4	4.2				
1963	13.7	2.0				
1964	14.1	3.3				
Oct 64	14.3	4.0	**Lab Govt**			
1965	14.8	4.8	1964-70			
1966	15.4	3.9	Average			
1967	15.8	2.5	4.4			
1968	16.5	4.7				
1969	17.4	5.4				
1970	18.5	6.4				
Jun 70	18.5	5.9	**Con Govt**			
1971	20.3	9.4	1970-74			
1972	21.7	7.1	Average			
1973	23.7	9.2	8.5			
1974	27.5	16.0				
Feb 74	25.8	13.2	**Lab Govt**			
1975	34.2	24.2	1974-79			
1976	39.8	16.6	Average			
1977	46.1	15.8	15.9			
1978	50.0	8.3				
1979	56.7	13.4				
May 79	54.7	10.3	**Con Govt**			£1.00
1980	66.8	18.0	1979-97	22.1		£0.82
1981	74.8	11.9	Average	36.6		£0.73
1982	81.2	8.6	6.5	48.4		£0.67
1983	85.0	4.6		55.2		£0.64
1984	89.2	5.0		62.9		£0.61
1985	94.6	6.1		72.8		£0.58
1986	97.8	3.4		78.7		£0.56
1987	101.9	4.2		86.2		£0.54
1988	106.9	4.9		95.3		£0.51
1989	115.2	7.8		110.5		£0.48
1990	126.1	9.5		130.5		£0.43
1991	133.5	5.9		143.9		£0.41
1992	138.5	3.7		153.0	0.0	£0.40
1993	140.7	1.6		157.0	1.6	£0.39
1994	144.1	2.5		163.4	4.1	£0.38
1995	149.1	3.4		172.4	7.6	£0.37
Nov 96	153.9	2.7		181.2	11.1	£0.36

USING THE SAME TABLE:

Government points
1. Inflation lowest since 1967.
2. Inflation fallen since start of decade.
3. Annual rate lower than during Labour Government of 1974-79.
4. Highest post-war inflation in 1975 under Labour.

Opposition points
1. Prices nearly trebled since 1979.
2. Value of pound fallen to 36p since 1979.
3. Tory average rate higher than during Labour Government of 1964-70.

Source: Labour Market Trends

Inflation 1960–94

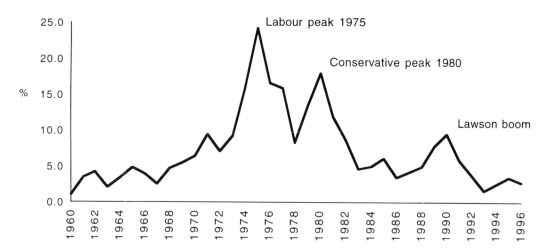

Unemployment 1971–96

Year	Seasonally adjusted current coverage	Rate %	Average rate %	Increase since 1979	Increase since 1992	% change since 1993
1971	652,900	2.6				
1972	723,900	2.8				
1973	514,700	2.0				
1974	518,100	2.0				
Feb 74	489,700	1.9	**Lab Govt**			
1975	796,000	3.1	1974-79			
1976	1,090,900	4.2	Average			
1977	1,160,400	4.4	967,250			
1978	1,143,600	4.3				
1979	1,073,900	4.0				
May 79	1,086,000	4.1	**Con Govt**			
1980	1,363,800	5.1	1979-96	277,800		
1981	2,171,500	8.1	Average	1,085,500		
1982	2,544,100	9.5	2,386,184	1,458,100		
1983	2,787,200	10.4		1,701,200		
1984	2,915,500	10.6		1,829,500		
1985	3,027, 000	10.9		1,941,000		
1986	3,096,900	11.1		2,010,900		
1987	2,804,900	9.9		1,718,900		
1988	2,272,800	8.0		1,186,800		
1989	1,782,100	6.2		696,100		
1990	1,660,800	5.8		574,800		
1991	2,286,100	8.0		1,200,100		
1992	2,765,000	9.7		1,679,000		
Apr 92	2,694,500	9.5		1,608,500		
1993	2,900,600	10.3		1,814,600	206,100	
1994	2,619,300	9.3		1,533,300	−75,200	−10
1995	2,308,200	8.2		1,222,200	−386,300	−20
Nov 96	1,929,400	6.9		843,000	−765,500	−33

USING THE SAME TABLE:

Government points
1. Unemployment down 765,500 since 1992.
2. Unemployment down more than a million in last decade.
3. Unemployment fallen 33% since 1993.

Opposition points
1. Unemployment nearly doubled since 1979.
2. Average unemployment less than half under Labour.
3. Unemployment reached highest post-war level under Tories.

Source: Labour Market Trends

Unemployment 1971–95

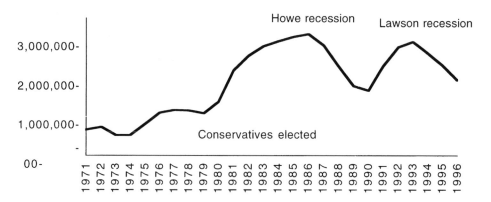

Growth and public spending 1960–97

Year	Gross domestic product £ billions 1995 prices	Growth rate %	Average growth rate %	Growth since 1979	Public spending £ billions (financial years)	Share of GDP %	Change since 1979
1960	272	5.5					
1961	279	2.7					
1962	283	1.5					
1963	295	4.0			125	35.50	
1964	311	5.6	**Lab Govt**		129	35.00	
1965	320	2.9	1964-70		136	36.50	
1966	326	1.9	Average 3.1		145	38.00	
1967	333	2.2			163	41.50	
1968	348	4.4			162	40.00	
1969	357	2.5			163	39.25	
1970	364	2.0	**Con Govt**		168	39.50	
1971	370	1.7	1970-74		173	40.00	
1972	380	2.8	Average 2.5		182	39.25	
1973	409	7.5			196	41.25	
1974	403	−1.5	**Lab Govt**		221	46.75	
1975	400	−0.7	1974-79		221	47.25	
1976	410	2.7	Average 1.4		216	44.75	
1977	421	2.6			205	41.25	
1978	433	2.8			216	42.25	
1979	445	2.7	**Con Govt**		223	42.50	
1980	435	−2.1	1979-97	−2	227	44.75	2
1981	430	−1.1	Average 1.8	−3	230	45.50	3
1982	438	1.8		−2	236	45.50	6
1983	454	3.7		2	241	44.75	8
1984	464	2.0		4	248	45.25	11
1985	482	4.0		8	246	43.25	11
1986	502	4.0		13	252	42.25	13
1987	525	4.6		18	254	40.50	14
1988	521	4.9		17	248	38.00	11
1989	563	2.3		27	259	38.25	14
1990	566	0.5		27	258	39.00	16
1991	554	−2.1		24	267	41.00	20
1992	552	−0.5		24	283	43.50	27
1993	564	2.2		27	289	43.25	30
1994	586	4.0		32	295	42.50	32
1995	601	2.5		35	300	42.25	34
1996 est	*616*	*2.5*		*38*	*300*	*41.25*	*35*
1997 est	*637*	*3.5*		*43*	*301*	*40.00*	*35*
1998 est					*302*	*39.00*	*36*

USING THE SAME TABLE:

Government points
1. Economy has grown in real terms by 38% since 1979.
2. Public spending has grown in real terms by 34% since 1979.
3. Public spending will have fallen from 42.5 to 40.50% of GDP.

Opposition points
1. Average growth rate was higher in 1960s.
2. Tories failed to cut public spending significantly as share of GDP.
3. Tories presided over two deep recessions.

GDP per capita

shown as £

Marginal tax rate

% paid by average worker

Govt spending

% of GDP

1995			1995			1995	
1 Luxembourg	30,570		1 Denmark	47		1 Sweden	68
2 Switzerland	27,195		2 Netherlands	38		2 Denmark	62
3 Japan	25,842		3 Hungary	35		3 Finland	58
4 Poland	21,233		4 France	35		4 Netherlands	57
5 Denmark	21,149		5 Italy	34		5 France	55
6 Germany	18,673		6 Australia	34		6 Hungary	55
7 Austria	18,296		7 Iceland	33		7 Austria	54
8 United States	17,425		8 Austria	32		8 Greece	54
9 Belgium	17,084		9 Sweden	31		9 Italy	52
10 France	17,076		10 Turkey	30		10 Belgium	52
11 Singapore	16,525		11 Russia	30		11 Czech Republic	51
12 Sweden	16,286		12 Israel	30		12 Germany	51
13 Netherlands	16,283		13 Germany	30		13 Poland	49
14 Iceland	16,020		14 United States	28		14 Norway	49
15 Finland	15,728		15 Norway	28		15 Canada	48
16 Hong Kong	15,466		16 Egypt	28		16 Portugal	47
17 Italy	12,261		17 Ireland	27		17 Israel	47
18 Canada	12,249		18 Finland	27		18 Spain	47
19 Australia	12,048		19 Belgium	27		19 Ireland	45
20 **United Kingdom**	12,015		20 **United Kingdom**	25		20 South Africa	43
21 Ireland	11,080		21 Spain	25		21 **United Kingdom**	43
22 New Zealand	10,523		22 Brazil	25		22 Switzerland	41
23 Israel	9,801		23 Venezuela	24		23 Iceland	40
24 Spain	9,079		24 New Zealand	24		24 Brazil	38
25 Taiwan	7,716		25 Poland	21		25 Luxembourg	37

Source: OECD

World competitiveness league Table 1

Economies ranked by ability to promote growth in national output and living standards

Ranking	Country	Ranking	Country
1	Singapore	26	Ireland
2	Hong Kong	27	Iceland
3	New Zealand	28	Jordan
4	United States	29	Egypt
5	Luxembourg	30	Indonesia
6	Switzerland	31	Philippines
7	Norway	32	Spain
8	Canada	33	Mexico
9	Taiwan	34	Portugal
10	Malaysia	35	Czech Republic
11	Denmark	36	China
12	Australia	37	Argentina
13	Japan	38	Peru
14	Thailand	39	Greece
15	**United Kingdom**	40	Colombia
16	Finland	41	Italy
17	Netherlands	42	Turkey
18	Chile	43	South Africa
19	Austria	44	Poland
20	Korea	45	India
21	Sweden	46	Hungary
22	**Germany**	47	Venezuela
23	France	48	Brazil
24	Israel	49	Russia
25	Belgium		

Source: World Economic Forum

Good for the Government:
Table1 shows the UK well placed above its main European Union rivals.
Only Denmark is better placed while Germany, the key European partner, is behind.

World competitiveness league Table 2: 1995–96

Economies ranked by ability to promote growth in national output and living standards

1995 Ranking	Country	1996 Ranking	Country
1	United States	1	United States
2	Singapore	2	Singapore
3	Hong Kong	3	Hong Kong
4	Japan	4	Japan
5	Switzerland	5	Denmark
6	Germany	6	Norway
7	Denmark	7	Netherlands
8	Netherlands	8	Luxembourg
9	New Zealand	9	Switzerland
10	Norway	10	Germany
11	Austria	11	New Zealand
12	Sweden	12	Canada
13	Canada	13	Chile
14	Taiwan	14	Sweden
15	**United Kingdom**	15	Finland
16	Australia	16	Austria
17	Luxembourg	17	Belgium
18	Finland	18	Taiwan
19	France	19	**United Kingdom**
20	Chile	20	France

Source: Institute for Management Development

Bad for the Government:

Table 2 shows UK overtaken by Chile and Finland in terms of competitiveness and UK well behind other members of the Group of Seven industrial nations.

Unemployment

Rates in the European Union – men and women
aged 16-54

Ranking	Country	Rate %
1	Germany (West)	6
2	Portugal	6
3	Germany (East)	6
4	Netherlands	7
5	Greece	9
6	Belgium	10
7	**United Kingdom**	10
8	France	10
9	Denmark	11
10	Italy	12
11	Ireland	16
12	Luxembourg	16
13	Spain	19

Education

Spending per student in primary and secondary
education in the European Union

Ranking	Country	Amount £
1	Ireland	3,310
2	France	2,949
3	Belgium	2,949
4	Germany (West)	2,911
5	Luxembourg	2,829
6	Germany (East)	2,772
7	Greece	2,443
8	Denmark	2,430
9	**United Kingdom**	2,392
10	Netherlands	1,892
11	Portugal	1,797
12	Spain	1,582
13	Italy	1,418

Source: OECD Survey 1993-94

Crime

Notifiable offences 1994-95 – England and Wales

Offence group	1994	1995	Change %
Violence against the person	219,200	217,500	−0.8
Sexual offences	31,900	30,400	−4.9
Robbery	59,800	68,400	14.5
Total violent crime	**310,900**	**316,300**	**1.7**
Burglary	1,257,900	1,244,200	−1.1
Total theft and handling stolen goods	2,557,800	2,459,600	−3.8
Vehicle crime	1,376,400	1,323,500	−3.8
Fraud and forgery	145,700	134,300	−7.8
Criminal damage	928,600	917,000	−1.3
Total property crime	**4,890,000**	**4,755,100**	**−2.8**
Other notifiable offences	48,600	52,200	7.6
Total all offences	**5, 249,500**	**5,100,200**	**−2.9**

Source: Home Office Statistical Bulletin

USING THE SAME TABLE:
Government points
1. Vehicle crime, theft and burglary down.
2. Crime rate falling overall.

Opposition points
1. Violent crimes rising.
2. Robbery up sharply.

Crime

Notifiable offences 1960-95

Year	Offences (old series)	Change %	Clear-up rate %	Offences (new series)	Change %	Change since 1979 %	Change since 1992 %
1960	800,323	1	43				
1961	870,894	9	44				
1962	965,699	11	43				
1963	1,060,071	10	42				
1964	1,171,176	10	38				
1965	1,243,463	6	38				
1966	1,315,662	6	39				
1967	1,316,761	0	40				
1968	1,407,774	7	41				
1969	1,498,703	6	42				
1970	1,568,375	5	45				
1971	1,665,663	6	45				
1972	1,690,219	1	46				
1973	1,657,669	−2	47				
1974	1,963,360	18	44				
1975	2,105,631	7	44				
1976	2,135,713	1	43				
1977	2,463,025	15	41				
1978	2,395,757	−3	42				
1979	2,376,666	−1	41	2,536,700			
1980	2,520,628	6	40	2,688,200	6	6	
1981	2,794,220	11	38	2,963,800	10	17	
1982	3,088,336	11	37	3,262,400	10	29	
1983	3,070,975	−1	37	3,427,000	5	35	
1984	3,313,807	8	35	3,499,100	2	38	
1985	3,426,433	3	35	3,611,900	3	42	
1986	3,660,004	7	32	3,847,400	7	52	
1987	3,716,186	2	33	3,892,200	1	53	
1988	3,550,179	−4	35	3,715,800	−5	46	
1989	3,706,217	4	34	3,870,700	4	53	
1990	4,363,632	18	32	4,543,600	17	79	
1991	5,075,343	16	29	5,276,200	16	108	
1992	5,383,485	6	26	5,591,700	6	120	
1993	5,317,110	−1	25	5,526,300	−1	118	−1
1994	5,035,954	−5	26	5,249,500	−5	107	−6
1995	4,909,419	−3	26	5,100,200	−3	101	−9

Source: Home Office

USING THE SAME TABLE:

Government points
1. Crime down 9% since 1992.
2. Crime falling three years running.

Opposition points
1. Crime more than doubled since 1979.
2. Clear-up rate fallen from 41 to 26.

Note: Old series offences exclude theft of goods valued at less than £20.

PART THREE

ELECTIONS

CONSTITUENCIES

How to read the Constituency Guide

The first line of each entry gives the name of the constituency, followed by the country or region and a short description.

The second line gives the constituency's three most distinctive characteristics in the 1991 census, and its place in an imaginary league table where all the seats in England and Wales are put in order from 1st to 569th. Thus Aberavon has the third highest proportion of its population suffering from long-term illness and the 14th highest percentage working in unskilled manual jobs. 'Mobility', as defined by the census, indicates having 'a different address a year ago'. There are, as yet, no census figures available for Scotland or Northern Ireland.

The next line shows the degree to which the constituency boundaries have been changed. Some, like Aberavon, have not been affected at all. Some, like Aberdeen Central, are entirely new seats which do not correspond to any existing seat. Others, like Aberdeen North, have changed a lot but are still based on an existing seat of the same name. (If a constituency has lost 40 per cent of its old voters or gained 40 per cent new voters, it is shown as a 40 per cent change. But if it has both gained and lost 40 per cent, it is shown as an 80 per cent change.

Where there is 'No change', as in Aberavon, we show the actual votes gained by the main parties in the 1992 election followed by their percentage share of the vote in 1992 and 1987.

Where there is an entirely new seat, as in Aberdeen Central, we show the notional votes and percentages that each party would have received if the 1992 election had been fought on the same boundaries as the new seat. These have been estimated by Colin Rallings and Michael Thrasher of Plymouth University.

Where the new seat is still largely based on an existing seat, like Aberdeen North, we show the notional votes and percentages if the 1992 election had been fought on the new boundaries, plus the actual percentages on the old boundaries in 1992 and 1987. This allows the reader to judge the political impact of the boundaries. The old Aberdeen North, for instance, was a strong Labour seat with a majority of 23 per cent. The new Aberdeen North is more marginal, with a Labour majority of 11 per cent.

The last line shows the 'swing' in the 1992 and 1987 elections – that is, the proportion of voters who switched parties. In Aberdeen North, for instance, there was a swing of 7 per cent to Labour in 1987 and a swing of 9 per cent to the Scottish National Party in 1992.

Where the seat is marginal, the last column of the last line shows the swing that the second party will need in order to win the seat from the leading party. In Aberdeen North the Lib Dems and the SNP are vying for second place. The Lib Dems need a 6 per cent swing to win the seat – it is 26th on their target list. The SNP also needs a 6 per cent swing to win it, and it is 8th on its target list.

For the sake of brevity, throughout this section 'Liberal Democrats' or 'Lib Dem' includes the Social Democrats (SDP) and the SDP–Liberal Alliance from previous elections.

Abbreviations

APNI	Alliance Party of Northern Ireland
by-	by-election
Con	Conservative
DUP	Democratic Unionist Party
IUP	Independent Unionist Party
Lab	Labour
Lib Dem/LD/Ldm	Liberal Democrat (also includes SDP and Alliance throughout this section)
PlC	Plaid Cymru
SDLP	Social Democratic and Labour Party
SF	Sinn Fein
SNP	Scottish Nationalist Party
UKUP	United Kingdom Unionist Party
UPUP	Ulster Popular Unionist Party
UUP	Ulster Unionist Party

Key

→	swing to

ABERAVON, West Glamorgan. 12th safest Labour seat, steel industry, includes Port Talbot
Govt schemes 2% (74th); Long-term ill 22% (3rd); Unskilled 8% (14th)

No change	Actual 92	%		87	Candidates
Conservative	5,567	14		14	Peter Harper, computer consultant
Labour	26,877	67		67	John Morris, MP, QC
Lib Dem	4,999	13		16	
Plaid Cymru	1,919	5		3	Phil Cockwell
Majority	21,310	Lab 53		Lab 51	
Swing		No swing		6 → Lab	

ABERDEEN CENTRAL, Grampian. New seat, should be Labour, oil industry

94% change	Notional 92	%	Candidates
Conservative	10,872	29	Jill Wesley
Labour	16,269	43	Frank Doran former MP
Lib Dem	3,985	11	John Brown
SNP	6,636	18	Brian Topping, councillor
Majority	5,397	Lab 14	

ABERDEEN NORTH, Grampian. New boundaries take in Lib Dem area, should stay Labour, oil industry

88% change	Notional 92	%	92	87	Candidates
Conservative	7,002	19	17	14	James Gifford
Labour	13,189	35	47	55	Malcolm Savidge, former council deputy leader
Lib Dem	8,952	24	12	18	Mike Rumbles, team leader, HRM
SNP	8,443	23	24	13	Brian Adam, councillor
Majority	4,237	Lab 11	Lab 23	Lab 37	
Swing			9 → SNP	7 → Lab	LD need 6 to win. 26th on LD list
					SNP needs 6 to win. 8th on SNP list

ABERDEEN SOUTH, Grampian. Tory marginal

90% change	Notional 92	%	92	87	Candidates
Conservative	16,487	37	39	35	Raymond Robertson, MP
Labour	10,545	24	35	38	Anne Begg, teacher
Lib Dem	11,762	27	12	21	Nicol Stephen, solicitor, management consultant
SNP	5,336	12	15	7	Jim Towers
Majority	4,725	Con 11	Con 4	Lab 3	
Swing			3 → Con	6 → Lab	LD need 5 to win. 25th on LD list
					Lab needs 7 to win. 79th on Lab list

ABERDEENSHIRE WEST & KINCARDINE, Grampian. Tory marginal, agricultural, based on Kincardine or Deeside

63% change	Notional 92	%	92	87	Candidates
Conservative	19,123	45	44	41	George Kynoch, MP
Labour	2,886	7	9	16	Qaisra Khan
Lib Dem	14,686	35	35	36	Sir Robert Smith, estate manager
SNP	5,280	13	11	6	Joy Mowatt
Majority	4,437	Con 11	Con 9	Con 4	
Swing			2 → Con	7 → LibAll	LD need 5 to win. 24th on LD list

AIRDRIE & SHOTTS, Strathclyde. Based on John Smith's old seat of Monklands East, agricultural, industrial, working class

53% change	Notional 92	%	94 by-	92	87	Candidates
Conservative	6,588	15	2	16	17	Nicholas Brook
Labour	27,678	63	50	61	61	Helen Liddell, MP
Lib Dem	1,997	5	3	5	9	Richard Wolseley
SNP	8,023	18	45	18	13	Keith Robertson, councillor
Majority	19,655	Lab 44	Lab 5	Lab 43	Lab 44	
Swing			19 → SNP	2 → SNP	8 → Lab	

ALDERSHOT, Hampshire. Strong Tory seat, military, middle-class, formerly held by maverick Sir Julian Critchley
Age 16-24 16% (6th); Mobility 14% (23rd); Professional 10% (95th)

8% change	Notional 92	%	92	87	Candidates
Conservative	34,300	58	58	59	Gerald Howarth, director public affairs, former M
Labour	8,154	14	13	12	Terence Bridgeman
Lib Dem	15,584	26	28	29	Adrian Collett
Majority	18,716	Con 32	Con 30	Con 30	
Swing			No swing	4 → Con	

ALDRIDGE-BROWNHILLS, West Midlands. Strong Tory seat, residential, middle-class, part of Walsall borough
Age 40-pension 31% (3rd); Council tenants 22% (190th); Skilled manual 34% (80th)

No Change	Actual 92	%		87	Candidates
Conservative	28,431	54		53	Richard Shepherd, MP
Labour	17,407	33		28	Janos Toth
Lib Dem	6,503	12		18	Celia Downie
Majority	11,024	Con 21		Con 25	
Swing		2 → Lab		No swing	

ALTRINCHAM & SALE WEST, Greater Manchester. Strong Tory seat, suburbs, middle-class
Owner-occupied 77% (110th); Professional 14% (12th); Managerial 41% (61st)

53% change	Notional 92	%	92	87	Candidates
Conservative	30,343	55	55	54	Graham Brady, transport consultant
Labour	14,727	26	23	21	Jane Baugh
Lib Dem	10,261	18	22	26	Marc Ramsbottom
Majority	15,616	Con 28	Con 32	Con 27	
Swing			1 → Lab	2 → Con	

ALYN & DEESIDE, Clwyd. Strong Labour seat, ex-steel industry, close to Liverpool
White 99.4% (78th); Owner-occupied 77% (121st); Skilled manual 33% (90th)

6% change	Notional 92	%	92	87	Candidates
Conservative	16,770	37	36	35	Timothy Roberts
Labour	23,157	51	52	49	Barry Jones, MP
Lib Dem	4,431	10	10	15	Eleanor Burnham
Plaid Cymru	517	1	1	1	Siw Hills
Majority	6,387	Lab 14	Lab 16	Lab 14	
Swing			1 → Lab	5 → Lab	

AMBER VALLEY, Derbyshire. Tory marginal, industrial, includes Alfreton, Heanor and Ripley
White 99% (94th); Owner-occupied 76% (144th); Skilled manual 38% (17th)

3% change	Notional 92	%	92	87	Candidates
Conservative	28,360	47	46	51	Phillip Oppenheim, MP
Labour	27,077	44	45	34	Judy Mallaber, researcher
Lib Dem	5,582	9	9	14	Roger Shelley, researcher
Majority	1,283	Con 2	Con 1	Con 17	
Swing			8 → Lab	5 → Con	Lab needs 1 to win. 17th on Lab list

ANGUS, Tayside. SNP marginal, agricultural, includes Montrose and Arbroath

23% change	Notional 92	%	92	87	Candidates
Conservative	16,801	38	3	39	Sebastian Leslie
Labour	5,708	13	13	11	Catherine Taylor
Lib Dem	3,878	9	8	8	Dick Speirs
SNP	17,274	39	40	42	Andrew Welsh
Majority	473	SNP 1	SNP 2	SNP 3	
Swing			1 → Con	6 → SNP	Con need 1 to win. 6th on Con list

ANTRIM EAST, Northern Ireland, Strong Unionist seat, includes Larne and Carrickfergus

22% change	Notional 92	%	92	87	Candidates
UUP	15,465	44	43	72	Roy Beggs, MP
APNI	8,919	25	23	26	Sean Neeson, marketing consultant
DUP	8,046	23	24	–	
Conservative	2,788	8	9	–	
Majority	6,546	UUP 19	UUP 19	UUP 46	
Swing			No swing	14 → UUP	

ANTRIM NORTH, Northern Ireland. Paisley's stronghold, includes Moyle, Ballymoney and Paisley's own Ballymena

No Change	Actual 92	%		87	Candidates
UUP	8,216	18		–	James Leslie
DUP	23,152	51		69	Rev. Ian Paisley, MP
SDLP	6,512	14		13	
Conservative	2,263	5		–	
Majority	14,936	DUP 33		56	

ANTRIM SOUTH, Northern Ireland. Safest Unionist seat, agricultural

5% change	Notional 92	%	92	87	Candidates
UUP	28,447	71	71	70	Clifford Forsythe, MP
SDLP	5,397	14	13	10	
APNI	4,362	11	12	16	David Ford, party official
SF	1,220	3	3	4	
Majority	23,050	UUP 58	UUP 58	UUP 54	
Swing			1 → SDLP	10 → UUP	

ARGYLL & BUTE, Strathclyde. Lib Dem marginal, 3rd most Gaelic speakers

No Change	Actual 92	%		87	Candidates
Conservative	10,117	28		34	Ralph Leishman
Labour	4,946	14		12	Ali Syed
Lib Dem	12,739	35		37	Ray Michie, MP
SNP	8,689	24		17	Neil MacCormick, professor
Majority	2,622	LD 7		LibAll 4	
Swing				7 → Lib All	Con need 4 to win. 54th on Con list
					SNP needs 6 to win. 6th on SNP list

ARUNDEL & SOUTH DOWNS, West Sussex. New strong Tory seat, rural, middle-class
Pensionable 24% (36th); Self-employed 19% (33rd); Managerial 42% (52nd)

105% change	Notional 92	%	Candidates
Conservative	33,365	63	Howard Flight, managing director, investment cons
Labour	4,957	9	Richard Black
Lib Dem	13,349	25	John Goss
Majority	20,016	Con 38	

ASHFIELD, Nottinghamshire. Strong Labour seat, mining, working class
Long-term ill 15% (92nd); Skilled manual 41% (6th); Unskilled 6% (164th)

0.1 % change	Notional 92	%	92	87	Candidates
Conservative	19,015	33	33	34	Mark Simmonds, management consultant
Labour	31,978	55	55	42	Geoff Hoon, MP
Lib Dem	7,285	13	13	25	Bill Smith
Majority	12,963	Lab 22	Lab 22	Lab 8	
Swing			7 → Lab	2 → Con	

ASHFORD, Kent. Strong Tory seat, commuting, middle-class, *Darling Buds of May* country
Self-employed 15% (96th); Second homes .4% (122nd); Mobility 11% (154th)

No Change	Actual 92	%		87	Candidates
Conservative	31,031	55		57	Damian Green, PA consultant
Labour	11,365	20		15	John Ennals
Lib Dem	13,672	24		27	John Williams
Majority	17,359	Con 31		Con 29	
Swing		1 → Con		No swing	

ASHTON-UNDER-LYNE, Greater Manchester. Strong Labour seat, textile industry, Asian minority
Asian 5% (95th); Unemployed 11% (156th); Skilled manual 36% (37th)

52% change	Notional 92	%	92	87	Candidates
Conservative	15,706	29	31	30	Richard Mayson
Labour	31,138	57	57	52	Robert Sheldon, MP
Lib Dem	6,519	12	9	18	Timothy Pickstone
Majority	15,432	Lab 28	Lab 25	Lab 22	
Swing			2 → Lab	2 → Lab	

AYLESBURY, Buckinghamshire. Strong Tory seat, commuting, middle-class
Age 16-24 14% (50th); Car owners 80% (94th); Managerial 37% (117th)

4% change	Notional 92	%	92	87	Candidates
Conservative	34,983	57	57	58	David Lidington, MP
Labour	8,205	13	13	14	Robert Langridge
Lib Dem	16,943	28	28	29	Sharon Bowles
Majority	18,040	Con 30	Con 30	Con 29	
Swing			No swing	No swing	

AYR, Strathclyde. Labour marginal, held by Con in 1992 but goes to Lab on boundary changes

17% change	Notional 92	%	92	87	Candidates
Conservative	17,417	39	41	39	Phil Gallie, MP
Labour	19,312	43	41	39	Sandra Osborn, councillor
Lib Dem	3,382	8	8	15	Clare Hamblen
SNP	5,057	11	11	17	Ian Blackford
Majority	1,895	Lab 4	Con 0.2	Con 0.3	
Swing			No swing	8 → Lab	

BANBURY, Oxfordshire. Strong Tory seat, mainly rural, middle-class
Age 25-39 25% (68th); Private tenants 9% (117th); Mobility 14% (24th)

4% change	Notional 92	%	92	87	Candidates
Conservative	30,886	55	55	56	Anthony Brian (Tony) Baldry, MP
Labour	15,155	27	27	20	Hazel Peperall
Lib Dem	10,027	18	18	23	Catherine Bearder
Majority	15,731	Con 28	Con 29	Con 33	
Swing			4 → Lab	3 → Con	

BANFF & BUCHAN, Grampian. Strong SNP seat, agricultural, includes Fraserburgh and Peterhead

12% change	Notional 92	%	92	87	Candidates
Conservative	14,156	35	39	39	William Frain-Bell
Labour	3,501	9	8	8	Megan Harris
Lib Dem	2,387	6	6	10	Neil Fletcher
SNP	20,724	51	48	44	Alex Salmond, MP
Majority	6,568	SNP 16	SNP 9	SNP 6	
Swing			2 → SNP	4 → SNP	

BARKING, East London. Strong Labour seat, industrial, skilled manual, Lab held in by-election
Black 3% (92nd); Unemployed 13% (96th); Council tenants 49% (9th)

11% change	Notional 92	%	94 by-	92	87	Candidates
Conservative	13,229	34	10	34	34	Keith Langford, property services
Labour	20,409	52	72	52	44	Margaret Hodge, MP
Lib Dem	5,436	14	12	15	21	Mark Marsh
Majority	7,180	Lab 18	Lab 60	Lab 18	Lab 10	
Swing			22 → Lab	4 → Lab	1 → Con	

BARNSLEY CENTRAL, South Yorkshire. Strong Labour seat, mining, working class
Govt schemes 3% (9th); Council tenants 33% (59th); Skilled manual 37% (26th)

14% change	Notional 92	%	92	87	Candidates
Conservative	8,340	19	20	18	Simon Gutteridge
Labour	31,844	71	69	67	Eric Illsley, MP
Lib Dem	4,823	11	11	15	
Majority	23,504	Lab 52	Lab 50	Lab 49	
Swing			1 → Lab	5 → Lab	

BARNSLEY EAST & MEXBOROUGH, South Yorkshire. 10th safest Labour seat, mining, working class
White 99.5% (38th); Govt schemes 3% (10th); Long-term ill 19% (10th)

57% change	Notional 92	%	96 by-	92	87	Candidates
Conservative	8,654	17	7	14	14	Jane Ellison, assist. to company c
Labour	36,375	73	76	77	75	Jeff Ennis, MP, teacher
Lib Dem	4,864	10	8	9	12	
Majority	27,721	Lab 56	Lab 68	Lab 63	Lab 61	
Swing			3 → Lab	1 → Lab	5 → Lab	

BARNSLEY WEST & PENISTONE, South Yorkshire. Strong Labour seat, mining, home of Arthur Scargill
Govt schemes 3% (45th); Long-term ill 16% (59th); Unskilled 6% (84th)

No Change	Actual 92	%		87	Candidates
Conservative	13,461	28		27	Paul Watkins, registered general nurse
Labour	27,965	58		57	Michael Clapham, MP
Lib Dem	5,610	12		16	
Majority	14,504	Lab 30		Lab 31	
Swing		No swing		4 → Lab	

BARROW & FURNESS, Cumbria. Labour marginal, shipbuilding, home of Trident
Owner-occupied 78% (81st); No central heating 40% (26th); Skilled manual 38% (15th)

No Change	Actual 92	%		87	Candidates
Conservative	22,990	41		47	Richard Hunt, chartered accountant
Labour	26,568	48		39	John Hutton, MP
Lib Dem	6,089	11		14	Anne Metcalfe
Majority	3,578	Lab 6		Con 7	
Swing				1 → Lab	Con needs 3 to win. 45th on Con list

BASILDON, Essex. Emblematic Tory win in 1992, highest proportion of *Sun* readers
Age 16-24 14% (72nd); Council tenants 30% (77th); Skilled manual 32% (118th)

68% change	Notional 92	%	92	87	Candidates
Conservative	27,291	45	45	44	John Baron, director, investment company
Labour	24,645	41	42	38	Angela Smith, political analyst & researcher
Lib Dem	8,599	14	13	18	~~Terry Marsh, former pro boxing champion~~
Majority	2,646	Con 4	Con 3	Con 5	
Swing			1 → Lab	1 → Con	Lab needs 2 to win. 29th on Lab list

BASINGSTOKE, Hampshire. Strong Tory seat, includes new town, middle-class
Age 16-24 14% (39th); Car owners 79% (111th); Professional 9% (114th)

10% change	Notional 92	%	92	87	Candidates
Conservative	33,695	54	55	56	Andrew Hunter, MP
Labour	15,809	25	24	18	Nigel Lickley
Lib Dem	12,819	20	21	26	Martin Rimmer
Majority	17,886	Con 28	Con 31	Con 30	
Swing			4 → Lab	4 → Con	

BASSETLAW, Nottinghamshire. Fairly solid Labour seat, ex-mining, skilled manual
Govt schemes 2% (86th); Skilled manual 36% (35th); Unskilled 5% (175th)

No Change	Notional 92	%	92	87	Candidates
Conservative	19,061	35	35	38	Martin Cleasby, teacher
Labour	29,056	53	53	48	Joe Ashton, MP
Lib Dem	6,339	12	12	14	Mike (Sean) Kerrigan
Majority	9,995	Lab 18	Lab 18	Lab 11	
Swing			4 → Lab	1 → Lab	

BATH, Avon. Lib Dem marginal, boundary changes help Con, retirement, professional
Pensionable 24% (40th); Private tenants 12% (58th); Professional 11% (51st)

11% change	Notional 92	%	92	87	Candidates
Conservative	25,289	43	42	45	Alison McNair, finance director
Labour	4,761	8	8	11	Tim Bush
Lib Dem	27,298	47	49	43	Don Foster, MP
Majority	2,009	LD 4	LD 7	Con 3	
Swing			5 → LD	4 → SDPAll	Con need 2 to win. 26th on Con list

BATLEY & SPEN, West Yorkshire. Tory marginal, very mixed area, Asian minority
Asian 10% (45th); No central heating 35% (46th); Skilled manual 34% (65th)

16% change	Notional 92	%	92	87	Candidates
Conservative	22,676	45	45	43	Elizabeth Peacock, MP
Labour	21,831	43	43	41	Mike Wood
Lib Dem	5,757	11	11	14	Kath Pinnock
Majority	845	Con 2	Con 2	Con 2	
Swing			No swing	No swing	Lab needs 1 to win. 15th on Lab list

BATTERSEA, South London. Tory marginal, middle-class influx in 1980s, Con gain in 87
Age 25-39 33% (1st); Black 14% (13th); Mobility 15% (12th)

0.3% change	Notional 92	%	92	87	Candidates
Conservative	26,411	50	51	44	John Bowis, MP
Labour	21,630	41	41	42	Martin Linton, *Guardian* journalist
Lib Dem	3,700	7	7	12	Paula Keaveney
Majority	4,781	Con 9	Con 9	Con 2	
Swing			4 → Con	5 → Con	Lab needs 5 to win. 62nd on Lab list

BEACONSFIELD, Buckinghamshire. 3rd safest Tory seat, stock-broker belt, middle-class
Age 40-pension 32% (2nd); Car owners 85% (6th); Managerial 47% (7th)

3% change	Notional 92	%	92	87	Candidates
Conservative	34,316	64	64	66	Timothy John Smith, MP, chartered accountant
Labour	7,371	14	14	10	Alastair Hudson
Lib Dem	10,452	19	19	24	Peter Mapp
Majority	23,864	Con 44	Con 45	Con 42	
Swing			1 → Con	2 → Con	

BECKENHAM, South London. Strong Tory seat, suburban, white collar
Age 25-39 25% (65th); Managerial 43% (34th); White collar 20% (14th)

25% change	Notional 92	%	92	87	Candidates
Conservative	35,154	60	57	56	Piers Merchant, MP
Labour	12,341	21	24	18	Robert Hughes
Lib Dem	9,765	17	17	26	Rosemary Vetterlein
Majority	22,813	Con 39	Con 33	Con 30	
Swing			3 → Lab	No swing	

BEDFORD, Bedfordshire. Tory marginal, mainly urban, large Asian community, based on Bedfordshire N
Age 16-24 14% (40th); Black 4% (63rd); Asian 9% (50th)

47% change	Notional 92	%	92	87	Candidates
Conservative	22,863	45	51	53	Robert Blackman, sales manager
Labour	18,318	36	31	23	Patrick Hall, planning officer
Lib Dem	8,263	16	17	24	Christopher Noyce
Majority	4,545	Con 9	Con 20	Con 29	
Swing			5 → Lab	2 → Con	Lab needs 5 to win. 61st on Lab list

BEDFORDSHIRE MID, Bedfordshire. 7th safest Tory seat, mainly rural, middle-class
Age 40-pension 29% (93rd); Car owners 84% (14th); Managerial 41% (54th)

99% change	Notional 92	%	92	87	Candidates
Conservative	31,561	62	58	59	Jonathan Sayeed, chairman of PA company
Labour	10,016	20	22	18	Neil Mallett
Lib Dem	7,973	16	17	23	Tim Hill
Majority	21,545	Con 43	Con 36	Con 36	
Swing			2 → Lab	3 → Con	

BEDFORDSHIRE NORTH EAST, Bedfordshire. New strong Tory seat, mainly rural, professional
Age 40-pension 29% (70th); Car owners 83% (27th); Professional 11% (56th)

78% change	Notional 92	%	Candidates
Conservative	31,081	59	Sir Nicholas Lyell, MP, QC
Labour	10,478	20	John Lehal
Lib Dem	9,706	19	Philip Bristow
Majority	20,603	Con 39	

BEDFORDSHIRE SOUTH WEST, Bedfordshire. Strong Tory seat, mainly rural, professional
Age 25-39 24% (71st); Owner-occupied 76% (125th); Mobility 10% (190th)

13% change	Notional 92	%	92	87	Candidates
Conservative	32,000	56	57	58	Sir David Madel, MP
Labour	14,660	26	25	18	Andrew Date
Lib Dem	9,475	17	17	22	Stephen Owen
Majority	17,340	Con 31	Con 32	Con 36	
Swing			4 → Lab	4 → Con	

BELFAST EAST, Northern Ireland. Democratic Unionist stronghold, inner city, shipbuilding

22% change	Notional 92	%	92	87	Candidates
DUP	22,635	55	52	62	Peter Robinson, MP
APNI	11,337	27	30	32	Jim Hendron, solicitor
SF	686	2	2	2	
Conservative	4,170	10	9	–	
Majority	11,298	DUP 27	DUP 22	DUP 30	
Swing			1 → APNI	4 → DUP	

BELFAST NORTH, Northern Ireland. Strong Unionist seat, includes Protestant Shankhill

24% change	Notional 92	%	92	87	Candidates
UUP	22,259	52	48	39	Cecil Walker, MP
SDLP	7,867	18	21	16	Alan Maginness, barrister
SF	4,882	11	13	14	
Conservative	2,678	6	6	–	
Majority	14,392	UUP 33	UUP 27	UUP 23	
Swing			2 → UUP	1 → UUP	

BELFAST SOUTH, Northern Ireland. Strongest Unionist seat in Belfast, urban, middle-class

26% change	Notional 92	%	92	87	Candidates
UUP	23,258	53	49	58	Rev William Smythe, MP
SDLP	6,266	14	19	13	
APNI	6,921	16	15	21	Steve McBride, barrister
Conservative	5,154	12	10	–	
Majority	16,337	UUP 37	UUP 30	UUP 37	
Swing			7 → SDLP	5 → UUP	

BELFAST WEST, Northern Ireland. SDLP seat, won from Gerry Adams

21% change	Notional 92	%	92	87	Candidates
UUP	5,275	12	12	19	
SDLP	20,045	44	44	36	Dr Joe Hendron, MP
SF	19,027	42	42	41	Gerry Adams, ex-MP
Majority	1,018	SDLP 2	SDLP 2	SF 5	
Swing			3 → SDLP	3 → SDLP	SF need 1 to win

BERWICK-UPON-TWEED, Northumberland. Lib Dem seat, Conservative second, ex-mining, working class
White 99.8% (1st); Second homes 3% (13th); Govt schemes 3% (53rd)

No Change	Actual 92	%		87	Candidates
Conservative	14,240	33		30	Nick Herbert
Labour	9,933	23		18	Paul Brannen
Lib Dem	19,283	44		52	Alan Beith, MP
Majority	5,043	LD 12		LD 23	
Swing		6 → Con		1 → LibAll	

BETHNAL GREEN & BOW, East London. Strong Labour seat, inner city, strongly Asian
Asian 29% (7th); Unemployed 23% (8th); Council tenants 57% (4th)

26% change	Notional 92	%	92	87	Candidates
Conservative	7,316	16	18	19	Kabir Choudhury, company director
Labour	23,863	54	56	48	Syed Nurul Islam
Lib Dem	11,498	26	22	32	
Majority	12,365	Lab 28	Lab 34	Lab 17	
Swing			9 → Lab	2 → LibAll	

(handwritten: (Jamaica))

(handwritten: OONA KING)

BEVERLEY & HOLDERNESS, Humberside. New strong Tory seat, mainly rural, professional
Age 40-pension 30% (30th); Owner-occupied 78% (88th); Second homes 1% (120th)

90% change	Notional 92	%	Candidates
Conservative	29,800	55	James Cran, MP
Labour	10,981	20	Norman O'Neill
Lib Dem	13,843	25	John Melling
Majority	15,957	Con 29	

BEXHILL & BATTLE, East Sussex. Strong Tory seat, seaside, managerial
Pensionable 34% (2nd); Self-employed 22% (13th); Second homes 2% (32nd)

0.1 % change	Notional 92	%	92	87	Candidates
Conservative	31,347	60	60	66	Charles Wardle, MP
Labour	4,877	9	9	8	Robert Beckwith
Lib Dem	15,007	29	29	26	Kathryn Field
Majority	16,340	Con 31	Con 31	Con 41	
Swing			5 → LD	2 → SDPAll	

BEXLEYHEATH & CRAYFORD, South London. Strong Tory seat, suburban, white collar
White collar 19% (19th); Owner-occupied 80% (51st); Mobility 6% (560th)

75% change	Notional 92	%	92	87	Candidates
Conservative	28,380	54	54	54	David Evennett, MP
Labour	16,377	31	24	18	Nigel Beard
Lib Dem	7,515	14	21	29	Françoise Montford
Majority	12,003	Con 23	Con 30	Con 25	
Swing			3 → Lab	1 → Con	

BILLERICAY, Essex. Strong Tory seat, commuting, middle-class
White collar 16% (91st); Professional 6% (268th); No central heating 4% (567th)

58% change	Notional 92	%	92	87	Candidates
Conservative	34,274	58	57	55	Teresa Gorman, MP
Labour	11,914	20	21	19	Paul Richards
Lib Dem	13,276	22	23	26	Geoff Williams
Majority	20,998	Con 35	Con 34	Con 29	
Swing			2 → Con	1 → Con	

BIRKENHEAD, Merseyside. Strong Labour seat, inner city, working class, high unemployment
Unemployed 19% (21st); Single parents 35% (27th); Govt schemes 3% (33rd)

No Change	Actual 92	%		87	Candidates
Conservative	11,485	25		26	John Crosby, financial manager
Labour	29,098	64		59	Frank Field, MP
Lib Dem	4,417	10		15	Roy Wood
Majority	17,613	Lab 39		Lab 32	
Swing		3 → Lab		6 → Lab	

BIRMINGHAM EDGBASTON, West Midlands. Tory marginal, urban, middle-class
Professional 14% (10th); Black 4% (60th); Single parents 28% (64th)

32% change	Notional 92	%	92	87	Candidates
Conservative	25,059	49	49	50	Andrew Marshall, account director
Labour	20,003	39	38	27	Gisela Stuart, lecturer in law
Lib Dem	5,158	10	12	21	Jock Gallagher
Majority	5,056	Con 10	Con 11	Con 23	
Swing		6 → Lab	5 → Lab		Lab needs 5 to win. 67th on Lab list

BIRMINGHAM ERDINGTON, West Midlands. Strong Labour seat, inner city, working class
No central heating 44% (13th); Unemployed 16% (41st); Council tenants 36% (47th)

40% change	Notional 92	%	92	87	Candidates
Conservative	18,498	37	38	39	Anthony Tompkins, legal recruitment consultant
Labour	27,021	53	51	46	Robin Corbett, MP
Lib Dem	5,187	10	12	15	Ian Garrett
Majority	8,523	Lab 17	Lab 13	Lab 7	
Swing			3 → Lab	3 → Lab	

BIRMINGHAM HALL GREEN, West Midlands. Tory marginal, outer suburbs, middle-class
No central heating 34% (52nd); Asian 6% (76th); Black 3% (96th)

No Change	Actual 92	%		87	Candidates
Conservative	21,649	46		45	Andrew Hargreaves, MP
Labour	17,984	38		28	Stephen McCabe, social work education adviser
Lib Dem	7,342	16		27	Christine Ransome-Wallis
Majority	3,665	Con 8		Con 17	
Swing		4 → Lab		3 → Lab	Lab needs 4 to win. 51st on Lab list

BIRMINGHAM HODGE HILL, West Midlands. Labour seat, inner city, skilled manual
No central heating 51% (4th); Skilled manual 37% (22nd); Asian 12% (36th)

No Change	Actual 92	%	87	Candidates
Conservative	14,827	36	37	Ed Grant, barrister
Labour	21,895	54	49	Terry Davis, MP
Lib Dem	3,740	9	14	Haydn Thomas
Majority	7,068	Lab 17	Lab 12	
Swing		3 → Lab	No swing	

BIRMINGHAM LADYWOOD, West Midlands. 16th safest Labour seat, inner city, strongly Asian
Unemployed 28% (2nd); Age 16-24 17% (2nd); Asian 33% (4th)

95% change	Notional 92	%	92	87	Candidates
Conservative	8,596	20	26	31	Shailesh Vara, solicitor
Labour	30,065	71	66	58	
Lib Dem	3,447	8	8	9	Sardul Singh Marwa
Majority	21,469	Lab 51	Lab 41	Lab 26	
Swing			7 → Lab	1 → Lab	

BIRMINGHAM NORTHFIELD, West Midlands. Labour marginal, car industry, skilled manual, Con gain in 92
No central heating 40% (25th); Council tenants 33% (61st); Single parents 27% (72nd)

24% change	Notional 92	%	92	87	Candidates
Conservative	17,273	43	44	45	Alan Blumenthal, retail manager
Labour	18,652	46	46	39	Richard Burden, MP
Lib Dem	4,692	12	10	16	Michael Ashall
Majority	1,379	Lab 3	Lab 1	Con 6	
Swing			4 → Lab	No swing	Con need 2 to win. 24th on Con list

BIRMINGHAM PERRY BARR, West Midlands. Labour seat, urban, outer ring council estates
Asian 24% (10th); No central heating 40% (24th); Black 11% (24th)

56% change	Notional 92	%	92	87	Candidates
Conservative	19,867	37	37	37	Andrew Dunnett, hospital development director
Labour	27,596	52	53	50	Jeffrey Rooker, MP
Lib Dem	5,720	11	10	13	Ray Hassall
Majority	7,729	Lab 15	Lab 17	Lab 14	
Swing			2 → Lab	No swing	

BIRMINGHAM SELLY OAK, West Midlands. Labour marginal, suburban, middle-class, Lab gain in 92
Age 16-24 14% (43rd); Asian 7% (68th); No central heating 30% (71st)

No Change	Actual 92	%	87	Candidates
Conservative	23,370	42	44	Graham Greene
Labour	25,430	46	39	Dr Lynne Jones, MP
Lib Dem	5,679	10	15	David Osborne
Majority	2,060	Lab 4	Con 5	
Swing		4 → Lab	3 → Lab	Con need 2 to win. 29th on Con list

BIRMINGHAM SPARKBROOK & SMALL HEATH, West Midlands. Strong Labour seat, inner city, strongly Asian
Asian 40% (1st); Overcrowding 10% (2nd); No central heating 53% (3rd)

40% change	Notional 92	%	92	87	Candidates
Conservative	12,604	26	25	26	
Labour	31,052	63	64	61	
Lib Dem	3,916	8	9	11	Roger Harmer
Majority	18,448	Lab 38	Lab 39	Lab 35	
Swing			2 → Lab	2 → Lab	

BIRMINGHAM YARDLEY, West Midlands. Labour marginal, outer ring, skilled manual, Lab gain in 92
No central heating 44% (11th); Skilled manual 35% (44th); Professional 3% (54th)

No Change	Actual 92	%	87	Candidates
Conservative	14,722	35	43	Anne Jobson, barrister
Labour	14,884	35	37	Estelle Morris, MP
Lib Dem	12,899	30	21	John Hemming, businessman
Majority	162	Lab 0.4	Con 6	
Swing		3 → Lab	No swing	Con need 0.2 to win. 3rd on Con list
				LD need 4 to win. 17th on LD list

BISHOP AUCKLAND, Durham. Labour seat, ex-mining, working class
White 99.6% (21st); Govt schemes 3% (41st); Long-term ill 16% (55th)

48% change	Notional 92	%	92	87	Candidates
Conservative	17,109	33	32	35	Josephine Fergus, self employed businesswor
Labour	24,825	48	50	48	Derek Foster, MP
Lib Dem	10,184	20	18	17	
Majority	7,716	Lab 15	Lab 18	Lab 13	
Swing			3 → Lab	2 → Lab	

BLABY, Leicestershire. Strong Tory seat, mainly suburban, middle-class
Owner-occupied 84% (17th); Car owners 83% (31st); Unemployed 5% (560th)

18% change	Notional 92	%	92	87	Candidates
Conservative	31,882	57	58	61	Andrew Robathan
Labour	12,213	22	21	15	Ross Willmott
Lib Dem	11,261	20	20	25	Geoffrey Welsh
Majority	19,669	Con 35	Con 37	Con 36	
Swing			4 → Lab	2 → Con	

BLACKBURN, Lancashire. Labour seat, industrial, large Asian community
Asian 18% (17th); Overcrowding 5% (27th); Age 16-24 14% (82nd)

No Change	Actual 92	%		87	Candidates
Conservative	20,606	38		40	Sangeeta Sidhu, solicitor
Labour	26,633	48		50	Jack Straw, MP
Lib Dem	6,332	12		10	Stephen Fenn
Majority	6,027	Lab 11		Lab 10	
Swing		1 → Lab		2 → Lab	

BLACKPOOL NORTH & FLEETWOOD, Lancashire. Tory marginal, seaside, retirement, white-collar
Pensionable 27% (20th); Long-term ill 17% (22nd); Owner-occupied 79% (57th)

99% change	Notional 92	%	92	87	Candidates
Conservative	29,838	50	48	48	Harold Elletson, MP
Labour	22,562	38	41	31	Joan Humble, councillor
Lib Dem	7,167	12	11	21	Beverley Hill
Majority	7,276	Con 12	Con 7	Con 17	
Swing			5 → Lab	6 → Lab	Lab needs 6 to win. 75th on Lab list

BLACKPOOL SOUTH, Lancashire. Tory marginal, seaside, working class
Long-term ill 17% (25th); No central heating 39% (28th); Private tenants 13% (47th)

35% change	Notional 92	%	92	87	Candidates
Conservative	25,957	44	45	48	Richard Booth, self-employed businessman
Labour	25,563	43	41	32	Gordon Marsden, editor of *History Today*
Lib Dem	7,148	12	13	20	Doreen Holt
Majority	394	Con 1	Con 4	Con 16	
Swing			6 → Lab	5 → Lab	Lab needs 0.3 to win. 8th on Lab list

BLAENAU GWENT, Gwent. Safest Labour seat, ex-mining, Michael Foot and Nye Bevan were MPs
Long-term ill 21% (4th); Unskilled 9% (7th); White 99.5% (41st)

No Change	Actual 92	%		87	Candidates
Conservative	4,266	10		12	Margrit Williams, global investment strategist
Labour	34,333	79		76	Llew Smith, MP
Lib Dem	2,774	6		9	Geraldine Layton
Plaid Cymru	2,099	5		4	
Majority	30,067	Lab 69		Lab 64	
Swing		2 → Lab		3 → Lab	

BLAYDON, Tyne and Wear. Strong Labour seat, ex-mining, partly rural
White 99.5% (53rd); Long-term ill 16% (72nd); Age 40-pension 29% (88th)

No Change	Actual 92	%		87	Candidates
Conservative	13,685	27		24	Mark Watson
Labour	27,028	53		50	John McWilliam, MP
Lib Dem	10,602	21		26	Peter Maughan
Majority	13,343	Lab 26		Lab 25	
Swing		No swing		3 → Lab	

BLYTH VALLEY, Northumberland. Labour seat, ex-mining, part new town
Govt schemes 3% (38th); White 99.4% (67th); Council tenants 28% (106th)

No Change	Actual 92	%		87	Candidates
Conservative	7,691	16		17	Barbara Musgrave
Labour	24,542	50		43	Ronnie Campbell, MP
Lib Dem	16,498	34		41	
Majority	8,044	Lab 16		Lab 2	
Swing		7 → Lab		3 → SDPAll	LD needs 8 to win. 45th on LD list

BOGNOR REGIS & LITTLEHAMPTON, West Sussex. Strong Tory seat, seaside, pensioners, based on Arundel
Pensionable 30% (8th); Second homes 2% (36th); Owner-occupied 80% (50th)

18% change	Notional 92	%	92	87	Candidates
Conservative	28,316	57	58	61	Nick Gibb, tax consultant, senior manager
Labour	6,700	14	14	11	Roger Nash
Lib Dem	13,309	27	26	28	James Walsh
Majority	15,007	Con 30	Con 33	Con 34	
Swing			1 → LD	2 → Con	

BOLSOVER, Derbyshire. Strong Labour seat, ex-mining, skilled manual
Skilled manual 41% (8th); White 99.5% (36th); Long-term ill 16% (48th)

0.1% change	Notional 92	%	92	87	Candidates
Conservative	13,339	25	25	28	Richard Harwood, barrister
Labour	34,018	65	65	56	Dennis Skinner, MP
Lib Dem	5,374	10	10	16	Ian Cox
Majority	20,679	Lab 39	Lab 39	Lab 28	
Swing			6 → Lab	1 → Con	

BOLTON NORTH EAST, Greater Manchester. Labour marginal, Tory target seat, industrial, urban
Asian 7% (58th); Long-term ill 14% (121st); Age 16-24 13% (139th)

16% change	Notional 92	%	92	87	Candidates
Conservative	23,477	42	45	44	Robert Wilson, director of PR company
Labour	26,494	48	45	43	David Crausby, engineer
Lib Dem	5,638	10	10	13	Edmund Critchley
Majority	3,017	Lab 5	Con 0.4	Con 2	
Swing			1 → Lab	2 → Lab	Con need 3 to win. 40th on Con list

BOLTON SOUTH EAST, Greater Manchester. Strong Labour seat, industrial, large Asian community
Unskilled 8% (27th); Asian 12% (38th); Skilled manual 35% (50th)

0.2 % change	Notional 92	%	92	87	Candidates
Conservative	14,192	29	29	31	Paul Carter, company director
Labour	26,863	54	54	54	Brian Iddon
Lib Dem	5,236	11	11	15	Frank Harasiwka
Majority	12,671	Lab 26	Lab 26	Lab 23	
Swing			1 → Lab	3 → Lab	

BOLTON WEST, Greater Manchester. Tory marginal, Labour target seat, residential
Owner-occupied 79% (73rd); Managerial 35% (156th); Professional 8% (164th)

13% change	Notional 92	%	92	87	Candidates
Conservative	24,619	47	44	44	Tom Sackville, MP
Labour	20,338	39	43	36	Ruth Kelly, economist
Lib Dem	6,862	13	13	20	Barbara Ronson
Majority	4,281	Con 8	Con 2	Con 8	
Swing			3 → Lab	3 → Lab	Lab needs 4 to win. 55th on Lab list

BOOTLE, Merseyside. 3rd safest Labour seat, inner city, high unemployment
Govt schemes 3% (8th); No central heating 45% (9th); Unskilled 9% (10th)

13% change	Notional 92	%	92	87	Candidates
Conservative	6,130	14	16	20	Rupert Mathews, freelance writer
Labour	33,250	77	75	67	Joe Benton, MP
Lib Dem	2,812	7	7	13	Kiron Reid
Majority	27,120	Lab 62	Lab 59	Lab 47	
Swing			6 → Lab	9 → Lab	

BOSTON & SKEGNESS, Lincolnshire. Strong Tory seat, mainly rural, working class
Pensionable 23% (49th); Self-employed 15% (91st); White 99.3% (107th)

73% change	Notional 92	%	92	87	Candidates
Conservative	25,721	51	55		Sir Richard Body, MP
Labour	14,299	28	29		Phil McCauley
Lib Dem	10,613	21	16		Jim Dodsworth
Majority	11,422	Con 23	Con 26	Con 37	
Swing			6 → Lab	6 → Con	

BOSWORTH, Leicestershire. Strong Tory seat, commuting
Owner-occupied 81% (34th); Skilled manual 32% (124th); Age 40-pensionable 28% (132nd)

18% change	Notional 92	%	92	87	Candidates
Conservative	28,863	52	54	54	David Tredinnick, MP
Labour	14,732	26	26	17	Andrew Furlong
Lib Dem	11,576	21	19	27	Jonathan Ellis
Majority	14,131	Con 25	Con 28	Con 27	
Swing			5 → Lab	2 → LibAll	

BOURNEMOUTH EAST, Dorset. Strong Tory seat, seaside, professional
Private tenants 16% (22nd); Pensionable 26% (23rd); Mobility 13% (52nd)

17% change	Notional 92	%	92	87	Candidates
Conservative	25,558	56	56	58	David Atkinson, MP
Labour	5,916	13	14	11	Jessica Stevens
Lib Dem	14,315	31	29	31	Douglas Eyre, councillor, chartered accountant
Majority	11,243	Con 24	Con 27	Con 28	
Swing			No swing	2 → Con	

BOURNEMOUTH WEST, Dorset. Strong Tory seat, seaside, retirement
Pensionable 30% (9th); Second homes 2% (20th); Mobility 14% (32nd)

50% change	Notional 92	%	92	87	Candidates
Conservative	24,532	53	53	55	John Butterfill, MP
Labour	9,110	20	17	13	Dennis Gritt
Lib Dem	12,815	27	30	32	Janet Dover, councillor, own employment agen
Majority	11,717	Con 25	Con 22	Con 23	
Swing			No swing	2 → SDPAll	

BRACKNELL, Berkshire. Strong Tory seat, partly new town, professional, based on Berkshire
Car owners 82% (42nd); Professional 11% (49th); Age 25-39 25% (50th)

52% change	Notional 92	%	92	87	Candidates
Conservative	35,916	60	60	60	Andrew Mackay, MP
Labour	12,036	20	20	60	Anne Snelgrove
Lib Dem	11,511	19	21	25	Alan Hilliar
Majority	23,880	Con 40	Con 39	Con 35	
Swing			2 → Con	4 → Con	

BRADFORD NORTH, West Yorkshire. Labour seat, textile industry, large Asian community
No central heating 43% (15th); Asian 18% (18th); Overcrowding 5% (28th)

No Change	Actual 92	%		87	Candidates
Conservative	15,756	32		40	Rasjid Skinner, clinical psychologist
Labour	23,420	48		43	Terry Rooney, MP
Lib Dem	9,133	19		18	Terry Browne
Majority	7,664	Lab 16		Lab 3	
Swing		No swing		3 → Lab	

BRADFORD SOUTH, West Yorkshire. Labour marginal, Tory target seat, inner city, working class
No central heating 40% (23rd); Asian 6% (70th); Overcrowding 3% (84th)

No Change	Actual 92	%	94 by-	87	Candidates
Conservative	20,283	38	18	41	Anne Hawksworth, businesswom
Labour	25,185	48	55	41	Gerry Sutcliffe, MP
Lib Dem	7,243	14	24	18	Alex Wilson-Fletcher
Majority	4,902	Lab 9	Lab 31	Lab 1	
Swing		4 → Lab	14 → Lab	No swing	Con needs 5 to win, 71st on Con

BRADFORD WEST, West Yorkshire. Labour seat, inner city, strongly Asian, Max Madden MP standing down
Asian 32% (5th); Overcrowding 7% (8th); Age 16-24 15% (13th)

No Change	Actual 92	%		87	Candidates
Conservative	16,544	34		37	Mohammed Riaz, business consultant
Labour	26,046	53		52	
Lib Dem	5,150	11		11	Helen Wright
Majority	9,502	Lab 19		Lab 15	
Swing		2 → Lab		4 → Lab	

BRAINTREE, Essex. Strong Tory seat, mainly rural, white collar
Car owners 76% (165th); Self-employed 12% (208th); Age 25-39 22% (208th)

23% change	Notional 92	%	92	87	Candidates
Conservative	29,278	51	52	54	Tony Newton, MP
Labour	15,890	27	26	19	Alan Hurst
Lib Dem	12,039	21	21	27	Trevor Ellis
Majority	13,388	Con 23	Con 27	Con 28	
Swing			4 → Lab	2 → Con	

BRECON & RADNORSHIRE, Powys. Tory seat, 3-way marginal, mainly rural, Con gain in 92
Self-employed 25% (2nd); Second homes 2% (31st); Pensionable 23% (58th)

No Change	Actual 92	%		87	Candidates
Conservative	15,977	36		35	Jonathan Evans, MP
Labour	11,634	26		29	Christopher Mann, probation officer
Lib Dem	15,847	36		35	Richard Livsey, lecturer, ex-MP
Plaid Cymru	418			1	Steve Cornilus
Majority	130	Con 0.3		LibAll 0.1	
Swing		0.2 → Con		12 → LibAll	Lab needs 10 to win. 110th on Lab list
					LD need 0.2 to win. 1st on LD list

BRENT EAST, North London. Labour seat, urban, large non-white population
Private tenants 22% (5th); Other non-white 7% (6th); Black 16% (12th)

% change	Notional 92	%	92	87	Candidates
Conservative	13,365	37	37	38	Mark Francois, company director
Labour	19,314	53	53	43	Ken Livingstone, MP
Lib Dem	3,237	9	9	15	Ian Hunter
Majority	5,949	Lab 16	Lab 16	Lab 4	
Swing			6 → Lab	4 → Con	

BRENT NORTH, North London. Strong Tory seat, suburban, strongly Asian
Other non-white 9% (1st); White collar 19% (31st); Black 7% (34th)

16% change	Notional 92	%	92	87	Candidates
Conservative	21,660	57	56	60	Sir Rhodes Boyson, MP
Labour	11,430	30	32	25	Barry Gardiner
Lib Dem	3,999	11	10	15	Paul Lorber
Majority	10,230	Con 27	Con 24	Con 35	
Swing			5 → Lab	1 → Con	

BRENT SOUTH, North London. Strong Labour seat, urban, large non-white population
Black 26% (3rd); Overcrowding 8% (5th); Age 16-24 15% (27th)

16% change	Notional 92	%	92	87	Candidates
Conservative	11,651	31	31	32	Stewart Jackson, business banking manager
Labour	21,568	58	58	52	Paul Boateng, MP
Lib Dem	3,551	10	10	16	Julian Brazil
Majority	9,917	Lab 27	Lab 27	Lab 20	
Swing			4 → Lab	3 → Con	

BRENTFORD & ISLEWORTH, West London. Tory marginal, Labour target seat, urban, large Asian community
Age 25-39 27% (30th); Private tenants 14% (35th); White collar 18% (48th)

15% change	Notional 92	%	92	87	Candidates
Conservative	26,994	46	46	48	Nirj Deva, MP
Labour	25,319	43	42	33	Ann Keen, former nursing director
Lib Dem	5,962	10	11	18	Gareth Hartwell
Majority	1,675	Con 3	Con 4	Con 15	
Swing			5 → Lab	2 → Lab	Lab needs 1 to win. 19th on Lab list

BRENTWOOD & ONGAR, Essex. Strong Tory seat, commuting, managerial
Age 40-pension 31% (8th); Managerial 46% (13th); Car owners 81% (54th)

0.1 % change	Notional 92	%	92	87	Candidates
Conservative	32,187	58	58	61	Eric Pickles, MP
Labour	6,102	11	11	13	Marc Young
Lib Dem	17,012	31	31	25	Elizabeth Bottomley
Majority	15,175	Con 27	Con 27	Con 36	
Swing			4 → LD	4 → Con	

BRIDGEND, Mid Glamorgan. Labour seat, mainly urban
Long-term ill 16% (53rd); Owner-occupied 78% (91st); Pensionable 21% (127th)

No Change	Actual 92	%	87	Candidates
Conservative	16,817	36	38	David Davies, distribution manager
Labour	24,143	51	48	Win Griffiths, MP
Lib Dem	4,827	10	12	Andrew McKinlay
Plaid Cymru	1,301	3	2	John Ball
Majority	7,326	Lab 16	Lab 10	
Swing		3 → Lab	6 → Lab	

BRIDGWATER, Somerset. Tory seat, Lib Dem long-shot, mainly rural, working class
White 99.5% (29th); Self-employed 17% (45th); Pensionable 23% (65th)

No Change	Actual 92	%	87	Candidates
Conservative	26,610	47	52	Tom King, MP
Labour	12,365	22	18	Roger Lavers
Lib Dem	16,894	30	30	Michael Hoban, business dev. consultant
Majority	9,716	Con 17	Con 21	
Swing		2 → Lib Dem	1 → SDPAll	LD need 9 to win. 48th on LD list

BRIGG & GOOLE, Humberside. New Tory seat, Labour long-shot, mainly urban, skilled manual
Skilled manual 35% (48th); Unskilled 7% (49th); White 99.5% (52nd)

86% change	Notional 92	%	Candidates
Conservative	25,499	50	Donald Stewart, farmer
Labour	18,258	36	Ian Cawsey
Lib Dem	7,406	15	Mary-Rose Hardy
Majority	7,241	Con 14	Lab needs 7 to win. 83rd on Lab list

BRIGHTON KEMPTOWN, East Sussex. Strong Tory seat, seaside, white collar
Pensionable 24% (41st); Second homes 1% (66th); White collar 17% (81st)

41% change	Notional 92	%	92	87	Candidates
Conservative	26,828	53	48	54	Andrew Bowden, MP
Labour	16,571	33	41	33	Desmond Turner
Lib Dem	7,056	14	10	14	Clive Gray
Majority	10,257	Con 20	Con 7	Con 21	
Swing			7 → Lab	1 → Lab	

BRIGHTON PAVILION, East Sussex. Tory marginal, Labour target seat, seaside, middle-class, moving towards Lab
Mobility 15% (13th); Private tenants 18% (16th); Age 25-39 26% (38th)

14% change	Notional 92	%	92	87	Candidates
Conservative	22,619	45	47	51	Sir Derek Spencer, MP, QC
Labour	20,089	40	38	30	David Lepper, teacher
Lib Dem	6,169	12	13	20	Ken Blanshard
Majority	2,530	Con 5	Con 8	Con 21	
Swing			6 → Lab	3 → Lab	Lab needs 3 to win. 34th on Lab list

BRISTOL EAST, Avon. Labour marginal, Tory target seat, inner city, white collar, Lab gain in 92
Black 4% (64th); White collar 17% (72nd); Age 25-39 24% (86th)

43% change	Notional 92	%	92	87	Candidates
Conservative	20,472	38	39	44	Eddie Vaizey, barrister
Labour	25,754	47	45	35	Jean Corston, MP
Lib Dem	8,025	15	16	20	Peter Tyzack
Majority	5,282	Lab 10	Lab 5	Con 8	
Swing			7 → Lab	2 → Con	Con needs 5 to win. 74th on Con list

BRISTOL NORTH WEST, Avon. Currently Tory, on new boundaries Labour marginal, urban, working class
Council tenants 30% (76th); Unskilled 6% (93rd); Single parents 24% (108th)

23% change	Notional 92	%	92	87	Candidates
Conservative	23,148	39	42	47	Michael Stern, MP
Labour	27,019	45	42	35	Douglas Naysmith
Lib Dem	8,849	15	14	19	Ian Parry
Majority	3,871	Lab 7	Con 0.1	Con 12	
Swing			6 → Lab	0.4 → Con	Con need 3 to win. 46th on Con list

BRISTOL SOUTH, Avon. Labour seat, inner city, working class
Skilled manual 33% (96th); Council tenants 29% (96th); Age 25-39 23% (113th)

16% change	Notional 92	%	92	87	Candidates
Conservative	19,144	33	32	38	Michael Roe, computer consultant
Labour	27,259	47	50	41	Dawn Primarolo, MP
Lib Dem	10,361	18	16	20	Steven Williams
Majority	8,115	Lab 14	Lab 18	Lab 3	
Swing			8 → Lab	3 → Con	

BRISTOL WEST, Avon. Tory seat, Lib Dem long-shot, inner city, university, professional
Professional 18% (2nd); Mobility 18% (4th); Private tenants 20% (9th)

12% change	Notional 92	%	92	87	Candidates
Conservative	26,850	45	42	46	William Waldegrave, MP
Labour	13,900	23	25	21	Valerie Davey
Lib Dem	17,356	29	31	31	Charles Boney, teacher
Majority	9,494	Con 16	Con 12	Con 14	
Swing			1 → LD	3 → LibAll	LD need 8 to win. 44th on LD list

BROMLEY & CHISLEHURST, South London. Strong Tory seat, outer suburbs, middle-class
White collar 19% (24th); Managerial 43% (35th); Age 40-pension 29% (90th)

82% change	Notional 92	%	92	87	Candidates
Conservative	36,028	62	58	58	Eric Forth, MP
Labour	10,027	17	22	19	Rob Yeldham
Lib Dem	10,370	18	16	23	Paul Booth, councillor
Majority	25,658	Con 44	Con 36	Con 35	
Swing			1 → Lab	2 → Con	

BROMSGROVE, Hereford and Worcester. Strong Tory seat, commuting, managerial
Age 40-pension 30% (20th); Car owners 80% (85th); Managerial 37% (114th)

0.2% change	Notional 92	%	92	87	Candidates
Conservative	31,773	54	54	55	Julie Kirkbride, journalist
Labour	18,021	31	31	23	Peter McDonald
Lib Dem	8,118	14	14	22	Jennette Davy
Majority	13,752	Con 23	Con 23	Con 31	
Swing			4 → Lab	2 → Lab	

BROXBOURNE, Hertfordshire. Strong Tory seat, stockbroker belt, white collar
Age 40-pension 29% (61st); Owner-occupied 79% (70th); Car owners 80% (86th)

9% change	Notional 92	%	92	87	Candidates
Conservative	32,518	62	63	63	Marion Roe, MP
Labour	11,168	21	21	17	Ben Coleman
Lib Dem	8,353	16	16	20	Julia Davies
Majority	21,350	Con 41	Con 42	Con 43	
Swing			2 → Lab	4 → Con	

BROXTOWE, Nottinghamshire. Tory seat, Labour long-shot, suburban
Owner-occupied 78% (86th); Age 40-pension 29% (113th); Professional 9% (128th)

0.2% change	Notional 92	%	92	87	Candidates
Conservative	31,033	51	51	54	Jim Lester, MP
Labour	21,162	35	35	24	Nick Palmer
Lib Dem	8,378	14	14	22	Terence Miller
Majority	9,871	Con 16	Con 16	Con 29	
Swing			7 → Lab	1 → Lab	Lab needs 8 to win. 94th on Lab list

BUCKINGHAM, Buckinghamshire. Strong Tory seat, mainly rural, professional
Car owners 86% (5th); Managerial 44% (23rd); Age 40-pension 30% (28th)

6% change	Notional 92	%	92	87	Candidates
Conservative	31,045	62	63	59	John Bercow, account director, public affairs
Labour	7,999	16	16	17	Robert Lehmann
Lib Dem	10,401	21	21	25	Neil Stuart
Majority	20,644	Con 41	Con 42	Con 34	
Swing			4 → Con	3 → Con	

BURNLEY, Lancashire. Strong Labour seat, industrial, working class
Long-term ill 16% (49th); No central heating 30% (69th); Asian 5% (90th)

No Change	Actual 92	%		87	Candidates
Conservative	15,693	31		34	Bill Wiggin
Labour	27,184	53		48	Peter Pike, MP
Lib Dem	8,414	16		18	Gordon Birtwistle
Majority	11,491	Lab 22		Lab 15	
Swing		4 → Lab		7 → Lab	

BURTON, Staffordshire. Tory marginal, Labour target seat, brewing industry, working class
No central heating 29% (77th); Skilled manual 34% (86th); Unskilled 6% (126th)

5% change	Notional 92	%	92	87	Candidates
Conservative	28,454	48	50	51	Sir Ivan Lawrence, MP
Labour	24,327	41	40	34	Janet Dean, Mayor of East Staffordshire
Lib Dem	6,219	11	10	16	David Fletcher
Majority	4,127	Con 7	Con 10	Con 17	
Swing			4 → Lab	2 → Lab	Lab needs 4 to win. 46th on Lab list

BURY NORTH, Greater Manchester. Tory marginal, Labour target seat, urban
Owner-occupied 79% (72nd); Asian 3% (125th); Age 40-pension 28% (155th)

No Change	Actual 92	%		87	Candidates
Conservative	29,266	50		50	Alistair Burt, MP
Labour	24,502	42		38	David Chaytor, councillor, former college lecturer
Lib Dem	5,010	9		12	Neville Kenyon
Majority	4,764	Con 8		Con 12	
Swing		2 → Lab		4 → Con	Lab needs 4 to win. 54th on Lab list

BURY SOUTH, Greater Manchester. Tory marginal, 11th on Labour target list, mainly urban
White collar 15% (131st); Age 25-39 23% (155th); Owner-occupied 75% (174th)

0.4% change	Notional 92	%	92	87	Candidates
Conservative	24,925	46	46	46	David Sumberg, MP
Labour	24,197	45	45	41	Ivan Lewis, chief executive, Jewish Social Service
Lib Dem	4,853	9	9	13	Victor D'Albert
Majority	728	Con 1	Con 2	Con 5	
Swing			2 → Lab	1 → Lab	Lab needs 1 to win. 11th on Lab list

BURY ST EDMUNDS, Suffolk. Tory seat, Lib Dem long-shot, mainly rural, middle-class
Mobility 12% (84th); Car owners 78% (120th); Second homes .4% (127th)

97% change	Notional 92	%	92	87	Candidates
Conservative	25,742	46	54	59	David Ruffley, political consultant
Labour	14,565	26	24	17	Mark Ereira-Guyer
Lib Dem	15,097	27	22	22	David Cooper, charity worker for TEAR Fund
Majority	10,645	Con 19	Con 30	Con 38	
Swing			6 → Lab	4 → Con	Lab needs 10 to win. 118th on Lab list
					LD needs 10 to win. 63rd on LD list

CAERNARFON, Gwynedd. Strong Plaid Cymru seat, Welsh-speaking
Second homes 8% (2nd); White 99.6% (17th); Self-employed 19% (27th)

No Change	Actual 92	%		87	Candidates
Conservative	6,963	19		21	Elwyn Williams
Labour	5,641	16		16	Eifion Williams
Lib Dem	2,101	6		6	
Plaid Cymru	21,439	59		57	Dafydd Wigley, MP
Majority	14,476	PIC 40		PIC 36	
Swing		2 → PIC		2 → PIC	

CAERPHILLY, Mid Glamorgan. Strong Labour seat, ex-mining, working class
Long-term ill 19% (11th); Skilled manual 34% (82nd); Unemployed 13% (100th)

No Change	Actual 92	%		87	Candidates
Conservative	9,041	18		19	Rhodri Harris, accountant
Labour	31,713	64		58	Ron Davies, MP
Lib Dem	4,247	9		14	Tony Ferguson
Plaid Cymru	4,821	10		8	Lindsay Whittle
Majority	22,672	Lab 46		Lab 39	
Swing		3 → Lab		7 → Lab	

CAITHNESS, SUTHERLAND & EASTER ROSS, Highland. Strong Lib Dem seat, rural

33% change	Notional 92	%	92	87	Candidates
Conservative	6,391	22	21	17	Tom Miers
Labour	4,629	16	16	15	James Hendry
Lib Dem	13,150	44	45	54	Robert Maclennan, MP
SNP	5,440	18	18	10	Euan Harper, councillor
Majority	6,759	LD 23	LD 24	LD 37	
Swing			6 → Con	4 → SPDAll	

CALDER VALLEY, West Yorkshire. Tory marginal, Labour target seat, mainly rural
No central heating 31% (62nd); Owner-occupied 76% (149th); Managerial 36% (150th)

No Change	Actual 92	%		87	Candidates
Conservative	27,753	45		44	Sir Donald Thompson, MP
Labour	22,875	37		33	Christine McCafferty, health centre manager, councillor
Lib Dem	9,842	16		23	Stephen Pearson, councillor
Majority	4,878	Con 8		Con 10	
Swing		1 → Lab		3 → Lab	Lab needs 4 to win. 52nd on Lab list

CAMBERWELL & PECKHAM, South London. Strong Labour seat, inner city, high unemployment
Council tenants 60% (1st); Black 27% (1st); Unskilled 10% (2nd)

35% change	Notional 92	%	92	87	Candidates
Conservative	7,841	24	24	26	Kim Humphreys, manager, overseas banking, councillor
Labour	19,891	60	62	55	Harriet Harman, MP
Lib Dem	4,974	15	14	18	Nigel Williams
Majority	12,050	Lab 37	Lab 38	Lab 29	
Swing			5 → Lab	1 → Lab	

CAMBRIDGE, Cambridgeshire. Labour marginal, Tory target seat, university, professional, Lab gain in 92
Professional 17% (3rd); Mobility 17% (6th); Age 16-24 15% (18th)

No Change	Actual 92	%		87	Candidates
Conservative	19,459	39		40	Martin Humphrys, teacher
Labour	20,039	40		28	Anne Campbell, MP
Lib Dem	10,037	20		31	Geoffrey Heathcock
Majority	580	Lab 1		Con 9	
Swing		5 → Lab		1 → SDPAll	Con need 1 to win. 7th on Con list

CAMBRIDGESHIRE NORTH EAST, Cambridgeshire. Strong Tory seat, rural, working class
Skilled manual 34% (74th); Self-employed 15% (92nd); Pensionable 21% (121st)

8% change	Notional 92	%	92	87	Candidates
Conservative	31,168	54	54	47	Malcolm Moss, MP
Labour	7,928	14	14	9	Virginia Bucknor
Lib Dem	18,007	31	30	45	Andrew Nash, social worker
Majority	13,161	Con 23	Con 24	Con 3	
Swing			11 → Con	6 → Con	

CAMBRIDGESHIRE NORTH WEST, Cambridgeshire. New strong Tory seat, rural, managerial
Mobility 13% (46th); Age 25-39 24% (83rd); Car owners 79% (103rd)

88% change	Notional 92	%	Candidates
Conservative	32,170	62	Dr Brian Mawhinney, MP
Labour	13,361	26	Lee Steptoe
Lib Dem	4,503	9	Barbara McCoy
Majority	18,809	Con 37	

CAMBRIDGESHIRE SOUTH, Cambridgeshire. Strong Tory seat, rural, professional
Professional 15% (5th); Car owners 83% (33rd); Age 40-pension 29% (77th)

49% change	Notional 92	%	92	87	Candidates
Conservative	32,914	59	57	58	Andrew Lansley, former director, Con Central Office
Labour	8,624	15	14	13	Tony Gray
Lib Dem	13,976	25	28	29	James Quinlan
Majority	18,938	Con 34	Con 29	Con 29	
Swing			No swing	2 → Con	

CAMBRIDGESHIRE SOUTH EAST, Cambridgeshire. Strong Tory seat, rural, professional
Car owners 82% (44th); Mobility 12% (61st); Professional 10% (84th)

23% change	Notional 92	%	92	87	Candidates
Conservative	33,080	58	58	59	Jim Paice, MP
Labour	11,205	20	20	14	Rex Collinson
Lib Dem	12,217	21	20	28	Sal Brinton
Majority	20,863	Con 36	Con 38	Con 31	
Swing			3 → Con	2 → Con	

CANNOCK CHASE, Staffordshire. Labour seat, ex-mining, working class
Skilled manual 40% (9th); Age 16-24 14% (97th); Govt schemes 2% (102nd)

60% change	Notional 92	%	92	87	Candidates
Conservative	22,790	38	44	45	John Backhouse, managing director, management
Labour	29,259	49	46	40	Dr Tony Wright, MP
Lib Dem	7,283	12	10	16	David Sanders
Majority	6,469	Lab 11	Lab 3	Con 5	
Swing			4 → Lab	1 → Con	

CANTERBURY, Kent. Tory seat, Lib Dem long-shot, mainly rural, university, middle-class
Pensionable 23% (50th); Second homes 1% (80th); Mobility 11% (117th)

4% change	Notional 92	%	92	87	Candidates
Conservative	28,290	50	51	54	Julian Brazier, MP
Labour	8,635	15	15	17	Cheryl Hall
Lib Dem	18,293	33	32	27	Martin Vye, retired schoolmaster
Majority	9,997	Con 18	Con 18	Con 27	
Swing			4 → LD	2 → LibAll	LD need 9 to win. 54th on LD list

CARDIFF CENTRAL, South Glamorgan. Labour marginal, Tory target seat, inner city, residential, middle-class, Lab gain in 92
Age 16-24 17% (1st); Private tenants 18% (18th); Mobility 14% (26th)

No Change	Actual 92	%		87	Candidates
Conservative	14,549	34		37	David Melding, deputy director, Int. affairs for Wales
Labour	18,014	42		32	Jon Owen Jones, MP
Lib Dem	9,170	21		29	Jenny Randerson, college lecturer
Plaid Cymru	748	2		1	Wayne Vernon
Majority	3,465	Lab 8		Con 5	
Swing		7 → Lab		6 → Lab	

CARDIFF NORTH, South Glamorgan. Tory marginal, Labour target seat, suburban, middle-class
Owner-occupied 83% (19th); Professional 13% (21st); White collar 18% (51st)

No Change	Actual 92	%		87	Candidates
Conservative	21,547	45		45	Gwilym Jones, MP
Labour	18,578	39		27	Julie Morgan, asst director of childcare
Lib Dem	6,487	14		27	Robyn Rowland
Plaid Cymru	916	2		2	Colin Palfrey
Majority	2,969	Con 6		Con 19	
Swing		6 → Lab		4 → Lab	Lab needs 3 to win. 40th on Lab list

CARDIFF SOUTH & PENARTH, South Glamorgan. Strong Labour seat, inner city, white collar
Single parents 28% (58th); Unemployed 13% (89th); White collar 17% (71st)

No Change	Actual 92	%		87	Candidates
Conservative	15,958	34		37	Caroline Roberts, public affairs director
Labour	26,383	56		47	Alun Michael, MP
Lib Dem	3,707	8		15	John Dixon
Plaid Cymru	776	2		1	David Haswell
Majority	10,425	Lab 22		Con 10	
Swing		6 → Lab		2 → Lab	

CARDIFF WEST, South Glamorgan. Strong Labour seat, inner city
Single parents 28% (57th); No central heating 27% (92nd); Overcrowding 3% (99th)

1% change	Notional 92	%	92	87	Candidates
Conservative	15,028	33	33	37	Simon Hoare, media and PR manager
Labour	24,319	53	53	46	Rhodri Morgan, MP
Lib Dem	5,005	11	11	16	Jacqui Gasson
Plaid Cymru	1,178	3	3	2	Gwenllian Carr
Majority	9,291	Lab 20	Lab 20	Lab 9	
Swing			6 < Lab	7 < Lab	

CARLISLE, Cumbria. Labour marginal, Tory target seat, mainly urban, working class
Skilled manual 34% (68th); No central heating 28% (79th); Unskilled 6% (87th)

9% change	Notional 92	%	92	87	Candidates
Conservative	19,746	41	40	40	Richard Lawrence, marketing consultant
Labour	21,667	45	47	42	Eric Martlew, MP
Lib Dem	6,232	13	13	18	
Majority	1,921	Lab 4	Lab 7	Lab 2	
Swing			3 → Lab	1 → Lab	Con need 2 to win. 31st on Con list

CARMARTHEN EAST & DINEFWR, Dyfed. New Labour seat, PLC second, mainly rural, Welsh-speaking
Self-employed 25% (7th); White 99.5% (25th); Long-term ill 17% (30th)

40% change	Notional 92	%	92	87	Candidates
Conservative	8,953	20	22	27	Edmund Hayward, self-employed business consultant
Labour	18,305	42	37	35	Dr Alan Wynne Williams, MP
Lib Dem	4,023	9	9	13	Juliana Hughes
Plaid Cymru	12,815	29	32	23	Rhodri Glyn Thomas
Majority	5,490	Lab 13	Lab 5	Lab 8	
Swing			4 → PLC	3 → Lab	Con need 2 to win. 21st on Con list
					PIC needs 6 to win. 1st on PIC list

CARMARTHEN WEST & PEMBROKESHIRE, Dyfed. New Labour marginal, mainly urban
Self-employed 22% (15th); Second homes 1% (42nd); Govt schemes 2% (50th)

85% change	Notional 92	%	Candidates
Conservative	15,278	36	Owen Williams, energy distribution company chairman
Labour	16,588	39	Nicholas Ainger, MP
Lib Dem	4,672	11	Keith Evans
Plaid Cymru	6,497	15	Roy Llewellyn
Majority	1,310	Lab 3	Con need 2 to win. 21st on Con list

CARRICK, CUMNOCK & DOON VALLEY, Strathclyde. Strong Labour seat, ex-mining

20% change	Notional 92	%	92	87	Candidates
Conservative	13,271	26	20	21	Alasdair Marshall
Labour	27,957	54	59	60	George Foulkes, MP
Lib Dem	2,690	5	5	10	Derek Young
SNP	7,802	15	16	10	Christine Hutchison
Majority	14,686	Lab 28	Lab 39	Lab 39	
Swing			No Swing	6 → Lab	

CARSHALTON & WALLINGTON, South London. Tory seat, Lib Dem long-shot, outer suburbs, white collar
White collar 20% (15th); Other non-white 2% (83rd); Black 2% (118th)

No Change	Actual 92	%	87	Candidates
Conservative	26,243	50	54	Nigel Forman, MP
Labour	9,333	18	18	Andrew Theobald
Lib Dem	16,300	31	26	Thomas Brake, software consultant
Majority	9,943	Con 19	Con 28	
Swing		3 → Lib Dem	3 → Con	LD need 9 to win. 61st on LD list

CASTLE POINT, Essex. Strong Tory seat, commuting, white collar
Owner-occupied 90% (2nd); Age 40-pension 30% (24th); White collar 16% (96th)

No Change	Actual 92	%	92	87	Candidates
Conservative	29,629	56		60	Dr Robert Spink, MP
Labour	12,799	24		19	Christine Butler
Lib Dem	10,208	19		21	David Baker
Majority	16,830	Con 32		Con 39	
Swing		5 → Lab		3 → Con	

CEREDIGION, Dyfed. Plaid Cymru marginal, Lib Dem target seat, rural, Welsh-speaking, PLC gain in 92
Self-employed 27% (1st); Second homes 3% (9th); Govt schemes 2% (52nd)

20% change	Notional 92	%	92	87	Candidates
Conservative	10,178	24	25	27	Dr Felix Aubel, lecturer, Welsh independent minist…
Labour	7,889	19	19	19	Robert Harris
Lib Dem	11,251	27	25	37	Dai Davies, chartered accountant
Plaid Cymru	13,144	31	31	16	Cynog Dafis, MP
Majority	1,893	5	PIC 6	LD 10	
Swing		13 → PIC		1 → Con	Con need 3 to win. 48th on Con list
					Lab needs 8 to win. 92nd on Lab list
					LD need 2 to win. 8th on LD list

CHARNWOOD, Leicestershire. New strong Tory seat, commuting, managerial
Owner-occupied 86% (4th); Age 40-pension 30% (35th); Car owners 82% (46th)

133% change	Notional 92	%	Candidates
Conservative	35,126	61	Stephen Dorrell, MP
Labour	12,526	22	David Knaggs
Lib Dem	10,345	18	Roger Wilson
Majority	22,600	Con 39	

CHATHAM & AYLESFORD, Kent. New strong Tory seat, mainly rural, white collar
Age 25-39 26% (43rd); Owner-occupied 79% (64th); Age 16-24 14% (76th)

75% change	Notional 92	%	Candidates
Conservative	28,056	51	Richard Knox-Johnston, actuarial consultant
Labour	14,633	27	Jonathon Shaw
Lib Dem	11,643	21	Robin Murray
Majority	13,423	Con 25	

CHEADLE, Greater Manchester. Strong Tory seat, commuting, professional
Owner-occupied 88% (3rd); Age 40-pension 31% (9th); Professional 14% (11th)

2% change	Notional 92	%	92	87	Candidates
Conservative	32,804	58	58	55	Stephen Day, MP
Labour	7,080	12	12	9	Paul Diggett
Lib Dem	16,828	30	30	36	Patsy Calton
Majority	15,976	Con 28	Con 28	Con 19	
Swing			5 → Con	No swing	

CHELMSFORD WEST, Essex. New strong Tory seat, mainly rural, professional
Professional 11% (54th); Age 25-39 24% (85th); White collar 16% (88th)

45% change	Notional 92	%	92	87	Candidates
Conservative	34,284	55	55	52	Simon Burns
Labour	9,443	15	14	7	Roy Chad
Lib Dem	18,098	29	29	41	Martin Bracken, senior treasury manager
Majority	16,186	Con 26	Con 26	Con 11	
Swing			7 → Con	5 → Con	

CHELTENHAM, Gloucestershire. Lib Dem marginal, Tory target seat, mainly urban, white collar, Lib Dem gain in 92
White collar 18% (37th); Mobility 13% (41st); Private tenants 11% (77th)

16% change	Notional 92	%	92	87	Candidates
Conservative	24,861	44	45	50	John Todman
Labour	3,769	7	6	8	Barry Leach
Lib Dem	26,808	48	47	42	Nigel Jones, MP
Majority	1,947	LD 4	LD 3	Con 8	
Swing			5 → Lib Dem	1 → LibAll	Con need 2 to win. 25th on Con list

CHESHAM & AMERSHAM, Buckinghamshire. Strong Tory seat, stockbroker belt, managerial
Age 40-pension 32% (1st); Managerial 48% (4th); Car owners 85% (8th)

5% change	Notional 92	%	92	87	Candidates
Conservative	35,207	63	63	62	Cheryl Gillan, MP
Labour	5,758	10	10	9	Paul Farrelly
Lib Dem	13,606	25	25	27	Michael Brand
Majority	21,601	Con 39	Con 39	Con 35	
Swing			2 → Con	3 → Con	

CHESTER, CITY OF, Cheshire. Tory marginal, Labour target seat, mainly urban, middle-class
Professional 10% (71st); Pensionable 20% (159th); Private tenants 8% (164th)

8% change	Notional 92	%	92	87	Candidates
Conservative	25,641	45	44	45	Gyles Brandreth, MP
Labour	23,281	41	42	36	Christine Russell, advocacy project co-ordinator, MIND
Lib Dem	7,808	14	13	20	David Simpson
Majority	2,360	Con 4	Con 2	Con 9	
Swing			4 → Lab	5 → Lab	Lab needs 2 to win. 27th on Lab list

CHESTERFIELD, Derbyshire. Labour seat, ex-mining, skilled manual
Skilled manual 34% (70th); Govt schemes 2% (97th); Council tenants 27% (107th)

No Change	Actual 92	%		87	Candidates
Conservative	9,473	17		25	Martin Potter, financial analyst
Labour	26,461	47		46	Tony Benn, MP
Lib Dem	20,047	36		30	Tony Rogers, professional interviewer
Majority	6,414	Lab 12		Lab 16	
Swing		2 → Lib Dem		6 → LibAll	LD need 6 to win. 27th on LD list

CHICHESTER, West Sussex. Strong Tory seat, mainly rural, middle-class
Second homes 3% (15th); Pensionable 27% (17th); Self-employed 18% (40th)

8% change	Notional 92	%	92	87	Candidates
Conservative	34,971	59	59	62	Anthony Nelson, MP
Labour	6,703	11	11	8	Andrew Emerson
Lib Dem	15,690	27	27	28	Peter Gardiner
Majority	19,281	Con 33	Con 33	Con 34	
Swing			No Swing	1 → LibAll	

CHINGFORD & WOODFORD GREEN, North London. New strong Tory seat, commuting, white collar
White collar 19% (18th); Black 3% (84th); Other non-white 2% (109th)

42% change	Notional 92	%	92	87	Candidates
Conservative	30,656	61	59	62	Iain Duncan-Smith, MP
Labour	10,455	21	25	15	Tommy Hutchinson
Lib Dem	7,154	14	13	21	Geoffrey Seeff
Majority	20,201	Con 41	Con 34	Con 41	
Swing			6 → Lab	5 → Con	

CHIPPING BARNET, North London. Strong Tory seat, commuting, middle-class
Managerial 44% (21st); Professional 12% (29th); Other non-white 4% (38th)

19% change	Notional 92	%	92	87	Candidates
Conservative	30,241	57	57	58	Sir Sydney Chapman, MP, RIBA, FRTPI
Labour	14,028	26	26	19	Geoff Cooke
Lib Dem	8,594	16	16	23	Sean Hooker
Majority	16,213	Con 30	Con 31	Con 35	
Swing			4 → Lab	2 → Con	

CHORLEY, Lancashire. Tory marginal, Labour target seat, mainly urban
Owner-occupied 79% (60th); Age 40-pension 28% (172nd); Managerial 34% (180th)

7% change	Notional 92	%	92	87	Candidates
Conservative	27,752	46	47	48	Den Dover, MP
Labour	25,228	42	41	35	Lindsay Hoyle, director, printing company
Lib Dem	7,249	12	12	16	
Majority	2,524	Con 4	Con 7	Con 13	
Swing			3 → Lab	2 → Lab	Lab needs 2 to win. 28th on Lab list

CHRISTCHURCH, Dorset. Strong Tory seat won by Lib Dems in 1993 by-election, seaside, middle-class
Pensionable 34% (4th); Owner-occupied 85% (7th); Second homes 1% (44th)

5% change	Notional 92	%	93 by-	92	87	Candidates
Conservative	35,237	64	31	64	66	Christopher Chope, ex-MP
Labour	6,678	12	3	12	10	Charles Mannam
Lib Dem	12,913	23	62	24	25	Diana Maddock, MP
Majority	22,324	Con 40	LD 31	Con 40	Con 41	
Swing			35 → LD	1 → LD	No swing	

CITIES OF LONDON & WESTMINSTER, Central London. Strong Tory seat, inner city, middle-class
Mobility 24% (1st); Private tenants 32% (2nd); Other non-white 9% (2nd)

20% change	Notional 92	%	92	87	Candidates
Conservative	25,512	59	60	58	Peter Brooke, MP
Labour	10,368	24	22	20	Kate Green
Lib Dem	6,077	14	16	22	Michael Dumigan
Majority	15,144	Con 35	Con 39	Con 36	
Swing			1 → Con	1 → SDPAll	

CLEETHORPES, Humberside. Tory seat, Labour long-shot, seaside, part of Brigg & Cleethorpes
Skilled manual 33% (100th); Age 40-pension 29% (122nd); Unskilled 6% (133rd)

17% change	Notional 92	%	92	87	Candidates
Conservative	25,582	48	49	49	Michael Brown, MP
Labour	19,169	36	35	23	Shona McIsaac, freelance journalist, councillor
Lib Dem	7,833	15	15	29	Keith Melton
Majority	6,413	Con 12	Con 14	Con 20	
Swing			6 → Lab	1 → LibAll	Lab needs 6 to win. 74th on Lab list

CLWYD SOUTH, Clwyd. Labour seat, partly Welsh-speaking, rural, working class
White 99.5% (27th); Govt schemes 3% (34th); Skilled manual 35% (54th)

68% change	Notional 92	%	92	87	Candidates
Conservative	12,897	30	34	33	Boris Johnson, journalist
Labour	21,229	50	44	35	Martyn Jones, MP
Lib Dem	4,727	11	12	23	Andrew Chadwick
Plaid Cymru	3,394	8	10	9	Gareth Williams
Majority	8,332	Lab 20	Lab 10	Lab 2	
Swing			4 → Lab	4 → LibAll	

CLWYD WEST, Clwyd. Tory seat, Labour long-shot, rural, seaside
Pensionable 27% (18th); Self-employed 20% (21st); Second homes 1% (50th)

66% change	Notional 92	%	92	87	Candidates
Conservative	20,132	49	46	49	Roderick Richards, MP
Labour	12,819	31	35	25	Gareth Thomas
Lib Dem	6,526	16	15	23	Gwyn Williams
Plaid Cymru	1,906	5	4	4	Eryl Williams
Majority	7,313	Con 18	Con 11	Con 24	
Swing			6 → Lab	6 → Lab	Lab needs 9 to win. 101st on Lab list
					PlC needs 26 to win. 7th on PlC list

CLYDEBANK & MILNGAVIE, Strathclyde. Strong Labour seat, shipbuilding

7% change	Notional 92	%	92	87	Candidates
Conservative	8,503	22	18	16	Nancy Morgan
Labour	19,923	50	53	57	Tony Worthington, MP
Lib Dem	3,778	10	9	15	Keith Moody
SNP	7,319	19	20	13	Jim Yuill
Majority	11,420	Lab 29	Lab 34	Lab 41	
Swing			5 < SNP	8 → Lab	

CLYDESDALE, Strathclyde. Strong Labour seat, ex-mining

No Change	Actual 92	%		87	Candidates
Conservative	11,231	23		24	Mark Izatt
Labour	21,418	45		45	Jimmy Hood, MP
Lib Dem	3,957	8		16	Sandra Grieve
SNP	11,084	23		15	Andrew Doig
Majority	10,187	Lab 21		Lab 22	
Swing		No swing		6 → Lab	SNP needs 11 to win. 17th on SNP list

COATBRIDGE & CHRYSTON, Strathclyde. Strong Labour seat, industrial, based on Monklands West

26% change	Notional 92	%	92	87	Candidates
Conservative	6,241	16	16	16	Andrew Wauchope
Labour	24,843	62	61	62	Tom Clarke, MP
Lib Dem	2,388	6	6	11	
SNP	6,743	17	17	11	Brian Nugent
Majority	18,100	Lab 45	Lab 45	Lab 47	
Swing			3 < SNP	7 → Lab	

COLCHESTER, Essex. New Tory seat, Lib Dem target seat, Labour long-shot, mainly urban
Age 16-24 15% (17th); Mobility 13% (34th); Other non-white 2% (111th)

81% change	Notional 92	%			Candidates
Conservative	23,692	42			Stephan Shakespeare, head of special needs
Labour	13,582	24			Roderick Green
Lib Dem	18,424	33			Bob Russell, publicity officer, University of Essex
Majority	5,268	Con 9			
Swing					Lab needs 9 to win. 103rd on Lab list
					LD need 5 to win. 18th on LD list

COLNE VALLEY, West Yorkshire. Tory seat, Labour long-shot, mainly urban
No central heating 36% (43rd); Owner-occupied 79% (65th); Asian 4% (113th)

No Change	Actual 92	%		87	Candidates
Conservative	24,804	42		36	Graham Riddick, MP
Labour	17,579	30		29	Kali Mountford, former civil servant, councillor
Lib Dem	15,953	27		33	Nigel Priestley, solicitor
Majority	7,225	Con 12		Con 3	
Swing		3 → Con		5 → Con	Lab needs 6 to win. 76th on Lab list
					LD need 8 to win. 40th on LD list

CONGLETON, Cheshire. Tory seat, Lib Dem long-shot, mainly rural, middle-class
Age 40-pension 30% (29th); Owner-occupied 81% (36th); Professional 10% (68th)

7% change	Notional 92	%	92	87	Candidates
Conservative	27,007	49	49	48	Ann Winterton, MP
Labour	10,684	19	20	18	Helen Scholey
Lib Dem	17,657	32	30	34	Joan Walmsley, PR consultant
Majority	9,350	Con 17	Con 19	Con 15	
Swing			2 → Con	1 → LibAll	LD need 8 to win. 46th on LD list

CONWY, Gwynedd. Tory marginal, Lib Dem target seat, Welsh-speaking, seaside
Pensionable 25% (28th); Second homes 1% (47th); No central heating 32% (56th)

No Change	Actual 92	%		87	Candidates
Conservative	14,250	34		39	David Jones, solicitor
Labour	10,883	26		22	Betty Williams, media researcher
Lib Dem	13,255	31		31	Roger Roberts, superintendent minister/broadcaster
Plaid Cymru	3,108	7		8	Rhodri Davies
Majority	995	Con 2		Con 7	
Swing		3 → Lib Dem		2 → LibAll	Lab needs 6 to win. 71st on Lab list
					LD need 1 to win. 6th on LD list

COPELAND, Cumbria. Labour marginal, Tory target seat, ex-mining, mainly rural, working class
White 99.6% (4th); Unskilled 7% (42nd) Second homes 1% (56th);

No Change	Actual 92	%		87	Candidates
Conservative	19,889	43		43	Andrew Cumpsty, communications officer
Labour	22,328	49		47	Dr Jack Cunningham, MP
Lib Dem	3,508	8		9	Roger Putnam
Majority	2,439	Lab 5		Lab 4	
Swing		1 → Lab		No swing	Con need 3 to win. 39th on Con list

CORBY, Northamptonshire. Tory marginal, ex-steel industry, working class
Council tenants 30% (83rd); Single parents 21% (179th); Skilled manual 35% (53rd)

No Change	Actual 92	%		87	Candidates
Conservative	25,203	45		44	William Powell, MP
Labour	24,861	44		41	Philip Hope, management consultant
Lib Dem	5,792	10		15	Ian Hankinson
Majority	342	Con 1		Con 3	
Swing		1 → Lab		2 → Lab	Lab needs 0.3 to win. 7th on Lab list

CORNWALL NORTH, Cornwall. Lib Dem marginal, Tory target seat, mainly rural, working class
Pensionable 23% (62nd); Self-employed 25% (3rd); Second homes 3% (12th)

No Change	Actual 92	%		87	Candidates
Conservative	27,775	44		52	Nigel Linacre, company director
Labour	4,103	7		6	Annie Lindo
Lib Dem	29,696	47		42	Paul Tyler, MP
Majority	1,921	LD 3		Con 10	
Swing		7 → Lib Dem		No swing	Con need 2 to win. 22nd on Con list

CORNWALL SOUTH EAST, Cornwall. Tory seat, Lib Dem long-shot, rural
White 99.6% (20th); Self-employed 20% (22nd); Second homes 2% (29th)

No Change	Actual 92	%		87	Candidates
Conservative	30,565	51		52	Warwick Lightfoot, economist
Labour	5,536	9		9	Dorothy Kirk
Lib Dem	22,861	38		40	Colin Breed, company director
Majority	7,704	Con 13		Con 12	
Swing		1 → Con		2 → LibAll	LD need 6 to win. 34th on LD list

COTSWOLD, Gloucestershire. Strong Tory seat, rural, professional, based on Cirencester & Tewkesbury
Pensionable 23% (64th); Self-employed 18% (35th); Second homes 2% (28th)

55% change	Notional 92	%	92	87	Candidates
Conservative	28,496	54	56	55	Geoffrey Clifton-Brown, MP
Labour	5,697	11	10	8	David Ellwell
Lib Dem	17,479	33	33	36	David Gayler, company director
Majority	11,017	Con 21	Con 22	Con 19	
Swing			1 → Con	2 → LibAll	

COVENTRY NORTH EAST, West Midlands. Strong Labour seat, urban, large Asian community
Asian 14% (25th); Unemployed 15% (58th); Overcrowding 4% (50th)

19% change	Notional 92	%	92	87	Candidates
Conservative	15,854	28	28	29	Michael Burnett, accountant
Labour	28,083	50	53	54	Bob Ainsworth, MP
Lib Dem	5,948	11	11	16	Geoffrey Sewards
Majority	12,229	Lab 22	Lab 25	Lab 25	
Swing			No swing	3 → Lab	

COVENTRY NORTH WEST, West Midlands. Labour seat, urban
Asian 6% (71st); Owner-occupied 77% (120th); No central heating 24% (122th)

55% change	Notional 92	%	92	87	Candidates
Conservative	22,425	37	35	35	Paul Bartlett, public relations manager
Labour	31,083	51	52	49	Geoffrey Robinson, MP
Lib Dem	7,152	12	13	16	Dr Napier Penington
Majority	8,658	Lab 14	Lab 16	Lab 14	
Swing			1 → Lab	3 → Lab	

COVENTRY SOUTH, West Midlands. New Tory marginal, Labour target seat, urban, professional
Age 16-24 14% (65th); Single parents 25% (86th); Professional 11% (57th)

99% change	Notional 92	%			Candidates
Conservative	22,674	40			Paul Ivey, engineer
Labour	19,770	35			Jim Cunningham, MP
Lib Dem	5,260	9			Gordon Macdonald
Majority	2,904	Con 5			Lab needs 3 to win. 35th on Lab list

CRAWLEY, West Sussex. Tory marginal, Labour target seat, new town, white collar
Age 25-39 25% (63rd); Asian 6% (73rd); Council tenants 31% (74th)

16% change	Notional 92	%	92	87	Candidates
Conservative	22,738	44	49	50	Josephine Crabb, solicitor
Labour	20,848	40	36	29	Laura Moffatt, nurse
Lib Dem	7,492	15	14	22	Harold de Souza
Majority	1,890	Con 4	Con 13	Con 21	
Swing			4 → Lab	1 → Lab	Lab needs 2 to win. 23rd on Lab list

CREWE & NANTWICH, Cheshire. Labour marginal, Tory target seat, mainly urban, working class
Owner-occupied 74% (193rd); No central heating 25% (109th); Skilled manual 31% (161st)

21% change	Notional 92	%	92	87	Candidates
Conservative	21,751	39	41	42	Michael Loveridge, self-employed businessman
Labour	26,622	48	46	44	Gwyneth Dunwoody, MP
Lib Dem	6,991	13	12	14	David Cannon
Majority	4,871	Lab 9	Lab 4	Lab 2	
Swing			1 → Lab	1 → Lab	

CROSBY, Merseyside. Strong Tory seat, urban, white collar
Owner-occupied 80% (48th); Managerial 39% (78th); White collar 20% (13th)

52% change	Notional 92	%	92	87	Candidates
Conservative	23,329	49	47	46	Sir Malcolm Thornton, MP
Labour	13,738	29	26	18	Clare Curtis-Tansley
Lib Dem	9,558	20	24	36	Paul McVey
Majority	9,591	Con 20	Con 22	Con 10	
Swing			3 → Lab	3 → Con	Lab needs 10 to win. 120th on Lab list

CROYDON CENTRAL, South London. Strong Tory seat, urban, white collar
Age 25-39 25% (49th); Black 6% (43rd); White collar 20% (7th)

88% change	Notional 92	%	92	87	Candidates
Conservative	33,940	56	55	57	David Congdon, MP
Labour	19,279	32	31	24	Geraint Davies
Lib Dem	7,934	13	13	19	George Schlich
Majority	14,661	Con 24	Con 24	Con 32	
Swing			4 → Lab	1 → Con	

CROYDON NORTH, South London. New Tory marginal, 5th on Labour target list, suburban, white collar, based on Croydon NW
Age 25-39 28% (21st); Black 14% (15th); White collar 21% (3rd)

45% change	Notional 92	%	92	87	Candidates
Conservative	25,865	45	44	47	Ian Martin, general manager, business development
Labour	25,705	44	47	37	Malcolm Wicks, MP
Lib Dem	6,340	11	9	16	Martin Morris
Majority	160	Con 0.3	Lab 4	Con 10	
Swing			7 → Lab	4 → Lab	Lab needs 0.1 to win. 5th on Lab list

CROYDON SOUTH, South London. Strong Tory seat, outer suburbs, managerial
Owner-occupied 82% (25th); Managerial 45% (17th); White collar 18% (46th)

17% change	Notional 92	%	92	87	Candidates
Conservative	35,937	62	64	64	Richard Ottoway, MP
Labour	9,513	16	13	10	Charles Burling
Lib Dem	12,599	22	23	24	Steven Gauge
Majority	23,338	Con 40	Con 41	Con 40	
Swing			1 → Con	1 → Con	

CUMBERNAULD & KILSYTH, Strathclyde. Strong Labour seat, partly new town

No Change	Actual 92	%	87	Candidates
Conservative	4,143	11	9	Ian Sewell
Labour	19,855	54	60	Norman Hogg, MP
Lib Dem	2,118	6	11	John Biggam
SNP	10,640	29	20	Colin Barrie
Majority	9,215	Lab 25	Lab 40	
Swing		7 → SNP	4 → Lab	SNP need 13 to win. 24th on SNP list

CUNNINGHAME NORTH, Strathclyde. Labour marginal, Tory target seat, ex-mining

No Change	Actual 92	%	87	Candidates
Conservative	14,625	34	34	Margaret Mitchell
Labour	17,564	41	44	Brian Wilson, MP
Lib Dem	2,864	7	12	Karen Freel
SNP	7,813	18	10	Kim Nicoll, councillor
Majority	2,939	Lab 7	Lab 10	
Swing		2 → Con	7 → Lab	Con need 3 to win. 47th on Con list

CUNNINGHAME SOUTH, Strathclyde. Strong Labour seat, industrial

No Change	Actual 92	%	87	Candidates
Conservative	6,070	16	16	Pamela Paterson
Labour	19,687	53	61	Brian Donohoe, MP
Lib Dem	2,299	6	12	
SNP	9,007	24	11	Margaret Burgess
Majority	10,680	Lab 29	Lab 45	
Swing		11 → SNP	6 → Lab	

CYNON VALLEY, Mid Glamorgan. Strong Labour seat, ex-mining, working class
Govt schemes 3% (35th); Unemployed 15% (55th); Long-term ill 21% (5th)

No Change	Actual 92	%	87	Candidates
Conservative	4,890	13	12	Andrew Smith, public affairs
Labour	26,254	69	69	Ann Clwyd, MP
Lib Dem	2,667	7	12	Huw Price
Plaid Cymru	4,186	11	7	Alun Davies
Majority	21,364	Lab 56	Lab 57	
Swing		No swing	11 → Lab	

DAGENHAM, East London. Labour seat, car industry, working class, Lab by-election held
Council tenants 38% (40th); White collar 19% (26th); Skilled manual 36% (32nd

3% change	Notional 92	%	94 by-	92	87	Candidates
Conservative	16,052	37	10	36	39	James Fairrie, export credit insura
Labour	22,499	52	72	52	44	Judith Church, MP
Lib Dem	4,992	12	8	11	17	Thomas Dobrashian
Majority	6,447	Lab 15	Lab 62	Lab 16	Lab 6	
Swing			23 → Lab	5 → Lab	1 → Con	

DARLINGTON, Durham. Labour marginal, Tory target seat, mainly urban, working class, Lab gain in 92
Govt schemes 3% (36th); Single parents 22% (141st); Unskilled 6% (103rd)

No Change	Actual 92	%	87	Candidates
Conservative	23,758	43	47	Peter Scrope, telecommunications company dire
Labour	26,556	48	42	Alan Milburn, MP
Lib Dem	4,586	8	12	
Majority	2,798	Lab 5	Con 5	
Swing		5 → Lab	1 → Lab	Con need 3 to win. 37th on Con list

DARTFORD, Kent. Tory seat, Labour long-shot, industrial, partly rural, white collar
Age 16-24 13% (151st); Other non-white 1% (138th); White collar 16% (87th)

8% change	Notional 92	%	92	87	Candidates
Conservative	28,796	51	52	54	Bob Dunn, MP
Labour	20,482	36	35	28	Howard Stoate
Lib Dem	6,873	12	13	18	Dorothy Webb
Majority	8,314	Con 15	Con 17	Con 26	
Swing		4 → Lab	1 → Con		Lab needs 7 to win. 86th on Lab list

DAVENTRY, Northamptonshire. Strong Tory seat, rural, middle-class
Age 40-pension 29% (112th); Self-employed 15% (109th); Car owners 83% (35th)

14% change	Notional 92	%	92	87	Candidates
Conservative	35,842	58	58	58	Timothy Boswell, MP
Labour	14,831	24	24	21	Ken Ritchie
Lib Dem	10,933	18	17	22	John Gordon
Majority	21,011	Con 34	Con 34	Con 36	
Swing			2 → Lab	5 → Con	

DELYN, Clwyd. Labour marginal, Tory target seat, industrial, working class, Lab gain in 92
Age 40-pension 29% (98th); White 99.6% (9th); Unskilled 6% (117th)

20% change	Notional 92	%	92	87	Candidates
Conservative	17,428	40	41	41	Karen Lumley, company secretary
Labour	20,606	47	45	39	David Hanson, MP
Lib Dem	4,822	11	11	17	Phil Lloyd
Plaid Cymru	1,116	3	3	3	Ashley Drake
Majority	3,178	Lab 7	Lab 4	Con 2	
Swing			3 → Lab	5 → Lab	Con need 4 to win. 55th on Con list

DENTON & REDDISH, Greater Manchester. Labour seat, urban, skilled manual
No central heating 23% (148th); Long-term ill 14% (161st); Skilled manual 36% (40th)

25% change	Notional 92	%	92	87	Candidates
Conservative	18,010	34	32	34	Barbara Nutt, self-employed businesswoman
Labour	28,164	53	55	50	Andrew Bennett, MP
Lib Dem	5,298	10	9	17	Iain Donaldson
Majority	10,154	Lab 19	Lab 23	Lab 16	
Swing			4 → Lab	3 → Lab	

DERBY NORTH, Derbyshire. Tory marginal, Labour target seat, mainly urban
No central heating 25.2% (111th); Professional 10% (98th); Unskilled 6% (139th)

No Change	Actual 92	%		87	Candidates
Conservative	28,574	48		49	Greg Knight, MP
Labour	24,121	41		37	Bob Laxton, Telecom engineer, council leader
Lib Dem	5,638	10		13	Bob Charlesworth
Majority	4,453	Con 8		Con 12	
Swing		2 → Lab		2 → Con	Lab needs 4 to win. 49th on Lab list

DERBY SOUTH, Derbyshire. Labour marginal, Tory target seat, urban, large Asian community
Age 16-24 14% (58th); Asian 13% (32nd); No central heating 28% (80th)

13% change	Notional 92	%	92	87	Candidates
Conservative	23,400	41	38	41	Javed Arain, marketing and management consultant
Labour	27,627	48	52	44	Margaret Beckett, MP
Lib Dem	6,195	11	10	16	Jeremy Beckett
Majority	4,227	Lab 7	Lab 14	Lab 3	
Swing			5 → Lab	1 → Lab	Con need 4 to win. 59th on Con list

DERBYSHIRE NORTH EAST, Derbyshire. Labour seat, ex-mining
Age 40-pension 29% (58th); White 99.4% (74th); Council tenants 27% (117th)

No Change	Actual 92	%		87	Candidates
Conservative	22,590	38		38	Simon Elliott, senior consultant, Shandwick PR
Labour	28,860	49		44	Harry Barnes, MP
Lib Dem	7,675	13		18	Stephen Hardy
Majority	6,270	Lab 11		Lab 7	
Swing		2 → Lab		1 → Lab	

DERBYSHIRE SOUTH, Derbyshire. Tory marginal, Labour target seat, mainly rural
Age 40-pension 28% (170th); Owner-occupied 76% (137th); Skilled manual 33% (99th)

10% change	Notional 92	%	92	87	Candidates
Conservative	29,825	47	49	49	Edwina Currie, MP
Labour	27,878	44	42	33	Mark Todd, businessman, former council leader
Lib Dem	5,235	8	9	18	Rob Renold
Majority	1,947	Con 3	Con 7	Con 16	
Swing			5 → Lab	1 → Con	Lab needs 2 to win. 20th on Lab list

DERBYSHIRE WEST, Derbyshire. Strong Tory seat, rural
Age 40-pension 31% (11th); White 99.5% (28th); Self-employed 16% (59th)

3% change	Notional 92	%	92	87	Candidates
Conservative	31,944	54	54	53	Patrick Mcloughlin, MP
Labour	13,164	22	22	12	Stephen Clamp
Lib Dem	13,824	24	23	35	Christopher Seeley
Majority	18,120	Con 31	Con 31	Con 18	
Swing			7 → Con	6 → LibAll	

DEVIZES, Wiltshire. Strong Tory seat, rural
Second homes 1% (87th); Car owners 79% (102nd); Mobility 13% (39th)

71% change	Notional 92	%	92	87	Candidates
Conservative	33,603	53	53	55	Earl of Ancram, Michael Ancram, MP
Labour	7,613	12	18	17	Frank Jeffrey
Lib Dem	20,584	33	26	28	Tony Vickers, chartered land surveyor
Majority	13,019	Con 21	Con 27	Con 27	
Swing			No swing	1 → Con	

DEVON EAST, Devon. Strong Tory seat, rural, retirement
Pensionable 34% (3th); White 99.6% (7th); Second homes 2% (27th)

15% change	Notional 92	%	92	87	Candidates
Conservative	28,895	53	52	59	Sir Peter Emery, MP
Labour	6,685	12	13	8	Andrew Siantonas
Lib Dem	14,902	27	27	31	Rachel Trethewey, freelance journalist
Majority	13,993	Con 25	Con 26	Con 28	
Swing			1 → Lib Dem	No swing	

DEVON NORTH, Devon. Lib Dem marginal, rural
White 99.5% (43rd); Self-employed 22% (14th); Second homes 1% (60th)

0.1% change	Notional 92	%	92	87	Candidates
Conservative	26,596	46	46	51	Richard Ashworth
Labour	3,406	6	6	6	Eithne Brenton
Lib Dem	27,389	47	47	43	Nick Harvey, MP
Majority	793	LD 1	LD 1	Con 8	
Swing			5 → Lib Dem	5 → LibAll	Con need 1 to win. 8th on Con list

DEVON SOUTH WEST, Devon. New strong Tory seat, mainly rural, part suburban
Owner-occupied 84% (13th); Car owners 84% (13th); Second homes 1% (86th)

79% change	Notional 92	%	Candidates
Conservative	30,796	58	Gary Streeter
Labour	8,470	16	Chris Mavin
Lib Dem	13,666	26	Keith Baldry
Majority	17,130	Con 32	

DEVON WEST & TORRIDGE, Devon. Tory marginal, Lib Dem target seat, rural, Emma Nicholson's old seat
White 99.6% (10th); Self-employed 25% (4th); Second homes 1% (46th)

4% change	Notional 92	%	92	87	Candidates
Conservative	28,458	47	47	50	Ian Liddell-Grainger
Labour	5,748	10	10	9	David Brenton
Lib Dem	25,187	42	42	39	John Burnett, solicitor, farmer
Majority	3,271	Con 5	Con 6	Con 11	
Swing			3 → Lib Dem	6 → LibAll	LD need 3 to win. 10th on LD list

DEWSBURY, West Yorkshire. Labour marginal, Tory target seat, urban, large Asian community
Asian 12% (34th); Overcrowding 4% (47th); No central heating 40% (22nd)

51% change	Notional 92	%	92	87	Candidates
Conservative	19,637	40	43	42	Paul McCormick, self-employed joiner & salesr
Labour	23,186	47	44	42	Ann Taylor, MP
Lib Dem	4,835	10	11	16	Kingsley Hill
Majority	3,549	Lab 7	Lab 1	Lab 1	
Swing			No swing	2 → Lab	Con needs 4 to win. 56th on Con list

DON VALLEY, South Yorkshire. Labour seat, ex-mining
Govt schemes 2% (66th); Unemployed 11% (143rd); Long-term ill 15% (105th)

45% change	Notional 92	%	92	87	Candidates
Conservative	18,927	37	32	32	Clare Gledhill, political adviser
Labour	26,046	51	55	53	
Lib Dem	5,718	11	12	15	Paul Johnston
Majority	7,119	Lab 14	Lab 23	Lab 21	
Swing			1 → Lab	4 → Lab	

DONCASTER CENTRAL, South Yorkshire. Strong Labour seat, industrial, working class
Govt schemes 2% (55th); Unemployed 14% (70th); Long-term ill 16% (70th)

No Change	Actual 92	%		87	Candidates
Conservative	17,113	34		35	David Turtle
Labour	27,795	54		51	Rosalie Winterton, researcher/lobbyist
Lib Dem	6,057	12		14	Simon Tarry
Majority	10,682	Lab 21		Lab 16	
Swing		3 → Lab		6 → Lab	

DONCASTER NORTH, South Yorkshire. Strong Labour seat, ex-mining, working class
Govt schemes 3% (30th); Long-term ill 17% (43rd); Skilled manual 38% (21st)

15% change	Notional 92	%	92	87	Candidates
Conservative	10,131	22	26	24	Peter Kennerley, solicitor
Labour	29,272	64	62	62	Kevin Hughes, MP
Lib Dem	6,022	13	12	14	Michael Cook
Majority	19,141	Lab 42	Lab 36	Lab 37	
Swing			1 → Con	6 → Lab	

DORSET MID & POOLE NORTH, Dorset. New Tory seat, Lib Dem long-shot, suburban and rural, middle-class
Owner-occupied 83% (22nd); Car owners 84% (10th); Professional 8% (142th)

120% chang	Notional 92	%			Candidates
Conservative	24,999	50			Christopher Fraser, managing director
Labour	5,959	12			David Collis
Lib Dem	18,945	38			Alan Leaman, party official
Majority	6,054	Con 12			
Swing					LD need 6 to win. 31st on LD list

DORSET NORTH, Dorset. Tory seat, Lib Dem long-shot, rural, middle-class
White 99.5% (24th); Self-employed 20% (25th); Car owners 82% (36th)

24% change	Notional 92	%	92	87	Candidates
Conservative	29,855	57	55	57	Robert Walter
Labour	3,195	6	7	7	John Fitzmaurice
Lib Dem	19,784	38	39	36	Paula Yates, local government consultant
Majority	10,071	Con 19	Con 16	Con 21	
Swing			2 → LD	1 → LibAll	

DORSET SOUTH, Dorset. Strong Tory seat, seaside
Pensionable 23% (71st); Second homes 2% (25th); Mobility 13% (40th)

11% change	Notional 92	%	92	87	Candidates
Conservative	26,405	51	50	55	Ian Bruce, MP
Labour	10,805	21	21	17	Jim Knight
Lib Dem	13,788	27	27	28	Kevin Hodder, self-employed businessman
Majority	12,617	Con 24	Con 23	Con 27	
Swing			2 → LD	1 → LibAll	

DORSET WEST, Dorset. Tory seat, Lib Dem target seat, rural, middle-class
Pensionable 27% (14th); Self-employed 21% (19th); Second homes 2% (18th)

No Change	Actual 92	%		87	Candidates
Conservative	27,766	51		56	Oliver Letwin, director, Rothschild
Labour	7,082	13		12	Robert Bygraves
Lib Dem	19,755	36		32	Robin Legg, local government solicitor
Majority	8,011	Con 15		Con 25	
Swing		5 → LD		3 → LibAll	LD need 7 to win. 37th on LD list

DOVER, Kent. Tory marginal, Labour target seat, port, ex-mining, working class
Pensionable 21% (92th); Second homes 1% (54th); Private tenants 9% (133rd)

0.2% change	Notional 92	%	92	87	Candidates
Conservative	25,443	44	44	46	David Shaw, MP
Labour	24,583	43	43	34	Gwyn Prosser, marine engineer
Lib Dem	6,234	11	11	20	Mark Corney
Majority	860	Con 2	Con 1	Con 12	
Swing		5 → Lab	3 → Lab		Lab needs 1 to win. 13th on Lab list

DOWN NORTH, Unionist marginal, Tory target, mainly urban, seaside, UKUP by-election gain

31% change	Notional 92	%	95 by-	92	87	
UPUP	15,298	41		43	45	
UKUP			37		35	Robert McCartney, MP
APNI	5,894	16	26	15	19	Oliver Napier, solicitor
UUP			26			Alan McFarland, researcher
DUP	3,153	8		10		
Conservative	13,033	35	2	32		
Majority	2,265	UPUP 6	UKUP 11	UPUP 11	UPUP 10	
Swing				1 → UPUP		

DOWN SOUTH, Strong SDLP seat, mainly rural

16% change	Notional 92	%	92	87	Candidates
UUP	18,531	35	41	46	Dermot Nesbitt
SDLP	29,408	56	51	47	Eddie McGrady, MP
SF	1,860	4	3	4	
APNI					Julian Crozier, retired civil servant
Conservative	1,262	2	2		
Majority	10,877	SDLP 21	SDLP 10	SDLP 1	
Swing		5 → SDLP	1 → SDLP		

DUDLEY NORTH, West Midlands. New Labour marginal, urban, working class
Council tenants 35% (52nd); No central heating 36% (36th); Skilled manual 37% (25th)

69% change	Notional 92	%	Candidates
Conservative	23,776	44	Charles MacNamara, solicitor
Labour	24,730	46	Dr John Gilbert, MP
Lib Dem	5,273	10	Gerry Lewis
Majority	954	Lab 2	Con needs 1 to win. 10th on Con list

DUDLEY SOUTH, West Midlands. Labour marginal, urban, working class, based on Dudley West, Lab by-election gain
Council tenants 27% (112th); No central heating 32% (55th); Skilled manual 39% (12th)

62% change	Notional 92	%	94 by-	92	87	Candidates
Conservative	22,296	42	19	49	50	Mark Simpson, publicity specialist
Labour	25,025	47	69	41	34	Ian Pearson, MP
Lib Dem	5,886	11	8	11	16	Richard Burt
Majority	2,729	Lab 5	Lab 50	Con 8	Con 16	
Swing			29 → Lab	4 → Lab	1 → Con	Con needs 3 to win. 38th on Con lis

DULWICH & WEST NORWOOD, South London.New Labour marginal, Tory target seat, suburban, middle-class
Age 25-39 29% (10th); Black 16% (11th); Single parents 38% (19th)

73% change	Notional 92	%	Candidates
Conservative	21,779	43	Roger Gough, investment analyst
Labour	23,582	46	Tessa Jowell, MP
Lib Dem	4,998	10	Susan Kramer
Majority	1,803	Lab 4	Con need 2 to win. 27th on Con list

DUMBARTON, Strathclyde. Labour seat, ex-textile industry

No Change	Actual 92	%	87	Candidates
Conservative	13,126	30	32	Peter Ramsay
Labour	19,255	44	43	John McFall, MP
Lib Dem	3,425	8	13	Alan Reid
SNP	8,127	18	12	Bill Mackechnie, councillor
Majority	6,129	Lab 14	Lab 11	
Swing		1 → Lab	3 → Lab	SNP need 13 to win. 26th on SNP list

DUMFRIES, Dumfries and Galloway. Tory seat, Labour long-shot, ex-mining

2% change	Notional 92	%	92	87
Conservative	21,597	43	43	42
Labour	14,831	30	30	25
Lib Dem	5,854	12	12	18
SNP	7,411	15	14	14
Majority	6,766	Con 14	Con 13	Con 17
Swing			2 → Lab	4 → Lab

Candidates
Struan Stevenson
Russell Brown, leader of Labour group on UA
Neil Wallace
Robert Higgins, councillor

Lab needs 7 to win. 80th on Lab list

DUNDEE EAST, Tayside. Labour seat, SNP long-shot, urban

12% change	Notional 92	%	92	87
Conservative	8,297	18	18	13
Labour	19,954	44	44	42
Lib Dem	1,939	4	4	5
SNP	14,437	32	33	40
Majority	5,517	Lab 12	Lab 11	Lab 2
Swing			4 → Lab	7 → Lab

Candidates
Bruce Mackie
John McAllion, MP

Shona Robison

SNP needs 6 to win.7th on SNP list

DUNDEE WEST, Tayside. Strong Labour seat, urban

9% change	Notional 92	%	92	87
Conservative	7,717	19	19	18
Labour	19,520	48	49	53
Lib Dem	3,071	8	8	13
SNP	10,056	25	24	15
Majority	9,464	Lab 23	Lab 25	Lab 35
Swing			6 → SNP	7 → Lab

Candidates
Neil Powrie
Ernie Ross, MP
Elizabeth Dick
John Dorward

SNP needs 12 to win. 21st on SNP list

DUNFERMLINE EAST, Fife. Strong Labour seat, urban

4% change	Notional 92	%	92	87
Conservative	6,211	16	17	15
Labour	23,966	63	62	65
Lib Dem	2,329	6	6	11
SNP	5,619	15	15	10
Majority	17,755	Lab 47	Lab 46	Lab 50
Swing			2 → Con	9 → Lab

Candidates
Iain Mitchell, QC
Dr Gordon Brown, MP
Jim Tolson
John Ramage

DUNFERMLINE WEST, Fife. Labour seat, urban

4% change	Notional 92	%	92	87
Conservative	8,948	23	23	23
Labour	16,132	42	42	47
Lib Dem	6,066	16	16	9
SNP	7,703	20	19	21
Majority	7,184	Lab 19	Lab 19	Lab 24
Swing			2 → Con	9 → Lab

Candidates
Kevin Newton
Rachel Squire, MP
Elizabeth Harris, councillor, teacher/education officer
John Lloyd

SNP needs 11 to win. 18th on SNP list

DURHAM NORTH, Durham. Strong Labour seat, mainly urban, working class
White 99.4% (64th); Govt schemes 3% (26th); Long-term ill 16% (60th)

10% change	Notional 92	%	92	87
Conservative	12,610	25	25	21
Labour	30,374	60	60	56
Lib Dem	7,755	15	15	23
Majority	17,764	Lab 35	Lab 35	Lab 34
Swing			No swing	4 → Lab

Candidates
Mark Hardy, commercial manager
Giles Radice, MP
Brian Moore

DURHAM NORTH WEST, Durham. Strong Labour seat, mainly urban
White 99.6% (6th); Govt schemes 3% (28th); Long-term ill 17% (38th)

10% change	Notional 92	%	92	87
Conservative	13,930	27	28	28
Labour	29,596	58	58	51
Lib Dem	7,458	15	15	21
Majority	15,666	Lab 31	Lab 30	Lab 23
Swing			4 → Lab	4 → Lab

Candidates
Louise St John Howe
Hilary Armstrong, MP
Anthony Gillings

DURHAM, CITY OF, Durham. Strong Labour seat, urban, middle-class
Age 40-pension 29% (76th); Govt schemes 2% (87th); Professional 10% (85th)

No Change	Actual 92	%	87	Candidates
Conservative	12,037	24	22	Richard Chalk, investment manager
Labour	27,095	53	45	Gerald Steinberg, MP
Lib Dem	10,915	22	33	Nigel Martin
Majority	15,058	Lab 30	Lab 12	
Swing		3 → Lab	4 → Lab	

EALING ACTON & SHEPHERD'S BUSH, West London. New Labour marginal, urban, large non-white population
Age 25-39 29% (11th); Other non-white 7% (10th); Mobility 15% (14th)

75% change	Notional 92	%		Candidates
Conservative	19,553	39		Barbara Yerolemou
Labour	23,024	46		Clive Soley, MP
Lib Dem	5,998	12		Andrew Mitchell
Majority	3,471	Lab 7		
Swing				Con need 4 to win. 49th on Con list

EALING NORTH, West London. Tory seat, Labour long-shot, large non-white population
Black 7% (38th); Other non-white 6% (13th); White collar 18% (36th)

16% change	Notional 92	%	92	87	Candidates
Conservative	29,917	51	50	56	Harry Greenway, MP
Labour	20,842	36	38	28	Shephen Pound
Lib Dem	6,266	11	11	15	Anjan Gupta
Majority	9,075	Con 16	Con 12	Con 28	
Swing			8 → Lab	8 → Con	Lab needs 8 to win. 90th on Lab list

EALING SOUTHALL, West London. Labour marginal, Tory target seat, urban, strongly Asian
Asian 35% (2nd); Other non-white 6% (16th); Overcrowding 7% (11th)

13% change	Notional 92	%	92	87	Candidates
Conservative	20,340	36	34	36	John Penrose, commercial director
Labour	25,371	45	47	51	Piara Khabra, MP
Lib Dem	4,567	8	8	13	Nikki Thomson
Majority	5,031	Lab 9	Lab 14	Lab 15	
Swing			1 → Con	3 → Con	

EASINGTON, Durham. 9th safest Labour seat, ex-mining, skilled manual
Govt schemes 4% (3rd); Long-term ill 21% (6th); Skilled manual 40% (11th)

No Change	Actual 92	%	87	Candidates
Conservative	7,879	17	16	Jason Hollands
Labour	34,269	73	68	John Cummings, MP
Lib Dem	5,001	11	16	
Majority	26,390	Lab 56	Lab 52	
Swing		2 → Lab	5 → Lab	

EAST HAM, East London. Strong Labour seat, urban, strongly Asian, based on Newham NE
Asian 31% (6th); Other non-white 6% (15th); Overcrowding 9% (3rd)

20% change	Notional 92	%	94 by-	92	87	Candidates
Conservative	13,751	32	15	31	31	Angela Bray, public affairs consultant
Labour	23,212	54	75	58	52	Stephen Timms, MP
Lib Dem	6,049	14	4	11	17	Paul Gentry
Majority	9,461	Lab 22	Lab 60	Lab 28	Lab 21	
Swing			16 → Lab	3 → Lab	0.4 → Con	

EAST KILBRIDE, Strathclyde. Strong Labour seat, part new town

2% change	Notional 92	%	92	87	Candidates
Conservative	9,365	19	19	15	Clifford Herbertson
Labour	23,795	47	47	49	Adam Ingram, MP
Lib Dem	5,221	10	11	24	
SNP	11,855	24	24	13	George Gebbie
Majority	11,940	Lab 24	Lab 23	Lab 25	
Swing			7 → SNP	8 → Lab	

EAST LOTHIAN, Lothian. Labour seat, ex-mining

17% change	Notional 92	%	92	87	Candidates
Conservative	14,024	30	28	28	Murdo Fraser
Labour	21,123	46	47	48	John Home Robertson, MP
Lib Dem	5,147	11	11	16	Alison MacAskill
SNP	6,171	13	14	7	David McCarthy
Majority	7,099	Lab 15	Lab 18	Lab 20	
Swing			1 → Con	3 → Lab	

EASTBOURNE, East Sussex. Tory seat, Lib Dem long-shot, seaside, white collar, Con regain in 92 from Lib Dem
Pensionable 33% (6th); Self-employed 15% (93rd); White collar 17% (53rd)

11% change	Notional 92	%	92	87	Candidates
Conservative	30,548	53	52	60	Nigel Waterson, MP
Labour	2,697	5	5	9	David Lines
Lib Dem	23,739	41	43	30	Chris Berry, chartered town planner
Majority	6,809	Con 12	Con 9	Con 30	
Swing			11 → Lib Dem	2 → Con	LD need 6 to win. 29th on LD list

EASTLEIGH, Hampshire. Strong Tory seat, mainly urban, white collar, Lib Dem by-election gain
Age 25-39 25% (60th); Owner-occupied 79% (66th); Car owners 81% (64th)

27% change	Notional 92	%	94 by-	92	87	Candidates
Conservative	28,620	51	25	51	51	Stephen Reid, data-processing manager
Labour	10,947	20	28	21	17	Alan Lloyd
Lib Dem	16,708	30	44	28	32	David Chidgey, MP, chartered civil engineer
Majority	11,912	Con 21	LD 17	Con 23	Con 19	
Swing			21 →Lib Dem	2 → Con	1 → LibAll	

EASTWOOD, Strathclyde. Strong Tory seat, stockbroker belt

2% change	Notional 92	%	92	87	Candidates
Conservative	24,544	47	47	40	Allan Stewart, MP
Labour	12,706	24	24	25	Jim Murphy
Lib Dem	8,651	16	17	27	Christopher Mason
SNP	6,589	13	12	8	Douglas Yates
Majority	11,838	Con 23	Con 23	Con 12	
Swing			4 → Con	3 → SDPAll	

ECCLES, Greater Manchester. Strong Labour seat, inner city, working class
Council tenants 31% (71st); Long-term ill 16% (63rd); Unskilled 6% (99th)

35% change	Notional 92	%	92	87	Candidates
Conservative	16,730	31	29	31	Gregory Barker, managing director, investment bank
Labour	30,960	58	57	51	Ian Stewart
Lib Dem	5,186	10	12	18	Bob Boyd
Majority	14,230	Lab 27	Lab 28	Lab 19	
Swing			4 → Lab	3 → Lab	

EDDISBURY, Cheshire. Strong Tory seat, mainly rural, middle-class
Age 40-pension 30% (46th); Self-employed 15% (94th); Car owners 81% (69th)

47% change	Notional 92	%	92	87	Candidates
Conservative	26,794	53	51	51	Alistair Goodlad, Mp
Labour	15,798	31	31	24	Margaret Hanson
Lib Dem	7,553	15	17	24	David Reaper
Majority	10,996	Con 22	Con 21	Con 28	
Swing			4 → Lab	No swing	

EDINBURGH CENTRAL, Lothian. Labour marginal, Tory target seat, inner city

38% change	Notional 92	%	92	87	Candidates
Conservative	12,013	29	33	35	Mike Scott-Hayward
Labour	15,770	39	39	40	Alistair Darling, MP
Lib Dem	6,073	15	12	18	Karen Utting
SNP	6,232	15	14	6	Fiona Hyslop
Majority	3,757	Lab 9	Lab 5	Lab 6	
Swing			No swing	6 → Lab	Con needs 5 to win. 70th on Con list

EDINBURGH EAST & MUSSELBURGH, Lothian. Strong Labour seat, urban

48% change	Notional 92	%	92	87	Candidates
Conservative	10,568	24	24	25	Kenneth Ward
Labour	19,669	45	46	50	Gavin Strang, MP
Lib Dem	5,075	12	10	15	Callum McKellar
SNP	7,890	18	18	10	James O'Neill, councillor
Majority	9,101	Lab 21	Lab 21	Lab 26	
Swing			2 → Con	5 → Lab	

EDINBURGH NORTH & LEITH, Lothian. Labour seat, urban

43% change	Notional 92	%	92	87	Candidates
Conservative	10,685	25	21	23	Ewen Stewart
Labour	15,019	35	34	49	Malcolm Chisholm, MP
Lib Dem	5,038	12	12	18	Hilary Campbell
SNP	8,749	20	22	10	Anne Dana
Majority	4,334	Lab 10	Lab 12	Lab 27	
Swing			14 → SNP	7 → Lab	SNP needs 7 to win. 10th on SNP list

EDINBURGH PENTLANDS, Lothian. Tory marginal, Labour target seat, suburban

8% change	Notional 92	%	92	87	Candidates
Conservative	18,474	40	41	38	Malcolm Rifkind, MP
Labour	14,326	31	31	30	Linda Clark, QC
Lib Dem	5,828	13	13	25	Jennifer Dawe
SNP	7,203	16	15	7	Stewart Gibb
Majority	4,148	Con 9	Con 10	Con 8	
Swing			1 → Con	4 → Lab	Lab needs 5 to win. 60th on Lab list

EDINBURGH SOUTH, Lothian. Labour marginal, Tory target seat, suburban

3% change	Notional 92	%	92	87	Candidates
Conservative	14,270	32	32	34	Elizabeth Smith
Labour	18,426	42	42	38	Nigel Griffiths, MP
Lib Dem	5,855	13	13	23	Mike Pringle
SNP	5,719	13	13	5	Dr John Hargreaves
Majority	4,156	Lab 9	Lab 9	Lab 4	
Swing			3 → Lab	6 → Lab	

EDINBURGH WEST, Lothian. Tory marginal, Lib Dem target

52% change	Notional 92	%	92	87	Candidates
Conservative	19,715	38	37	37	Lord James Douglas-Hamilton, MP
Labour	8,961	17	18	22	Lesley Hinds
Lib Dem	15,424	30	35	35	Donald Gorrie, councillor
SNP	6,471	13	8	6	Graham Sutherland
Majority	4,291	Con 8	Con 2	Con 3	
Swing			No swing	1 → Con	LD need 4 to win. 16th on LD list

EDMONTON, North London. Tory marginal, large black population
Black 11% (25th); Other non-white 4% (40th); White collar 18% (42nd)

No Change	Actual 92	%		87	Candidates
Conservative	22,076	46		51	Dr Ian Twinn, MP
Labour	21,483	45		36	Andy Love, Co-op parliamentary officer
Lib Dem	3,940	8		13	Andrew Wiseman
Majority	593	Con 1		Con 15	
Swing		7 → Lab		6 → Con	Lab needs 1 to win. 10th on Lab list

ELLESMERE PORT & NESTON, Cheshire. Labour marginal, Tory target seat, commuting, working class, Lab gain in 92
Age 40-pension 28% (187th); White 99.3% (92nd); Govt schemes 2% (120th)

7% change	Notional 92	%	92	87	Candidates
Conservative	23,603	42	43	44	Lynn Turnbull, complementary health clinic own
Labour	26,836	48	46	41	Andrew Miller, MP
Lib Dem	5,012	9	10	14	Joanna Pemberton
Majority	3,233	Lab 6	Lab 3	Con 3	
Swing			3 → Lab	5 → Lab	Con need 3 to win. 42nd on Con list

ELMET, West Yorkshire. Tory marginal, Labour target seat, outer suburbs, white collar
Age 40-pension 30% (36th); Council tenants 22% (185th); White collar 15% (149th)

No Change	Actual 92	%		87	Candidates
Conservative	27,677	48		47	Spencer Batiste, MP
Labour	24,416	42		37	Colin Burgon, former teacher
Lib Dem	6,144	11		16	Brian Jennings
Majority	3,261	Con 6		Con 10	
Swing		2 → Lab		3 → Lab	Lab needs 3 to win. 38th on Lab list

ELTHAM, South London. Tory marginal, Labour target seat, suburban, white collar
Black 3% (88th); Other non-white 2% (81st); White collar 19% (17th)

26% change	Notional 92	%	92	87	Candidates
Conservative	20,384	44	46	48	Clive Blackwood, barrister
Labour	18,604	40	42	32	Clive Efford, taxi drive
Lib Dem	7,213	16	12	21	Amanda Taylor
Majority	1,780	Con 4	Con 4	Con 16	
Swing			6 → Lab	2 → Lab	Lab needs 2 to win. 25th on Lab list

ENFIELD NORTH, North London. Tory seat, Labour long-shot, outer suburbs, white collar
Age 25-39 24% (80th); Black 4% (62nd); White collar 17% (59th)

No Change	Actual 92	%		87	Candidates
Conservative	27,789	53		56	Mark Field, partner in consultancy firm
Labour	18,359	35		29	Joan Ryan
Lib Dem	5,817	11		15	Michael Hopkins
Majority	9,430	Con 18		Con 27	
Swing		5 → Lab		2 → Con	Lab needs 9 to win. 104th on Lab list

ENFIELD SOUTHGATE, North London. Strong Tory seat, outer suburbs, middle-class
Other non-white 4% (53rd); Self-employed 17% (49th); White collar 18% (41st)

0.1% change	Notional 92	%	92	87	Candidates
Conservative	28,390	58	58	59	Michael Portillo, MP
Labour	12,845	26	26	19	Stephen Twigg
Lib Dem	7,072	14	14	21	Jeremy Browne
Majority	15,545	Con 32	Con 32	Con 38	
Swing			4 → Lab	2 → Con	

EPPING FOREST, Essex. Strong Tory seat, commuting, white collar
Age 40-pension 29% (96th); Self-employed 16% (74th); White collar 19% (25th)

8% change	Notional 92	%	92	87	Candidates
Conservative	34,034	60	60	61	Eleanor Laing, business and political consultant
Labour	12,851	23	22	18	Stephen Murray
Lib Dem	9,520	17	17	19	Stephen Robinson
Majority	21,183	Con 37	Con 37	Con 42	
Swing			3 → Lab	5 → Con	

EPSOM & EWELL, Surrey. Strong Tory seat, stockbroker belt, managerial
Owner-occupied 83% (23rd); Professional 12% (40th); Managerial 45% (18th)

25% change	Notional 92	%	92	87	Candidates
Conservative	35,621	61	60	62	Archie Hamilton, MP
Labour	8,789	15	16	15	Philip Woodford
Lib Dem	13,561	23	24	23	John Vincent
Majority	22,060	Con 38	Con 37	Con 39	
Swing			1 → LD	3 → Con	

EREWASH, Derbyshire. Tory marginal, Labour target seat, mainly urban, skilled manual
Owner-occupied 76% (133rd); No central heating 21% (173rd); Skilled manual 35% (43rd)

0.2% change	Notional 92	%	92	87	Candidates
Conservative	29,970	47	47	49	Angela Knight, MP
Labour	24,247	38	38	32	Elizabeth Blackman, teacher, council deputy leader
Lib Dem	8,623	14	14	19	Martin Garnett
Majority	5,723	Con 9	Con 9	Con 17	
Swing			4 → Lab	2 → Lab	Lab needs 5 to win. 59th on Lab list

ERITH & THAMESMEAD, South London. New Labour seat, outer suburbs, white collar
Age 25-39 27% (34th); Black 5% (48th); White collar 20% (8th)

94% change	Notional 92	%			Candidates
Conservative	15,615	32			Nadhim Zahawi, sales director, manufacturing
Labour	21,245	43			John Austin-Walker, MP
Lib Dem	12,555	25			Alexander Grigg, marketing director, printing co
Majority	5,630	Lab 11			

ESHER & WALTON, Surrey. Strong Tory seat, stockbroker belt, managerial
Car owners 83% (32nd); Professional 12% (31st); Managerial 48% (6th)

65% change	Notional 92	%	92	87	Candidates
Conservative	33,237	61	65	66	Ian Taylor, MP
Labour	9,513	17	12	9	Julie Reay
Lib Dem	12,013	22	23	26	Gary Miles
Majority	21,224	Con 39	Con 43	Con 40	
Swing			2 → Con	2 → Con	

ESSEX NORTH, Essex. New strong Tory seat, mainly rural, managerial
Age 40-pension 30% (27th); Self-employed 17% (44th); Owner-occupied 82% (24th)

80% change	Notional 92	%			Candidates
Conservative	31,309	58			Bernard Jenkin, MP
Labour	10,347	19			Timothy Young
Lib Dem	12,059	22			Andrew Phillips
Majority	19,250	Con 36			

EXETER, Devon. Tory marginal, Labour target seat, mainly urban, white collar
No central heating 34% (51st); Mobility 13% (42nd); White collar 18% (33rd)

1% change	Notional 92	%	92	87	Candidates
Conservative	25,693	41	41	44	Dr Adrian Rogers, GP
Labour	22,629	36	36	23	Ben Bradshaw
Lib Dem	12,129	19	19	32	Dennis Brewer
Majority	3,064	Con 5	Con 5	Con 13	
Swing			9 → Lab	2 → SDPAll	Lab needs 2 to win. 32nd on Lab list

FALKIRK EAST, Central. Labour seat, mainly urban

29% change	Notional 92	%	92	87	Candidates
Conservative	8,771	20	21	19	Malcolm Nicol
Labour	19,183	44	46	54	Michael Connarty, MP
Lib Dem	3,159	7	7	12	Roger Spillane
SNP	12,327	28	26	15	Keith Brown
Majority	6,856	Lab 16	Lab 20	Lab 36	
Swing			10 → SNP	4 → Lab	SNP needs 8 to win. 12th on SNP list

FALKIRK WEST, Central. Strong Labour seat, urban

15% change	Notional 92	%	92	87	Candidates
Conservative	7,719	19	20	17	Carol Buchanan
Labour	21,065	52	50	53	Dennis Canavan, MP
Lib Dem	2,522	6	6	13	Derek Houston
SNP	9,635	24	24	17	David Alexander, councillor
Majority	11,430	Lab 28	Lab 26	Lab 35	
Swing			5 → SNP	5 → Lab	

FALMOUTH & CAMBORNE, Cornwall. Tory seat, 3-way marginal, mainly urban
Self-employed 16% (68th); Second homes 1% (62nd); No central heating 32% (59th)

No Change	Actual 92	%		87	Candidates
Conservative	21,150	37		44	Sebastian Coe, MP
Labour	16,732	29		35	Candy Atherton, journalist
Lib Dem	17,883	31		21	Terrye Jones, manager/partner in printing comp
Majority	3,267	Con 6		Con 9	
Swing		2 → Lib Dem		7 → SDPAll	Lab needs 4 to win. 50th on Lab list
					LD need 3 to win. 13th on LD list

FAREHAM, Hampshire. Strong Tory seat, seaside, professional
Age 40-pension 29% (53rd); Owner-occupied 86% (5th); Professional 10% (66th)

19% change	Notional 92	%	92	87	Candidates
Conservative	32,588	61	61	61	Peter Lloyd, MP
Labour	7,980	15	13	9	Michael Prior
Lib Dem	12,489	23	25	30	Grace Hill
Majority	20,099	Con 37	Con 36	Con 31	
Swing			3 → Con	No swing	

FAVERSHAM & KENT MID, Kent. New strong Tory seat, mainly rural, middle-class
Self-employed 14% (130th); Professional 9% (123rd); Managerial 36% (133th)

125% change	Notional 92	%			Candidates
Conservative	32,047	59			Andrew Rowe, MP
Labour	12,448	23			Alan Stewart
Lib Dem	9,225	17			Bruce Parmenter
Majority	19,599	Con 36			

FELTHAM & HESTON, West London. Labour marginal, outer suburbs, white collar
Asian 21% (14th); Overcrowding 5% (24th); White collar 18% (35th)

12% change	Notional 92	%	92	87	Candidates
Conservative	22,894	43	43	47	Patrick Ground, former MP
Labour	24,294	46	46	37	Alan Keen, MP
Lib Dem	6,189	12	11	16	Colin Penning
Majority	1,400	Lab 3	Lab 3	Con 9	
Swing			6 → Lab	3 → Con	Con need 1 to win. 19th on Con list

FERMANAGH & SOUTH TYRONE, Northern Ireland. Strong Unionist seat, rural

13% change	Notional 92	%	92	87	Candidates
UUP	25,071	52	49	50	Ken Maginnis, MP
SDLP	10,982	23	23	19	Thomas Gallagher, teacher
APNI	830	2	2	2	Steven Farry, researcher
SF	9,143	19	23	26	
Majority	14,089	UUP 29	UUP 26	UUP 23	
Swing			2 → SDLP	5 → UUP	

FIFE CENTRAL, Fife. Strong Labour seat, industrial

2% change	Notional 92	%	92	87	Candidates
Conservative	7,440	18	18	17	Francis Murray
Labour	21,627	51	50	53	Henry McLeish, MP
Lib Dem	2,937	7	7	15	Ross Laird
SNP	10,636	25	25	15	Tricia Marwick
Majority	10,991	Lab 26	Lab 25	Lab 37	
Swing			7 → SNP	8 → Lab	

FIFE NORTH EAST, Fife. Lib Dem marginal, Tory target seat, rural

No Change	Actual 92	%		87	Candidates
Conservative	16,129	39		41	Adam Bruce
Labour	2,337	6		7	Charles Milne
Lib Dem	19,432	46		45	Menzies Campbell, MP, QC
SNP	3,598	9		7	Colin Welsh
Majority	3,303	LD 8		LD 4	
Swing		2 → LD		5 → LibAll	

FINCHLEY & GOLDERS GREEN, North London. New strong Tory seat, suburban, middle-class,
Other non-white 8% (4th); Private tenants 20% (10th); Managerial 47% (10th)

73% change	Notional 92	%			Candidates
Conservative	28,623	55			John Marshall, MP
Labour	16,149	31			Rudolph Vis
Lib Dem	6,690	13			Jonathan Davies
Majority	12,474	Con 24			

FOLKESTONE & HYTHE, Kent. Tory seat, Lib Dem long-shot, seaside
Pensionable 25% (32nd); Private tenants 12% (59th); Second homes 2% (33rd)

No Change	Actual 92	%		87	Candidates
Conservative	27,435	52		55	Michael Howard, MP
Labour	6,347	12		7	Peter Doherty
Lib Dem	18,527	35		37	David Laws
Majority	8,908	Con 17		Con 18	
Swing		1 → LD		3 → LibAll	LD need 8 to win. 47th on LD list

FOREST OF DEAN, Gloucestershire. New Labour marginal, Tory target seat, rural
Age 40-pension 29% (71st); White 99.6% (11th); Self-employed 16% (65th)

22% change	Notional 92	%	Candidates
Conservative	21,444	41	Paul Marland, MP
Labour	22,176	43	Diana Organ, former deputy head of primary sc
Lib Dem	8,422	16	Dr Anthony Lynch
Majority	732	Lab 1	Con need 1 to win. 9th on Con list

FOYLE, Northern Ireland. Strong SDLP seat, urban, based on Derry

17% change	Notional 92	%	92	87	Candidates
DUP	10,809	25	26	29	
SDLP	23,291	54	52	49	John Hume, MP
APNI	866	2	3	3	
SF	7,475	17	18	18	
UUP					Andrew Davidson
Majority	12,482	SDLP 29	SDLP 25	SDLP 20	
Swing			2 → SDLP	2 → SDLP	

FYLDE, Lancashire. Strong Tory seat, seaside, middle-class
Pensionable 25% (29th); Second homes 1% (83rd); Professional 11% (62nd)

13% change	Notional 92	%	92	87	Candidates
Conservative	31,849	60	61	61	Michael Jack, MP
Labour	9,827	19	19	14	John Garrett, MP
Lib Dem	10,937	21	19	24	Bill Greene
Majority	20,912	Con 40	Con 42	Con 37	
Swing			3 → Con	1 → LibAll	

GAINSBOROUGH, Lincolnshire. Strong Tory seat, mainly rural
Age 40-pension 30% (39th); White 99.4% (73rd); Car owners 78% (128th)

13% change	Notional 92	%	92	87	Candidates
Conservative	26,919	53	54	53	Edward Leigh, MP
Labour	10,533	21	20	12	Paul Taylor
Lib Dem	12,993	26	26	35	Neil Taylor
Majority	13,926	Con 28	Con 28	Con 18	

GALLOWAY & UPPER NITHSDALE, Dumfries and Galloway. Tory marginal, SNP target, rural

3% change	Notional 92	%	92	87	Candidates
Conservative	18,173	42	42	40	Ian Lang, MP
Labour	5,609	13	13	13	Katy Clark
Lib Dem	3,721	9	9	15	John McKerchar
SNP	15,773	37	36	32	Alasdair Morgan
Majority	2,400	Con 6	Con 6	Con 9	
Swing			2 → SNP	3 → SNP	SNP needs 3 to win. 2nd on SNP list

GATESHEAD EAST & WASHINGTON WEST, Tyne and Wear. Strong Labour seat, urban
Govt schemes 2% (49th); Council tenants 44% (15th); Single parents 23% (127th)

69% change	Notional 92	%	92	87	Candidates
Conservative	13,492	28	24	24	Jacqueline Burns, self-employed accountant
Labour	28,192	58	64	59	Joyce Quin, MP
Lib Dem	6,963	14	12	17	Alan Ord
Majority	14,700	Lab 30	Lab 39	Lab 35	
Swing			2 → Lab	7 → Lab	

GEDLING, Nottinghamshire. Tory seat, Labour long-shot, commuting
Age 40-pension 29% (118th); Owner-occupied 80% (49th); Skilled manual 31% (154th)

No Change	Actual 92	%	92	87	Candidates
Conservative	30,191	53		55	Andrew Mitchell, MP
Labour	19,554	34		24	Vernon Coaker
Lib Dem	6,863	12		22	Ray Poynter
Majority	10,637	Con 19		Con 31	
Swing		6 → Lab		2 → Lab	Lab needs 9 to win. 108th on Lab list

GILLINGHAM, Kent. Strong Tory seat, mainly urban, working class
Age 25-39 24% (94th); Owner-occupied 80% (44th); White collar 15% (135th)

3% change	Notional 92	%	92	87	Candidates
Conservative	29,092	52	52	53	James Couchman, MP
Labour	13,332	24	24	17	Paul Clark
Lib Dem	13,150	24	23	30	Robert Sayer
Majority	15,760	Con 28	Con 29	Con 23	
Swing			4 → Lab	1 → Con	

GLASGOW ANNIESLAND, Strathclyde. New strong Labour seat, outer suburbs

29% change	Notional 92	%	92	87	Candidates
Conservative	5,895	16	12	11	Andrew Brocklehurst
Labour	20,000	53	64	68	Donald Dewar, MP
Lib Dem	5,166	14	5	9	Christopher McGinty
SNP	6,411	17	19	12	Dr William Wilson
Majority	13,589	Lab 36	Lab 45	Lab 55	
Swing			5 → SNP	5 → Lab	

GLASGOW BAILLIESTON, Strathclyde. New strong Labour seat, outer suburbs

94% change	Notional 92	%	Candidates
Conservative	3,448	10	Malcolm Kelly
Labour	22,030	63	James Wray, MP
Lib Dem	1,505	4	
SNP	7,865	23	Patsy Thomson
Majority	14,165	Lab 41	

GLASGOW CATHCART, Strathclyde. Strong Labour seat, suburban

46% change	Notional 92	%	92	87	Candidates
Conservative	8,167	22	25	22	Alistair Muir
Labour	18,719	49	48	52	John Maxton, MP
Lib Dem	2,732	7	8	15	
SNP	7,244	19	18	10	Maire Whitehead
Majority	10,552	Lab 28	Lab 24	Lab 30	
Swing			3 → Con	9 → Lab	

GLASGOW GOVAN, Strathclyde. Labour seat, shipbuilding

123% change	Notional 92	%	92	87	Candidates
Conservative	7,165	20	10	12	William Thomas
Labour	15,665	43	49	65	Mohammed Sarwar
Lib Dem	2,033	6	4	12	Bob Stewart
SNP	10,056	28	37	10	Nicola Sturgeon
Majority	5,609	Lab 15	Lab 12	Lab 53	
Swing			21 → SNP	9 → Lab	SNP needs 8 to win. 11th on SNP list

GLASGOW KELVIN, Strathclyde. Strong Labour seat, inner city

35% change	Notional 92	%	92	87	Candidates
Conservative	4,765	13	17	14	Duncan McPhie
Labour	16,971	47	39	43	George Galloway, MP
Lib Dem	6,848	19	26	35	Elspeth Buchanan
SNP	6,982	19	17	7	Sandra White, councillor
Majority	9,989	Lab 28	Lab 12	Lab 8	
Swing			2 → Lab	5 → Lab	

GLASGOW MARYHILL, Strathclyde. Strong Labour seat, suburban

17% change	Notional 92	%	92	87
Conservative	3,241	10	10	9
Labour	21,042	63	62	66
Lib Dem	2,238	7	7	12
SNP	6,530	19	19	11
Majority	14,512	Lab 43	Lab 43	Lab 55
Swing			6 → SNP	11 → Lab

Candidates
Stuart Baldwin
Maria Fyfe, MP
Elspeth Attwool
John Wailes, councillor

GLASGOW POLLOK, Strathclyde. Strong Labour seat, inner city

100% change	Notional 92	%	92	87
Conservative	3,107	8	16	14
Labour	18,945	50	43	63
Lib Dem	1,648	4	6	12
SNP	9,492	25	16	10
Majority	9,453	Lab 25	Lab 24	Lab 49
Swing			No swing	9 → Lab

Candidates
Edwin Hamilton
Ian Davidson, MP
David Jago
David Logan

GLASGOW RUTHERGLEN, Strathclyde. Strong Labour seat, outer suburbs

16% change	Notional 92	%	92	87
Conservative	7,443	19	17	12
Labour	20,742	53	55	56
Lib Dem	4,529	12	11	24
SNP	6,052	16	16	8
Majority	13,299	Lab 34	Lab 39	Lab 32
Swing			3 → Con	6 → Lab

Candidates
David Bannerman
Thomas McAvoy, MP
Robert Brown
Ian Gray, councillor

GLASGOW SHETTLESTON, Strathclyde. Strong Labour seat, inner city

100% change	Notional 92	%	92	87
Conservative	3,876	12	15	13
Labour	20,767	66	61	64
Lib Dem	1,939	6	5	10
SNP	5,123	16	19	13
Majority	15,644	Lab 49	Lab 42	Lab 50
Swing			5 → SNP	8 → Lab

Candidates
Colin Simpson
David Marshall, MP

Humayun Hanif

GLASGOW SPRINGBURN, Strathclyde. Strong Labour seat, inner city

44% change	Notional 92	%	92	87
Conservative	3,909	11	9	8
Labour	23,347	65	68	74
Lib Dem	1,559	4	4	8
SNP	7,150	20	20	10
Majority	16,197	Lab 45	Lab 48	Lab 63
Swing			8 → SNP	3 → Lab

Candidates
Mark Holdsworth
Michael Martin, MP
Erlend Watson
John Brady

GLOUCESTER, Gloucestershire. Tory marginal, Labour target seat, urban
Black 2.7% (90th); Mobility 12% (78th); White collar 16% (103rd)

6% change	Notional 92	%	92	87
Conservative	28,274	46	46	50
Labour	22,867	37	37	30
Lib Dem	10,961	18	17	21
Majority	5,407	Con 9	Con 9	Con 20
Swing			5 → Lab	1 → Lab

Candidates
Douglas French, MP
Tess Kingham, PR, War on Want
Peter Munisamy

Lab needs 4 to win. 58th on Lab list

GORDON, Grampian. Strong Tory seat, rural, based on Lib Dem seat

64% change	Notional 92	%	92	87
Conservative	19,596	48	37	32
Labour	2,561	6	11	50
Lib Dem	11,110	27	37	12
SNP	7,593	19	14	7
Majority	8,486	Con 21	LD 1	Lab 18
Swing			9 → Con	8 → LibAll

Candidates
John Porter
Lindsey Kirkhill
Malcolm Bruce, MP, barrister
Richard Lochhead

GOSPORT, Hampshire. Strong Tory seat, seaside, working class
Age 16-24 14% (109th); Second homes .3% (168th); Mobility 13% (44th)

No Change	Actual 92	%	87	Candidates
Conservative	31,094	58	59	Peter Viggers, MP
Labour	7,275	14	10	Ivan Gray
Lib Dem	14,776	28	32	Brian Dash
Majority	16,318	Con 31	Con 27	
Swing		2 → Con	2 → LibAll	

GOWER, West Glamorgan. Labour seat, Welsh-speaking
Owner-occupied 80% (55th); Second homes 1% (52nd); Long-term ill 16% (47th)

No Change	Actual 92	%	87	Candidates
Conservative	16,437	35	35	Alun Cairns, business consultant
Labour	23,455	50	47	Martin Caton
Lib Dem	4,655	10	16	Howard Evans
Plaid Cymru	1,658	4	3	Elwyn Williams
Majority	7,018	Lab 15	Lab 12	
Swing		1 → Lab	5 → Lab	

GRANTHAM & STAMFORD, Lincolnshire. New strong Tory seat, mainly rural
Private tenants 8% (159th); Car owners 74% (214th); Mobility 12% (93rd)

91% change	Notional 92	%		Candidates
Conservative	31,263	58		Quentin Davies, MP
Labour	14,105	26		Peter Denning
Lib Dem	8,663	16		John Sellick
Majority	17,158	Con 32		

GRAVESHAM, Kent. Tory marginal, Labour target seat, mainly urban, working class
Age 16-24 13% (173rd); Asian 7% (60th); Skilled manual 31% (164th)

1% change	Notional 92	%	92	87	Candidates
Conservative	29,031	50	50	50	Jacques Arnold, MP
Labour	23,663	40	40	35	Chris Pond, director, Low Pay Unit
Lib Dem	5,207	9	9	15	(Jean) Merilyn Canet
Majority	5,368	Con 9	Con 9	Con 15	
Swing		3 → Lab		No swing	Lab needs 5 to win. 64th on Lab list

GREAT GRIMSBY, Humberside. Labour seat, fishing, working class
No central heating 31% (61st); Single parents 27% (73rd); Unskilled 7% (45th)

No Change	Actual 92	%	87	Candidates
Conservative	18,391	36	28	Dean Godson
Labour	25,895	51	46	Austin Mitchell, MP
Lib Dem	6,475	13	26	Andrew de Freitas
Majority	7,504	Lab 15	Lab 17	
Swing		1 → Con	8 → Lab	

GREAT YARMOUTH, Norfolk. Tory seat, Labour long-shot, urban, working class
Pensioners 22% (80th); Second homes 1% (88th); Skilled manual 32% (122nd)

No Change	Actual 92	%	87	Candidates
Conservative	25,505	48	52	Michael Carttiss
Labour	20,196	38	31	Tony Wright, council leader, director GY tourist authority
Lib Dem	7,225	14	17	
Majority	5,309	Con 10	Con 21	
Swing		5 → Lab	2 → Lab	Lab needs 5 to win. 68th on Lab list

GREENOCK & INVERCLYDE, Strathclyde. Strong Labour seat, industrial

54% change	Notional 92	%	92	87	Candidates
Conservative	8,081	21	12	10	Hugo Swire
Labour	18,319	48	58	64	Dr Norman Godman, MP
Lib Dem	5,324	14	11	18	Rod Ackland
SNP	6,621	17	19	9	Brian Goodall
Majority	10,238	Lab 27	Lab 39	Lab 46	
Swing			8 → SNP	18 → Lab	

GREENWICH & WOOLWICH, South London. Labour marginal, Lib Dem target seat, urban, large black population
Council tenants 48% (10th); Single parents 37% (22nd); Unskilled 8% (28th)

38% change	Notional 92	%	92	87	Candidates
Conservative	8,565	18	20	23	Michael Mitchell, finance director
Labour	20,951	45	41	35	Nick Raynsford, MP
Lib Dem	16,478	35	37	41	Cherry Luxton, teacher
Majority	4,473	Lab 10	Lab 4	SDP 6	
Swing			5 → Lab	9 → SDP	LD need 5 to win. 19th on LD list

GUILDFORD, Surrey. Strong Tory seat, mainly urban, professional
Mobility 12% (75th); Professional 13% (23rd); Managerial 40% (69th)

2% change	Notional 92	%	92	87	Candidates
Conservative	32,820	55	55	56	Nick St Aubyn, investment banker
Labour	6,732	11	11	11	Joseph Burns
Lib Dem	19,478	33	33	34	Margaret Sharp, university lecturer
Majority	13,342	Con 23	Con 22	Con 22	
Swing			No swing	No swing	

HACKNEY NORTH & STOKE NEWINGTON, North London. Strong Labour seat, inner city, high unemployment
Black 21% (7th); Unemployed 23% (6th); Overcrowding 8% (4th)

No Change	Actual 92	%		87	Candidates
Conservative	9,356	27		29	Michael Lavender
Labour	20,083	58		49	Diane Abbott, MP
Lib Dem	3,996	12		19	Douglas Taylor
Majority	10,727	Lab 31		Lab 20	
Swing		6 → Lab		2 → Con	

HACKNEY SOUTH & SHOREDITCH, North London. Strong Labour seat, inner city, high unemployment
Unemployed 23% (7th); Single parents 45% (5th); Unskilled 10% (4th)

0.1% change	Notional 92	%	92	87	Candidates
Conservative	10,699	29	29	29	Christopher O'Leary, university administrator
Labour	19,702	53	53	48	Brian Sedgemore, MP
Lib Dem	5,525	15	15	22	Martin Pantling
Majority	9,003	Lab 24	Lab 24	Lab 19	
Swing			3 → Lab	1 → Con	

HALESOWEN & ROWLEY REGIS, West Midlands. Tory marginal, mainly urban, working class
Council tenants 27% (114th); No central heating 24% (118th); Skilled manual 35% (59th)

88% change	Notional 92	%	92	87	Candidates
Conservative	24,306	45	51	50	John Kennedy, company director
Labour	24,181	45	36	28	Sylvia Heal, officer, Carers' National Association
Lib Dem	5,384	10	12	22	
Majority	125	Con 0.2	Con 15	Con 22	
Swing			4 → Lab	1 → Lab	Lab needs 0.1 to win. 3rd on Lab list

HALIFAX, West Yorkshire. Labour marginal, urban, skilled manual
Asian 7% (67th); Overcrowding 3% (82nd); No central heating 36% (42nd)

No Change	Actual 92	%		87	Candidates
Conservative	24,637	43		41	Robert Light, farmer, businessman
Labour	25,115	44		43	Alice Mahon, MP
Lib Dem	7,364	13		15	Edgar Waller
Majority	478	Lab 1		Lab 2	
Swing		1 → Con		3 → Lab	Con need 0.4 to win. 5th on Con list

HALTEMPRICE & HOWDEN, Humberside. Strong Tory seat, rural, middle-class, based on Beverley
Age 40-pension 31% (5th); Owner-occupied 83% (18th); Car owners 81% (59th)

68% change	Notional 92	%	92	87	Candidates
Conservative	30,085	59	53	52	David Davis, MP
Labour	7,774	15	19	16	George McManus
Lib Dem	12,772	25	28	31	Diana Wallis
Majority	17,313	Con 34	Con 26	Con 21	
Swing			2 → Con	2 → Lib Dem	

HALTON, Cheshire. Strong Labour seat, industrial, working class
White 99.4% (84th); No central heating 32% (57th); Skilled manual 35% (57th)

13% change	Notional 92	%	92	87	Candidates
Conservative	15,426	30	29	30	Philip Balmer
Labour	30,363	60	60	56	Derek Twigg
Lib Dem	4,499	9	10	14	
Majority	14,937	Lab 29	Lab 31	Lab 25	
Swing			3 → Lab	6 → Lab	

HAMILTON NORTH & BELLSHILL, Strathclyde. Strong Labour seat, industrial, based on Motherwell N

62% change	Notional 92	%	92	87	Candidates
Conservative	6,115	15	11	11	Gordon McIntosh
Labour	23,422	58	63	67	Dr John Reid, MP
Lib Dem	2,715	7	5	8	
SNP	7,932	20	20	14	Michael Mathieson
Majority	15,490	Lab 39	Lab 43	Lab 53	
Swing			5 → SNP	4 → Lab	

HAMILTON SOUTH, Strathclyde. Strong Labour seat, industrial

25% change	Notional 92	%	92	87	Candidates
Conservative	5,596	16	18	14	Robert Kilgour
Labour	19,816	57	55	60	George Robertson, MP
Lib Dem	2,308	7	8	13	
SNP	7,074	20	20	13	Ian Black
Majority	12,742	Lab 37	Lab 35	Lab 45	
Swing			6 → SNP	6 → Lab	

HAMMERSMITH & FULHAM, West London. Tory seat, Labour long-shot, urban, middle-class
Age 25-39 32% (4th); Private tenants 24% (4th); Mobility 18% (3rd)

39% change	Notional 92	%	92	87	Candidates
Conservative	28,487	52	53	52	Matthew Carrington, MP
Labour	21,313	39	37	37	Iain Colman
Lib Dem	4,553	8	8	10	Alexi Sugden
Majority	7,174	Con13	Con 16	Con 15	
Swing			1 → Con	1 → Con	Lab needs 7 to win. 77th on Lab list

HAMPSHIRE EAST, Hampshire. Strong Tory seat, rural, middle-class
Age 40-pension 30% (42nd); Owner-occupied 80% (47th); Car owners 83% (30th)

110% change	Notional 92	%	92	87	Candidates
Conservative	35,960	61	64	65	Michael Mates, MP
Labour	5,605	10	9	7	Robert Hoyle
Lib Dem	16,303	28	25	29	Robert Booker
Majority	19,657	Con 33	Con 39	Con 36	
Swing			2 → Con	2 → Con	

HAMPSHIRE NORTH EAST, Hampshire. Strong Tory seat, rural, professional
Car owners 87% (2nd); Professional 12% (36th); Managerial 42% (46th)

43% change	Notional 92	%	92	87	Candidates
Conservative	33,782	64	64	65	James Arbuthnot, MP
Labour	4,854	9	9	7	Peter Dare
Lib Dem	13,242	25	25	29	Ian Mann
Majority	20,540	Con 39	Con 39	Con 36	
Swing			2 → Con	2 → Con	

HAMPSHIRE NORTH WEST, Hampshire. Strong Tory seat, mainly rural, middle-class
Age 40-pension 29% (95th); Car owners 81% (61st); Mobility 12% (85th)

26% change	Notional 92	%	92	87	Candidates
Conservative	33,154	58	58	58	Sir George Young, MP
Labour	7,175	13	13	9	Michael Mumford
Lib Dem	15,990	28	28	33	Charlie Fleming
Majority	17,164	Con 30	Con 30	Con 25	
Swing			3 → Con	No swing	

HAMPSTEAD & HIGHGATE, North London. Labour marginal, Tory target seat, urban, middle-class
Private tenants 26% (3rd); Mobility 18% (5th); Managerial 47% (8th)

7% change	Notional 92	%	92	87	Candidates
Conservative	18,582	41	42	43	Elizabeth Gibson, part-time teacher, director
Labour	21,059	46	45	38	Glenda Jackson, MP
Lib Dem	5,028	11	11	19	Bridget Fox
Majority	2,477	Lab 5	Lab 3	Con 5	
Swing			4 → Lab	1 → Lab	Con need 3 to win. 41st on Con list

HARBOROUGH, Leicestershire. Tory seat, Lib Dem long-shot, rural, middle-class
Age 40-pension 29% (79th); Asian 4% (100th); Owner-occupied 84% (16th)

12% change	Notional 92	%	92	87	Candidates
Conservative	29,274	53	55	59	Edward Garnier, MP
Labour	6,828	12	12	13	Nick Holden
Lib Dem	19,122	35	33	28	Mark Cox
Majority	10,152	Con 18	Con 22	Con 32	
Swing			5 → Lib Dem	1 → LibAll	LD need 9 to win. 55th on LD list

HARLOW, Essex. Tory marginal, Labour target seat, new town, skilled manual
Age 25-39 24% (89th); Council tenants 42% (23rd); Overcrowding 3% (69th)

6% change	Notional 92	%	92	87	Candidates
Conservative	24,568	46	47	47	Jerry Hayes, MP
Labour	22,881	43	42	37	Bill Rammell, commercial manager
Lib Dem	6,002	11	11	16	Lorna Spenceley
Majority	1,687	Con 3	Con 5	Con 11	
Swing			3 → Lab	2 → Con	Lab needs 2 to win. 21st on Lab list

HARROGATE & KNARESBOROUGH, North Yorkshire. Tory seat, Lib Dem long-shot, mainly urban, middle-class
Pensionable 22% (79th); Managerial 40% (67th); White collar 17% (54th)

16% change	Notional 92	%	92	87	Candidates
Conservative	25,909	52	54	56	Norman Lamont, MP
Labour	6,777	14	12	10	Barbara Boyce
Lib Dem	16,698	33	33	34	Phil Willis, head teacher
Majority	9,211	Con 18	Con 21	Con 21	
Swing			No swing	5 → SDPAll	LD need 9 to win. 57th on LD list

HARROW EAST, North London. Tory seat, Labour long-shot, suburban, large Asian community
Asian 21% (15th); Other non-white 5% (29th); White collar 18% (38th)

2% change	Notional 92	%	92	87	Candidates
Conservative	31,624	53	53	54	Hugh Dykes, MP
Labour	20,219	34	34	24	Tony McNulty
Lib Dem	6,471	11	11	23	Baldev Sharma
Majority	11,405	Con 19	Con 19	Con 31	
Swing			6 → Lab	2 → Con	Lab needs 10 to win. 112th on Lab list

HARROW WEST, North London. Strong Tory seat, outer suburbs, large non-white population
Asian 14% (26th); Other non-white 5% (25th); Managerial 42% (47th)

No Change	Actual 92	%	87	Candidates
Conservative	30,227	55	55	Bob Hughes, MP
Labour	12,337	23	18	Gareth Thomas
Lib Dem	11,045	20	27	Pash Nandhra
Majority	17,890	Con 33	Con 28	
Swing		3 → Lab	4 → Con	

HARTLEPOOL, Cleveland. Labour seat, urban, working class
Govt schemes 4% (5th); Long-term ill 16% (66th); Unskilled 7% (58th)

No Change	Actual 92	%	87	Candidates
Conservative	18,034	35	34	Michael Horsley, political researcher
Labour	26,816	52	49	Peter Mandelson, MP
Lib Dem	6,860	13	14	Reg Clark
Majority	8,782	Lab 17	Lab 15	
Swing		1 → Lab	4 → Lab	

HARWICH, Essex. Strong Tory seat, mainly rural, working class
Pensionable 34% (5th); Second homes 2% (16th); Long-term ill 17% (36th)

8% change	Notional 92	%	92	87	Candidates
Conservative	29,372	52	52	52	Iain Sproat, MP
Labour	14,047	25	23	18	Ivan Henderson
Lib Dem	13,187	23	24	31	Ann Elvin
Majority	15,325	Con 27	Con 28	Con 21	
Swing			3 → Con	2 → LibAll	

HASTINGS & RYE, East Sussex. Tory seat, Lib Dem long-shot, seaside, white collar
Pensionable 24% (37th); Private tenants 14% (43rd); Second homes 1% (38th)

No Change	Actual 92	%	92	87	Candidates
Conservative	25,573	48		50	Jacqui Lait, MP
Labour	8,458	16		13	Michael Foster
Lib Dem	18,939	35		36	Monroe Palmer, chartered accountant
Majority	6,634	Con 12		Con 14	
Swing		1 → Lib Dem		4 → Lib All	LD need 6 to win. 33rd on LD list

HAVANT, Hampshire. Strong Tory seat, mainly urban, working class
Second homes 1% (82nd); Overcrowding 3% (122nd); No central heating 25% (114th)

50% change	Notional 92	%	92	87	Candidates
Conservative	27,981	53	55	57	David Willetts, MP
Labour	13,812	20	19	14	Lynne Armstrong
Lib Dem	10,465	26	25	28	Mike Kooner
Majority	14,169	Con 27	Con 30	Con 29	
Swing			1 → Con	3 → Con	

HAYES & HARLINGTON, West London. Tory marginal, airport, large Asian community
Age 25-39 26% (42nd); Asian 15% (23rd); Overcrowding 5% (30th)

0.1% change	Notional 92	%	92	87	Candidates
Conservative	19,511	45	45	49	Andrew Retter, accounts & logistics manager
Labour	19,467	45	45	36	John McDonnell, former GLC councillor
Lib Dem	4,477	10	10	15	Tony Little
Majority	44	Con 0.1	Con 0.1	Con 14	
Swing			7 → Lab	2 → Con	Lab needs 0.1 to win. 2nd on Lab list

HAZEL GROVE, Greater Manchester. Tory marginal, Lib Dem target seat, commuting, middle-class
Age 40-pension 29% (64th); Professional 10% (93rd); Managerial 38% (96th)

No Change	Actual 92	%		87	Candidates
Conservative	24,479	45		46	Brendan Murphy, councillor
Labour	6,390	12		12	
Lib Dem	23,550	43		42	Andrew Stunell, special projects officer for ALDC
Majority	929	Con 2		Con 3	
Swing		1 → Lib Dem		No swing	LD need 1 to win. 4th on LD list

HEMEL HEMPSTEAD, Hertfordshire. Tory seat, Labour long-shot, new town, white collar
Age 25-39 24% (90th); Council tenants 31% (73rd); White collar 15% (140th)

19% change	Notional 92	%	92	87	Candidates
Conservative	29,248	50	52	50	Robert Jones, MP
Labour	19,090	33	30	24	Tony McWalter
Lib Dem	9,005	15	16	26	Patricia Lindsley
Majority	10,158	Con 17	Con 22	Con 23	
Swing			2 → Lab	4 → Con	Lab needs 9 to win. 99th on Lab list

HEMSWORTH, West Yorkshire. Strong Labour seat, mining, skilled manual
Council tenants 29% (94th); Long-term ill 16% (67th); Skilled manual 35% (45th)

21% change	Notional 92	%	96 by-	92	87	Candidates
Conservative	13,428	26	9	19	17	Norman Hazell
Labour	33,229	64	72	71	67	Jon Trickett, MP
Lib Dem	5,424	10	7	11	16	
Majority	19,801	Lab 38	Lab 63	Lab 52	Lab 50	
Swing			5 → Lab	1 → Lab	5 → Lab	

HENDON, North London. Strong Tory seat, suburban, large non-white population
Asian 11% (41st); Other non-white 6% (12th); White collar 19% (32nd)

41% change	Notional 92	%	92	87	Candidates
Conservative	28,916	54	53	56	Sir John Gorst, MP
Labour	18,068	34	35	26	Andrew Dismore
Lib Dem	6,289	12	11	19	Wayne Casey
Majority	10,848	Con 20	Con 18	Con 30	
Swing			6 → Lab	2 → Con	

HENLEY, Oxfordshire. Strong Tory seat, mainly rural, middle-class
Age 40-pension 30% (25th); Car owners 85% (7th); Managerial 44% (29th)

3% change	Notional 92	%	92	87	Candidates
Conservative	31,651	60	60	61	Michael Heseltine, MP
Labour	7,802	15	15	13	Duncan Enright
Lib Dem	12,608	24	24	26	Timothy Horton
Majority	19,043	Con 36	Con 36	Con 35	
Swing			No swing	2 → Con	

HEREFORD, Hereford and Worcester. Tory marginal, Lib Dem target seat, mainly rural
White 99.3% (109th); Self-employed 15% (84th); Second homes 1% (96th)

1% change	Notional 92	%	92	87	Candidates
Conservative	26,217	47	47	48	Colin Shepherd, MP
Labour	5,910	11	11	8	Chris Chapell
Lib Dem	23,063	41	41	45	Paul Keetch
Majority	3,154	Con 6	Con 6	Con 3	
Swing			2 → Con	1 → LibAll	LD need 3 to win. 12th on LD list

HERTFORD & STORTFORD, Hertfordshire. Strong Tory seat, mainly rural, managerial
Car owners 81% (57th); Professional 10% (69th); Managerial 42% (45th)

26% change	Notional 92	%	92	87	Candidates
Conservative	31,942	57	58	58	Bowen Wells, MP
Labour	9,529	17	16	13	
Lib Dem	14,408	26	25	28	Michael Wood
Majority	17,534	Con 31	Con 33	Con 29	
Swing			2 → Con	2 → Con	

HERTFORDSHIRE NORTH EAST, Hertfordshire. Strong Tory seat, part new town, managerial
Age 40-pension 29% (109th); Car owners 79% (105th); Managerial 38% (92nd)

63% change	Notional 92	%	92	87	Candidates
Conservative	28,911	52	50	50	Oliver Heald, MP
Labour	11,908	21	24	19	Ivan Gibbons
Lib Dem	14,775	26	25	32	Steve Jarvis, product marketing manager
Majority	14,136	Con 25	Con 24	Con 18	
Swing			3 → Con	1 → Con	

HERTFORDSHIRE SOUTH WEST, Hertfordshire. Strong Tory seat, stockbroker belt, managerial
Age 40-pension 29% (87th); Managerial 45% (19th); Professional 11% (47th)

38% change	Notional 92	%	92	87	Candidates
Conservative	34,189	59	57	56	Richard Page, MP
Labour	10,062	17	19	15	Mark Wilson
Lib Dem	13,034	23	23	29	Ann Shaw
Majority	21,155	Con 37	Con 34	Con 27	
Swing			4 → Con	3 → Con	

HERTSMERE, Hertfordshire. Strong Tory seat, stockbroker belt, white collar
Professional 10% (94th); Managerial 39% (86th); White collar 17% (64th)

9% change	Notional 92	%	92	87	Candidates
Conservative	30,439	58	57	57	James Clappison, MP
Labour	11,473	22	24	20	Beth Kelly
Lib Dem	10,364	20	19	24	Ann Gray
Majority	18,966	Con 36	Con 33	Con 33	
Swing			2 → Lab	3 → Con	

HEXHAM, Northumberland. Strong Tory seat, rural, middle-class
Age 40-pension 30% (22nd); Second homes 1% (55th); Managerial 41% (58th)

No Change	Actual 92	%	92	87	Candidates
Conservative	24,967	52		50	Peter Atkinson, MP
Labour	11,529	24		18	Ian McMinn
Lib Dem	10,344	22		32	Philip Carr
Majority	13,438	Con 28		Con 18	
Swing		2 → Lab		1 → LibAll	

HEYWOOD & MIDDLETON, Greater Manchester. Labour seat, mainly urban
Council tenants 27% (108th); Single parents 24% (116th); White collar 15% (162nd)

30% change	Notional 92	%	92	87	Candidates
Conservative	17,591	32	33	34	Sebastian Grigg, merchant banker
Labour	25,885	47	52	50	Jim Dobbin
Lib Dem	11,119	20	12	16	David Clayton
Majority	8,294	Lab 15	Lab 19	Lab 16	
Swing			2 → Lab	3 → Lab	

HIGH PEAK, Derbyshire. Tory marginal, Labour target seat, mainly rural, middle-class
White 99.4% (80th); Self-employed 14% (133rd); Second homes .4% (132nd)

No Change	Actual 92	%		87	Candidates
Conservative	27,535	46		46	Charles Hendry, MP
Labour	22,717	38		29	Tom Levitt, research consultant, teacher
Lib Dem	8,860	15		26	Susan Barber
Majority	4,818	Con 8		Con 17	
Swing		4 → Lab		2 → Lab	Lab needs 4 to win. 53rd on Lab list

HITCHIN & HARPENDEN, Hertfordshire. New strong Tory seat, mainly rural, managerial
Car owners 81% (78th); Professional 12% (28th); Managerial 46% (12th)

102% change	Notional 92	%	Candidates
Conservative	33,402	61	Peter Lilley, MP
Labour	9,711	18	Rosemary Sanderson
Lib Dem	10,766	20	Chris White
Majority	22,636	Con 42	

HOLBORN & ST PANCRAS, Central London. Strong Labour seat, inner city, large non-white population
Other non-white 6% (11th); Single parents 39% (13th); Mobility 16% (9th)

7% change	Notional 92	%	92	87	Candidates
Conservative	10,590	28	28	31	Julian Smith, chartered accountant
Labour	20,377	54	55	51	Frank Dobson, MP
Lib Dem	5,213	14	14	18	Justine McGuiness
Majority	9,787	Lab 26	Lab 27	Lab 20	
Swing			4 → Lab	1 → Lab	

HORNCHURCH, East London. Tory seat, Labour long-shot, outer suburbs, white collar
Age 40-pension 29% (116th); Owner-occupied 82% (26th); White collar 20% (10th)

No Change	Actual 92	%		87	Candidates
Conservative	25,817	54		51	Robin Squire, MP
Labour	16,652	35		28	John Cryer
Lib Dem	5,366	11		20	Rabi Martins
Majority	9,165	Con 19		Con 23	
Swing		2 → Lab		1 → Con	Lab needs 9 to win. 109th on Lab list

HORNSEY & WOOD GREEN, North London. Labour marginal, Tory target seat, suburban, middle-class
Age 25-39 30% (8th); Private tenants 21% (7th); Mobility 15% (16th)

No Change	Actual 92	%	92	87	Candidates
Conservative	21,843	39		43	Helena Hart, PA in advertising
Labour	27,020	49		40	Barbara Roche, MP
Lib Dem	5,547	10		15	Lynne Featherstone
Majority	5,177	Lab 9		Con 3	
Swing		6 → Lab		2 → Lab	Con need 5 to win. 72nd on Con list

HORSHAM, West Sussex. Strong Tory seat, mainly rural, managerial
Car owners 84% (12th); Professional 9% (106th); Managerial 42% (43rd)

57% change	Notional 92	%	92	87	Candidates
Conservative	35,769	62	62	64	Francis Maude, ex-MP, merchant banker
Labour	6,858	12	10	9	Maureen Walsh
Lib Dem	13,078	23	25	25	Morwen Millson
Majority	22,691	Con 40	Con 37	Con 38	
Swing			1 → LD	1 → Con	

HOUGHTON & WASHINGTON EAST, Tyne and Wear. Strong Labour seat, industrial, skilled manual
Govt schemes 3% (22nd); Council tenants 42% (22nd); Long-term ill 17% (32nd)

42% change	Notional 92	%	92	87	Candidates
Conservative	10,046	22	25	23	Philip Booth, university lecturer
Labour	30,995	67	62	59	Fraser Kemp
Lib Dem	5,221	11	13	18	
Majority	20,949	Lab 45	Lab 37	Lab 36	
Swing			No swing	4 → Lab	

HOVE, East Sussex. Strong Tory seat, seaside, white collar
Pensionable 27% (15th); Private tenants 18% (14th); White collar 21% (4th)

No Change	Actual 92	%	87	Candidates
Conservative	24,525	49	59	Robert Guy
Labour	12,257	25	18	Ivor Caplin
Lib Dem	9,709	19	22	Sue Bucknall
Majority	12,268	Con 25	Con 37	
Swing		8 → Lab	No swing	

HUDDERSFIELD, West Yorkshire. Labour seat, urban, working class
Age 16-24 14% (42nd); No central heating 45% (10th); Black 6% (42nd)

No Change	Actual 92	%	87	Candidates
Conservative	16,574	34	31	Bill Forrow, psychiatric nurse
Labour	23,832	49	46	Barry Sheerman, MP
Lib Dem	7,777	16	22	Gordon Beever, councillor
Majority	7,258	Lab 15	Lab 15	
Swing		No swing	3 → Lab	

HULL EAST, Humberside. Strong Labour seat, urban, working class
Council tenants 41% (27th); No central heating 44% (12th); Unskilled 9% (6th)

No Change	Actual 92	%	87	Candidates
Conservative	11,373	24	26	Angus West, MD, manufacturing company
Labour	30,092	63	56	John Prescott, MP
Lib Dem	6,050	13	18	
Majority	18,719	Lab 39	Lab 30	
Swing		4 → Lab	5 → Lab	

HULL NORTH, Humberside. Strong Labour seat, urban, working class
Age 16-24 15% (20th); Council tenants 38% (39th); Unskilled 8% (22nd)

No Change	Actual 92	%	87	Candidates
Conservative	11,235	24	27	David Lee, sales & marketing consultant
Labour	26,619	56	51	Kevin McNamara, MP
Lib Dem	9,504	20	22	David Nolan
Majority	15,384	Lab 32	Lab 24	
Swing		4 → Lab	6 → Lab	

HULL WEST & HESSLE, Humberside. Strong Labour seat, mainly urban, working class
Private tenants 13% (46th); No central heating 40% (21st); Unskilled 7% (47th)

19% change	Notional 92	%	92	87	Candidates
Conservative	13,634	30	29	30	Cormach Moore, marketing strategist
Labour	23,251	52	57	52	Stuart Randall, MP
Lib Dem	7,837	17	13	18	Bob Tress
Majority	9,617	Lab 21	Lab 29	Lab 22	
Swing			4 → Lab	6 → Lab	

HUNTINGDON, Cambridgeshire. Strong Tory seat, rural, middle-class
Age 16-24 14% (81st); Car owners 81% (74th); Mobility 13% (35th)

85% change	Notional 92	%	92	87	Candidates
Conservative	34,124	60	66	64	John Major, MP
Labour	8,234	15	17	14	Jason Reece
Lib Dem	12,153	21	13	21	Matthew Owen
Majority	21,971	Con 39	Con 49	Con 42	
Swing			No swing	3 → Con	

HYNDBURN, Lancashire. Labour marginal, Tory target seat, mainly urban, skilled manual, Lab gain in 92
Asian 5% (79th); No central heating 31% (63rd); Skilled manual 34% (77th)

13% change	Notional 92	%	92	87	Candidates
Conservative	23,995	43	43	44	Peter Britcliffe, councillor
Labour	26,026	47	47	40	Greg Pope, MP
Lib Dem	5,314	10	10	15	Les Jones
Majority	2,031	Lab 4	Lab 4	Con 5	
Swing			4 → Lab	2 → Con	Con need 2 to win. 28th on Con list

ILFORD NORTH, East London. Strong Tory seat, suburban, white collar
Asian 7% (57th); Other non-white 3% (61st); White collar 20% (5th)

76% change	Notional 92	%	92	87	Candidates
Conservative	29,076	58	54	55	Vivian Bendall, MP
Labour	15,027	30	34	27	Linda Perham
Lib Dem	6,174	12	12	18	Alan Dean
Majority	14,049	Con 28	Con 20	Con 28	
Swing			4 → Lab	1 → Con	

ILFORD SOUTH, East London. Currently Labour, under new boundaries Tory marginal, Labour target seat
Asian 23% (11th); Overcrowding 4% (38th); White collar 20% (11th)

39% change	Notional 92	%	92	87	Candidates
Conservative	24,677	47	44	48	Sir Neil Thorne, chartered surveyor
Labour	22,147	42	45	38	Mike Gapes, MP
Lib Dem	5,493	11	10	14	Aina Khan
Majority	2,530	Con 5	Lab 1	Con 11	
Swing			6 → Lab	No swing	Lab needs 2 to win. 30th on Lab list

INVERNESS EAST, NAIRN & LOCHABER, Highland. Lib Dem seat, 4-way marginal, mainly rural

12% change	Notional 92	%	92	87	Candidates
Conservative	10,777	24	23	23	Mary Scanlon
Labour	10,633	23	25	25	David Stewart, social worker
Lib Dem	12,249	27	26	37	Stephen Gallagher
SNP	11,513	25	25	15	Fergus Ewing
Majority	736	LD 2	LD 1	LD 12	
Swing			5 → Lab	10 → Lab	Con need 2 to win. 23rd on Con list
					Lab needs 2 to win. 24th on Lab list
					SNP needs 1 to win. 1st on SNP list

IPSWICH, Suffolk. Labour marginal, Tory target seat, urban, working class, Lab gain in 92
Black 3% (95th); No central heating 31% (64th); Mobility 11% (113th)

0.4% change	Notional 92	%	92	87	Candidates
Conservative	23,288	43	43	44	Stephen Castle, head of marketing, opticians
Labour	23,623	44	44	43	Jamie Cann, MP
Lib Dem	6,135	11	11	13	Nigel Roberts
Majority	335	Lab 1	Lab 1	Con 2	
Swing			1 → Lab	2 → Con	Con need 0.3. to win.4th on Con list

ISLE OF WIGHT, Tory marginal, Lib Dem target seat, mainly rural
Pensionable 26% (21st); Self-employed 17% (46th); Second homes 3% (14th)

No Change	Actual 92	%		87	Candidates
Conservative	38,163	48		51	Barry Field, MP
Labour	4,784	6		6	Deborah Gardiner
Lib Dem	36,336	46		43	Dr Peter Brand, GP
Majority	1,827	Con 2		Con 8	
Swing		3 → LD		6 → Con	LD need 1 to win. 5th on LD list

ISLINGTON NORTH, North London. Strong Labour seat, inner city, high unemployment
Age 25-39 30% (7th); Black 13% (17th); Single parents 42% (8th)

No Change	Actual 92	%		87	Candidates
Conservative	8,958	24		25	Simon Fawthrop, civil servant
Labour	21,742	57		50	Jeremy Corbyn, MP
Lib Dem	5,732	15		22	James Kempton
Majority	12,784	Lab 34		Lab 25	
Swing		5 → Lab		5 → Lab	

ISLINGTON SOUTH & FINSBURY, North London. Strong Labour seat, inner city, high unemployment
Age 25-39 27% (26th); Council tenants 55% (6th); Single parents 41% (10th)

2% change	Notional 92	%	92	87	Candidates
Conservative	9,818	25	25	21	David Berens, solicitor
Labour	20,369	51	51	40	Chris Smith, MP
Lib Dem	9,232	23	23	38	Sarah Ludford, councillor
Majority	10,551	Lab 27	Lab 26	Lab 2	
Swing			4 → Lab	1 → Lab	

ISLWYN, Gwent. 6th safest Labour seat, mainly urban, working class, Labour by-election hold, formerly Neil Kinnock's seat
Long-term ill 19% (12th); Skilled manual 36% (41st); Unskilled 8% (30th)

No Change	Actual 92	%	95 by-		87	Candidates
Conservative	6,180	15	4		15	Russell Walters, PR director
Labour	30,908	74	69		71	Don Touhig, MP
Lib Dem	2,352	6	11		9	Chris Worker
Plaid Cymru	1,636	4	13		5	Darren Jones
Majority	24,728	Lab 59	Lab 57		Lab 57	
Swing			7 → PIC		6 → Lab	

JARROW, Tyne and Wear. Strong Labour seat, ex-shipbuilding, skilled manual
Govt schemes 3% (27th); Council tenants 42% (25th); Skilled manual 35% (47th)

22% change	Notional 92	%	92	87	Candidates
Conservative	11,243	23	24	23	Mark Allatt, PR director
Labour	29,978	63	62	63	Stephen Hepburn
Lib Dem	6,749	14	14	13	
Majority	18,735	Lab 39	Lab 38	Lab 40	
Swing			1 → Con	5 → Lab	

KEIGHLEY, West Yorkshire. Tory marginal, Labour target seat, mainly rural
Asian 7% (62nd); Owner-occupied 79% (75th); No central heating 33% (53rd)

No Change	Actual 92	%		87	Candidates
Conservative	25,983	47		46	Gary Waller, MP
Labour	22,387	41		35	Ann Cryer, former researcher, councillor
Lib Dem	5,793	11		19	Michael Doyle
Majority	3,596	Con 7		Con 11	
Swing		2 → Lab		3 → Con	Lab needs 3 to win. 43rd on Lab list

KENSINGTON & CHELSEA, West London. Safest Conservative seat, inner city, managerial, based on Chelsea
Private tenants 35% (1st); Mobility 22% (2nd); Managerial 54% (1st)

50% change	Notional 92	%	92	87	Candidates
Conservative	28,979	68	65	65	Alan Clark, diarist, ex-MP
Labour	7,080	17	18	15	Robert Atkinson
Lib Dem	5,590	13	15	18	Robert Woodthorpe Browne
Majority	21,899	Con 52	Con 48	Con 47	
Swing		1 → Lab	3 → Con		

KETTERING, Northamptonshire. Strong Tory seat, mainly urban
Owner-occupied 76% (129th); Car owners 75% (194th); Skilled manual 31% (158th)

5% change	Notional 92	%	92	87	Candidates
Conservative	30,884	53	52	51	Roger Freeman, MP
Labour	18,697	32	32	20	Philip Sawford
Lib Dem	9,012	15	16	29	Roger Aron
Majority	12,187	Con 21	Con 20	Con 22	
Swing			6 → Lab	2 → Con	

KILMARNOCK & LOUDOUN, Strathclyde. Labour seat, SNP long-shot, mainly urban

No Change	Actual 92	%		87	Candidates
Conservative	9,438	19		20	Douglas Taylor
Labour	22,210	45		49	Willie McKelvey, MP
Lib Dem	2,722	6		14	John Stewart
SNP	15,231	31		18	Alex Neil
Majority	6,979	Lab 14		Lab 29	
Swing		8 → SNP		5 → Lab	SNP needs 7 to win. 9th on SNP list

KINGSTON & SURBITON, South London. Strong Tory seat, outer suburbs, white collar
Private tenants 11% (69th); Managerial 41% (63rd); White collar 19% (23rd)

65% change	Notional 92	%	92	87	Candidates
Conservative	29,674	53	54	56	Richard Tracey, MP
Labour	10,991	20	18	14	Sheila Griffin
Lib Dem	14,510	26	27	29	Edward Davey
Majority	15,164	Con 27	Con 28	Con 27	
Swing			No swing	1 → Con	

KINGSWOOD, Avon. Currently Labour, under new boundaries Tory marginal, Labour target seat, suburban
Skilled manual 34% (87th); Owner-occupied 77% (111th); White collar 16% (108th)

51% change	Notional 92	%	92	87	Candidates
Conservative	29,562	46	41	45	Jon Howard, businessman and solicitor
Labour	26,222	41	45	37	Dr Roger Berry, MP
Lib Dem	8,771	14	15	18	Jeanne Pinkerton
Majority	3,340	Con 5	Lab 4	Con 8	
Swing			6 → Lab	2 → Con	Lab needs 3 to win. 36th on Lab list

KIRKCALDY, Fife. Strong Labour seat, industrial

3% change	Notional 92	%	92	87	Candidates
Conservative	8,361	22	22	21	Charlotte Black
Labour	17,246	46	46	50	Dr Lewis Moonie, MP
Lib Dem	3,671	10	10	17	John Mainland
SNP	8,561	23	23	12	Stewart Hosie
Majority	8,685	Lab 23	Lab 24	Lab 28	
Swing			7 → SNP	7 → Lab	

KNOWSLEY NORTH & SEFTON EAST, Merseyside. Strong Labour seat, outer suburbs, high unemployment
Govt schemes 3% (24th); Unemployment 19% (26th); No central heating 36% (38th)

88% change	Notional 92	%	92	87	Candidates
Conservative	14,930	27	14	13	Carl Doran, assistant producer, BBC
Labour	30,316	54	78	70	George Howarth, MP
Lib Dem	8,670	16	4	16	David Bamber
Majority	15,386	Lab 28	Lab 63	Lab 54	
Swing			3 → Lab	2 → Lab	

KNOWSLEY SOUTH, Merseyside. Strong Labour seat, car industry, high unemployment
Govt schemes 3% (23rd); Unemployed 19% (24th); No central heating 46% (7th)

15% change	Notional 92	%	92	87	Candidates
Conservative	10,936	21	21	22	Gary Robertson
Labour	37,071	70	69	65	Eddie O'Hara, MP
Lib Dem	4,818	9	10	14	Clifford Mainey
Majority	26,135	Lab 49	Lab 47	Lab 43	
Swing			2 → Lab	9 → Lab	

LAGAN VALLEY, Northern Ireland. Strong Unionist seat, mainly urban

27% change	Notional 92	%	92	87	Candidates
UUP	30,957	67	61	70	Jeffrey Donaldson
SDLP	4,192	9	9	7	
APNI	5,453	12	13	14	Seamus Close, accountant
Conservative	4,170	9	9		
Majority	25,504	UUP 55	UUP 48	UUP 56	
Swing			4 → APNI	4 → UUP	

LANCASHIRE WEST, Lancashire. Labour marginal, Tory target seat, mainly urban, Lab gain in 92
Age 16-24 14% (101st); Age 40-pension 29% (107th); White 99.2% (132nd)

21% change	Notional 92	%	92	87	Candidates
Conservative	25,243	42	44	44	Chris Varley, computer consultant
Labour	29,470	49	47	42	Colin Pickthall, MP
Lib Dem	4,147	7	8	15	
Majority	4,227	Lab 7	Lab 3	Con 2	
Swing			3 → Lab	5 → Lab	Con needs 4 to win. 53rd on Con list

LANCASTER & WYRE, Lancashire. Tory seat, Labour long-shot, mainly urban
Pensionable 23% (55th); Self-employed 16% (66th); Owner-occupied 84% (14th)

76% change	Notional 92	%	92	87	Candidates
Conservative	30,838	52	46	47	Keith Mans, MP
Labour	19,554	33	39	32	Hilton Dawson
Lib Dem	8,264	14	14	20	John Humberstone
Majority	11,284	Con 19	Con 6	Con 14	
Swing			4 → Lab	6 → Lab	Lab needs 10 to win. 111th on Lab list

LEEDS CENTRAL, West Yorkshire. Strong Labour seat, inner city, high unemployment
Age 16-24 15% (10th); No central heating 41% (19th); Unskilled 9% (5th)

19% change	Notional 92	%	92	87	Candidates
Conservative	10,281	22	23	26	Edward Wild, religious studies teacher
Labour	29,273	64	62	56	Derek Fatchett, MP
Lib Dem	6,416	14	15	18	David Freeman
Majority	18,992	Lab 41	Lab 40	Lab 30	
Swing			5 → Lab	3 → Lab	

LEEDS EAST, West Yorkshire. Strong Labour seat, inner city, working class
Council tenants 38% (37th); No central heating 49% (6th); Unskilled 8% (36th)

No Change	Actual 92	%		87	Candidates
Conservative	12,232	28		27	John Emsley
Labour	24,929	58		49	George Mudie, MP
Lib Dem	6,040	14		25	Madeleine Kirk
Majority	12,697	Lab 29		Lab 22	
Swing		4 → Lab		4 → Lab	

LEEDS NORTH EAST, West Yorkshire. Tory marginal, middle-class, the seat that gives Labour a majority
Black 6% (45th); Asian 7% (56th); Professional 12% (37th)

No Change	Actual 92	%		87	Candidates
Conservative	22,462	45		46	Timothy Kirkhope, MP
Labour	18,218	37		25	Fabian Hamilton
Lib Dem	8,274	17		28	Bill Winlow
Majority	4,244	Con 9		Con 17	
Swing		6 → Lab		1 → SDP	Lab needs 4 to win. 57th on Lab list

LEEDS NORTH WEST, West Yorkshire. Tory seat, Lib Dem and Labour long-shot, outer suburbs, professional
Age 16-24 14% (52nd); Private tenants 13% (52nd); Professional 13% (22nd

No Change	Actual 92	%		87	Candidates
Conservative	21,750	43		44	Dr Keith Hampson, MP
Labour	13,782	27		22	Harold Best
Lib Dem	14,079	28		34	Barbara Pearce
Majority	7,671	Con 15		Con 10	
Swing		6 → Lab		4 → Lib All	Lab needs 8 to win. 91st on Lab list
					LD need 8 to win. 42nd on LD list

LEEDS WEST, West Yorkshire. Strong Labour seat, inner city, working class
Council tenants 35% (49th); No central heating 45% (8th); Unskilled 6% (90th)

No Change	Actual 92	%	92	87	Candidates
Conservative	12,482	26		23	John Whelan, freelance journalist & broadcaster
Labour	26,310	55		43	John Battle, MP
Lib Dem	4,252	9		34	
Majority	13,828	Lab 29		Lab 10	
Swing		5 → Lab		7 → Lab	

LEICESTER EAST, Leicestershire. Strong Labour seat, inner city, strongly Asian
Asian 34% (3rd); Overcrowding 4% (39th); Skilled manual 35% (52nd)

No Change	Actual 92	%	92	87	Candidates
Conservative	16,807	34		43	Simon Milton
Labour	28,123	57		46	Keith Vaz, MP
Lib Dem	4,043	8		11	
Majority	11,316	Lab 23		Lab 4	
Swing		10 → Lab		3 → Lab	

LEICESTER SOUTH, Leicestershire. Labour seat, residential, strongly Asian, Lab gain in 87
Age 16-24 16% (7th); Asian 26% (8th); Overcrowding 4% (46th)

No Change	Actual 92	%		87	Candidates
Conservative	18,494	35		41	Christopher Heaton-Harris
Labour	27,934	52		44	James Marshall, MP
Lib Dem	6,271	12		14	Barry Coles
Majority	9,440	Lab 18		Lab 3	
Swing		7 → Lab		2 → Lab	

LEICESTER WEST, Leicestershire. Labour marginal, Tory target seat, large Asian community
Age 16-24 14% (53rd); Asian 12% (37th); Single parents 29% (51st)

No Change	Actual 92	%		87	Candidates
Conservative	18,596	39		42	Richard Thomas, senior manager, chemical company
Labour	22,574	47		45	Patricia Hewitt
Lib Dem	6,402	13		14	Mark Jones
Majority	3,978	Lab 8		Lab 2	
Swing		3 → Lab		1 → Con	Con need 4 to win. 67th on Con list

LEICESTERSHIRE NORTH WEST, Leicestershire. Tory marginal, Labour target seat, ex-mining, Tory MP David, Ashby deselected
Age 40-pension 29% (125th); Professional 7% (189th); Skilled manual 34% (79th)

14% change	Notional 92	%	92	87	Candidates
Conservative	24,735	45	46	48	Robert Goodwill, farmer
Labour	23,869	44	44	34	David Taylor, computer manager
Lib Dem	5,648	10	10	17	Stan Heptinstall
Majority	866	Con 2	Con 2	Con 13	
Swing			6 → Lab	1 → Con	Lab needs 1 to win. 14th on Lab list

LEIGH, Greater Manchester. Strong Labour seat, ex-mining, working class
Long-term ill 16% (56th); Skilled manual 34% (83rd); Unskilled 6% (78th)

31% change	Notional 92	%	92	87	Candidates
Conservative	14,341	27	26	26	Edward Young, corporate export adviser
Labour	31,196	59	61	59	Lawrence Cunliffe, MP
Lib Dem	6,539	12	13	15	
Majority	16,855	Lab 32	Lab 36	Lab 32	
Swing			2 → Lab	4 → Lab	

LEOMINSTER, Hereford and Worcester. Strong Tory seat, mainly rural, managerial
White 99.6% (12th); Self-employed 24% (9th); Car owners 83% (28th)

20% change	Notional 92	%	92	87	Candidates
Conservative	28,837	56	57	58	
Labour	6,294	12	12	8	Richard Westwood
Lib Dem	14,236	28	28	32	Terence James
Majority	14,601	Con 29	Con 29	Con 26	
Swing			1 → Con	3 → Con	

LEWES, East Sussex. Tory seat, Lib Dem long-shot, mainly rural, managerial
Pensionable 28% (12th); Self-employed 16% (63rd); Managerial 41% (56th)

32% change	Notional 92	%	92	87	Candidates
Conservative	26,638	51	55	57	Tim Rathbone, MP
Labour	4,270	8	10	9	Mark Patton
Lib Dem	20,301	39	35	33	Norman Baker, teacher
Majority	6,337	Con 12	Con 20	Con 24	
Swing			2 → Lib Dem	2 → LibAll	LD need 6 to win. 32nd on LD list

LEWISHAM DEPTFORD, South London. Strong Labour seat, inner city, large black population
Age 25-39 30% (6th); Black 25% (4th); Single parents 43% (6th)

2% change	Notional 92	%	92	87	Candidates
Conservative	10,395	28	28	32	Irene Kimm, clothing company manager
Labour	22,816	61	61	50	Joan Ruddock, MP
Lib Dem	4,432	12	11	17	Kofi Appiah
Majority	12,421	Lab 33	Lab 33	Lab 18	
Swing			8 → Lab	1 → Lab	

LEWISHAM EAST, South London. Labour marginal, Tory target seat, suburban, large black population, Lab gain in 92
Age 25-39 26% (44th); Black 10% (28th); Single parents 33% (35th)

% change	Notional 92	%	92	87	Candidates
Conservative	18,510	43	43	45	Philip Hollobone, research analyst
Labour	19,633	45	45	34	Bridget Prentice, MP
Lib Dem	4,935	11	11	21	David Buxton
Majority	1,123	Lab 3	Lab 3	Con 11	
Swing			7 → Lab	3 → Con	Con need 1 to win. 18th on Con list

LEWISHAM WEST, South London. Labour marginal, Tory target seat, suburban, large black population, Lab gain in 92
Black 14% (16th); Single parents 36% (24th); White collar 20% (9th)

No Change	Actual 92	%		87	Candidates
Conservative	18,569	43		46	Clare Whelan, PA to Edwina Currie, MP
Labour	20,378	47		38	Jim Dowd, MP
Lib Dem	4,295	10		16	Kathy McGrath
Majority	1,809	Lab 4		Con 8	
Swing		6 → Lab		1 → Con	Con need 2 to win. 33rd on Con list

LEYTON & WANSTEAD, North London. Labour seat, urban, large non-white population
Black 14% (14th); Asian 13% (30th); Overcrowding 5% (26th)

41% change	Notional 92	%	92	87	Candidates
Conservative	14,006	31	23	29	Robert Vaudry, banker
Labour	20,775	46	53	41	Harry Cohen, MP
Lib Dem	9,300	21	21	30	Charles Anglin, PR consultant
Majority	6,769	Lab 15	Lab 30	Lab 12	
Swing			9 → Lab	4 → LibAll	

LICHFIELD, Staffordshire. New strong Tory seat, mainly urban, managerial
Age 40-pension 31% (13th); Owner-occupied 79% (85th); Car owners 81% (72nd)

103% change	Notional 92	%	Candidates
Conservative	29,583	57	Michael Fabricant, MP
Labour	18,993	37	Susan Woodward
Lib Dem	2,970	6	Phillip Bennion
Majority	10,590	Con 20	

LINCOLN, Lincolnshire. Currently Tory seat, under new boundaries Labour marginal, Tory target seat, urban, working-class
Govt schemes 2% (115th); Unemployed 13% (113th); Mobility 12% (90th)

17% change	Notional 92	%	92	87	Candidates
Conservative	22,905	44	46	47	Anthony Brown, PR company partner
Labour	23,869	46	43	34	Gillian Merron, trade union official
Lib Dem	4,561	9	10	19	Lisa Gabriel
Majority	964	Lab 2	Con 3	Con 13	
Swing			5 → Lab	3 → Lab	Con need 1 to win. 13th on Con list

LINLITHGOW, Lothian. Labour seat, SNP long-shot, ex-mining

15% change	Notional 92	%	92	87	Candidates
Conservative	5,613	14	18	15	Tom Kerr
Labour	20,137	49	45	47	Tam Dalyell, MP
Lib Dem	2,843	7	7	13	Andrew Duncan
SNP	12,340	30	30	25	Kenny MacAskill
Majority	7,797	Lab 19	Lab 15	Lab 23	
Swing			4 → SNP	2 → SNP	SNP needs 10 to win. 14th on SNP list

LIVERPOOL GARSTON, Merseyside. Strong Labour seat, suburban, high unemployment
Govt schemes 3% (37th); Unemployed 17% (34th); No central heating 41% (18th)

21% change	Notional 92	%	92	87	Candidates
Conservative	12,340	25	27	24	Nigel Gordon-Johnson, technical sales consultant
Labour	25,214	51	57	54	Maria Eagle, solicitor
Lib Dem	10,680	22	13	22	Flo Clucas
Majority	12,874	Lab 26	Lab 30	Lab 30	
Swing			No swing	11 → Lab	

LIVERPOOL RIVERSIDE, Merseyside. Strong Labour seat, inner city, high unemployment
Govt schemes 4% (2nd); Unemployed 29% (1st); Single parents 49% (3rd)

45% change	Notional 92	%	92	87	Candidates
Conservative	4,572	11	12	14	David Sparrow, solicitor, company director
Labour	28,760	68	76	73	Louise Ellman, councillor, Open University counsellor
Lib Dem	7,744	18	9	11	
Majority	21,016	Lab 50	Lab 64	Lab 59	
Swing			3 → Lab	7 → Lab	

LIVERPOOL WALTON, Merseyside. 5th safest Labour seat, suburban, high unemployment
Unemployed 22% (13th); No central heating 53% (2nd); Unskilled 9% (12th)

No Change	Actual 92	%		87	Candidates
Conservative	5,915	13		14	Mark Kotecha, director, national training co.
Labour	34,214	72		64	Peter Kilfoyle, MP
Lib Dem	5,672	12		21	
Majority	28,299	Lab 60		43	
Swing		5 → Lab		6 → LibAll	

LIVERPOOL WAVERTREE, Merseyside. Labour marginal, suburban, working class, based on Broadgreen
Private tenants 14% (42nd); No central heating 49% (5th); Single parents 29% (53rd)

63% change	Notional 92	%	92	87	Candidates
Conservative	6,422	13	13	16	Christopher Malthouse, accountant, financial director
Labour	21,237	41	43	49	Jane Kennedy, MP
Lib Dem	17,857	35	26	36	Richard Kemp, economic development adviser
Majority	3,380	Lab 7	Lab 17	Lab 13	
Swing			2 → Lab	9 → Lib All	LD need 3 to win. 14th on LD list

LIVERPOOL WEST DERBY, Merseyside. Strong Labour seat, outer suburbs, working class
Govt schemes 3% (12th); Unemployed 24% (4th); No central heating 54% (1st)

21% change	Notional 92	%	92	87	Candidates
Conservative	6,975	15	17	19	Neil Morgan
Labour	30,830	65	68	65	Robert Wareing, MP
Lib Dem	7,297	15	12	16	
Majority	23,533	Lab 49	Lab 52	Lab 46	
Swing			3 → Lab	10 → Lab	

LIVINGSTON, Lothian. Labour seat, SNP long-shot, new town

13% change	Notional 92	%	92	87	Candidates
Conservative	7,689	18	19	19	Hugh Halkett
Labour	19,461	46	44	46	Robin Cook, MP
Lib Dem	3,857	9	9	19	Ewan Hawthorn
SNP	11,013	26	27	17	Peter Johnston, councillor
Majority	8,448	Lab 20	Lab 18	Lab 27	
Swing			6 → SNP	7 → Lab	SNP needs 10 to win. 16th on SNP list

LLANELLI, Dyfed. Strong Labour seat, ex-mining, working class
Pensionable 23% (48th); Govt schemes 3% (32nd); Long-term ill 21% (7th)

9% change	Notional 92	%	92	87	Candidates
Conservative	7,851	17	17	17	Andrew Hayes, founder of publishing co.
Labour	25,122	55	55	59	Denzil Davies, MP
Lib Dem	5,884	13	13	14	Nick Burree
Plaid Cymru	7,253	16	–	10	Marc Phillips
Majority	17,271	Lab 38	Lab 38	Lab 42	
Swing			2 → Con	7 → Lab	

LONDONDERRY EAST, Northern Ireland. Strong Unionist seat, rural

27% change	Notional 92	%	92	87	Candidates
UUP	23,287	65	58	61	William Ross, MP
SDLP	7,134	20	23	19	Arthur Doherty, public servant
APNI	2,634	7	7	7	Yvonne Boyle, social worker
Conservative	1,589	4	3	–	
Majority	16,153	UUP 45	UUP 35	UUP 41	
Swing			3 → SDLP	11 → UUP	

LOUGHBOROUGH, Leicestershire. Tory marginal, Labour target seat, suburban, boundaries help Labour
Asian 5% (80th); Other non-white 2% (115th); Professional 9% (121st)

40% change	Notional 92	%	92	87	Candidates
Conservative	23,412	47	51	55	Kenneth Andrew, company director
Labour	19,920	40	32	25	Andy Reed, local government officer
Lib Dem	5,635	11	15	20	Diana Brass
Majority	3,492	Con 7	Con 18	Con 30	
Swing			6 → Lab	No swing	Lab needs 3 to win. 45th on Lab list

LOUTH & HORNCASTLE, Lincolnshire. Strong Tory seat, rural, based on Lindsey East
Pensionable 24% (35th); Self-employed 19% (32nd); Second homes 2% (19th)

42% change	Notional 92	%	92	87	Candidates
Conservative	27,499	53	51	52	Sir Peter Tapsell, MP
Labour	7,122	14	15	11	John Hough
Lib Dem	16,529	32	32	37	Fiona Martin, councillor
Majority	10,970	Con 21	Con 19	Con 16	
Swing			2 → Con	No swing	

LUDLOW, Shropshire. Strong Tory seat, rural, managerial
Age 40-pension 30% (26th); White 99.5% (46th); Self-employed 21% (16th)

15% change	Notional 92	%	92	87	Candidates
Conservative	24,415	52	52	54	Christopher Gill, MP
Labour	10,134	21	21	15	Nuala O'Kane
Lib Dem	12,108	26	26	31	Ian Huffer
Majority	12,307	Con 26	Con 25	Con 23	
Swing			1 → Con	1 → LibAll	

LUTON NORTH, Bedfordshire. Tory seat, Labour long-shot, mainly urban, large non-white population
Age 16-24 14% (68th); Black 6% (44th); Asian 10% (43rd)

36% change	Notional 92	%	92	87	Candidates
Conservative	26,853	51	54	54	David Senior
Labour	19,496	37	33	27	Kelvin Hopkins, economist, former lecturer
Lib Dem	5,311	10	12	19	Kathryn Newbound
Majority	7,357	Con 14	Con 21	Con 27	
Swing			3 → Lab	2 → Con	Lab needs 7 to win. 81st on Lab list

LUTON SOUTH, Bedfordshire. Tory marginal, car industry, large Asian community
Age 25-39 25% (48th); Asian 15% (22nd); Overcrowding 5% (35th)

10% change	Notional 92	%	92	87	Candidates
Conservative	22,928	44	45	46	Graham Bright, MP
Labour	22,396	43	44	37	Margaret Moran, former council leader
Lib Dem	5,795	11	10	17	
Majority	532	Con 1	Con 1	Con 10	
Swing			4 → Lab	1 → Con	Lab needs 1 to win. 9th on Lab list

MACCLESFIELD, Cheshire. Strong Tory seat, mainly rural, middle-class
Age 40-pension 29% (66th); Professional 11% (61st); Managerial 43% (37th)

8% change	Notional 92	%	92	87	Candidates
Conservative	32,332	56	58	56	Nicholas Winterton, MP
Labour	13,202	23	22	20	Janet Jackson, housing association director
Lib Dem	11,958	21	20	24	Mike Flynn
Majority	19,130	Con 33	Con 36	Con 32	
Swing			No swing	3 → LibAll	

MAIDENHEAD, Berkshire. Strong Tory seat, mainly urban, managerial, based on Windsor & Maidenhead
Age 40-pension 31% (14th); Car owners 84% (11th); Managerial 46% (11th)

62% change	Notional 92	%	92	87	Candidates
Conservative	33,958	62	56	57	Theresa May, head of a European Affairs Unit
Labour	4,741	9	8	11	Denise Robson
Lib Dem	16,462	30	35	27	Andrew Ketteringham
Majority	17,496	Con 32	Con 21	Con 30	
Swing			5 → LD	2 → LibAll	

MAIDSTONE & THE WEALD, Kent. Strong Tory seat, mainly urban, managerial
Age 40-pension 29% (91st); Car owners 78% (130th); Managerial 38% (90th)

63% change	Notional 92	%	92	87	Candidates
Conservative	31,951	56	54	52	Anne Widdecombe, MP
Labour	7,097	13	18	13	John Morgan
Lib Dem	17,237	30	26	34	Jane Nelson, IT consultant
Majority	14,714	Con 26	Con 28	Con 19	
Swing			5 → Con	2 → Con	

MAKERFIELD, Greater Manchester. Strong Labour seat, mainly urban, skilled manual
Age 16-24 14% (67th); White 99.4% (71st); Skilled manual 39% (13th)

26% change	Notional 92	%	92	87	Candidates
Conservative	12,640	24	27	27	Michael Winstanley
Labour	32,787	63	60	56	Ian McCartney, MP
Lib Dem	4,751	9	9	17	
Majority	20,147	Lab 39	Lab 33	Lab 29	
Swing			2 → Lab	4 → Lab	

MALDON & CHELMSFORD EAST, Essex. New strong Tory seat, mainly rural, managerial
Age 40-pension 31% (12th); Car owners 81% (63rd); Managerial 41% (62nd)

81% change	Notional 92	%	Candidates
Conservative	32,944	64	John Whittingdale, MP
Labour	6,592	13	Kevin Freeman
Lib Dem	11,359	22	Graham Pooley
Majority	21,585	Con 42	

MANCHESTER BLACKLEY, Greater Manchester. Strong Labour seat, inner city, high unemployment
Unemployed 19% (19th); Single parents 39% (14th); Unskilled 8% (18th)

18% change	Notional 92	%	92	87	Candidates
Conservative	11,285	26	28	29	Stephen Barclay, postgraduate law student
Labour	26,977	62	60	52	Graham Stringer
Lib Dem	4,786	11	11	19	Simon Wheale
Majority	15,692	Lab 36	Lab 32	Lab 24	
Swing			4 → Lab	4 → Lab	

MANCHESTER CENTRAL, Greater Manchester. Strong Labour seat, inner city, high unemployment
Unemployed 27% (3rd); Single parents 53% (2nd); Unskilled 10% (3rd)

49% change	Notional 92	%	92	87	Candidates
Conservative	7,581	19	17	19	Simon McIlwaine
Labour	27,009	69	73	68	Tony Lloyd, MP
Lib Dem	4,105	11	10	13	Alison Firth
Majority	19,428	Lab 50	Lab 56	Lab 49	
Swing			3 → Lab	3 → Lab	

MANCHESTER GORTON, Greater Manchester. Strong Labour seat, inner city, high unemployment
Age 16-24 16% (3rd); Private tenants 19% (12th); Single parents 39% (15th)

0.1% change	Notional 92	%	92	87	Candidates
Conservative	7,388	20	20	23	Guy Senior
Labour	23,658	62	62	54	Gerald Kaufman, MP
Lib Dem	5,324	14	14	22	Jackie Pearcey, councillor
Majority	16,270	Lab 43	Lab 43	Lab 31	
Swing			6 → Lab	4 → Lab	

MANCHESTER WITHINGTON, Greater Manchester. Strong Labour seat, suburban, Lab gain in 87
Private tenants 19% (13th); Single parents 33% (32nd); Mobility 14% (28th)

0.2% change	Notional 92	%	92	87	Candidates
Conservative	14,193	31	31	36	Jonathan Smith, barrister
Labour	23,907	53	53	43	Keith Bradley, MP
Lib Dem	6,442	14	14	20	Yasmen Zalzala
Majority	9,714	Lab 21	Lab 21	Lab 7	
Swing			7 → Lab	6 → Lab	

MANSFIELD, Nottinghamshire. Strong Labour seat, mining, skilled manual
Govt schemes 2% (84th); Long-term ill 16% (75th); Skilled manual 37% (27th)

No Change	Actual 92	%		87	Candidates
Conservative	18,208	33		37	Tim Frost, merchant banker
Labour	29,932	54		38	Alan Meale, MP
Lib Dem	6,925	13		22	Philip Smith
Majority	11,724	Lab 21		Lab 0.1	
Swing		11 → Lab		2 → Con	

MEDWAY, Kent. Tory seat, Labour long-shot, urban, white collar
Age 25-39 23% (126th); Asian 3% (122nd); Skilled manual 34% (76th)

No Change	Actual 92	%		87	Candidates
Conservative	25,924	52		51	Dame Peggy Fenner, MP
Labour	17,138	35		30	Robert Marshall-Andrews
Lib Dem	4,751	10		18	Roger Roberts
Majority	8,786	Con 18		Con 21	
Swing		2 → Lab		1 → Con	Lab needs 9 to win. 102nd on Lab list

MEIRIONNYDD NANT CONWY, Gwynedd. PLC seat, Tory long-shot, white collar
Self-employed 25% (8th); Second homes 9% (1st); No central heating 35% (45th)

No Change	Actual 92	%		87	Candidates
Conservative	6,995	27		28	Jeremy Quin, corporate stockbroker
Labour	4,978	19		17	Hefin Rees
Lib Dem	2,358	9		15	Robina Feeley
Plaid Cymru	11,608	44		40	Elfyn Llwyd, MP
Majority	4,613	PIC 18		PIC 12	
Swing		3 → PIC		1 → PIC	

MERIDEN, West Midlands. Strong Tory seat, mainly rural
Age 16-24 14% (41st); Age 40-pension 30% (37th); Black 2% (120th)

No Change	Actual 92	%		87	Candidates
Conservative	33,462	55		55	
Labour	18,763	31		26	Brian Seymour-Smith
Lib Dem	8,489	14		19	Tony Dupont
Majority	14,699	Con 24		Con 29	
Swing		2 → Lab		No swing	

MERTHYR TYDFIL & RHYMNEY, Mid Glamorgan. 4th safest Labour seat, ex-mining, high unemployment
Unemployed 16% (46th); Long-term ill 22% (2nd); Unskilled 10% (1st)

No Change	Actual 92	%		87	Candidates
Conservative	4,904	11		12	Jonathan Morgan, postgraduate law student
Labour	31,710	72		75	Ted Rowlands, MP
Lib Dem	4,997	11		8	Steve Beizak
Plaid Cymru	2,704	6		5	Alan Cox
Majority	26,713	Lab 60		Lab 64	
Swing		4 → Lib Dem		4 → Lab	

MIDDLESBROUGH, Cleveland. Strong Labour seat, urban, high unemployment
Govt schemes 4% (6th); Unemployed 19% (20th); Unskilled 9% (9th)

25% change	Notional 92	%	92	87	Candidates
Conservative	16,424	30	26	25	Liam Bentham, political liaison officer
Labour	33,543	61	64	60	Stuart Bell, MP
Lib Dem	4,925	9	10	15	
Majority	17,119	Lab 31	Lab 38	Lab 35	
Swing			2 → Lab	6 → Lab	

MIDDLESBROUGH SOUTH & CLEVELAND EAST, Cleveland. Based on Langbaurgh, Tory marginal
White 99.2% (133rd); Govt schemes 3% (16th); Unemployed 11% (150th)

13% change	Notional 92	%	92	87	Candidates
Conservative	25,802	46	45	42	Michael Bates, MP
Labour	24,401	43	43	38	Ashok Kumar, research scientist, former MP
Lib Dem	6,163	11	12	20	Hamish Garrett
Majority	1,401	Con 3	Con 2	Con 3	
Swing			1 → Lab	4 → Lab	Lab needs 1 to win. 18th on Lab list

MIDLOTHIAN, Lothian. Strong Labour seat, industrial

22% change	Notional 92	%	92	87	Candidates
Conservative	6,242	18	20	18	Anne Harper
Labour	17,120	48	44	48	Eric Clarke, MP
Lib Dem	3,552	10	13	22	Richard Pinnock
SNP	8,256	23	22	11	Lawrence Millar
Majority	8,864	Lab 25	Lab 22	Lab 26	
Swing			8 → SNP	6 → Lab	SNP needs 13 to win. 25th on SNP list

MILTON KEYNES NORTH EAST, Bucks. Strong Tory seat, part new town, white collar, new seat in 92
Age 25-39 27% (27th); Other non-white 2% (97th); Mobility 12% (80th)

No Change	Actual 92	%			Candidates
Conservative	26,212	52			Peter Butler, MP
Labour	12,036	24			Brian White
Lib Dem	11,693	23			Graham Mabbutt
Majority	14,176	Con 28			

MILTON KEYNES SOUTH WEST, Buckinghamshire. Tory marginal, new town, new seat in 92
Age 25-39 26% (45th); Other non-white 2% (112th); Mobility 12% (91st)

No Change	Actual 92	%			Candidates
Conservative	23,840	47			Barry Legg, MP
Labour	19,153	37			Phyllis Starkey, scientist, former lecturer
Lib Dem	7,429	15			Peter Jones, scientist, former council leader
Majority	4,687	Con 9			Lab needs 5 to win. 63rd on Lab list

MITCHAM & MORDEN, South London. Tory marginal, Labour target seat, outer suburbs, white collar
Black 10% (30th); Other non-white 5% (28th); White collar 20% (16th)

No Change	Actual 92	%		87	Candidates
Conservative	23,789	47		48	Dame Angela Rumbold, MP
Labour	22,055	43		35	Siobhain McDonagh, housing officer, councillor
Lib Dem	4,687	9		17	Nicholas Harris
Majority	1,734	Con 3		Con 13	
Swing		5 → Lab		1 → Lab	Lab needs 2 to win. 22nd on Lab list

MOLE VALLEY, Surrey. Strong Tory seat, mainly rural, middle-class
Age 40-pension 31% (4th); Car owners 84% (16th); Professional 13% (16th)

36% change	Notional 92	%	92	87	Candidates
Conservative	35,313	61	59	61	Sir Paul Beresford, MP
Labour	5,386	9	10	9	Christopher Payne
Lib Dem	16,486	29	30	30	Stephen Cooksey
Majority	18,827	Con 33	Con 29	Con 31	
Swing			1 → Lib Dem	No swing	

MONMOUTH, Gwent. Tory marginal, Labour target seat, mainly rural, middle-class, Lab by-election gain in 1991, Con regain in 9
Age 40-pension 30% (18th); Self-employed 17% (53rd); Managerial 40% (74th)

No Change	Actual 92	%		87	Candidates
Conservative	24,059	47		48	Roger Evans, MP
Labour	20,855	41		28	Huw Edwards, Open University tutor
Lib Dem	5,562	11		24	Mark Williams
Plaid Cymru	431	1		1	
Majority	3,204	Con 6		Con 20	
Swing		7 → Lab		4 → Lab	Lab needs 3 to win. 41st on Lab list

MONTGOMERYSHIRE, Powys. Lib Dem seat, Tory long-shot, rural
White 99.4% (61st); Self-employed 25% (5th); Second homes 2% (23rd)

No Change	Actual 92	%		87	Candidates
Conservative	10,822	33		39	Glyn Davies, systems analyst
Labour	4,115	12		11	Angharad Davies
Lib Dem	16,031	49		47	Lembit Opik
Plaid Cymru	1,581	5		5	Helen Jones
Majority	5,209	LD 16		LD 8	
Swing		4 → Lib Dem		3 → Lib Dem	

MORAY, Grampian. SNP marginal, Tory target seat, rural

10% change	Notional 92	%	92	87	Candidates
Conservative	15,517	38	38	35	Andrew Finlay
Labour	4,913	12	12	11	Lewis Macdonald
Lib Dem	2,466	6	6	11	Debra Storr
SNP	18,444	45	44	43	Margaret Anne Ewing, MP
Majority	2,927	SNP 7	SNP 6	SNP 8	
Swing			1 → Con	6 → SNP	Con need 4 to win. 52nd on Con list

MORECAMBE & LUNESDALE, Lancashire. Tory seat, Labour long-shot, seaside
Pensionable 24% (34th); Private tenants 11% (70th); No central heating 29% (76th)

20% change	Notional 92	%	92	87	Candidates
Conservative	26,292	49	51	53	Mark Lennox-Boyd, MP
Labour	15,720	29	25	23	Geraldine Smith
Lib Dem	10,183	19	22	25	Dexter Bracey
Majority	10,572	Con 20	Con 26	Con 28	
Swing			2 → Lab	2 → SDPAll	Lab needs 10 to win. 114th on Lab list

MORLEY & ROTHWELL, West Yorkshire. Labour seat, urban, skilled manual, based on Leeds South
Council tenants 27% (119th); No central heating 33% (54th); Skilled manual 35% (51st)

44% change	Notional 92	%	92	87	Candidates
Conservative	18,523	37	36	34	Alan Barraclough
Labour	24,843	50	52	50	John Gunnell, MP
Lib Dem	6,506	13	11	16	Mitchell Galdas
Majority	6,320	Lab 13	Lab 16	Lab 15	
Swing			No swing	1 → Lab	

MOTHERWELL & WISHAW, Strathclyde. Strong Labour seat, steel industry, based on Motherwell South

5% change	Notional 92	%	92	87	Candidates
Conservative	6,264	16	16	15	Scott Dickson
Labour	22,691	57	57	58	Frank Roy, asst to Helen Liddle, MP
Lib Dem	2,433	6	6	11	Alex Mackie
SNP	8,601	21	20	15	James McGuigan
Majority	14,090	Lab 35	Lab 37	Lab 43	
Swing			3 → SNP	No swing	

NEATH, West Glamorgan. Strong Labour seat, ex-mining, working class
Govt schemes 2% (69th); Long-term ill 20% (8th); Pensionable 21% (106th)

No Change	Actual 92	%		87	Candidates
Conservative	6,928	15		16	David Evans
Labour	30,903	68		63	Peter Hain, MP
Lib Dem	2,467	5		14	Frank Little
Plaid Cymru	5,145	11		6	Trefor Jones
Majority	23,975	Lab 53		Lab 47	
Swing		3 → Lab		6 → Lab	

NEW FOREST EAST, Hampshire. Tory seat, rural, middle-class, based on Romsey & Waterside
Owner-occupied 81% (37th); Second homes 1% (68th); Car owners 84% (15th)

51% change	Notional 92	%	92	87	Candidates
Conservative	27,980	53	54	56	Julian Lewis, deputy dir, Conservative Research Dept
Labour	6,704	13	13	12	Malcolm Leatherdale
Lib Dem	17,632	33	32	32	George Dawson, chemical engineer
Majority	10,348	Con 20	Con 22	Con 24	
Swing			1 → Lib Dem	1 → SDPAll	

NEW FOREST WEST, Hampshire. Strong Tory seat, rural, managerial, based on New Forest
Pensionable 32% (7th); Self-employed 19% (28th); Second homes 2% (30th)

16% change	Notional 92	%	92	87	Candidates
Conservative	30,982	61	62	65	Desmond Swayne, bank manager
Labour	4,179	8	8	8	Dave Griffiths
Lib Dem	15,583	31	29	27	Bob Hale
Majority	15,399	Con 30	Con 34	Con 38	
Swing			2 → Lib Dem	1 → LibAll	

NEWARK, Nottinghamshire. Tory seat, Labour long-shot, mainly rural, skilled manual
Age 40-pension 29% (105th); White 99.1% (160th); Govt schemes 2% (185th)

No Change	Actual 92	%		87	Candidates
Conservative	28,494	50		54	Richard Alexander, MP
Labour	20,265	36		28	Fiona Jones
Lib Dem	7,342	13		19	Peter Harris
Majority	8,229	Con 15		Con 26	
Swing		6 → Lab		2 → Lab	Lab needs 7 to win. 84th on Lab list

NEWBURY, Berkshire. Tory seat, Lib Dem long-shot, mainly rural, professional, Lib Dem by-election gain in 1993
Car owners 82% (49th); Mobility 12% (72nd); Professional 11% (48th)

12% change	Notional 92	%	93 by-	92	87	Candidates
Conservative	32,898	56	27	56	60	Richard Benyon, farmer
Labour	3,584	6	2	6	8	Paul Hannon
Lib Dem	21,841	37	65	37	32	David Rendel, MP
Majority	11,057	Con 19	LD 38	Con 19	Con 28	
Swing			28 → Lib Dem	5 → Lib Dem	2 → Con	LD need 9 to win. 59th on LD list

NEWCASTLE UPON TYNE CENTRAL, Tyne and Wear. Labour seat, residential, professional
Age 16-24 14% (47th); Mobility 13% (49th); Professional 15% (7th)

14% change	Notional 92	%	92	87	Candidates
Conservative	17,393	36	37	39	Brooks Newmark, businessman
Labour	25,281	52	49	44	Jim Cousins, MP
Lib Dem	6,208	13	14	16	
Majority	7,888	Lab 16	Lab 12	Lab 5	
Swing			4 → Lab	5 → Lab	

NEWCASTLE UPON TYNE EAST & WALLSEND, Tyne and Wear. Strong Labour seat, inner city, working class
Council tenants 39% (36th); Long-term ill 16% (46th); Unskilled 8% (26th)

45% change	Notional 92	%	92	87	Candidates
Conservative	10,421	23	26	27	Jeremy Middleton, company director
Labour	26,466	57	60	56	Nick Brown, MP
Lib Dem	8,628	19	12	16	
Majority	16,045	Lab 35	Lab 34	Lab 30	
Swing			2 → Lab	6 → Lab	

NEWCASTLE UPON TYNE NORTH, Tyne and Wear. Labour seat, suburban, white collar
Council tenants 32% (69th); Single parents 24% (103rd); White collar 17% (69th)

No Change	Actual 92	%	87	Candidates
Conservative	16,175	32	25	Gregory White, company director, food and drink
Labour	25,121	49	43	Doug Henderson, MP
Lib Dem	9,542	19	33	Lembit Opik
Majority	8,946	Lab 18	Lab 10	
Swing		No swing	1 → Lab	

NEWCASTLE-UNDER-LYME, Staffordshire. Labour seat, urban, working class
Long-term ill 15% (96th); Skilled manual 34% (75th); Unskilled 6% (120th)

No Change	Actual 92	%	87	Candidates
Conservative	15,813	30	28	Marcus Hayes, solicitor
Labour	25,652	48	41	Llin Golding, MP
Lib Dem	11,727	22	31	Elizabeth Jewkes
Majority	9,839	Lab 18	Lab 10	
Swing		3 → Lab	5 → LibAll	

NEWPORT EAST, Gwent. Strong Labour seat, urban, working class
Long-term ill 14% (131st); Skilled manual 32% (133rd); Unskilled 7% (44th)

No Change	Actual 92	%	87	Candidates
Conservative	13,151	31	32	David Evans
Labour	23,050	55	49	Roy Hughes, MP
Lib Dem	4,991	12	18	Alastair Cameron
Plaid Cymru	716	2	1	Chris Holland
Majority	9,899	Lab 24	Lab 17	
Swing		3 → Lab	5 → Lab	

NEWPORT WEST, Gwent. Labour seat, urban
Single paremts 24% (100th); Long-term ill 15% (108th); Professional 8% (140th)

No Change	Actual 92	%	87	Candidates
Conservative	16,360	36	40	Peter Clarke
Labour	24,139	53	46	Paul Flynn, MP
Lib Dem	4,296	10	13	Stan Wilson
Plaid Cymru	653	1	1	Huw Jackson
Majority	7,779	Lab 17	Lab 6	
Swing		6 → Lab	4 → Lab	

NEWRY & ARMAGH, Northern Ireland. SDLP seat, rural

1% change	Notional 92	%	92	87	Candidates
UUP	18,930	36	36	38	
SDLP	25,740	49	50	48	Seamus Mallon, MP
APNI	972	2	2	1	Pete Whitcroft, sales manager
SF	6,530	13	13	12	
Majority	6,810	SDLP 13	SDLP 14	SDLP 10	
Swing			2 → SDLP	7 → SDLP	

NORFOLK MID, Norfolk. Strong Tory seat, rural, managerial
Age 40-pension 29% (55th); White 99.5% (50th); Car owners 83% (24th)

10% change	Notional 92	%	92	87	Candidates
Conservative	32,481	55	54	57	Keith Simpson
Labour	15,537	26	25	18	Daniel Zeichner
Lib Dem	11,316	19	20	26	Richard Williams
Majority	16,944	Con 29	Con 29	Con 31	
Swing			5 → Lab	1 → Con	

NORFOLK NORTH, Norfolk. Strong Tory seat, rural, working class
Pensionable 28% (13th); Self-employed 19% (30th); Second homes 5% (4th)

No Change	Actual 92	%	87	Candidates
Conservative	28,810	48	53	David Prior, company chairman
Labour	13,850	23	20	Michael Cullingham
Lib Dem	16,265	27	25	Norman Lamb, solicitor
Majority	12,545	Con 21	Con 28	
Swing		4 → Lab	1 → Con	

NORFOLK NORTH WEST, Norfolk. Tory seat, Labour long-shot, mainly rural, working class
Pensionable 23% (56th); Second homes 3% (10th); Self-employed 14% (154th)

No Change	Actual 92	%	87	Candidates
Conservative	32,554	52	51	Henry Bellingham, MP
Labour	20,990	34	18	George Turner
Lib Dem	8,599	14	32	Evelyn Knowles
Majority	11,564	Con 19	Con 19	
Swing		7 → Lab	6 → Con	Lab needs 9 to win. 107th on Lab list

NORFOLK SOUTH, Norfolk. Strong Tory seat, rural, middle-class
Age 40-pension 30% (40th); White 99.5% (31st); Car owners 82% (37th)

7% change	Notional 92	%	92	87	Candidates
Conservative	33,669	52	53	53	John MacGregor, MP
Labour	11,841	18	18	13	Jane Ross
Lib Dem	17,305	27	27	34	Barbara Hacker, radiographer
Majority	16,364	Con 25	Con 26	Con 20	
Swing			3 → Con	1 → LibAll	

NORFOLK SOUTH WEST, Norfolk. Strong Tory seat, rural, working class
Pensionable 21% (95th); Second homes 1% (85th); Car owners 79% (98th)

1% change	Notional 92	%	92	87	Candidates
Conservative	34,098	55	55	58	Gillian Shephard, MP
Labour	16,848	27	27	21	Adrian Heffernan
Lib Dem	11,343	18	18	21	David Buckton
Majority	17,250	Con 28	Con 28	Con 36	
Swing			5 → Lab	4 → Con	

NORMANTON, West Yorkshire. Labour seat, ex-mining, skilled manual
Age 25-39 23% (109th); White 99.1% (154th); Skilled manual 35% (55th)

41% change	Notional 92	%	92	87	Candidates
Conservative	16,467	36	34	34	Fiona Bulmer, political researcher
Labour	23,659	51	52	50	Bill O'Brien, MP
Lib Dem	6,155	13	14	16	
Majority	7,192	Lab 16	Lab 18	Lab 16	
Swing			1 → Lab	3 → Lab	

NORTHAMPTON NORTH, Northamptonshire. Tory marginal, Labour target seat, part new town, working class
Black 3% (94th); Skilled manual 31% (139th); White collar 15% (145th)

5% change	Notional 92	%	92	87	Candidates
Conservative	25,972	46	46	48	Tony Marlow, MP
Labour	21,905	39	39	30	Sally Keeble, journalist, former council leader
Lib Dem	8,630	15	15	21	Lesley Dunbar
Majority	4,067	Con 7	Con 7	Con 18	
Swing			5 → Lab	1 → Lab	Lab needs 4 to win. 47th on Lab list

NORTHAMPTON SOUTH, Northamptonshire. Strong Tory seat, mainly urban
Age 25-39 24% (75th); Black 2% (119th); Mobility 11% (120th)

12% change	Notional 92	%	92	87	Candidates
Conservative	32,898	56	55	56	Michael Morris, MP
Labour	17,854	30	30	25	Tony Clark
Lib Dem	8,355	14	15	19	Anthony Worgan
Majority	15,044	Con 26	Con 25	Con 31	
Swing			3 → Lab	No swing	

NORTHAVON, Avon. Tory seat, Lib Dem long-shot, commuting, middle-class
Owner-occupied 84% (11th); Car owners 87% (3rd); Professional 9% (100th)

11% change	Notional 92	%	92	87	Candidates
Conservative	32,700	52	50	54	Sir John Cope, MP
Labour	7,625	12	15	14	Ron Stone
Lib Dem	21,759	35	33	32	Steven Webb, university professor
Majority	10,941	Con 17	Con 17	Con 23	
Swing			3 → LD	No swing	LD needs 9 to win. 50th on LD list

NORWICH NORTH, Norfolk. Tory marginal, Labour target seat, urban, white collar
Mobility 10% (215th); White collar 17% (70th); Skilled manual 31% (155th)

12% change	Notional 92	%	92	87	Candidates
Conservative	25,558	44	43	46	Robert Kinghorn, oil and gas exploration speci
Labour	23,288	40	43	30	Ian Gibson, dean of biology, University of E An
Lib Dem	8,462	15	13	24	Paul Young
Majority	2,270	Con 4	Con 1	Con 16	
Swing			8 → Lab	2 → Con	Lab needs 2 to win. 26th on Lab list

NORWICH SOUTH, Norfolk. Labour marginal, Tory target seat, urban, middle-class, Lab gain in 87
Age 16-24 14% (63rd); Council tenants 33% (57th); Mobility 13% (43rd)

8% change	Notional 92	%	92	87	Candidates
Conservative	21,196	38	37	37	Bashir Khanbhai, industrial pharmacist & econ
Labour	25,546	46	49	38	Charles Clarke
Lib Dem	7,820	14	13	25	
Majority	4,350	Lab 8	Lab 12	Lab 1	
Swing			6 → Lab	2 → Lab	Con need 4 to win. 62nd on Con list

NOTTINGHAM EAST, Nottinghamshire. Labour seat, inner city, high unemployment, Lab gain in 92
Age 16-24 16% (8th); Unemployed 18% (27th); Mobility 14% (31st)

No Change	Actual 92	%		87	Candidates
Conservative	17,346	36		43	Andrew Raca, senior executive, stockbroker
Labour	25,026	53		42	John Heppell, MP
Lib Dem	3,695	8		15	Kevin Mulloy
Majority	7,680	Lab 16		Con 1	
Swing		9 → Lab		1 → Lab	

NOTTINGHAM NORTH, Nottinghamshire. Strong Labour seat, suburban, working class, Lab gain in 87
Council tenants 43% (17th); Skilled manual 37% (29th); Unskilled 8% (34th)

No Change	Actual 92	%		87	Candidates
Conservative	18,309	35		42	Gillian Shaw, solicitor
Labour	29,052	56		45	Graham Allen, MP
Lib Dem	4,477	9		12	
Majority	10,743	Lab 21		Lab 3	
Swing		9 → Lab		2 → Lab	

NOTTINGHAM SOUTH, Nottinghamshire. Labour marginal, Tory target seat, suburban, working class, Lab gain in 92
Age 16-24 15% (26th); Black 4% (59th); Asian 6% (74th)

No Change	Actual 92	%		87	Candidates
Conservative	22,590	42		45	Brian Kirsch, commercial insurance
Labour	25,771	48		41	Alan Simpson, MP
Lib Dem	5,408	10		14	Gary Long
Majority	3,181	Lab 6		Con 4	
Swing		5 → Lab		4 → Lab	Con need 3 to win. 43rd on Con list

NUNEATON, Warwickshire. Labour marginal, Tory target seat, mainly urban, Lab gain in 92
Skilled manual 34% (81st); Owner-occupied 77% (117th); Asian 3% (143rd)

No Change	Actual 92	%		87	Candidates
Conservative	25,526	43		45	Richard Blunt, restoration company owner
Labour	27,157	46		35	Bill Olner, MP
Lib Dem	6,671	11		19	Ron Cockings
Majority	1,631	Lab 3		Con 10	
Swing		7 → Lab		No swing	Con need 1 to win. 20th on Con list

OCHIL, Central/Tayside. Labour seat, SNP long-shot, mainly urban, based on Clackmannan

44% change	Notional 92	%	92	87	Candidates
Conservative	10,367	24	17	15	Allan Hogarth
Labour	18,620	43	49	54	Martin O'Neill, MP
Lib Dem	2,984	7	7	11	Ann Watters
SNP	11,270	26	27	21	George Reid
Majority	7,350	Lab 17	Lab 22	Lab 33	
Swing			5 → SNP	3 → Lab	SNP needs 9 to win. 13th on SNP list

OGMORE, Mid Glamorgan. 7th safest Labour seat, ex-mining, working class
Long-term ill 19% (9th); Skilled manual 38% (18th); Unskilled 7% (43rd)

No Change	Actual 92	%		87	Candidates
Conservative	6,359	15		15	David Unwin
Labour	30,186	72		69	Ray Powell, MP
Lib Dem	2,868	7		10	Kirsty Williams
Plaid Cymru	2,667	6		4	John Rogers
Majority	23,827	Lab 57		Lab 54	
Swing		1 → Lab		5 → Lab	

OLD BEXLEY & SIDCUP, South London. Strong Tory seat, suburban, white collar
Other non-white 2% (123rd); Owner-occupied 85% (8th); White collar 22% (1st)

39% change	Notional 92	%	92	87	Candidates
Conservative	31,340	56	60	62	Sir Edward Heath, MP
Labour	11,768	21	22	17	Richard Justham
Lib Dem	11,642	21	16	21	Iain King
Majority	19,572	Con 35	Con 39	Con 42	
Swing			3 → Lab	4 → Con	

OLDHAM EAST & SADDLEWORTH, Greater Manchester. New Tory marginal, mainly urban
Asian 4% (109th); Overcrowding 3% (112th); Skilled manual 31% (152nd)

59% change	Notional 92	%	Candidates
Conservative	20,271	35	John Hudson, party agent
Labour	17,300	30	Phil Woolas, union official
Lib Dem	19,712	34	Chris Davies, MP
Majority	559	Con 1	Lab needs 4 to win. 56th on Lab list
			LD need 0.5 to win. 3rd on LD list

OLDHAM WEST & ROYTON, Greater Manchester. New Labour seat, urban, large Asian community
Asian 12% (35th); Overcrowding 4% (48th); Skilled manual 32% (117th)

89% change	Notional 92	%	Candidates
Conservative	20,093	38	Jonathan Lord
Labour	25,887	49	Michael Meacher, MP
Lib Dem	6,031	11	
Majority	5,794	Lab 11	

ORKNEY & SHETLAND, Islands. Strong Lib Dem seat, islands

No Change	Actual 92	%		87	Candidates
Conservative	4,542	22		23	Hope Vere Anderson
Labour	4,093	20		19	James Paton
Lib Dem	9,575	46		42	James Wallace, MP
SNP	2,301	11		–	Willie Ross
Majority	5,033	LD 24		LD 18	
Swing		3 → Lib Dem		1 → Con	

ORPINGTON, South London. Strong Tory seat, suburban, white collar
Age 40-pension 30% (50th); Owner-occupied 81% (32nd); White collar 19% (21st)

41% change	Notional 92	%	92	87	Candidates
Conservative	36,770	55	57	58	John Horam, MP
Labour	9,837	15	12	11	Sue Polydorou
Lib Dem	18,840	28	30	31	Chris Maines
Majority	17,930	Con 27	Con 27	Con 27	
Swing			No swing	2 → Con	

OXFORD EAST, Oxfordshire. Labour seat, car industry, working class
Age 16-24 15% (35th); Mobility 15% (21st); Unskilled 9% (13th)

13% change	Notional 92	%	92	87	Candidates
Conservative	16,718	34	34	40	Jonathan Djanogly, solicitor
Labour	25,031	50	50	43	Andrew Smith, MP
Lib Dem	6,971	14	13	16	
Majority	8,313	Lab 17	Lab 16	Lab 3	
Swing			7 → Lab	3 → Lab	

OXFORD WEST & ABINGDON, Oxfordshire. Tory seat, Lib Dem long-shot, mainly urban, professional
Mobility 15% (20th); Professional 15% (6th); Private tenants 13% (51st)

24% change	Notional 92	%	92	87	Candidates
Conservative	27,630	46	45	46	Laurence Harris, solicitor
Labour	9,642	16	14	15	Susan Brown
Lib Dem	21,408	36	39	37	Dr Evan Harris, GP
Majority	6,222	Con 10	Con 6	Con 9	
Swing			1 → LD	3 → SDPAll	LD need 5 to win. 23rd on LD list

PAISLEY NORTH, Strathclyde. Strong Labour seat, mainly urban

32% change	Notional 92	%	92	87	Candidates
Conservative	5,757	16	16	16	Kenneth Brookes
Labour	19,043	52	51	56	
Lib Dem	2,828	8	8	16	Alan Jelfs
SNP	8,629	24	23	13	Ian Mackay
Majority	10,414	Lab 28	Lab 27	Lab 40	
Swing			8 → SNP	8 → Lab	

PAISLEY SOUTH, Strathclyde. Strong Labour seat, mainly urban

15% change	Notional 92	%	92	87	Candidates
Conservative	6,129	15	16	15	Robert Reid
Labour	20,268	51	51	56	Gordon McMaster, MP
Lib Dem	3,548	9	9	15	Eileen McCartin
SNP	9,799	25	24	14	Bill Martin, councillor
Majority	10,469	Lab 26	Lab 27	Lab 41	
Swing			8 → SNP	12 → Lab	SNP needs 13 to win. 30th on SNP list

PENDLE, Lancashire. Labour marginal, Tory target seat, mainly urban, working class, Lab gain in 92
Asian 10% (47th); Owner-occupied 79% (67th); Skilled manual 34% (66th)

No Change	Actual 92	%		87	Candidates
Conservative	21,384	40		40	John Midgley, solicitor
Labour	23,497	44		35	Gordon Prentice, MP
Lib Dem	7,976	15		24	
Majority	2,113	Lab 4		Con 5	
Swing		5 → Lab		3 → Lab	Con need 2 to win. 30th on Con list

PENRITH & THE BORDER, Cumbria. Strong Tory seat, rural
White 99.7% (2nd); Self-employed 23% (11th); Second homes 2% (26th)

25% change	Notional 92	%	92	87	Candidates
Conservative	30,030	59	58	60	David Maclean, MP
Labour	5,644	11	15	11	Alan Marsden
Lib Dem	14,848	29	26	29	Geyve Walker
Majority	15,182	Con 30	Con 31	Con 32	
Swing			No swing	No swing	

PERTH, Tayside. Tory marginal, SNP target seat, mainly rural, SNP by-election gain in 95

21% change	Notional 92	%	95 by-	92	87	Candidates
Conservative	18,159	41	21	40	40	John Godfrey
Labour	5,922	13	23	13	16	Douglas Alexander
Lib Dem	5,366	12	12	11	17	
SNP	15,433	34	40	36	28	Roseanna Cunningham, MP
Majority	2,726	Con 6	SNP17	Con 4	Con 12	
Swing			12 → SNP	4 → SNP	2 → SNP	SNP needs 3 to win. 3rd on SNP lis

PETERBOROUGH, Cambridgeshire. Tory seat, Labour long-shot, new town, working class
Asian 7% (55th); Age 16-24 14% (84th); Mobility 12% (83rd)

44% change	Notional 92	%	92	87	Candidates
Conservative	26,455	50	48	49	Jacqueline Foster, airline stewardess
Labour	20,201	38	40	34	Helen Brinton, teacher
Lib Dem	4,973	9	8	16	David Howarth
Majority	6,254	Con 12	Con 8	Con 16	
Swing			4 → Lab	1 → Lab	Lab needs 6 to win. 73rd on Lab list

PLYMOUTH DEVONPORT, Devon. Labour seat, urban, working class, Lab gain in 92
Govt schemes 2% (57th); Council tenants 32% (64th); No central heating 31% (65th)

15% change	Notional 92	%	92	87	Candidates
Conservative	21,111	36	34	29	Anthony Johnson, company secretary
Labour	27,877	47	49	29	David Jamieson, MP
Lib Dem	7,830	13	12	42	Richard Copus
Majority	6,766	Lab 11	Lab 15	LD 13	
Swing			8 → Lab	1 → SDPAll	

PLYMOUTH SUTTON, Devon. Tory marginal, Labour target seat, urban
Age 16-24 15% (22nd); Private tenants 19% (11th); No central heating 42% (17th)

34% change	Notional 92	%	92	87	Candidates
Conservative	22,049	42	50	46	Andrew Crisp, account director, corp. comms.
Labour	20,989	40	28	16	Linda Gilroy, head, Gas Consumers' Council, SW
Lib Dem	8,673	16	23	38	Steve Melia
Majority	1,060	Con 2	Con 22	Con 8	
Swing			4 → Lab	9 → LibAll	Lab needs 1 to win. 16th on Lab list

PONTEFRACT & CASTLEFORD, West Yorkshire. Strong Labour seat, ex-mining, working class
Long-term ill 17% (41st); Skilled manual 38% (16th); Council tenants 36% (46th)

No Change	Actual 92	%		87	Candidates
Conservative	10,051	21		21	Adrian Flook, investment banker
Labour	33,546	70		67	Geoffrey Lofthouse, MP
Lib Dem	4,410	9		11	
Majority	23,495	Lab 49		Lab 46	
Swing		2 → Lab		7 → Lab	

PONTYPRIDD, Mid Glamorgan. Strong Labour seat, ex-mining
Owner-occupied 77% (105th); Long-term ill 16% (45th); Unskilled 6% (144th)

No Change	Actual 92	%		87	Candidates
Conservative	9,925	20		20	Jonathan Cowen
Labour	29,722	61		56	Dr Kim Howells, MP
Lib Dem	4,180	9		19	David Rich
Plaid Cymru	4,448	9		5	Owain Llewelyn
Majority	19,797	Lab 41		Lab 37	
Swing		2 → Lab		7 → Lab	PlC needs 26 to win. 6th on PlC list

POOLE, Dorset. Strong Tory seat, urban, retirement
White 99% (185th); Second homes 2% (34th); Mobility 12% (73rd)

42% change	Notional 92	%	92	87	Candidates
Conservative	27,768	55	53	58	Robert Syms, managing director
Labour	5,880	12	11	10	Hadyn White
Lib Dem	14,787	29	33	33	Alan Tetlow
Majority	12,981	Con 26	Con 20	Con 25	
Swing			2 → LD	1 → SDPAll	

POPLAR & CANNING TOWN, East London. New strong Labour seat, docklands, high unemployment
Unemployed 22% (12th); Council tenants 60% (2nd); Overcrowding 8% (7th)

66% change	Notional 92	%	Candidates
Conservative	10,517	26	Bene't Steinberg, counsellor
Labour	20,935	51	Jim Fitzpatrick, union official
Lib Dem	7,986	20	Janet Ludlow
Majority	10,418	Lab 26	

PORTSMOUTH NORTH, Hampshire. Tory seat, Labour long-shot, urban, working class
Age 25-39 23% (145th); No central heating 36% (40th); Unskilled 6% (147th)

19% change	Notional 92	%	92	87	Candidates
Conservative	25,368	51	53	55	Peter Griffiths, MP
Labour	16,610	33	30	20	Syd Rapson
Lib Dem	7,529	15	17	25	Steve Sollitt
Majority	8,758	Con 18	Con 23	Con 31	
Swing			6 → Lab	1 → SDPAll	Lab needs 9 to win. 100th on Lab list

PORTSMOUTH SOUTH, Hampshire. Tory marginal, Lib Dem target seat, urban, white collar
Age 16-24 15% (19th); Private tenants 15% (32nd); No central heating 37% (34th)

No Change	Actual 92	%	92	87	Candidates
Conservative	22,798	43		43	David Martin, MP
Labour	7,857	15		13	Alan Burnett
Lib Dem	22,556	42		43	Mike Hancock
Majority	242	Con 1		Con 0.4	
Swing		No swing		12 → SDPAll	LD need 0.2 to win. 2nd on LD list

PRESELI PEMBROKESHIRE, Dyfed. Tory marginal, mainly rural, based on Pembroke
Self-employed 21% (17th); Govt schemes 3% (29th); Second homes 2% (21st)

63% change	Notional 92	%	92	87	Candidates
Conservative	17,270	40	42	41	Robert Buckland, barrister
Labour	16,667	38	43	31	Jackie Lawrence, political adviser
Lib Dem	5,379	12	11	26	Jeffrey Clarke
Plaid Cymru	3,773	9	3	2	Alun Lloyd Jones
Majority	603	Con 1	Lab 1	Con 10	
Swing			6 → Lab	4 → Lab	Lab needs 1 to win. 12th on Lab list

PRESTON, Lancashire. Strong Labour seat, cotton industry, working class
Age 16-24 15% (31st); No central heating 37% (31st); Unskilled 9% (8th)

31% change	Notional 92	%	92	87	Candidates
Conservative	17,876	32	28	29	Paul Gray, new business director, PR co.
Labour	29,342	53	54	53	Audrey Wise, MP
Lib Dem	7,644	14	17	19	Bill Chadwick, councillor
Majority	11,466	Lab 21	Lab 27	Lab 24	
Swing			1 → Lab	5 → Lab	

PUDSEY, West Yorkshire. Tory seat, Labour and Lib Dem long-shot, commuting, white collar
Age 40-pension 28% (134th); Owner-occupied 76% (143rd); No central heating 32% (58th)

No Change	Actual 92	%	92	87	Candidates
Conservative	25,067	44		46	Peter Bone, MD, international travel company
Labour	16,095	28		21	Paul Truswell
Lib Dem	15,153	27		34	Jonathan Brown
Majority	8,972	Con 16		Con 12	
Swing		5 → Lab		1 → Con	Lab needs 7 to win. 85th on Lab list
					LD needs 9 to win. 49th on LD list

PUTNEY, South London. Tory seat, Labour long-shot, suburban, middle-class
Age 25-39 27% (22nd); Mobility 14% (29th); Managerial 44% (26th)

No Change	Actual 92	%		87	Candidates
Conservative	25,188	52		51	David Mellor, MP
Labour	17,662	37		36	Anthony Colman
Lib Dem	4,636	10		12	Russell Pyne
Majority	7,526	Con 16		Con 14	
Swing		1 → Con		2 → Con	Lab needs 8 to win. 89th on Lab list

RAYLEIGH, Essex. Strong Tory seat, suburban, white collar, based on Rochford
Age 40-pension 29% (54th); Owner-occupied 90% (1st); Car owners 84% (20th)

19% change	Notional 92	%	92	87	Candidates
Conservative	33,065	61	61	60	Dr Michael Clark, MP
Labour	8,032	15	17	12	Raymond Ellis
Lib Dem	11,868	22	20	27	Sid Cumberland
Majority	21,197	Con 39	Con 41	Con 33	
Swing			4 → Con	4 → Con	

READING EAST, Berkshire. Strong Tory seat, mainly urban, professional
Age 16-24 15% (15th); Age 25-39 26% (40th); Professional 12% (34th)

67% change	Notional 92	%	92	87	Candidates
Conservative	25,699	49	54	54	John Watts, MP
Labour	15,115	29	27	22	Jane Griffiths
Lib Dem	10,684	20	18	23	Sam Samuel
Majority	10,584	Con 20	Con 27	Con 31	
Swing			3 → Lab	3 → Con	

READING WEST, Berkshire. Strong Tory seat, mainly urban, professional
Age 16-24 14% (93rd); Age 25-39 25% (67th); Black 3% (78th)

19% change	Notional 92	%	92	87	Candidates
Conservative	27,888	52	53	55	Nicholas Bennett, political adviser to accountancy firm
Labour	15,256	29	28	21	Martin Salter
Lib Dem	9,461	18	18	22	Dee Tomlin
Majority	12,632	Con 24	Con 25	Con 33	
Swing			5 → Lab	5 → Con	

REDCAR, Cleveland. Labour seat, chemical industry, working class
Govt schemes 3% (11th); Long-term ill 16% (52nd); Unskilled 7% (59th)

16% change	Notional 92	%	92	87	Candidates
Conservative	19,823	34	32	31	Andrew Isaacs, solicitor
Labour	31,237	54	56	47	Dr Mo Mowlam, MP
Lib Dem	7,241	12	12	21	Joyce Benbow
Majority	11,414	Lab 20	Lab 24	Lab 16	
Swing			4 → Lab	5 → Lab	

REDDITCH, Hereford and Worcester. Tory marginal, Labour target seat, new town, mainly rural
Age 25-39 24% (76th); Council tenants 28% (103rd); Black 1% (145th)

36% change	Notional 92	%	92	87	Candidates
Conservative	22,930	47	50	52	Anthea McIntyre
Labour	19,643	40	35	27	Jacqui Smith, teacher
Lib Dem	5,716	12	14	21	Malcolm Hall
Majority	3,287	Con 7	Con 14	Con 24	
Swing			5 → Lab	1 → Lab	Lab needs 3 to win. 44th on Lab list

REGENT'S PARK & KENSINGTON NORTH, North London. New Labour marginal, inner city
Other non-white 9% (3rd); Private tenants 20% (8th); Overcrowding 6% (14th)

55% change	Notional 92	%	Candidates
Conservative	21,503	41	Paul McGuinness, contracts manager
Labour	25,317	48	Karen Buck, party official
Lib Dem	4,163	8	Emily Gasson
Majority	3,814	Lab 7	Con need 4 to win. 57th on Con list

REIGATE, Surrey. Strong Tory seat, mainly urban, managerial
Car owners 81% (70th); Professional 11% (58th); Managerial 45% (16th)

29% change	Notional 92	%	92	87	Candidates
Conservative	29,148	58	57	59	Sir George Gardiner, MP
Labour	8,870	18	16	14	Andrew Howard
Lib Dem	12,208	24	26	24	Peter Samuel
Majority	16,940	Con 33	Con 31	Con 35	
Swing			2 → LD	1 → Con	

RENFREWSHIRE WEST, Strathclyde. Labour seat, commuting

63% change	Notional 92	%	92	87	Candidates
Conservative	11,128	28	33	30	Charles Cormack
Labour	17,174	43	37	39	Thomas Graham, MP
Lib Dem	3,375	8	10	21	
SNP	8,258	21	20	10	Colin Campbell
Majority	6,046	Lab 15	Lab 4	Lab 9	
Swing			3 → Con	6 → Lab	SNP needs 11 to win. 19th on SNP list

RHONDDA, Mid Glamorgan. 2nd safest Labour seat, ex-mining, working class
Unemployed 17% (39th); Long-term ill 26% (1st); Skilled manual 37% (28th)

No Change	Actual 92	%		87	Candidates
Conservative	3,588	8		8	Stephen Whiting
Labour	34,243	75		73	Allan Rogers, MP
Lib Dem	2,431	5		8	Rodney Berman
Plaid Cymru	5,427	12		9	Leanne Wood
Majority	28,816	Lab 63		Lab 65	
Swing		1 → PlC		7 → Lab	

RIBBLE SOUTH, Lancashire. Tory seat, Labour long-shot, car industry
Owner-occupied 84% (12th); Car owners 79% (101st); White collar 15% (170th)

36% change	Notional 92	%	92	87	Candidates
Conservative	29,366	50	48	47	Robert Atkins, MP
Labour	20,526	35	38	33	Dennis Golden
Lib Dem	8,695	15	14	20	Tim Farron
Majority	8,840	Con 15	Con 9	Con 14	
Swing			3 → Lab	4 → Lab	Lab needs 8 to win. 87th on Lab list

RIBBLE VALLEY, Lancashire. Strong Tory seat, rural, middle-class, Lib Dem by-election gain in 90, Con regain in 92
Age 40-pension 30% (32nd); Owner-occupied 85% (9th); Managerial 42% (50th)

12% change	Notional 92	%	92	87	Candidates
Conservative	31,629	53	52	61	Nigel Evans, MP
Labour	5,254	9	7	18	Marcus Johnstone
Lib Dem	23,000	38	41	21	Michael Carr, teacher
Majority	8,629	Con 14	Con 12	Con 39	
Swing			14 → Lib Dem	1 → SDPAll	LD need 7 to win. 36th on LD list

RICHMOND, North Yorkshire. Strong Tory seat, rural, middle-class
Self-employed 16% (64th); Second homes 2% (35th); Mobility 11% (62nd)

23% change	Notional 92	%	92	87	Candidates
Conservative	30,333	60	62	61	William Hague, MP
Labour	5,797	12	12	12	Steven Merritt
Lib Dem	13,626	27	26	27	Jane Harvey
Majority	16,707	Con 33	Con 36	Con 34	
Swing			1 → Con	No swing	

RICHMOND PARK, South London. Tory seat, Lib Dem long-shot, suburban.
Private tenants 15% (29th); Professional 17% (4th); Managerial 50% (2nd)

57% change	Notional 92	%	92	87	Candidates
Conservative	30,609	52	51	48	Jeremy Hanley, MP
Labour	5,211	9	6	7	Sue Jenkins
Lib Dem	22,225	38	42	44	Dr Jenny Tonge
Majority	8,384	Con 14	Con 9	Con 4	
Swing			2 → Con	2 → Con	LD needs 7 to win. 35th on LD list

ROCHDALE, Greater Manchester. Lib Dem marginal, urban, large Asian community, new boundaries help Labour
Asian 13% (29th); Overcrowding 5% (33rd); Unskilled 7% (62nd)

47% change	Notional 92	%	92	87	Candidates
Conservative	12,378	23	16	19	Mervyn Turnberg
Labour	20,076	38	39	38	Lorna Fitzsimmons, PR consultant
Lib Dem	20,204	38	43	43	Liz Lynne, MP
Majority	128	LD 0.2	LD 4	LD 5	
Swing			1 → Lab	5 → Lab	Lab needs 0.1 to win. 4th on Lab list

ROCHFORD & SOUTHEND EAST, Essex. Strong Tory seat, suburban, white collar, based on Southend East
Pensionable 22% (74th); Private tenants 11% (68th); White collar 19% (22nd)

19% change	Notional 92	%	92	87	Candidates
Conservative	30,096	59	59	58	Teddy Taylor, MP
Labour	14,019	28	27	18	Nigel Smith
Lib Dem	6,011	12	12	24	Paula Smith
Majority	16,077	Con 32	Con 31	Con 34	
Swing			4 → Lab	3 → Con	

ROMFORD, North London. Strong Tory seat, outer suburbs
Black 1% (157th); Owner-occupied 81% (42nd); White collar 21% (2nd)

12% change	Notional 92	%	92	87	Candidates
Conservative	27,462	58	57	56	Sir Michael Neubert, MP
Labour	13,398	28	30	23	Eileen Gordon
Lib Dem	5,865	12	13	20	Nigel Meyer
Majority	14,064	Con 30	Con 27	Con 33	
Swing			3 → Lab	1 → Lab	

ROMSEY, Hampshire. New strong Tory seat, mainly rural, professional
Age 40-pension 30% (23rd); Car owners 84% (9th); Professional 12% (33rd)

105% change	Notional 92	%	Candidates
Conservative	34,218	63	Michael Colvin, MP
Labour	6,982	13	Joanne Ford
Lib Dem	12,496	23	Mark Cooper
Majority	21,722	Con 40	

ROSS, SKYE & INVERNESS WEST, Highland. Lib Dem seat, Tory long-shot, rural

33% change	Notional 92	%	92	87	Candidates
Conservative	8,452	22	23	20	Mary MacLeod
Labour	7,296	19	15	19	Donnie Munro, lead singer, *Runrig*
Lib Dem	14,957	39	42	49	Charles Kennedy, MP
SNP	7,276	19	19	12	Margaret Paterson, councillor
Majority	6,505	LD 17	LD 19	LD 30	
Swing			6 → Con	12 → SDPAll	Lab needs 10 to win. 116th on Lab list
					SNP needs 10 to win. 15th on SNP list

ROSSENDALE & DARWEN, Lancashire. Labour marginal, mainly urban, skilled manual
Owner-occupied 77% (115th); No central heating 21% (186th); Skilled manual 33% (91st)

10% change	Notional 92	%	92	87	Candidates
Conservative	24,995	44	44	47	Tricia Buzzard, advertising/marketing
Labour	25,044	44	44	38	Janet Anderson, MP
Lib Dem	6,798	12	11	15	Brian Dunning
Majority	49	Lab 0.1	Lab 0.2	Con 8	
Swing			4 → Lab	4 → Lab	Con need 0.04 to win. 2nd on Con list

ROTHER VALLEY, South Yorkshire. Strong Labour seat, ex-mining, skilled manual
White 99.3% (118th); Govt schemes 2% (92nd); Skilled manual 36% (36th)

No Change	Actual 92	%		87	Candidates
Conservative	13,755	27		25	Steven Stanbury
Labour	30,977	61		56	Kevin Barron, MP
Lib Dem	6,483	13		18	
Majority	17,222	Lab 34		Lab 32	
Swing		1 → Lab		7 → Lab	

ROTHERHAM, South Yorkshire. Strong Labour seat, ex-steel industry, working class
Govt schemes 3% (40th); Long-term ill 17% (39th); Unskilled 7% (39th)

No Change	Actual 92	%	94 by-	87	Candidates
Conservative	10,372	24	10	22	John Fareham
Labour	27,933	64	56	60	Denis MacShane, MP
Lib Dem	5,375	12	30	18	David Wildgoose
Majority	17,561	Lab 40	Lab 26	Lab 38	
Swing		1 → Lab	13 → LD	5 → Lab	

ROXBURGH & BERWICKSHIRE, Borders. Lib Dem, Tory long-shot, rural

7% change	Notional 92	%	92	87	Candidates
Conservative	12,354	34	34	37	Douglas Younger
Labour	3,167	9	9	9	Helen Eadie
Lib Dem	16,807	47	47	49	Archy Kirkwood, MP
SNP	3,844	11	10	5	Malcolm Balfour
Majority	4,453	LD 12	LD 13	LD 12	
Swing			No swing	1 → LibAll	

RUGBY & KENILWORTH, Warwickshire. Strong Tory seat, mainly urban, professional
Black 1% (143rd); Owner-occupied 77% (104th); Professional 10% (64th)

0.3% change	Notional 92	%	92	87	Candidates
Conservative	34,218	52	52	52	James Pawsey, MP
Labour	20,894	32	32	25	Andy King
Lib Dem	9,971	15	15	24	Jerry Roodhouse, councillor
Majority	13,324	Con 20	Con 20	Con 27	
Swing			3 → Lab	1 → Lab	

RUISLIP-NORTHWOOD, North London. Strong Tory seat, outer suburbs
Other non-white 2% (74th); White collar 18% (45th); Professional 10% (74th)

9% change	Notional 92	%	92	87	Candidates
Conservative	30,130	63	63	63	John Wilkinson, MP
Labour	9,521	20	19	14	Paul Barker
Lib Dem	7,981	17	17	24	Chris Edwards
Majority	20,609	Con 43	Con 45	Con 39	
Swing			2 → Lab	4 → Con	

RUNNYMEDE & WEYBRIDGE, Surrey. New strong Tory seat, stockbroker belt, managerial
Car owners 82% (47th); Professional 10% (83rd); Managerial 42% (49th)

69% change	Notional 92	%	Candidates
Conservative	34,645	61	Philip Hammond, business consultant
Labour	9,004	16	Ian Peacock
Lib Dem	11,905	21	Geoffrey Taylor
Majority	22,740	Con 40	

RUSHCLIFFE, Nottinghamshire. Strong Tory seat, commuting, middle-class
Owner-occupied 79% (58th); Professional 12% (38th); Managerial 42% (40th)

No Change	Actual 92	%	87	Candidates
Conservative	34,448	54	59	Kenneth Clarke, MP
Labour	14,682	23	17	Jocelyn Pettit
Lib Dem	12,660	20	23	
Majority	19,766	Con 31	Con 36	
Swing		6 → Lab	1 → SDPAll	

RUTLAND & MELTON, Leicestershire. Strong Tory seat, rural, middle-class
Age 40-pension 29% (62nd); Self-employed 14% (118th); Car owners 81% (81st)

39% change	Notional 92	%	92	87	Candidates
Conservative	34,137	61	59	62	Alan Duncan, MP
Labour	8,730	16	20	15	John Meads
Lib Dem	11,556	21	19	24	Kim Lee
Majority	22,581	Con 41	Con 39	Con 39	
Swing			4 → Lab	3 → Con	

RYEDALE, North Yorkshire. Strong Tory seat, rural, working class
Age 40-pension 30% (31st); White 99.6% (14th); Second homes 2% (22nd)

38% change	Notional 92	%	92	87	Candidates
Conservative	28,338	55	56	53	John Greenway, MP
Labour	7,497	15	14	8	Alison Hiles
Lib Dem	15,340	30	30	39	Keith Orrell
Majority	12,998	Con 25	Con 26	Con 15	
Swing			6 → Con	7 → LibAll	

SAFFRON WALDEN, Essex. Strong Tory seat, managerial, rural
Age 40-pension 30% (43rd); Car owners 83% (26th); Managerial 41% (57th)

5% change	Notional 92	%	92	87	Candidates
Conservative	33,378	57	57	58	Alan Hazelhurst, MP
Labour	8,468	14	14	12	Malcolm Fincken
Lib Dem	16,885	29	29	29	Melvin Caton
Majority	16,493	Con 28	Con 28	Con 29	
Swing			No swing	No swing	

SALFORD, Greater Manchester. Strong Labour seat, inner city, high unemployment
Unemployed 19% (25th); Single parents 38% (16th); Long-term ill 18% (16th)

15% change	Notional 92	%	92	87	Candidates
Conservative	10,545	27	27	27	Elliot Bishop, trainee solicitor
Labour	23,532	59	60	59	Hazel Blears, solicitor
Lib Dem	5,017	13	11	13	Norman Owen
Majority	12,987	Lab 33	Lab 33	Lab 31	
Swing			1 → Lab	4 → Lab	

SALISBURY, Wiltshire. Tory seat, Lib Dem long-shot, mainly urban
Private tenants 10% (112th); Second homes 1% (107th); Mobility 13% (48th)

No Change	Actual 92	%		87	Candidates
Conservative	31,546	52		55	Robert Key, MP
Labour	5,483	9		10	Ricky Rogers
Lib Dem	22,573	37		35	Yvonne Emmerson-Pierce
Majority	8,973	Con 15		Con 20	
Swing		3 → Lib Dem		3 → Con	LD need 7 to win. 39th on LD list

SCARBOROUGH & WHITBY, North Yorkshire. Tory seat, Labour long-shot, seaside, working class
Pensionable 24% (38th); Self-employed 17% (42nd); Second homes 2% (24th)

No Change	Actual 92	%		87	Candidates
Conservative	29,334	50		51	John Sykes, MP
Labour	17,600	30		24	Lawrence Quinn
Lib Dem	11,133	19		26	Martin Allinson
Majority	11,734	Con 20		Con 25	
Swing		4 → Lab		1 → SDPAll	Lab needs 10 to win. 117th on Lab list

SCUNTHORPE, Humberside. Labour seat, industrial, skilled manual, based on Glanford
Govt schemes 2% (101st); Skilled manual 41% (7th); Unskilled 8% (21st)

27% change	Notional 92	%	92	87	Candidates
Conservative	17,467	36	38	43	Martyn Fisher
Labour	26,370	54	53	44	Elliot Morley, MP
Lib Dem	3,727	8	7	14	Gordon Smith
Majority	8,903	Lab 18	Lab 15	Lab 1	
Swing			7 → Lab	1 → Lab	

SEDGEFIELD, Durham. Strong Labour seat, ex-mining, working class
White 99.6% (18th); Govt schemes 3% (39th); Long-term ill 17% (35th)

57% change	Notional 92	%	92	87	Candidates
Conservative	14,161	28	29	28	Elizabeth Noel, author
Labour	31,391	62	61	56	Tony Blair, MP
Lib Dem	4,897	10	11	16	Ron Beadle
Majority	17,230	Lab 34	Lab 32	Lab 28	
Swing			2 → Lab	5 → Lab	

SELBY, North Yorkshire. Tory seat, Labour long-shot, mining
Age 40-pension 29% (78th); White 99.4% (58th); Owner-occupied 77% (113th)

6% change	Notional 92	%	92	87	Candidates
Conservative	29,739	51	50	52	Ken Hind, barrister
Labour	20,752	36	35	27	John Grogan
Lib Dem	7,595	13	15	22	Ted Batty
Majority	8,987	Con 16	Con 15	Con 25	
Swing			5 → Lab	6 → Lab	Lab needs 8 to win. 88th on Lab list

SEVENOAKS, Kent. Strong Tory seat, stockbroker belt, managerial
Age 40-pension 30% (33rd); Car owners 82% (38th); Managerial 41% (60th)

22% change	Notional 92	%	92	87	Candidates
Conservative	30,847	58	57	59	Michael Fallon, ex-MP
Labour	8,626	16	16	13	John Hayes
Lib Dem	13,160	25	24	28	Roger Walshe, councillor
Majority	17,687	Con 33	Con 33	Con 31	
Swing			1 → Con	1 → Con	

SHEFFIELD ATTERCLIFFE, South Yorkshire. Strong Labour seat, ex-steel industry, skilled manual
Council tenants 32% (66th); Long-term ill 16% (58th); Skilled manual 37% (30th)

No Change	Actual 92	%		87	Candidates
Conservative	13,083	17		23	Brendan Doyle, company MD
Labour	28,563	69		58	Clive Betts, MP
Lib Dem	7,283	12		20	
Majority	15,480	Lab 31		Lab 35	
Swing		2 → Con		5 → Lab	

SHEFFIELD BRIGHTSIDE, South Yorkshire. Strong Labour seat, outer suburbs, working class
Council tenants 53% (7th); Long-term ill 18% (13th); Skilled manual 38% (20th)

No Change	Actual 92	%		87	Candidates
Conservative	7,090	17		16	Christopher Buckwell, law lecturer
Labour	29,771	70		70	David Blunkett, MP
Lib Dem	5,273	13		14	
Majority	22,681	Lab 54		Lab 54	
Swing		No swing		7 → Lab	

SHEFFIELD CENTRAL, South Yorkshire. Strong Labour seat, inner city, high unemployment
Age 16-24 16% (4th); Unemployed 22% (14th); Mobility 15% (10th)

25% change	Notional 92	%	92	87	Candidates
Conservative	7,983	19	17	17	Martin Hess
Labour	25,448	60	69	68	Richard Caborn, MP
Lib Dem	8,068	19	12	14	Ali Qadar
Majority	17,380	Lab 41	Lab 52	Lab 51	
Swing			1 → Lab	5 → Lab	

SHEFFIELD HALLAM, South Yorkshire. Tory seat, Lib Dem long-shot, residential, professional
Pensionable 22% (82nd); Professional 20% (1th); Managerial 48% (5th)

19% change	Notional 92	%	92	87	Candidates
Conservative	22,180	50	46	46	Irvine Patnick, MP
Labour	8,246	18	20	20	Stephen Conquest
Lib Dem	13,740	31	33	33	Richard Allan, NHS computer manager
Majority	8,440	Con 19	Con 12	Con 14	
Swing			1 → Lib Dem	4 → LibAll	

SHEFFIELD HEELEY, South Yorkshire. Strong Labour seat, outer suburbs, working class
Pensionable 24% (46th); Council tenants 41% (26th); Long-term ill 17% (33rd)

No Change	Actual 92	%		87	Candidates
Conservative	13,051	26		26	John Harthman, planning officer
Labour	28,005	56		53	Bill Michie, MP
Lib Dem	9,247	18		20	Roger Davison
Majority	14,954	Lab 30		Lab 27	
Swing		1 → Lab		6 → Lab	

SHEFFIELD HILLSBOROUGH, South Yorkshire. Labour seat, Lib Dem long-shot, suburban, skilled manual
Govt schemes 2% (141st); Long-term ill 14% (178th); Skilled manual 33% (89th)

No Change	Actual 92	%	87	Candidates
Conservative	11,640	20	18	David Nuttall, solicitor
Labour	27,568	46	44	Helen Jackson, MP
Lib Dem	20,500	34	39	Arthur Dunworth
Majority	7,068	Lab 12	Lab 6	
Swing		3 → Lab	1 → Lab	LD need 6 to win. 30th on LD list

SHERWOOD, Nottinghamshire. Labour marginal, Tory target seat, mining, skilled manual, Lab gain in 92
Owner-occupied 77% (108th); Skilled manual 35% (56th); Age 40-pension 28% (141st)

No Change	Actual 92	%	87	Candidates
Conservative	26,878	43	46	Roland Spencer
Labour	29,788	48	38	Paddy Tipping, MP
Lib Dem	6,039	10	16	Bruce Moult
Majority	2,910	Lab 5	Con 8	
Swing		6 → Lab	3 → Con	Con need 2 to win. 35th on Con list

SHIPLEY, West Yorkshire. Strong Tory seat, mainly rural, middle-class
Owner-occupied 78% (94th); No central heating 27% (90th); Managerial 39% (84th)

No Change	Actual 92	%	87	Candidates
Conservative	28,463	50	50	Sir Marcus Fox, MP
Labour	16,081	29	23	Christopher Leslie
Lib Dem	11,288	20	26	John Cole
Majority	12,382	Con 22	Con 23	
Swing		2 → Lab	1 → Con	

SHREWSBURY & ATCHAM, Shropshire. Tory seat, Lib Dem long-shot, mainly urban
Age 40-pension 28% (175th); White 99% (183rd); Self-employed 14% (153rd)

No Change	Actual 92	%	87	Candidates
Conservative	26,681	46	48	Derek Conway, MP
Labour	15,157	26	20	Paul Marsden
Lib Dem	15,716	27	31	Anne Woolland, laboratory technician
Majority	10,965	Con 19	Con 17	
Swing		2 → Con	No swing	Lab needs 10 to win. 115th on Lab list
				LD needs 9 to win. 60th on LD list

SHROPSHIRE NORTH, Shropshire. Strong Tory seat, rural
White 99.5% (35th); Self-employed 18% (37th); No central heating 24% (131st)

17% change	Notional 92	%	92	87	Candidates
Conservative	27,159	51	51	52	Owen Patterson, managing director, leather company
Labour	13,978	26	24	20	Ian Lucas
Lib Dem	12,283	23	25	27	John Stevens
Majority	13,181	Con 25	Con 25	Con 25	
Swing			No swing	1 → Con	

SITTINGBOURNE & SHEPPEY, Kent. Strong Tory seat, rural, white collar
Second homes 1% (108th); Skilled manual 35% (49th); Unskilled 6% (97th)

27% change	Notional 92	%	92	87	Candidates
Conservative	24,669	49	50	51	Sir Roger Moate, MP
Labour	12,106	24	25	21	Derek Wyatt
Lib Dem	13,541	27	24	28	Roger Truelove, retired teacher
Majority	11,128	Con 22	Con 25	Con 23	
Swing			3 → Lab	2 → SDPAll	

SKIPTON & RIPON, North Yorkshire. Strong Tory seat, rural, managerial
Self-employed 21% (18th); Second homes 1% (48th); Managerial 41% (55th)

8% change	Notional 92	%	92	87	Candidates
Conservative	32,944	58	58	59	David Curry, MP
Labour	8,442	15	15	11	Robert Marchant
Lib Dem	15,547	27	27	28	Thomas Mould
Majority	17,397	Con 31	Con 31	Con 31	
Swing			No swing	1 → Con	

SLEAFORD & NORTH HYKEHAM, Lincolnshire. Strong Tory seat, rural, based on Grantham
Age 40-pension 30% (47th); Car owners 81% (76th); Mobility 12% (81st)

52% change	Notional 92	%	92	87	Candidates
Conservative	31,180	58	56	57	Douglas Hogg, MP
Labour	11,698	22	27	21	Sean Harriss
Lib Dem	8,873	17	15	21	John Marriott
Majority	19,482	Con 37	Con 30	Con 36	
Swing			4 → Lab	1 → Con	

SLOUGH, Berkshire. Currently Tory but under new boundaries Labour marginal, Tory target seat, new town
Age 25-39 26% (37th); Asian 22% (12th); Overcrowding 6% (18th)

7% change	Notional 92	%	92	87	Candidates
Conservative	23,544	44	45	47	Peta Buscombe
Labour	23,580	44	44	40	Fiona Mactaggart, lecturer in primary education
Lib Dem	3,841	7	7	13	Chris Bushill
Majority	36	Lab 0.1	Con 1	Con 7	
Swing			3 → Lab	1 → Con	Con need 0.04 to win. 1st on Con list

SOLIHULL, West Midlands. Strong Tory seat, stockbroker belt, middle-class
Age 40-pension 30% (19th); Owner-occupied 85% (6th); Professional 11% (50th)

% change	Notional 92	%	92	87	Candidates
Conservative	38,277	61	61	61	John Taylor, MP
Labour	10,512	17	17	15	Rachel Harris
Lib Dem	13,202	21	21	24	Michael Southcombe
Majority	25,075	Con 40	Con 40	Con 37	
Swing			1 → Con	2 → Con	

SOMERTON & FROME, Somerset. Tory marginal, Lib Dem target seat, mainly rural, middle-class
White 99.6% (15th); Self-employed 19% (31st); Car owners 82% (41st)

1% change	Notional 92	%	92	87	Candidates
Conservative	28,287	47	48	54	Mark Robinson, MP
Labour	6,217	10	10	10	Bob Ashford
Lib Dem	24,036	40	40	36	David Heath, consultant optician
Majority	4,251	Con 7	Con 7	Con 18	
Swing			5 → Lib Dem	1 → LibAll	LD need 4 to win. 15th on LD list

SOUTH HOLLAND & THE DEEPINGS, Lincolnshire. New strong Tory seat, rural
Age 40-pension 29% (72nd); White 99.4% (62nd); Self-employed 16% (77nd)

84% change	Notional 92	%	Candidates
Conservative	29,017	57	John Hayes, sales director
Labour	12,254	24	John Lewis
Lib Dem	9,619	19	Peter Millen
Majority	16,763	Con 33	

SOUTH SHIELDS, Tyne and Wear. Strong Labour seat, ex-shipbuilding, skilled manual
Govt schemes 3% (17th); Unemployed 17% (37th); Long-term ill 17% (37th)

10% change	Notional 92	%	92	87	Candidates
Conservative	12,220	27	27	26	Mark Hoban
Labour	28,041	61	60	58	Dr David Clark, MP
Lib Dem	5,626	12	13	16	
Majority	15,821	Lab 35	Lab 32	Lab 32	
Swing			No swing	8 → Lab	

SOUTHAMPTON ITCHEN, Hampshire. Labour marginal, Tory target seat, urban, working class, Lab gain in 92
Single parents 24% (98th); Skilled manual 33% (95th); Unskilled 6% (76th)

28% change	Notional 92	%	92	87	Candidates
Conservative	24,065	42	43	44	Peter Fleet, advertising manager
Labour	25,118	44	44	32	John Denham, MP
Lib Dem	7,924	14	13	24	David Harrison
Majority	1,053	Lab 2	Lab 1	Con 12	
Swing			7 → Lab	1 → Lab	Con needs 1 to win. 12th on Con list

SOUTHAMPTON TEST, Hampshire. New Labour marginal, currently Tory, suburban, middle-class
Age 16-24 15% (33rd); Private tenants 14% (39th); Unskilled 7% (64th)

29% change	Notional 92	%	92	87	Candidates
Conservative	21,843	40	43	46	James Hill, MP
Labour	24,565	46	42	33	Alan Whitehead, professor of public policy
Lib Dem	7,087	13	13	21	Alan Dowden
Majority	2,722	Lab 5	Con 1	Con 12	
Swing			6 → Lab	2 → Lab	Con need 3 to win. 36th on Con list

SOUTHEND WEST, Essex. Strong Tory seat, seaside, white collar
Pensionable 25% (30th); Owner-occupied 82% (29th); White collar 20% (12th)

No Change	Actual 92	%		87	Candidates
Conservative	27,319	55		54	David Amess, MP for Basildon
Labour	6,139	12		8	Alan Harley
Lib Dem	15,417	31		38	Nina Stimson
Majority	11,902	Con 24		Con 16	
Swing		4 → Con		No swing	

SOUTHPORT, Merseyside. Tory marginal, Lib Dem target seat, seaside, white collar
Pensionable 26% (24th); Owner-occupied 80% (43rd); Private tenants 12% (64th)

No Change	Actual 92	%		87	Candidates
Conservative	26,081	47		45	Matthew Banks, MP
Labour	5,637	10		6	Sarah Norman
Lib Dem	23,018	42		48	Ronnie Fearn, ex-MP
Majority	3,063	Con 6		LD 3	
Swing		5 → Con		7 → LibAll	LD need 3 to win. 11th on LD list

SOUTHWARK NORTH & BERMONDSEY, South London. Lib Dem seat, Labour long-shot, inner city
Council tenants 59% (3rd); Single parents 43% (7th); Unskilled 8% (16th)

16% change	Notional 92	%	92	87	Candidates
Conservative	5,170	12	10	13	Grant Shapps, company director
Labour	14,889	35	31	40	Jeremy Fraser
Lib Dem	22,158	51	57	47	Simon Hughes, MP
Majority	7,269	LD 17	LD 26	LD 8	
Swing			9 → Lib Dem	4 → Lab	Lab needs 8 to win. 98th on Lab list

SPELTHORNE, Surrey. Strong Tory seat, mainly urban, white collar
Owner-occupied 80% (54th); Car owners 83% (34th); White collar 18% (40th)

No Change	Actual 92	%		87	Candidates
Conservative	32,627	59		60	David Wilshire, MP
Labour	12,784	23		17	Keith Dibble
Lib Dem	9,202	17		23	Edward Glynn
Majority	19,843	Con 36		Con 37	
Swing		4 → Lab		5 → Con	

ST ALBANS, Hertfordshire. Tory seat, Lib Dem long-shot, commuting, middle-class
Other non-white 2% (80th); Professional 12% (25th); Managerial 44% (30th)

62% change	Notional 92	%	92	87	Candidates
Conservative	23,586	46	53	53	David Rutley
Labour	12,932	25	19	12	Kerry Pollard
Lib Dem	14,452	28	26	35	Anthony Rowland, teacher
Majority	9,134	Con 18	Con 27	Con 18	
Swing			4 → Con	2 → Con	LD need 9 to win. 53rd on LD list

ST HELENS NORTH, Merseyside. Strong Labour seat, industrial, skilled manual
White 99.5% (26th); Govt schemes 2% (67th); Skilled manual 36% (34th)

No Change	Actual 92	%		87	Candidates
Conservative	15,686	29		27	Pelham Walker, chartered surveyor
Labour	31,930	58		54	John Evans, MP
Lib Dem	7,224	13		19	John Beirne
Majority	16,244	Lab 30		Lab 26	
Swing		2 → Lab		5 → Lab	

ST HELENS SOUTH, Merseyside. Strong Labour seat, glass industry, skilled manual
Govt schemes 3% (25th); Long-term ill 16% (50th); Skilled manual 35% (42nd)

1% change	Notional 92	%	92	87	Candidates
Conservative	12,263	25	25	27	Mary Russell, solicitor
Labour	30,572	61	61	55	Gerry Bermingham, MP
Lib Dem	6,961	14	14	19	Brian Spencer
Majority	18,309	Lab 37	Lab 37	Lab 28	
Swing			4 → Lab	4 → Lab	

ST IVES, Cornwall. Tory marginal, Lib Dem target seat, seaside, retirement
Pensionable 24% (45th); Self-employed 23% (10th); Second homes 2% (17th)

No Change	Actual 92	%		87	Candidates
Conservative	24,528	43		48	William Rogers, insurance broker
Labour	9,144	16		18	Christopher Fegan
Lib Dem	22,883	40		34	Andrew George, charity worker
Majority	1,645	Con 3		Con 15	
Swing		6 → Lib Dem		1 → SDPAll	LD need 1 to win. 7th on LD list

STAFFORD, Staffordshire. Tory seat, Labour long-shot, mainly rural
Age 16-24 13% (153rd); Age 40-pension 29% (97th); Professional 8% (153rd)

51% change	Notional 92	%	92	87	Candidates
Conservative	26,464	48	50	51	David Cameron, corporate affairs executive
Labour	19,229	35	32	21	David Kidney
Lib Dem	9,097	17	17	28	Pam Hornby
Majority	7,235	Con 13	Con 18	Con 24	
Swing			6 → Lab	1 → SDPAll	Lab needs 7 to win. 78th on Lab list

STAFFORDSHIRE MOORLANDS, Staffordshire. Labour marginal, Tory target seat, mainly rural, working class
Age 40-pension 30% (41st); White 99.6% (8th); Skilled manual 37% (24th)

60% change	Notional 92	%	92	87	Candidates
Conservative	20,787	39	47	53	Dr Andrew Ashworth, GP
Labour	21,972	41	35	29	Charlotte Atkins, parliamentary officer, Unison
Lib Dem	9,381	18	15	18	Christina Jebb
Majority	1,185	Lab 2	Con 12	Con 24	
Swing			6 → Lab	3 → Lab	Con need 1 to win. 15th on Con list

STAFFORDSHIRE SOUTH, Staffordshire. Strong Tory seat, mainly rural
Age 40-pension 31% (10th); Owner-occupied 79% (59th); Car owners 83% (25th)

17% change	Notional 92	%	92	87	Candidates
Conservative	32,982	59	60	61	Patrick Cormack, MP
Labour	14,367	26	26	19	Judith LeMaistre
Lib Dem	8,391	15	14	20	
Majority	18,615	Con 33	Con 34	Con 41	
Swing			4 → Lab	3 → Con	

STALYBRIDGE & HYDE, Greater Manchester. Labour seat, outer suburbs, working class
Council tenants 29% (99th); Overcrowding 2% (143rd); Skilled manual 33% (112th)

25% change	Notional 92	%	92	87	Candidates
Conservative	17,708	36	35	37	Nick De Bois
Labour	25,435	52	52	48	Tom Pendry, MP
Lib Dem	4,443	9	10	15	Martin Cross
Majority	7,727	Lab 16	Lab 18	Lab 11	
Swing			3 → Lab	1 → Lab	

STEVENAGE, Hertfordshire. Tory marginal, Labour target seat, new town, professional
Age 25-39 25% (55th); Council tenants 36% (48th); Professional 10% (91st)

6% change	Notional 92	%	92	87	Candidates
Conservative	24,078	44	46	42	Timothy Wood, MP
Labour	21,159	39	37	25	Barbara Follett, founder of Emily's list, media tra
Lib Dem	9,379	17	17	33 ·	Alex Wilcock
Majority	2,919	Con 5	Con 8	Con 10	
Swing			4 → Lab	3 → Con	Lab needs 3 to win. 37th on Lab list

STIRLING, Central. Tory marginal, mainly urban

12% change	Notional 92	%	92	87	Candidates
Conservative	16,607	39	40	38	Michael Forsyth, MP
Labour	16,371	39	39	36	Anne McGuire, dep. director SCVO
Lib Dem	2,854	7	7	15	Alistair Tough
SNP	6,145	15	14	11	Ewan Dow
Majority	236	Con 1	Con 2	Con 2	
Swing			No swing	5 → Lab	Lab needs 0.3 to win. 6th on Lab list

STOCKPORT, Greater Manchester. Labour seat, urban, Lab gain in 92
Age 25-39 25% (62nd); No central heating 23% (133rd); Single parents 22% (140th)

14% change	Notional 92	%	92	87	Candidates
Conservative	20,384	38	41	41	Stephen Fitzsimmons, general manager
Labour	25,852	48	44	35	Ann Coffey, MP
Lib Dem	6,894	13	14	22	Sylvia Roberts
Majority	5,468	Lab 10	Lab 3	Con 6	
Swing			5 → Lab	4 → Lab	

STOCKTON NORTH, Cleveland. Strong Labour seat, chemical industry, working class
Govt schemes 3% (21st); Council tenants 31% (72nd); Unskilled 8% (33rd)

5% change	Notional 92	%	92	87	Candidates
Conservative	16,666	33	33	33	Bryan Johnston
Labour	27,332	54	52	49	Frank Cook, MP
Lib Dem	6,060	12	14	18	Suzanne Fletcher
Majority	10,666	Lab 21	Lab 20	Lab 17	
Swing			2 → Lab	6 → Lab	

STOCKTON SOUTH, Cleveland. Tory marginal, Labour target seat, residential
Age 25-39 23% (123rd); Govt schemes 2% (76th); Professional 9% (116th)

24% change	Notional 92	%	92	87	Candidates
Conservative	23,331	45	45	35	Tim Devlin, MP
Labour	18,435	36	40	31	Dari Taylor, union official, councillor
Lib Dem	10,080	19	15	34	Peter Monck
Majority	4,896	Con 9	Con 5	Con 1	
Swing			1 → Con	1 → Con	Lab needs 5 to win. 65th on Lab list

STOKE-ON-TRENT CENTRAL, Staffordshire. Strong Labour seat, pottery industry, skilled manual
Long-term ill 17% (29th); Skilled manual 40% (10th); Unskilled 7% (46th)

No Change	Actual 92	%		87	Candidates
Conservative	12,477	28		31	Mio Sylvester, barrister
Labour	25,897	58		53	Mark Fisher, MP
Lib Dem	6,073	14		16	Edward Fordham
Majority	13,420	Lab 30		Lab 22	
Swing		4 → Lab		1 → Lab	

STOKE-ON-TRENT NORTH, Staffordshire. Strong Labour seat, mainly urban, skilled manual
Long-term ill 17% (34th); Skilled manual 46% (1st); Unskilled 7% (69th)

32% change	Notional 92	%	92	87	Candidates
Conservative	15,189	34	29	31	Christopher Day
Labour	24,693	55	57	47	Joan Walley, MP
Lib Dem	4,718	11	13	22	Henry Jebb
Majority	9,504	Lab 21	Lab 28	Lab 16	
Swing			6 → Lab	No swing	

STOKE-ON-TRENT SOUTH, Staffordshire. Labour seat, suburban, skilled manual
Long-term ill 16% (64th); Skilled manual 43% (2nd); Unskilled 6% (131st)

No Change	Actual 92	%	92	87	Candidates
Conservative	19,471	37		38	Sheila Scott, chief executive
Labour	26,380	50		48	George Stevenson, MP
Lib Dem	6,870	13		15	Peter Barnett
Majority	6,909	Lab 13		Lab 10	
Swing		2 → Lab		2 → Con	

STONE, Staffordshire. New strong Tory seat, mainly rural, managerial
Age 40-pension 31% (6th); Owner-occupied 80% (52nd); Car owners 82% (45th)

127% change	Notional 92	%	Candidates
Conservative	31,156	56	William Cash, MP
Labour	16,077	29	John Wakefield
Lib Dem	7,554	14	Barry Stamp
Majority	15,079	Con 27	

STOURBRIDGE, West Midlands. New Tory seat, Labour long-shot, mainly urban
Age 25-39 23% (154th); Asian 2.4% (156th); No central heating 24% (127th)

83% change	Notional 92	%	Candidates
Conservative	24,907	49	Warren Hawksley, MP
Labour	19,519	38	Debra Shipley, author
Lib Dem	6,011	12	Chris Bramall
Majority	5,388	Con 11	Lab needs 5 to win. 70th on Lab list

STRANGFORD, Northern Ireland. Strong Unionist seat, commuting

65% change	Notional 92	%	92	87	Candidates
UUP	20,473	49	44	76	John Taylor, MP
DUP	8,295	20	24	–	Iris Robinson
APNI	6,736	16	17	20	Kieran McCarthy, shopkeeper
Conservative	5,945	14	15	–	
Majority	12,178	UUP 29	UUP 20	UUP 56	
Swing			No swing	11 → UUP	

STRATFORD-ON-AVON, Warwickshire. Strong Tory seat, mainly rural, managerial
Age 40-pension 31% (16th); Car owners 81% (56th); Managerial 41% (64th)

7% change	Notional 92	%	92	87	Candidates
Conservative	37,252	59	59	62	John Maples, advertising chairman
Labour	8,512	13	13	10	
Lib Dem	16,247	26	26	28	Susan Juned
Majority	21,005	Con 33	Con 34	Con 34	
Swing			No swing	1 → Con	

STRATHKELVIN & BEARSDEN, Strathclyde. Labour seat, outer suburbs

14% change	Notional 92	%	92	87	Candidates
Conservative	16,710	33	36	33	David Sharpe
Labour	23,658	46	42	38	Sam Galbraith, MP
Lib Dem	4,252	8	9	21	John Morrison
SNP	6,621	13	13	7	Graeme McCormick
Majority	6,948	Lab 14	Lab 6	Lab 5	
Swing			1 → Lab	8 → Lab	

STREATHAM, South London. Labour seat, suburban, Lab gain in 92
Age 25-39 32% (3rd); Black 19% (8th); Private tenants 18% (17th)

27% change	Notional 92	%	92	87	Candidates
Conservative	19,114	38	41	45	Ernest Noad, financial adviser
Labour	24,585	49	47	39	Keith Hill, MP
Lib Dem	4,966	10	10	16	Roger O'Brien
Majority	5,471	Lab 11	Lab 6	Con 6	
Swing			6 → Lab	5 → Lab	

STRETFORD & URMSTON, Greater Manchester. Labour marginal, Tory target seat, suburban, white collar
Black 4% (67th); Asian 4% (108th); White collar 17% (62nd)

98% change	Notional 92	%	Candidates
Conservative	22,443	41	John Gregory, barrister
Labour	26,925	49	Beverley Hughes
Lib Dem	5,084	9	John Bridges
Majority	4,482	Lab 8	Con need 4 to win. 66th on Con list

STROUD, Gloucestershire. Tory seat, Labour long-shot, mainly rural, middle-class
White 99.4% (76th); Self-employed 14% (113th); Car owners 79% (104th)

19% change	Notional 92	%	92	87	Candidates
Conservative	29,032	46	46	50	Roger Knapman, MP
Labour	18,451	29	27	19	David Drew
Lib Dem	13,582	22	24	31	Paul Hodgkinson, training manager
Majority	10,581	Con 17	Con 19	Con 19	
Swing			6 → Lab	No swing	Lab needs 8 to win. 97th on Lab list

SUFFOLK CENTRAL & IPSWICH NORTH, Suffolk. Strong Tory seat, mainly urban, middle-class
Age 40-pension 29% (81st); Second homes 1% (89th); Car owners 80% (95th)

68% change	Notional 92	%	92	87	Candidates
Conservative	29,610	56	50	54	Michael Lord, MP
Labour	10,980	21	24	20	Carole Jones
Lib Dem	11,604	22	25	27	Madeline Goldspink
Majority	18,006	Con 34	Con 24	Con 27	
Swing			1 → LD	No swing	

SUFFOLK COASTAL, Suffolk. Strong Tory seat, rural
Pensionable 24% (43rd); Second homes 3% (11th); Mobility 13% (45th)

38% change	Notional 92	%	92	87	Candidates
Conservative	30,030	52	54	56	John Gummer, MP
Labour	13,325	23	21	13	Mark Campbell
Lib Dem	13,008	23	24	30	Alexandra Jones
Majority	16,705	Con 29	Con 30	Con 26	
Swing			2 → Con	2 → SDPAll	

SUFFOLK SOUTH, Suffolk. Strong Tory seat, rural, middle-class
Age 40-pension 29% (94th); Second homes 1% (69th); Car owners 80% (90th)

24% change	Notional 92	%	92	87	Candidates
Conservative	27,036	51	50	53	Tim Yeo, MP
Labour	11,504	22	24	19	Paul Bishop
Lib Dem	13,828	26	25	28	Kathy Pollard
Majority	13,208	Con 25	Con 25	Con 26	
Swing			No swing	3 → Con	

SUFFOLK WEST, Suffolk. New strong Tory seat, mainly urban, working class
Age 16-24 14% (44th); Age 25-39 23% (106th); Mobility 15% (11th)

68% change	Notional 92	%	Candidates
Conservative	28,455	54	Richard Spring, MP
Labour	12,692	24	Michael Jefferys
Lib Dem	11,283	21	Adrian Rogers
Majority	15,763	Con 30	

SUNDERLAND NORTH, Tyne and Wear. Strong Labour seat, inner city, skilled manual
Govt schemes 4% (4th); Council tenants 35% (51st); Long-term ill 18% (14th)

11% change	Notional 92	%	92	87	Candidates
Conservative	12,423	28	27	28	Andrew Selous, reinsurance underwriter
Labour	26,649	60	61	56	William Etherington, MP
Lib Dem	4,895	11	11	16	
Majority	14,226	Lab 32	Lab 34	Lab 28	
Swing			3 → Lab	7 → Lab	

SUNDERLAND SOUTH, Tyne and Wear. Strong Labour seat, ex-mining, high unemployment
Govt schemes 4% (1st); Unemployed 18% (28th); Long-term ill 18% (20th)

26% change	Notional 92	%	92	87	Candidates
Conservative	14,706	29	29	30	Tim Schofield, sales & marketing manager
Labour	28,829	58	58	54	Chris Mullin, MP
Lib Dem	5,933	12	12	15	
Majority	14,123	Lab 28	Lab 29	Lab 24	
Swing			3 → Lab	6 → Lab	

SURREY EAST, Surrey. Strong Tory seat, commuting, managerial
Age 40-pension 29% (52nd); Car owners 83% (22nd); Managerial 42% (42nd)

26% change	Notional 92	%	92	87	Candidates
Conservative	35,676	61	62	63	Peter Ainsworth, MP
Labour	6,135	11	11	10	David Ross
Lib Dem	15,704	27	25	24	Belinda Ford
Majority	19,972	Con 34	Con 37	Con 39	
Swing			1 → Lib Dem	2 → Con	

SURREY HEATH, Surrey. Strong Tory seat, stockbroker belt, middle-class
Age 40-pension 30% (34th); Owner-occupied 81% (41st); Car owners 87% (4th)

47% change	Notional 92	%	92	87	Candidates
Conservative	35,731	64	64	64	Nick Hawkins, MP
Labour	6,326	11	14	11	Susan Jones
Lib Dem	12,977	23	20	25	David Newman
Majority	22,754	Con 41	Con 43	Con 39	
Swing			2 → Con	1 → Con	

SURREY SOUTH WEST, Surrey. Strong Tory seat, rural, middle-class
Car owners 81% (55th); Professional 13% (24th); Managerial 44% (24th)

No Change	Actual 92	%		87	Candidates
Conservative	35,008	59		60	Virginia Bottomley, MP
Labour	3,840	6		6	Margaret Leicester
Lib Dem	20,033	34		34	Neil Sherlock, communications director
Majority	14,975	Con 25		Con 25	
Swing		No swing		1 → LibAll	

SUSSEX MID, Sussex. Strong Tory seat, rural, managerial
Owner-occupied 80% (53rd); Managerial 44% (32nd); Professional 10% (92nd)

15% change	Notional 92	%	92	87	Candidates
Conservative	33,415	59	59	61	Nicholas Soames, MP
Labour	6,034	11	10	7	Mervyn Hamilton
Lib Dem	16,008	28	28	32	Margaret Collins
Majority	17,407	Con 31	Con 31	Con 30	
Swing			1 → Con	No swing	

SUTTON & CHEAM, South London. Strong Tory seat, suburban
Other non-white 3% (66th); Owner-occupied 82% (27th); White collar 19% (20th)

No Change	Actual 92	%		87	Candidates
Conservative	27,710	55		61	Lady Olga Maitland, MP
Labour	4,980	10		11	Mark Allison
Lib Dem	16,954	34		29	Paul Burstow, councillor
Majority	10,756	Con 21		Con 32	
Swing		5 → Lib Dem		5 → Con	

SUTTON COLDFIELD, West Midlands. Strong Tory seat, stockbroker belt, middle-class
Age 40-pension 31% (7th); Owner-occupied 84% (10th); Managerial 44% (22nd)

No Change	Actual 92	%		87	Candidates
Conservative	37,001	65		64	Sir Norman Fowler, MP
Labour	8,490	15		1	Alan York
Lib Dem	10,965	19		25	Jim Whorwood
Majority	26,036	Con 46		Con 39	
Swing		3 → Con		No swing	

SWANSEA EAST, West Glamorgan. Strong Labour seat, inner city, working class
Govt schemes 3% (46th); Long-term ill 18% (19th); Unskilled 8% (24th)

No Change	Actual 92	%		87	Candidates
Conservative	7,697	17		19	Catherine Dibble
Labour	31,179	70		64	Donald Anderson, MP
Lib Dem	4,248	10		15	Elwyn Jones
Plaid Cymru	1,607	4		–	Rhodri Thomas
Majority	23,482	Lab 53		Lab 45	
Swing		4 → Lab		5 → Lab	

SWANSEA WEST, West Glamorgan. Strong Labour seat, suburban
Pensionable 23% (69th); Single parents 26% (74th); Long-term ill 18% (17th)

No Change	Actual 92	%		87	Candidates
Conservative	13,760	31		33	Andrew Baker, business consultant
Labour	23,238	53		49	Alan Williams, MP
Lib Dem	4,620	11		15	John Newbury
Plaid Cymru	1,668	4		2	Dai Lloyd
Majority	9,478	Lab 22		Lab 16	
Swing		3 → Lab		5 → Lab	PIC needs 28 to win. 9th on PIC list

SWINDON NORTH, Wiltshire. New Labour marginal, Tory target seat, mainly urban, working class
Age 16-24 13% (170th); Age 25-39 23% (105th); White collar 15% (172nd)

100% change	Notional 92	%			Candidates
Conservative	20,391	41			Guy Opperman, barrister
Labour	21,273	43			Michael Wills, TV producer
Lib Dem	7,299	15			Mike Evemy
Majority	882	Lab 2			Con need 1 to win. 11th on Con list

SWINDON SOUTH, Wiltshire. Tory seat, Labour long-shot, mainly urban, white collar
Age 16-24 14% (90th); Age 25-39 27% (35th); Mobility 13% (47th)

47% change	Notional 92	%	92	87	Candidates
Conservative	27,312	49	43	44	Simon Coombs, MP
Labour	17,209	31	39	37	Julia Drown
Lib Dem	10,439	19	16	20	Stanley Pajak
Majority	10,103	Con 18	Con 4	Con 7	
Swing			2 → Lab	2 → Con	Lab needs 9 to win. 105th on Lab list

TAMWORTH, Staffordshire. Tory seat, mainly rural, Labour by-election gain in Staffs SE
Age 16-24 14% (112th); Govt schemes 1.8% (116th); Skilled manual 33% (101st)

8% change	Notional 92	%	96 by-	92	87	Candidates
Conservative	26,209	49	29	51	48	Lady Ann Lightbown
Labour	20,804	39	60	38	25	Brian Jenkins, MP
Lib Dem	5,275	10	5	10	27	Jennifer Pinkett
Majority	5,405	Con 10	Lab 31	Con 13	Con 21	
Swing			22 → Lab	4 → Lab	4 → SDPAII	Lab needs 5 to win. 69th on Lab list

TATTON, Cheshire. Strong Tory seat, stockbroker belt, middle-class, includes Knutsford, Wilmslow
Age 40-pension 31% (15th); Professional 13% (17th); Managerial 45% (14th)

29% change	Notional 92	%	92	87	Candidates
Conservative	32,235	62	55	55	Neil Hamilton, MP
Labour	9,870	19	28	21	~~Jonathan Kelly~~
Lib Dem	9,387	18	17	24	~~Roger Barlow~~ } Martin Bell
Majority	22,365	Con 43	Con 28	Con 31	
Swing			3 → Lab	2 → Con	

TAUNTON, Somerset. Tory marginal, Lib Dem target seat, mainly rural
Pensionable 22% (73rd); White 99.3% (111th); Self-employed 15% (88th)

No Change	Actual 92	%		87	Candidates
Conservative	29,576	46		51	David Nicholson, MP
Labour	8,151	13		15	Elizabeth Lisgo
Lib Dem	26,240	41		34	Jackie Ballard, local government adviser
Majority	3,336	Con 5		Con 18	
Swing		6 → Lib Dem		3 → SDPAII	LD need 3 to win. 9th on LD list

TAYSIDE NORTH, Tayside. Tory marginal, SNP target seat, rural

22% change	Notional 92	%	92	87	Candidates
Conservative	21,036	46	47	45	Bill Walker, MP
Labour	3,156	7	9	9	Ian McFatridge
Lib Dem	3,579	8	7	13	Simon Horner
SNP	17,597	39	38	33	John Swinney
Majority	3,439	Con 8	Con 9	Con 12	
Swing			2 → SNP	7 → SNP	SNP needs 4 to win. 4th on SNP list

TEIGNBRIDGE, Devon. Tory seat, Lib Dem long-shot, rural
Pensionable 26% (22nd); Self-employed 19% (29th); Second homes 1% (53rd)

24% change	Notional 92	%	92	87	Candidates
Conservative	31,740	50	50	53	Patrick Nicholls, MP
Labour	8,181	13	13	11	Sue Dann
Lib Dem	22,192	35	36	35	Richard Younger-Ross, design consultant
Majority	9,548	Con 15	Con 14	Con 18	
Swing			2 → Lib Dem	1 → Con	LD need 8 to win. 41st on LD list

TELFORD, Shropshire. Labour seat, new town, working class,
Age 16-24 14% (37th); Age 25-39 24% (95th); Council tenants 29% (98th)

37% change	Notional 92	%	92	87	Candidates
Conservative	13,546	33	39	41	Bernard Gentry
Labour	21,473	53	48	43	Bruce Grocott, MP
Lib Dem	5,049	12	12	17	Nathaniel Green
Majority	7,927	Lab 20	Lab 10	Lab 2	
Swing			4 → Lab	2 → Lab	

TEWKESBURY, Gloucestershire. New Tory seat, Lib Dem long-shot, mainly urban, middle-class
Age 40-pension 29% (92nd); Owner-occupied 79% (79th); Car owners 81% (66th)

93% change	Notional 92	%	Candidates
Conservative	28,300	54	Laurence Robertson, company director
Labour	5,297	10	
Lib Dem	18,503	35	John Sewell, engineer
Majority	9,797	Con 19	LD need 9 to win. 58th on LD list

THANET NORTH, Kent. Strong Tory seat, seaside, white collar
Pensionable 29% (10th); Self-employed 15% (83rd); Second homes 1% (45th)

No Change	Actual 92	%	87	Candidates
Conservative	30,867	57	58	Roger Gale, MP
Labour	12,657	24	17	Iris Johnson
Lib Dem	9,563	18	23	Paul Kendrick
Majority	18,210	Con 34	Con 35	
Swing		4 → Lab	2 → Con	

THANET SOUTH, Kent. Strong Tory seat, seaside, white collar
Pensionable 26% (25th); Self-employed 15% (95th); Second homes 1% (41st)

0.1% change	Notional 92	%	92	87	Candidates
Conservative	25,222	52	52	54	Jonathan Aitken, MP
Labour	13,723	28	28	21	Stephen Ladyman
Lib Dem	8,936	18	18	25	Barbara Hewett-Silk
Majority	11,499	Con 24	Con 24	Con 30	
Swing			5 → Lab	1 → LibAll	

THURROCK, Essex. Labour marginal, Tory target seat, mainly urban, working class, Lab gain in 92
Age 25-39 24% (73rd); Skilled manual 34% (72nd); White collar 15% (161st)

No Change	Actual 92	%	87	Candidates
Conservative	23,619	44	43	Andrew Rosindell, freelance journalist
Labour	24,791	46	41	Andrew MacKinlay, MP
Lib Dem	5,145	10	17	
Majority	1,172	Lab 2	Con 1	
Swing		2 → Lab	3 → Con	Con need 1 to win. 14th on Con list

TIVERTON & HONITON, Devon. New Tory seat, Lib Dem long-shot, mainly rural
Pensionable 22% (76th); White 99.6% (16th); Self-employed 22% (12th)

31% change	Notional 92	%			Candidates
Conservative	30,536	51			Angela Browning, MP
Labour	6,524	11			John King
Lib Dem	18,872	32			Jim Barnard, forensic scientist, farmer
Majority	11,664	Con 20			

TONBRIDGE & MALLING, Kent. Strong Tory seat, commuting, managerial
Age 40-pension 30% (44th); Car owners 79% (99th); Managerial 42% (41st)

46% change	Notional 92	%	92	87	Candidates
Conservative	31,462	61	57	57	Sir John Stanley, MP
Labour	8,841	17	18	13	Barbara Withstandley
Lib Dem	10,721	21	24	29	Keith Brown
Majority	20,741	Con 40	Con 34	Con 28	
Swing			3 → Con	1 → Con	

TOOTING, South London. Labour marginal, Tory target seat, urban
Age 25-39 32% (2nd); Private tenants 21% (6th); White collar 19% (30th)

No Change	Actual 92	%	92	87	Candidates
Conservative	20,494	40		41	James Hutchings, company director
Labour	24,601	48		44	Tom Cox, MP
Lib Dem	3,776	7		13	Simon James
Majority	4,107	Lab 8		Lab 3	
Swing		3 → Lab		1 → Con	Con need 4 to win. 64th on Con list

TORBAY, Devon. Tory seat, Lib Dem long-shot, seaside, retirement
Pensionable 28% (11th); Self-employed 20% (24th); Second homes 1% (51st)

No Change	Actual 92	%		87	Candidates
Conservative	28,624	50		54	Rupert Allason, MP
Labour	5,503	10		8	Mike Morey
Lib Dem	22,837	40		38	Adrian Sanders, European funding adviser
Majority	5,787	Con 10		Con 16	
Swing		3 → Lib Dem		2 → Con	LD need 5 to win. 21st on LD list

TORFAEN, Gwent. Strong Labour seat, part new town, working class, based on Pontypool
Council tenants 35% (54th); Long-term ill 17% (26th); Unskilled 7% (51st)

No Change	Actual 92	%		87	Candidates
Conservative	9,598	20		19	Neil Parish
Labour	30,352	64		59	Paul Murphy, MP
Lib Dem	6,178	13		20	Jean Gray
Plaid Cymru	1,210	3		1	
Majority	20,754	Lab 44		Lab 39	
Swing		2 → Lab		10 → Lab	

TOTNES, Devon. New Tory seat, Lib Dem long-shot, rural, retirement, based on South Hams
Pensionable 27% (16th); Self-employed 25% (6th); Second homes 4% (5th)

38% change	Notional 92	%			Candidates
Conservative	28,736	51			Anthony Steen, MP
Labour	6,842	12			Victor Ellery
Lib Dem	20,110	36			Rob Chave, accountant
Majority	8,626	Con 15			LD need 8 to win. 43rd on LD list

TOTTENHAM, North London. Strong Labour seat, inner city
Black 25% (5th); Other non-white 7% (9th); Unemployed 22% (11th)

No Change	Actual 92	%		87	Candidates
Conservative	13,341	30		35	Derek Laud
Labour	25,309	57		44	Bernie Grant, MP
Lib Dem	5,120	11		18	Neil Hughes
Majority	11,968	Lab 27		Lab 8	
Swing		9 → Lab		7 → Con	

TRURO & ST AUSTELL, Cornwall. Lib Dem seat, Tory long-shot, mainly urban, retirement
Pensionable 24% (47th); Self-employed 19% (34th); Second homes 2% (37th)

No Change	Actual 92	%		87	Candidates
Conservative	23,660	38		41	Neil Badcock, farmer
Labour	6,078	10		10	Michael Dooley
Lib Dem	31,230	51		49	Matthew Taylor, MP
Majority	7,570	LD 12		LD 8	
Swing		2 → Lib Dem		6 → Con	

TUNBRIDGE WELLS, Kent. Strong Tory seat, commuting, managerial
Self-employed 14% (121st); Private tenants 10% (97th); Managerial 42% (51st)

14% change	Notional 92	%	92	87	Candidates
Conservative	28,297	55	57	58	Archie Norman, Asda chief executive
Labour	7,563	15	14	12	Peter Warner
Lib Dem	15,151	30	28	30	Tony Clayton, industrial economist
Majority	13,146	Con 26	Con 29	Con 29	
Swing			No swing	No swing	

TWEEDDALE, ETTRICK & LAUDERDALE, Borders/Lothian. Lib Dem marginal, Tory target seat, rural

41% change	Notional 92	%	92	87	Candidates
Conservative	12,218	31	32	30	Alister Jack
Labour	6,538	16	11	11	Keith Geddes
Lib Dem	13,953	35	40	50	Michael Moore
SNP	6,835	17	17	–	Ian Goldie
Majority	1,735	LD 4	LD 8	LD 20	
Swing			6 → Con	5 → Con	Con need 2 to win. 34th on Con list

TWICKENHAM, South London. Tory seat, Lib Dem long-shot, suburban
Age 25-39 25% (51st); Professional 12% (41st); Managerial 49% (3rd)

14% change	Notional 92	%	92	87	Candidates
Conservative	29,652	50	50	52	Toby Jessel, MP
Labour	6,194	10	9	8	Eva Tutchell
Lib Dem	23,531	39	40	38	Vincent Cable
Majority	6,121	Con 10	Con 11	Con 14	
Swing			1 → Lib Dem	2 → Con	LD need 5 to win. 22nd on LD list

TYNE BRIDGE, Tyne and Wear. Strong Labour seat, inner city, high unemployment
Govt schemes 3% (13th); Unemployed 22% (10th); Unskilled 9% (11th)

24% change	Notional 92	%	92	87	Candidates
Conservative	9,443	22	21	21	Adrian Lee, parliamentary researcher
Labour	28,520	67	67	63	David Clelland, MP
Lib Dem	4,755	11	11	16	Mary Wallace
Majority	19,077	Lab 45	Lab 46	Lab 42	
Swing			2 → Lab	6 → Lab	

TYNEMOUTH, Tyne and Wear. Tory marginal, Labour target seat, seaside, white collar
Pensionable 22% (77th); White collar 17% (58th); Professional 8% (131st)

9% change	Notional 92	%	92	87	Candidates
Conservative	27,056	49	46	43	Martin Callanan, engineering projects manager
Labour	23,527	42	45	39	Alan Campbell, teacher
Lib Dem	4,507	8	8	18	Andrew Duffield
Majority	3,529	Con 6	Con 1	Con 4	
Swing			2 → Lab	6 → Lab	Lab needs 3 to win. 42nd on Lab list

TYNESIDE NORTH, Tyne and Wear. Strong Labour seat, inner city, working class
Council tenants 40% (28th); Long-term ill 16% (57th); Unskilled 8% (20th)

31% change	Notional 92	%	92	87	Candidates
Conservative	13,130	26	24	23	Michael McIntyre
Labour	30,764	61	58	57	Stephen Byers, MP
Lib Dem	6,580	13	18	20	
Majority	17,634	Lab 35	Lab 34	Lab 34	
Swing			No swing	5 → Lab	

TYRONE WEST, Northern Ireland. DUP marginal, SDLP in 2nd place, rural, based on Mid-Ulster

56% change	Notional 92	%	92	87	Candidates
DUP	15,738	39	42	44	Oliver Gibson
UUP					William Thompson
SDLP	12,590	31	31	26	Joe Byrne, teacher
APNI	1,900	5	3	4	Ann Gormley, dental hygienist
SF	8,102	20	19	24	
Majority	3,148	DUP 8	DUP 11	DUP 18	
Swing			3 → SDLP	5 → DUP	

ULSTER MID, Northern Ireland. New DUP seat, SDLP in 2nd place, rural

106% change	Notional 92	%	92	87	Candidates
DUP	19,274	41	42	44	Rev. Robert McCrea, MP
SDLP	14,360	31	31	26	Denis Haughey, former teacher
SF	11,340	24	19	24	
Majority	4,914	DUP 11	DUP 11	DUP 18	
Swing			3 → SLDP	5 → DUP	

UPMINSTER, North London. Strong Tory seat, outer suburbs
Age 40-pension 28% (130th); Pensionable 21% (101st); White collar 18% (34th)

10% change	Notional 92	%	92	87	Candidates
Conservative	25,121	54	56	56	Sir Nicholas Bonsor, MP
Labour	13,964	30	29	22	Keith Darvil
Lib Dem	7,300	16	15	22	Pamela Peskett
Majority	11,157	Con 24	Con 27	Con 34	
Swing			4 → Lab	3 → Con	

UPPER BANN, Northern Ireland. Strong Unionist seat, rural

No Change	Actual 92	%		87	Candidates
Conservative	1,556	3		–	
UUP	26,824	59		62	David Trimble, MP
SDLP	10,661	23		21	Brid Rodgers, former teacher
SF	2,777	6		7	
APNI					William Ramsay, retired GP
Majority	16,163	UUP 36		UUP 41	
Swing		3 → SDLP		1 → UUP	

UXBRIDGE, North London. Strong Tory seat, outer suburbs
Age 25-39 25% (57th); Other non-white 2% (73rd); Overcrowding 3% (73rd)

8% change	Notional 92	%	92	87	Candidates
Conservative	25,467	56	56	57	Michael Shersby, MP
Labour	13,099	29	29	23	David Williams
Lib Dem	5,663	13	12	19	Andrew Malyan
Majority	12,368	Con 27	Con 27	Con 33	
Swing			3 → Lab	1 → Con	

VALE OF CLWYD, Clwyd. New Tory marginal, Labour target seat, rural
Pensionable 25% (27th); Private tenants 10% (87th); Long-term ill 17% (21st)

91% change	Notional 92	%	Candidates
Conservative	19,118	44	David Edwards, consultant
Labour	16,941	39	Chris Ruane, deputy headteacher
Lib Dem	5,435	12	Daniel Munford
Plaid Cymru	2,095	5	Gwyneth Kensler
Majority	2,177	Con 5	Lab needs 2 to win. 33rd on Lab list

VALE OF GLAMORGAN, South Glamorgan. Tory marginal, commuting
Car owners 74% (202nd); Professional 8% (181st); Managerial 33% (222nd)

1% change	Notional 92	%	92	87	Candidates
Conservative	24,207	44	44	47	Walter Sweeney, MP
Labour	24,188	44	44	35	John Smith, ex-MP
Lib Dem	5,042	9	9	17	Suzanne Campbell
Plaid Cymru	1,159	2	–	2	Melanie Corp
Majority	19	0	0	Con 12	
Swing			6 → Lab	5 → Lab	Lab needs 0.02 to win. 1st on Lab list

VALE OF YORK, North Yorkshire. New strong Tory seat, rural, middle-class
White 99.5% (32nd); Self-employed 17% (55th); Car owners 82% (40th)

109% change	Notional 92	%			Candidates
Conservative	31,854	61			Ann McIntosh, MEP
Labour	5,837	11			Matthew Carter
Lib Dem	14,626	28			Charles Hall
Majority	17,228	Con 33			

VAUXHALL, South London. Strong Labour seat, inner city
Age 25-39 31% (5th); Black 26% (2nd); Single parents 53% (1st)

13% change	Notional 92	%	92	87	Candidates
Conservative	11,517	27	28	29	Richard Bacon, trade association
Labour	24,278	56	55	50	Kate Hoey, MP
Lib Dem	6,247	14	15	18	Keith Kerr
Majority	12,761	Lab 30	Lab 27	Lab 21	
Swing			3 → Lab	1 → Lab	

WAKEFIELD, West Yorkshire. Labour marginal, Tory target seat, urban, skilled manual
Govt schemes 2% (145th); Council tenants 29% (88th); Skilled manual 31% (149th)

69% change	Notional 92	%	92	87	Candidates
Conservative	21,983	41	38	41	Jonathan Peacock, barrister
Labour	26,207	48	51	47	David Hinchliffe, MP
Lib Dem	6,128	11	11	12	
Majority	4,224	Lab 8	Lab 12	Lab 5	
Swing			4 → Lab	2 → Lab	Con need 4 to win. 61st on Con list

WALLASEY, Merseyside. Labour marginal, Tory target seat, suburban, working class
Govt schemes 2% (64th); No central heating 39% (29th); Single parents 29% (55th)

No Change	Actual 92	%		87	Candidates
Conservative	22,722	42		43	Patricia Wilcock, fenestration specialist
Labour	26,531	49		42	Angela Eagle, MP
Lib Dem	4,177	8		16	Neil Thomas
Majority	3,809	Lab 7		Con 1	
Swing		4 → Lab		7 → Lab	Con need 4 to win. 50th on Con list

WALSALL NORTH, West Midlands. Labour marginal, Tory target seat, urban, working class
Council tenants 43% (16th); No central heating 36% (35th); Skilled manual 43% (3rd)

No Change	Actual 92	%		87	Candidates
Conservative	20,563	39		39	Mike Bird, credit manager
Labour	24,387	47		43	David Winnick, MP
Lib Dem	6,629	13		18	Tracy O'Brien
Majority	3,824	Lab 7		Lab 4	
Swing		2 → Lab		1 → Con	Con need 4 to win. 58th on Con list

WALSALL SOUTH, West Midlands. Labour marginal, Tory target seat, residential, large Asian community
Age 16-24 14% (49th); Asian 17% (19th); Overcrowding 4% (44th)

No Change	Actual 92	%		87	Candidates
Conservative	20,955	42		43	Leslie Leek, company director
Labour	24,133	48		45	Bruce George, MP
Lib Dem	4,132	8		12	Harry Harris
Majority	3,178	Lab 6		Lab 2	
Swing		2 → Lab		No swing	Con need 3 to win. 44th on Con list

WALTHAMSTOW, North London. Labour marginal, Tory target seat, outer suburbs
Age 25-39 28% (20th); Black 12% (21st); White collar 20% (6th)

33% change	Notional 92	%	92	87	Candidates
Conservative	17,650	37	37	39	Jill Andrew, management consultant
Labour	21,001	44	46	35	Neil Gerrard, MP
Lib Dem	7,489	16	15	25	Jane Jackson
Majority	3,351	Lab 7	Lab 9	Con 4	
Swing			6 → Lab	4 → Con	Con need 4 to win. 51st on Con list

WANSBECK, Northumberland. Strong Labour seat, ex-mining, working class
White 99.5% (47th); Govt schemes 3% (18th); Long-term ill 16% (54th)

No Change	Actual 92	%	87	Candidates
Conservative	11,872	24	19	Paul Green, assistant to Sir Paul Beresford, MP
Labour	30,046	60	58	Dennis Murphy
Lib Dem	7,691	15	23	
Majority	18,174	Lab 36	Lab 34	
Swing		1 → Con	9 → Lab	

WANSDYKE, Avon. Tory seat, Labour long-shot, commuting, middle-class
Owner-occupied 81% (39th); Car owners 83% (29th); Self-employed 14% (138th)

59% change	Notional 92	%	92	87	Candidates
Conservative	27,852	47	48	52	Mark Prisk, business consultant
Labour	16,082	27	28	23	Dan Norris
Lib Dem	13,921	24	23	25	Jeff Manning, business consultant
Majority	11,770	Con 20	Con 21	Con 26	
Swing			4 → Lab	2 → Con	Lab needs 10 to win. 119th on Lab list

WANTAGE, Oxfordshire. Strong Tory seat, rural, professional
Car owners 82% (43rd); Mobility 12% (97th); Professional 13% (14th)

No Change	Actual 92	%	87	Candidates
Conservative	30,575	54	54	Robert Jackson, MP
Labour	10,955	19	16	Celia Wilson
Lib Dem	14,102	25	31	Jenny Riley
Majority	16,473	Con 29	Con 24	
Swing		3 → Con	1 → Con	

WARLEY, West Midlands. Labour seat, urban, large Asian community, based on Warley East
Asian 17% (21st); No central heating 36% (41st); Skilled manual 36% (39th)

19% change	Notional 92	%	92	87	Candidates
Conservative	15,334	34	33	36	Christopher Pincher, management consultant
Labour	23,743	53	54	50	John Spellar, MP
Lib Dem	5,112	11			Jeremy Pursehouse
Majority	8,409	Lab 19	Lab 12	Lab 14	
Swing		3 → Lab	3 → Lab		

WARRINGTON NORTH, Cheshire. Labour seat, inner city
Age 25-39 24% (91st); No central heating 22% (153rd); Professional 8% (182nd)

10% change	Notional 92	%	92	87	Candidates
Conservative	19,420	35	34	34	Ray Lacey, partner in family business
Labour	29,626	53	54	48	Doug Hoyle, MP
Lib Dem	6,307	11	12	18	Ian Greenhalgh
Majority	10,206	Lab 18	Lab 21	Lab 14	
Swing		3 → Lab	2 → Lab		

WARRINGTON SOUTH, Cheshire. Currently Labour but under new boundaries Tory marginal, Labour target
Age 40-pension 29% (73rd); Owner-occupied 79% (61st); Professional 9% (130th)

30% change	Notional 92	%	92	87	Candidates
Conservative	25,698	46	43	42	Christopher Grayling, executive
Labour	22,945	41	44	36	Helen Southworth, director, Age Concern
Lib Dem	7,316	13	13	22	Peter Walker
Majority	2,753	Con 5	Lab 0.3	Con 6	
Swing		3 → Lab	3 → Lab		Lab needs 2 to win. 31st on Lab list

WARWICK & LEAMINGTON, Warwickshire. Tory seat, Labour long-shot, mainly urban, professional
Asian 5% (87th); Professional 11% (52nd); Managerial 36% (140th)

8% change	Notional 92	%	92	87	Candidates
Conservative	31,028	50	48	50	Sir Dudley Smith, MP
Labour	19,564	31	33	24	James Plaskitt
Lib Dem	10,729	17	17	25	Nigel Hicks
Majority	11,464	Con 18	Con 15	Con 25	
Swing		5 → Lab	No swing		Lab needs 9 to win. 106th on Lab list

WARWICKSHIRE NORTH, Warwickshire. Labour marginal, Tory target seat, ex-mining, working class, Lab gain in 92
Age 40-pension 28% (129th); Skilled manual 35% (46th); Age 16-24 13% (184th)

0.1% change	Notional 92	%	92	87	Candidates
Conservative	26,124	44	44	45	Stephen Hamond, company director
Labour	27,577	46	46	40	Michael O'Brien, MP
Lib Dem	6,161	10	10	15	Bill Powell
Majority	1,453	Lab 2	Lab 2	Con 5	
Swing			4 → Lab	No swing	Con need 1 to win. 16th on Con list

WATFORD, Hertfordshire. Tory seat, Labour long-shot, mainly urban, white collar
Age 25-39 25% (69th); Asian 5% (89th); White collar 17% (66th)

25% change	Notional 92	%	92	87	Candidates
Conservative	28,159	48	49	49	Robert Gordon
Labour	19,896	34	33	28	Claire Ward
Lib Dem	9,807	17	17	23	Andy Canning
Majority	8,263	Con 14	Con 16	Con 21	
Swing			2 → Lab	1 → Lab	Lab needs 7 to win. 82nd on Lab list

WAVENEY, Suffolk. Tory marginal, Labour target seat, fishing, skilled manual
Pensionable 23% (51st); Second homes 1% (79th); Skilled manual 34% (62nd)

12% change	Notional 92	%	92	87	Candidates
Conservative	28,352	47	48	48	David Porter, MP
Labour	23,976	40	38	30	Robert Blizzard, teacher
Lib Dem	7,728	13	13	22	Christopher Thomas
Majority	4,376	Con 7	Con 10	Con 18	
Swing			4 → Lab	3 → Lab	Lab needs 4 to win. 48th on Lab list

WEALDEN, East Sussex. Strong Tory seat, rural, managerial
Self-employed 20% (26th); Car owners 84% (17th); Managerial 44% (27th)

0.2% change	Notional 92	%	92	87	Candidates
Conservative	37,256	62	62	64	Sir Geoffrey Johnson-Smith, MP
Labour	5,578	9	9	8	Nicholas Levine
Lib Dem	16,328	27	27	28	Michael Skinner, councillor
Majority	20,928	Con 35	Con 35	Con 37	
Swing			1 → Lib Dem	1 → Con	

WEAVER VALE, Cheshire. New Labour seat, salt-mining, includes Northwich
White 99.1% (150th); Govt schemes 2% (154th); Age 16-24 13% (165th)

122% change	Notional 92	%			Candidates
Conservative	18,515	36			James Byrne
Labour	25,265	49			Mike Hall, MP
Lib Dem	7,506	15			
Majority	6,750	Lab 13			

WELLINGBOROUGH, Northamptonshire. Tory seat, Labour long-shot, mainly urban, skilled manual
Age 16-24 14% (130th); Black 2% (112th); Skilled manual 35% (60th)

No Change	Actual 92	%		87	Candidates
Conservative	32,302	53		53	Sir Peter Fry, MP
Labour	20,486	34		27	Paul Stinchcombe
Lib Dem	7,714	13		20	Peter Smith
Majority	11,816	Con 20		Con 26	
Swing		3 → Lab		1 → Con	Lab needs 10 to win. 113th on Lab list

WELLS, Somerset. Tory seat, Lib Dem long-shot, mainly rural
Pensionable 23% (54th); White 99.4% (59th); Self-employed 18% (38th)

No Change	Actual 92	%		87	Candidates
Conservative	28,620	50		54	David Heathcoat-Amory, MP
Labour	6,126	11		9	Michael Eavis, farmer
Lib Dem	21,971	38		38	Dr Peter Gold, university lecturer
Majority	6,649	Con 12		Con 16	
Swing		2 → Lib Dem		1 → Con	LD need 6 to win. 28th on LD list

WELWYN HATFIELD, Hertfordshire. Tory seat, Labour long-shot, new town, professional
Other non-white 1% (139th); Council tenants 33% (58th); Professional 10% (80th)

7% change	Notional 92	%	92	87	Candidates
Conservative	27,139	48	48	46	David Evans, MP
Labour	20,556	36	35	26	Melanie Johnson, schools inspector, councillor
Lib Dem	9,147	16	17	27	Rodney Schwartz
Majority	6,583	Con 12	Con 14	Con 18	
Swing			3 → Lab	2 → SDPAll	Lab needs 6 to win. 72nd on Lab list

WENTWORTH, South Yorkshire. Strong Labour seat, ex-mining, skilled manual
White 99.6% (22nd); Long-term ill 17% (40th); Skilled manual 37% (23rd)

No Change	Actual 92	%		87	Candidates
Conservative	10,490	22		22	Karl Hamer
Labour	32,939	69		65	John Healey, TUC official
Lib Dem	4,629	10		13	
Majority	22,449	Lab 47		Lab 43	
Swing		2 → Lab		3 → Lab	

WEST BROMWICH EAST, West Midlands. Labour seat, mainly urban, working class
Asian 10% (42nd); Council tenants 38% (38th); Skilled manual 36% (31st)

16% change	Notional 92	%	92	87	Candidates
Conservative	18,797	38	40	40	Brian Matsell, chief executive
Labour	23,782	48	47	43	Peter Snape, MP
Lib Dem	6,591	13	13	17	Martyn Smith
Majority	4,985	Lab 10	Lab 7	Lab 2	
Swing			2 → Lab	1 → Lab	

WEST BROMWICH WEST, West Midlands. Labour seat, industrial, working class
Council tenants 45% (14th); No central heating 37% (33rd); Skilled manual 42% (5th)

18% change	Notional 92	%	92	87	Candidates
Conservative	17,763	38	36	37	None
Labour	23,937	51	55	51	Betty Boothroyd, speaker
Lib Dem	5,577	12	10	12	None
Majority	6,174	Lab 13	Lab 19	Lab 13	
Swing			3 → Lab	2 → Con	

WEST HAM, East London. Strong Labour seat, inner city
Black 18% (9th); Unemployed 19% (18th); Overcrowding 7% (9th)

39% change	Notional 92	%	92	87	Candidates
Conservative	11,229	30	26	25	Mark MacGregor, company director
Labour	21,717	58	61	55	Tony Banks, MP
Lib Dem	3,602	10	9	17	Elizabeth Lutzeier
Majority	10,488	Lab 28	Lab 35	Lab 30	
Swing			3 → Lab	3 → Lab	

WESTBURY, Wiltshire. Tory seat, Lib Dem long-shot, mainly urban
Second homes 1% (97th); Car owners 79% (116th); Mobility 11% (111th)

16% change	Notional 92	%	92	87	Candidates
Conservative	31,821	52	50	52	David Faber, MP
Labour	6,457	11	13	12	Kevin Small
Lib Dem	20,668	34	33	36	John Miller, graphic designer, lecturer
Majority	11,153	Con 18	Con 17	Con 15	
Swing			1 → Con	1 → Con	LD need 9 to win. 56th on LD list

WESTERN ISLES, Islands. Labour seat, SNP long-shot, Gaelic-speaking

No Change	Actual 92	%		87	Candidates
Conservative	1,362	9		8	
Labour	7,664	48		43	Calum Macdonald, MP
Lib Dem	552	3		21	Neil Mitchison
SNP	5,961	37		29	Anne Lorne Gillies
Majority	1,703	Lab 11		Lab 14	
Swing		2 → SNP		19 → Lab	SNP needs 5 to win. 5th on SNP list

WESTMORLAND & LONSDALE, Cumbria. Strong Tory seat, rural
White 99.6% (13th); Self-employed 20% (23rd); Second homes 4% (7th)

6% change	Notional 92	%	92	87	Candidates
Conservative	29,775	57	57	58	Tim Collins, media consultant
Labour	7,898	15	15	13	John Harding
Lib Dem	14,381	28	28	29	Stan Collins
Majority	15,394	Con 29	Con 29	Con 28	
Swing			1 → Con	3 → LibAll	

WESTON-SUPER-MARE, Avon. Tory marginal, Lib Dem target seat, seaside, retirement
Pensionable 25% (31st); Mobility 12% (92nd); Second homes 1% (113th)

11% change	Notional 92	%	92	87	Candidates
Conservative	27,063	48	48	49	Margaret Daly, company director, MEP
Labour	6,420	11	11	11	Derek Kraft
Lib Dem	21,691	39	39	36	Brian Cotter
Majority	5,372	Con 10	Con 9	Con 14	
Swing			3 → Lib Dem	2 → SDPAll	LD need 5 to win. 20th on LD list

WIGAN, Greater Manchester. Strong Labour seat, mainly urban, working class
Council tenants 27% (111th); Long-term ill 16% (61st); Skilled manual 33% (91st)

11% change	Notional 92	%	92	87	Candidates
Conservative	12,538	25	24	25	Mark Loveday, barrister
Labour	30,028	61	63	62	Roger Stott, MP
Lib Dem	5,787	12	11	14	Trevor Beswick
Majority	17,490	Lab 35	Lab 39	Lab 37	
Swing			1 → Lab	3 → Lab	

WILTSHIRE NORTH, Wiltshire. Strong Tory seat, mainly rural, managerial
Second homes .4% (125th); Car owners 81% (62nd); Mobility 13% (60th)

16% change	Notional 92	%	92	87	Candidates
Conservative	33,626	56	56	55	James Gray, public affairs consultant
Labour	6,087	10	10	7	Nigel Knowles
Lib Dem	18,866	32	32	38	Simon Cordon, management consultant
Majority	14,760	Con 25	Con 23	Con 17	
Swing			3 → Con	2 → Con	

Handwritten margin notes: 1997 / 21,915 / 8,261 / 25,390 / → 3,475 Redwood / Con 23 Ref 1774 / Lib Ind 410 / NAT LAH 263

WIMBLEDON, South London. Strong Tory seat, suburban
Other non-white 6% (17th); Professional 13% (15th); Managerial 45% (15th)

No Change	Actual 92	%		87	Candidates
Conservative	26,331	53		51	Dr Charles Goodson-Wickes, MP
Labour	11,570	23		22	Roger Casale
Lib Dem	10,569	21		28	Alison Willott
Majority	14,761	Con 30		Con 23	
Swing		No swing		1 → LibAll	

WINCHESTER, Hampshire. Tory seat, Lib Dem long-shot, mainly urban, professional
Age 40-pension 30% (48th); Professional 13% (20th); Managerial 41% (59th)

44% change	Notional 92	%	92	87	Candidates
Conservative	32,604	52	50	52	Gerry Malone, MP
Labour	4,734	8	7	7	Patrick Davies
Lib Dem	23,286	37	38	40	Mark Oaten, PR consultant
Majority	9,318	Con 15	Con 12	Con 12	
Swing		No swing		6 → SDPAll	LD need 7 to win. 38th on LD list

WINDSOR, Berkshire. New strong Tory seat, stockbroker belt, managerial
Car owners 82% (48th); Mobility 12% (76th); Managerial 43% (38th)

106% change	Notional 92	%			Candidates
Conservative	30,138	56			Michael Trend, MP
Labour	6,645	12			Amanda Williams
Lib Dem	15,587	29			Chris Fox
Majority	14,551	Con 27			

WIRRAL SOUTH, Merseyside. Tory seat, Labour long-shot, mainly rural, middle-class
Age 40-pension 29% (56th); Owner-occupied 81% (33rd); Professional 10% (97th)

0.1% change	Notional 92	%	92	87	Candidates
Conservative	25,550	51	51	50	Les Byrom, councillor
Labour	17,382	35	35	28	Ben Chapman
Lib Dem	6,572	13	13	22	
Majority	8,168	Con 16	Con 16	Con 22	
Swing			3 → Lab	5 → Lab	Lab needs 8 to win. 96th on Lab list

WIRRAL WEST, Merseyside. Strong Tory seat, commuting, middle-class
Pensionable 23% (70th); Owner-occupied 82% (28th); Professional 10% (63rd)

No Change	Actual 92	%		87	Candidates
Conservative	26,852	53		52	David Hunt, MP
Labour	15,788	31		26	Stephen Hesford
Lib Dem	7,420	15		20	John Thornton
Majority	11,064	Con 22		Con 26	
Swing		2 → Lab		4 → Lab	

WITNEY, Oxfordshire. Strong Tory seat, mainly rural, managerial
Second homes 1% (71st); Car owners 84% (19th); Mobility 13% (57th)

18% change	Notional 92	%	92	87	Candidates
Conservative	33,743	58	56	58	Shaun Woodward, broadcaster, university lecturer
Labour	10,582	18	21	17	Alexander Hollingsworth
Lib Dem	13,150	23	21	26	Angela Lawrence
Majority	20,593	Con 35	Con 35	Con 32	
Swing			3 → Lab	4 → Con	

WOKING, Surrey. Strong Tory seat, stockbroker belt, professional
Car owners 81% (60th); Professional 12% (27th); Managerial 39% (77th)

15% change	Notional 92	%	92	87	Candidates
Conservative	32,718	59	59	58	Humphrey Malins, solicitor, ex-MP
Labour	7,398	13	13	11	Catherine Hanson
Lib Dem	14,987	27	28	31	Philip Goldenberg
Majority	17,731	Con 32	Con 31	Con 27	
Swing			2 → Con	1 → LibAll	

WOKINGHAM, Berkshire. Strong Tory seat, stockbroker belt, managerial
Car owners 88% (1st); Professional 13% (13th); Managerial 47% (9th)

68% change	Notional 92	%	92	87	Candidates
Conservative	32,692	62	61	61	John Redwood, MP
Labour	5,987	11	13	9	Patricia Colling
Lib Dem	13,575	26	25	30	Royce Longton
Majority	19,117	Con 36	Con 36	Con31	
Swing			2 → Con	1 → Con	

WOLVERHAMPTON NORTH EAST, West Midlands. Labour marginal, Tory target seat, mainly urban, working class, Lab gain in 92.
Unemployed 15% (53rd); Council tenants 40% (31st); Skilled manual 38% (19th)

2% change	Notional 92	%	92	87	Candidates
Conservative	20,528	41	41	42	David Harvey, head of business policy
Labour	24,275	49	49	42	Kenneth Purchase, MP
Lib Dem	3,657	7	7	16	Brian Niblett
Majority	3,747	Lab 8	Lab 8	Con 0.4	
Swing			4 → Lab	1 → Con	Con need 4 to win. 60th on Con list

WOLVERHAMPTON SOUTH EAST, West Midlands. Strong Labour seat, industrial, working class
Asian 17% (20th); Council tenants 43% (18th); Skilled manual 42% (4th)

No Change	Actual 92	%		87	Candidates
Conservative	12,975	32		33	William Hanbury, barrister
Labour	23,215	57		49	Dennis Turner, MP
Lib Dem	3,881	10		18	Richard Whitehouse
Majority	10,240	Lab 25		Lab 16	
Swing		5 → Lab		2 → Lab	

WOLVERHAMPTON SOUTH WEST, West Midlands. Tory marginal, Labour target seat, inner city, suburban, large Asian commu
Black 5% (54th); Asian 15% (24th); Govt schemes 2% (103rd)

No Change	Actual 92	%		87	Candidates
Conservative	25,969	49		51	Nick Budgen, MP
Labour	21,003	40		31	Jenny Jones, director, management consultanc
Lib Dem	4,470	9		19	Matthew Green
Majority	4,966	Con 9		Con 20	
Swing		5 → Lab		2 → Lab	Lab needs 5 to win. 66th on Lab list

WOODSPRING, Avon. Strong Tory seat, commuting, managerial
Age 40-pension 31% (17th); Owner-occupied 84% (15th); Car owners 84% (18th)

34% change	Notional 92	%	92	87	Candidates
Conservative	29,529	53	55	57	Dr Liam Fox, MP
Labour	6,863	12	15	14	Deborah Sander
Lib Dem	17,523	32	27	27	Nan Kirsen
Majority	12,006	Con 22	Con 27	Con 30	
Swing			1 → LD	1 → Con	

WORCESTER, Hereford and Worcester. Tory marginal, Labour target seat, urban, middle-class
Age 25-39 23% (118th); No central heating 22% (166th); Mobility 10% (174th)

16% change	Notional 92	%	92	87	Candidates
Conservative	23,960	46	46	48	Nicholas Bourne, professor in law
Labour	21,013	40	36	28	Michael Foster, lecturer
Lib Dem	6,890	13	16	23	Paul Chandler, councillor
Majority	2,947	Con 6	Con 10	Con 20	
Swing			5 → Lab	4 → Lab	Lab needs 3 to win. 39th on Lab list

WORCESTERSHIRE MID, Hereford and Worcester. Strong Tory seat, mainly rural, managerial
Age 40-pension 29% (57th); White 99.4% (55th); Car owners 81% (67th)

108% change	Notional 92	%	92	87	Candidates
Conservative	27,535	55	50	52	Peter Luff, MP
Labour	8,832	18	35	27	Diane Smith
Lib Dem	13,081	26	14	21	David Barwick
Majority	14,454	Con 29	Con 14	Con 24	
Swing			5 → Lab	1 → Lab	

WORCESTERSHIRE WEST, Hereford and Worcester. Strong Tory seat, rural, middle-class, based on Worcestershire S
Age 40-pension 30% (21st); Self-employed 17% (47th); Car owners 81% (53rd)

50% change	Notional 92	%	92	87	Candidates
Conservative	27,654	55	54	55	Sir Michael Spicer, MP
Labour	6,967	14	15	11	Neil Stone
Lib Dem	14,785	29	29	32	Mike Hadley, pharmacist
Majority	12,869	Con 26	Con 25	Con 23	
Swing			1 → Con	1 → Con	

WORKINGTON, Cumbria. Labour seat, industrial, working class
White 99.7% (3rd); Second homes 1% (73rd); Unskilled 6% (77th)

16% change	Notional 92	%	92	87	Candidates
Conservative	19,696	37	35	37	Robert Blunden
Labour	29,296	54	57	52	Dale Campbell-Savours, MP
Lib Dem	4,028	8	6	11	Phillip Roberts
Majority	9,600	Lab 18	Lab 22	Lab 15	
Swing			4 → Lab	No swing	

WORSLEY, Greater Manchester. Strong Labour seat, mainly urban
Council tenants 30% (75th); Long-term ill 15% (90th); White collar 14% (208th)

35% change	Notional 92	%	92	87	Candidates
Conservative	16,888	32	35	35	Damien Garrido, barrister
Labour	28,291	54	52	48	Terry Lewis, MP
Lib Dem	6,661	13	12	17	Robert Bleakley
Majority	11,403	Lab 22	Lab 18	Lab 13	
Swing			2 → Lab	3 → Lab	

WORTHING EAST & SHOREHAM, West Sussex. New Tory seat, Lib Dem long-shot, seaside, pensioners
Pensionable 26% (26th); Owner-occupied 81% (35th); White collar 16% (105th)

71% change	Notional 92	%			Candidates
Conservative	28,824	51			Tim Loughton, director, asset management
Labour	7,476	13			Mark Williams
Lib Dem	18,919	34			Martin King, management consultant
Majority	9,905	Con 18			LD need 9 to win. 52nd on LD list

WORTHING WEST, West Sussex. Strong Tory seat, seaside, white collar
Pensionable 35% (1st); Owner-occupied 81% (31st); White collar 19% (28th)

57% change	Notional 92	%	92	87	Candidates
Conservative	34,762	62	57	62	Peter Bottomley, MP
Labour	4,883	9	11	10	John Adams
Lib Dem	15,483	28	29	29	Christopher Hare
Majority	19,279	Con 34	Con 28	Con 33	
Swing			3 → LD	2 → Con	

WREKIN, THE, Shropshire. Tory seat, Labour long-shot, part new town, working class
Age 16-24 14% (131st); Age 40-pension 28% (140th); Council tenants 24% (162nd)

90% change	Notional 92	%	92	87	Candidates
Conservative	23,259	48	39	41	Peter Bruinvels, media consultant, ex-MP
Labour	15,539	32	48	43	Peter Bradley, director, PA consultancy
Lib Dem	9,391	19	12	17	Ian Jenkins
Majority	7,720	Con 16	Lab 10	Lab 2	
Swing			4 → Lab	2 → Lab	Lab needs 8 to win. 93rd on Lab list

WREXHAM, Clwyd. Labour seat, mainly urban, working class
Govt schemes 2% (82nd); Council tenants 30% (79th); No central heating 24% (130th)

32% change	Notional 92	%	92	87	Candidates
Conservative	13,101	32	35	36	Stuart Andrew, charity organiser
Labour	20,191	50	48	44	Dr John Marek, MP
Lib Dem	6,054	15	14	19	Andrew Thomas
Plaid Cymru	1,075	3	3	1	James Hack
Majority	7,090	Lab 18	Lab 13	Lab 8	
Swing			2 → Lab	4 → Lab	

WYCOMBE, Buckinghamshire. Strong Tory seat, mainly urban, middle-class
Age 16-24 14% (48th); Black 4% (65th); Asian 7% (61st)

4% change	Notional 92	%	92	87	Candidates
Conservative	30,040	53	53	54	Ray Whitney, MP
Labour	12,096	21	22	19	Chris Bryant
Lib Dem	12,982	23	23	28	Paul Bensilum
Majority	17,058	Con 30	Con 30	Con 26	
Swing			2 → Con	No swing	

WYRE FOREST, Hereford and Worcester. Tory seat, Labour long-shot, mainly urban
Age 40-pension 29% (65th); Owner-occupied 75% (168th); Skilled manual 32% (135th)

3% change	Notional 92	%	92	87	Candidates
Conservative	27,999	48	48	47	Anthony Coombs, MP
Labour	18,414	31	31	19	David Lock
Lib Dem	12,551	21	21	34	David Cropp
Majority	9,585	Con 16	Con 17	Con 13	
Swing			6 → Lab	1 → SDPAll	Lab needs 8 to win. 95th on Lab list

WYTHENSHAWE & SALE EAST, Greater Manchester. New Labour seat, outer suburbs, working class
Council tenants 46% (12th); Single parents 32% (41st); Unskilled 8% (23rd)

48% change	Notional 92	%			Candidates
Conservative	18,977	35			Paul Fleming, aviation security officer
Labour	26,935	50			Paul Goggins
Lib Dem	7,869	15			Vanessa Tucker
Majority	7,958	Lab 15			

YEOVIL, Somerset. Lib Dem seat, Tory long-shot, mainly urban
Pensionable 22% (87th); White 99.4% (69th); Second homes .4% (135th)

1% change	Notional 92	%	92	87	Candidates
Conservative	21,890	37	37	41	Nicholas Cambrook, financial adviser
Labour	5,702	10	10	7	Patrick Conway
Lib Dem	30,634	52	52	51	Paddy Ashdown, MP
Majority	8,744	LD 15	LD 15	LD 10	
Swing			2 → Lib Dem	2 → LibAll	

YNYS MÔN (ANGLESEY), Gwynedd. PIC marginal, Tory target, Welsh-speaking
White 99.5% (39th); Govt schemes 3% (20th); Second homes 4% (8th)

No Change	Actual 92	%	92	87	Candidates
Conservative	14,878	35		33	Gwilym Owen, bank director
Labour	10,126	24		17	Owen Edwards
Lib Dem	1,891	4		7	
Plaid Cymru	15,984	37		43	Ieuan Wyn Jones, MP
Majority	1,106	PIC3		PIC 10	
Swing		4 → Con		7 → PIC	Con need 1 to win. 17th on Con list

YORK, CITY OF, North Yorkshire. Labour marginal, Tory target seat, railway industry, working class
No central heating 28% (82nd); Mobility 12% (74th); Unskilled 7% (54th)

No Change	Actual 92	%	87	Candidates
Conservative	25,183	39	42	Simon Mallett, barrister
Labour	31,525	49	41	Hugh Bayley, MP
Lib Dem	6,811	11	16	Andrew Waller
Majority	6,342	Lab 10	Con 0.2	
Swing		5 → Lab	3 → Lab	

YORKSHIRE EAST, Humberside. New strong Tory seat, rural, working class
Pensionable 23% (53rd); White 99.6% (5th); Self-employed 16% (58th)

71% change	Notional 92	%	Candidates
Conservative	25,759	51	John Townend, MP
Labour	13,487	27	Ian Male
Lib Dem	11,629	23	David Leadley
Majority	12,272	Con 24	

POLLS AND ELECTIONS

Conservative Target List

Ranking	Constituency	Held by	% swing needed
1	Slough	Lab	0.0
2	Rossendale & Darwen	Lab	0.0
3	Birmingham Yardley	Lab	0.2
4	Ipswich	Lab	0.3
5	Halifax	Lab	0.4
6	Angus	SNP	0.5
7	Cambridge	Lab	0.6
8	Devon North	Lib Dem	0.7
9	Forest of Dean	Lab	0.7
10	Dudley North	Lab	0.9
11	Swindon North	Lab	0.9
12	Southampton Itchen	Lab	0.9
13	Lincoln	Lab	0.9
14	Thurrock	Lab	1.1
15	Staffordshire Moorlands	Lab	1.1
16	Warwickshire North	Lab	1.2
17	Ynys Môn (Anglesey)	PIC	1.3
18	Lewisham East	Lab	1.3
19	Feltham & Heston	Lab	1.3
20	Nuneaton	Lab	1.4
21	Carmarthen West & Pembrokeshire	Lab	1.5
22	Cornwall North	Lib Dem	1.5
23	Inverness East, Nairn & Lochaber	Lib Dem	1.6
24	Birmingham Northfield	Lab	1.7
25	Cheltenham	Lib Dem	1.7
26	Bath	Lib Dem	1.7
27	Dulwich & West Norwood	Lab	1.8
28	Hyndburn	Lab	1.8
29	Birmingham Selly Oak	Lab	1.9
30	Pendle	Lab	2.0

31	Carlisle	Lab	2.0
32	Ayr	Lab	2.1
33	Lewisham West	Lab	2.1
34	Tweeddale, Ettrick & Lauderdale	Lib Dem	2.2
35	Sherwood	Lab	2.3
36	Southampton Test	Lab	2.5
37	Darlington	Lab	2.5
38	Dudley South	Lab	2.6
39	Copeland	Lab	2.7
40	Bolton North East	Lab	2.7
41	Hampstead & Highgate	Lab	2.7
42	Ellesmere Port & Neston	Lab	2.9
43	Nottingham South	Lab	3.0
44	Walsall South	Lab	3.2
45	Barrow & Furness	Lab	3.2
46	Bristol North West	Lab	3.2
47	Cunninghame North	Lab	3.4
48	Ceredigion	PIC	3.5
49	Ealing Acton & Shepherd's Bush	Lab	3.5
50	Wallasey	Lab	3.5
51	Walthamstow	Lab	3.5
52	Moray	SNP	3.5
53	Lancashire West	Lab	3.5
54	Argyll & Bute	Lib Dem	3.6
55	Delyn	Lab	3.6
56	Dewsbury	Lab	3.6
57	Regent's Park & Kensington North	Lab	3.6
58	Walsall North	Lab	3.7
59	Derby South	Lab	3.7
60	Wolverhampton North East	Lab	3.8

Labour Target List

Ranking	Constituency	Held by	% swing needed
1	Vale of Glamorgan	Con	0.0
2	Hayes & Harlington	Con	0.1
3	Halesowen & Rowley Regis	Con	0.1
4	Rochdale	Lib Dem	0.1
5	Croydon North	Con	0.1
6	Stirling	Con	0.3
7	Corby	Con	0.3
8	Blackpool South	Con	0.3
9	Luton South	Con	0.5
10	Edmonton	Con	0.6
11	Bury South	Con	0.7
12	Preseli Pembrokeshire	Con	0.7
13	Dover	Con	0.8
14	Leicestershire North West	Con	0.8
15	Batley & Spen	Con	0.8
16	Plymouth Sutton	Con	1.0
17	Amber Valley	Con	1.1
18	Middlesbrough South & Cleveland East	Con	1.3
19	Brentford & Isleworth	Con	1.4
20	Derbyshire South	Con	1.5
21	Harlow	Con	1.6
22	Mitcham & Morden	Con	1.7
23	Crawley	Con	1.8
24	Inverness East, Nairn & Lochaber	Lib Dem	1.9
25	Eltham	Con	1.9
26	Norwich North	Con	2.0
27	Chester, City of	Con	2.1
28	Chorley	Con	2.1
29	Basildon	Con	2.2
30	Ilford South	Con	2.4
31	Warrington South	Con	2.5
32	Exeter	Con	2.5
33	Vale of Clwyd	Con	2.5
34	Brighton Pavilion	Con	2.5
35	Coventry South	Con	2.6
36	Kingswood	Con	2.6
37	Stevenage	Con	2.7
38	Elmet	Con	2.8
39	Worcester	Con	2.8
40	Cardiff North	Con	3.1
41	Monmouth	Con	3.2

42	Tynemouth	Con	3.2
43	Keighley	Con	3.3
44	Redditch	Con	3.4
45	Loughborough	Con	3.5
46	Burton	Con	3.5
47	Northampton North	Con	3.6
48	Waveney	Con	3.6
49	Derby North	Con	3.8
50	Falmouth & Camborne	Con	3.9
51	Birmingham Hall Green	Con	3.9
52	Calder Valley	Con	4.0
53	High Peak	Con	4.0
54	Bury North	Con	4.0
55	Bolton West	Con	4.1
56	Oldham East & Saddleworth	Con	4.2
57	Leeds North East	Con	4.3
58	Gloucester	Con	4.4
59	Erewash	Con	4.5
60	Edinburgh Pentlands	Con	4.5
61	Bedford	Con	4.5
62	Battersea	Con	4.6
63	Milton Keynes South West	Con	4.6
64	Gravesham	Con	4.6
65	Stockton South	Con	4.7
66	Wolverhampton South West	Con	4.7
67	Birmingham Edgbaston	Con	5.0
68	Great Yarmouth	Con	5.0
69	Tamworth	Con	5.1
70	Stourbridge	Con	5.3
71	Conwy	Con	5.6
72	Welwyn Hatfield	Con	5.8
73	Peterborough	Con	5.9
74	Cleethorpes	Con	6.0
75	Blackpool North & Fleetwood	Con	6.1
76	Colne Valley	Con	6.1
77	Hammersmith & Fulham	Con	6.5
78	Stafford	Con	6.6
79	Aberdeen South	Con	6.7
80	Dumfries	Con	6.8
81	Luton North	Con	7.0
82	Watford	Con	7.1
83	Brigg & Goole	Con	7.1
84	Newark	Con	7.3
85	Pudsey	Con	7.3

86	Dartford	Con	7.3
87	Ribble South	Con	7.5
88	Selby	Con	7.7
89	Putney	Con	7.8
90	Ealing North	Con	7.8
91	Leeds North West	Con	7.9
92	Ceredigion	PIC	7.9
93	Wrekin, The	Con	7.9
94	Broxtowe	Con	8.1
X 95	Wyre Forest	Con	8.1
X 96	Wirral South	Con	8.1
97	Stroud	Con	8.4
98	Southwark North & Bermondsey	Lib Dem	8.4
99	Hemel Hempstead	Con	8.7
100	Portsmouth North	Con	8.8
101	Clwyd West	Con	8.8
102	Medway	Con	8.9
103	Colchester	Con	9.0
104	Enfield North	Con	9.0
X 105	Swindon South	Con	9.1
106	Warwick & Leamington	Con	9.2
107	Norfolk North West	Con	9.3
108	Gedling	Con	9.4
109	Hornchurch	Con	9.5
110	Brecon & Radnorshire	Con	9.5
111	Lancaster & Wyre	Con	9.5
112	Harrow East	Con	9.6
113	Wellingborough	Con	9.8
114	Morecambe & Lunesdale	Con	9.9
115	Shrewsbury & Atcham	Con	9.9
116	Ross, Skye & Inverness West	Lib Dem	9.9
117	Scarborough & Whitby	Con	10.0
118	Bury St Edmunds	Con	10.0
119	Wansdyke	Con	10.0
120	Crosby	Con	10.0

Plaid Cymru Target List

Ranking	Constituency	Held by	% swing needed
1	Carmarthen East & Dinefwr	Lab	6.2
2	Llanelli	Lab	19.4
3	Carmarthen West & Pembrokeshire	Lab	20.4
4	Clwyd South	Lab	22.3
5	Conwy	Con	24.0
6	Pontypridd	Lab	25.9
7	Clwyd West	Con	26.3
8	Caerphilly	Lab	27.0
9	Swansea West	Lab	27.6
10	Montgomeryshire	Lib Dem	28.0

Liberal Democrat Target List

Ranking	Constituency	Held by	% swing needed
1	Brecon & Radnorshire	Con	0.2
2	Portsmouth South	Con	0.2
3	Oldham East & Saddleworth	Con	0.5
4	Hazel Grove	Con	0.9
5	Isle of Wight	Con	1.2
6	Conwy	Con	1.2
7	St Ives	Con	1.4
8	Ceredigion	PIC	2.2
9	Taunton	Con	2.6
10	Devon West & Torridge	Con	2.7
11	Southport	Con	2.8
12	Hereford	Con	2.8
13	Falmouth & Camborne	Con	2.9
14	Liverpool Wavertree	Lab	3.3
15	Somerton & Frome	Con	3.6
16	Edinburgh West	Con	4.2
17	Birmingham Yardley	Lab	4.3
18	Colchester	Con	4.7
19	Greenwich & Woolwich	Lab	4.8
20	Weston-super-Mare	Con	4.8
21	Torbay	Con	5.1
22	Twickenham	Con	5.1

23	Oxford West & Abingdon	Con	5.2
24	Aberdeenshire West & Kincardine	Con	5.2
25	Aberdeen South	Con	5.4
26	Aberdeen North	Lab	5.6
27	Chesterfield	Lab	5.7
28	Wells	Con	5.8
29	Eastbourne	Con	5.9
30	Sheffield Hillsborough	Lab	5.9
31	Dorset Mid & Poole North	Con	6.1
32	Lewes	Con	6.1
33	Hastings & Rye	Con	6.2
34	Cornwall South East	Con	6.4
35	Richmond Park	Con	7.1
36	Ribble Valley	Con	7.2
37	Dorset West	Con	7.3
38	Winchester	Con	7.4
39	Salisbury	Con	7.4
40	Colne Valley	Con	7.5
41	Teignbridge	Con	7.6
42	Leeds North West	Con	7.6
43	Totnes	Con	7.6
44	Bristol West	Con	8.0
45	Blyth Valley	Lab	8.2
46	Congleton	Con	8.4
47	Folkestone & Hythe	Con	8.5
48	Bridgwater	Con	8.5
49	Pudsey	Con	8.6
50	Northavon	Con	8.7
51	Erith & Thamesmead	Lab	8.8
52	Worthing East & Shoreham	Con	8.8
53	St Albans	Con	8.8
54	Canterbury	Con	8.9
55	Harborough	Con	9.1
56	Westbury	Con	9.2
57	Harrogate & Knaresborough	Con	9.2
58	Tewkesbury	Con	9.3
59	Newbury	Con	9.4
60	Shrewsbury & Atcham	Con	9.4
61	Carshalton & Wallington	Con	9.4

SNP Target List

Ranking	Constituency	Held by	% swing needed
1	Inverness East, Nairn & Lochaber	Lib Dem	0.8
2	Galloway & Upper Nithsdale	Con	2.8
3	Perth	Con	3.0
4	Tayside North	Con	3.8
5	Western Isles	Lab	5.3
6	Argyll & Bute	Lib Dem	5.6
7	Dundee East	Lab	6.1
8	Aberdeen North	Lab	6.3
9	Kilmarnock & Loudoun	Lab	7.0
10	Edinburgh North & Leith	Lab	7.3
11	Glasgow Govan	Lab	7.7
12	Falkirk East	Lab	7.9
13	Ochil	Lab	8.5
14	Linlithgow	Lab	9.5
15	Ross, Skye & Inverness West	Lib Dem	9.9
16	Livingston	Lab	9.9
17	Clydesdale	Lab	10.8
18	Dunfermline West	Lab	10.9
19	Renfrewshire West	Lab	11.1
20	Kirkcaldy	Lab	11.5
21	Dundee West	Lab	11.6
22	East Kilbride	Lab	11.9
23	Glasgow Pollok	Lab	12.4
24	Cumbernauld & Kilsyth	Lab	12.5
25	Midlothian	Lab	12.5
26	Dumbarton	Lab	12.6
27	Aberdeen Central	Lab	12.8
28	Fife Central	Lab	12.9
29	Caithness, Sutherland & Easter Ross	Lib Dem	13.0
30	Paisley South	Lab	13.1

Top Tens

Which constituency has the highest percentage of unskilled workers, or unemployed, or households with cars, or professional people? The 1991 census figures have been broken down into the new constituencies by the House of Commons Library to provide league tables of constituencies on every census heading. They cover the 569 constituencies of England and Wales only.

	%		%
Professionals		Ashfield	41.2
Sheffield Hallam	20.2	Scunthorpe	40.7
Bristol West	17.8	Bolsover	40.5
Cambridge	16.7	Cannock Chase	40.4
Richmond Park	16.5	Stoke-on-Trent Central	40.2
Cambridgeshire South	15.1		
Oxford West & Abingdon	14.7	**Unskilled**	
Newcastle-upon-Tyne Central	14.7	Merthyr Tydfil & Rhymney	10.2
Kensington & Chelsea	14.4	Camberwell & Peckham	10.0
Hampstead & Highgate	14.0	Manchester Central	9.7
Birmingham Edgbaston	13.6	Hackney South & Shoreditch	9.5
Cheadle	13.6	Leeds Central	9.4
		Hull East	9.3
Managerial and technical		Blaenau Gwent	9.2
Kensington & Chelsea	54.3	Preston	9.2
Richmond Park	49.7	Bootle	9.0
Twickenham	49.2	Middlesbrough	9.0
Chesham & Amersham	48.4		
Sheffield Hallam	48.1	**Self-employed**	
Esher & Walton	47.6	Ceredigion	27.2
Beaconsfield	47.4	Brecon & Radnorshire	25.0
Hampstead & Highgate	47.0	Cornwall North	24.9
Finchley & Golders Green	46.8	Devon West & Torridge	24.8
Wokingham	46.8	Montgomeryshire	24.8
		Totnes	24.7
Clerical		Carmarthen East & Dinefwr	24.6
Old Bexley & Sidcup	21.8	Meirionnydd Nant Conwy	24.5
Romford	21.0	Leominster	23.6
Croydon North	20.7	St Ives	22.9
Hove	20.6		
Ilford North	20.4	**Government schemes**	
Walthamstow	20.3	Sunderland South	4.1
Croydon Central	20.3	Easington	3.8
Erith & Thamesmead	20.2	Liverpool Riverside	3.8
Lewisham West	20.1	Sunderland North	3.7
Hornchurch	19.9	Hartlepool	3.7
		Middlesbrough	3.5
Skilled manual		Bootle	3.4
Stoke-on-Trent North	46.1	Birmingham Ladywood	3.4
Stoke-on-Trent South	42.7	Barnsley Central	3.3
Walsall North	42.6	Liverpool West Derby	3.2
Wolverhampton South East	42.4	Redcar	3.2
West Bromwich West	41.5	Barnsley East & Mexborough	3.2

Unemployed	%
Liverpool Riverside	29.4
Birmingham Ladywood	27.9
Manchester Central	26.5
Liverpool West Derby	23.6
Birmingham Sparkbrook & Small Heath	23.5
Hackney North & Stoke Newington	22.9
Hackney South & Shoreditch	22.9
Bethnal Green & Bow	22.7
Camberwell & Peckham	22.6
Tyne Bridge	22.1

Mobility (different address a year ago)	
Cities of London & Westminster	23.9
Kensington & Chelsea	22.4
Hammersmith & Fulham	17.8
Bristol West	17.7
Hampstead & Highgate	17.5
Cambridge	16.6
Manchester Central	16.1
Tooting	15.6
Holborn & St Pancras	15.5
Battersea	15.4
Suffolk West	15.4
Sheffield Central	15.4

Availability of 1+ cars	
Wokingham	88.4
Hampshire North East	87.1
Northavon	87.0
Surrey Heath	86.5
Buckingham	86.0
Beaconsfield	85.1
Henley	84.8
Chesham & Amersham	84.7
Romsey	84.4
Dorset Mid & Poole North	84.3

No central heating	
Liverpool West Derby	54.4
Liverpool Walton	52.9
Birmingham Sparkbrook	52.7
Birmingham Hodge Hill	50.6
Liverpool Wavertree	49.3
Leeds East	48.5
Knowsley South	45.5
Leeds West	45.4
Bootle	45.4
Huddersfield	45.3

Limiting long-term illness	%
Rhondda	25.8
Merthyr Tydfil & Rhymney	22.4
Aberavon	22.0
Cynon Valley	21.3
Blaenau Gwent	21.3
Easington	21.2
Llanelli	21.0
Neath	20.1
Ogmore	19.3
Barnsley East & Mexborough	19.2

Lone-parent families	
Vauxhall	52.8
Manchester Central	52.6
Liverpool Riverside	48.8
Camberwell & Peckham	48.0
Hackney South & Shoreditch	44.7
Lewisham Deptford	43.4
Southwark North & Bermondsey	43.0
Islington North	42.0
Birmingham Ladywood	41.5
Islington South & Finsbury	40.8

Over 1 person per room	
Bethnal Green & Bow	12.0
Birmingham Sparkbrook	10.2
East Ham	8.9
Hackney North & Stoke Newington	8.1
Brent South	8.1
Poplar & Canning Town	8.0
Birmingham Ladywood	8.0
Bradford West	7.4
West Ham	7.2
Brent East	7.1
Ealing Southall	7.1

Black	
Camberwell & Peckham	26.5
Vauxhall	26.4
Brent South	25.7
Tottenham	24.8
Lewisham Deptford	24.8
Hackney South & Shoreditch	23.1
Hackney North & Stoke Newington	20.8
Streatham	18.5
West Ham	17.6
Birmingham Ladywood	16.8

Indian/Pakistani/Bangladeshi	
Birmingham Sparkbrook & Small Heath	40.3
Ealing Southall	35.1

	%
Leicester East	33.5
Birmingham Ladywood	33.1
Bradford West	31.9
East Ham	31.0
Bethnal Green & Bow	29.1
Leicester South	26.1
Brent North	26.0
Birmingham Perry Barr	23.8

White

Berwick-upon-Tweed	99.8
Penrith & the Border	99.7
Workington	99.7
Cornwall South East	99.6
Delyn	99.6
Somerton & Frome	99.6
Caernarfon	99.6
Sedgefield	99.6
Forest of Dean	99.6
Durham North West	99.6

Owner occupiers

Rayleigh	89.8
Castle Point	89.5
Cheadle	87.8
Charnwood	86.0
Fareham	85.6
Solihull	85.4
Christchurch	85.2
Old Bexley & Sidcup	85.1
Ribble Valley	84.9
Northavon	84.3
Sutton Coldfield	84.3

Private tenants

Kensington & Chelsea	34.7
Cities of London & Westminster	31.6
Hampstead & Highgate	25.7
Hammersmith & Fulham	23.5
Brent East	22.3
Tooting	21.3
Hornsey & Wood Green	20.6
Regent's Park & Kensington North	20.3
Bristol West	20.2
Finchley & Golders Green	20.0

Students

Cambridge	21.0
Oxford West & Abingdon	17.0
Leeds North West	17.0
Cardiff Central	16.0
Newcastle Central	15.0

	%
Bristol West	14.0
Liverpool Riverside	14.0
Sheffield Hallam	13.0
Manchester Gorton	13.0
Oxford East	12.0
Sheffield Central	12.0

Council or new town tenants

Camberwell & Peckham	59.7
Poplar & Canning Town	59.5
Southwark North & Bermondsey	59.3
Bethnal Green & Bow	57.2
Hackney South & Shoreditch	55.8
Islington South & Finsbury	55.1
Sheffield Brightside	53.4
Vauxhall	50.3
Barking	49.2
Greenwich & Woolwich	48.3

Second homes

Meirionnydd Nant Conwy	9.3
Caernarfon	7.8
Cities of London & Westminster	6.8
Norfolk North	4.7
Totnes	4.3
Kensington & Chelsea	4.2
Westmorland & Lonsdale	3.9
Ynys Môn (Anglesey)	3.6
Ceredigion	3.4
Norfolk North West	3.2

Pensionable age

Worthing West	35.4
Bexhill & Battle	34.4
Christchurch	34.3
Devon East	34.3
Harwich	33.7
Eastbourne	32.8
New Forest West	31.7
Bognor Regis & Littlehampton	29.8
Bournemouth West	29.6
Thanet North	29.4

By-elections

NEWBURY 6 May 1993
Elected: David Rendel

Lib Dem	37,590	65.1%
Con	15,535	26.9%
Lab	1,151	2.0%
Majority	22,055	
Swing	28.4% to Lib Dem	

CHRISTCHURCH 29 July 1993
Elected: Diana Maddock

Lib Dem	33,164	62.2%
Con	16,737	31.4%
Lab	1,453	2.7%
Majority	16,433	
Swing	35.4% to Lib Dem	

ROTHERHAM 5 May 1994
Elected: Denis MacShane

Lab	14,912	55.6%
Lib Dem	7,958	29.7%
Con	2,649	9.9%
Majority	6,954	
Swing	12.9% to Lib Dem	

EASTLEIGH 9 June 1994
Elected: David Chidgey

Lib Dem	24,473	44.3%
Lab	15,234	27.6%
Con	13,675	24.7%
Majority	9,239	
Swing	21.4% to Lib Dem	

BRADFORD SOUTH 9 June 1994
Elected: Gerry Sutcliffe

Lab	17,014	55.3%
Lib Dem	7,350	23.9%
Con	5,475	17.8%
Majority	9,664	
Swing	14.1% to Lab	

BARKING 9 June 1994
Elected: Margaret Hodge

Lab	13,704	72.0%
Lib Dem	2,290	12.0%
Con	1,976	10.4%
Majority	11,414	
Swing	22.0% to Lab	

NEWHAM NORTH EAST 9 June 1994
Elected: Stephen Timms

Lab	14,668	74.9%
Con	2,850	14.6%
Lib Dem	821	4.2%
Majority	11,818	
Swing	16.3% to Lab	

DAGENHAM 9 June 1994
Elected: Judith Church

Lab	15,474	72.0%
Con	2,130	9.9%
Lib Dem	1,804	8.4%
Majority	13,344	
Swing	23.1% to Lab	

MONKLANDS EAST 30 June 1994
Elected: Helen Liddell

Lab	16,960	49.8%
SNP	15,320	44.9%
Lib Dem	878	2.6%
Con	799	2.3%
Majority	1,640	
Swing	19.3% to SNP	

DUDLEY WEST 15 Dec 1994
Elected: Ian Pearson

Lab	28,400	68.8%
Con	7,706	18.7%
Lib Dem	3,154	7.6%
Majority	20,694	
Swing	29.1% to Lab	

ISLWYN 16 February 1995
Elected: Don Touhig

Lab	16,030	69.0%
PlC	2,933	12.7%
Lib Dem	2,448	10.6%
Con	913	3.9%
Majority	13,097	
Swing	6.9% to PlC	

PERTH & KINROSS 25 May 1995
Elected: Roseanna Cunningham

SNP	16,931	40.4%
Lab	9,620	22.9%
Con	8,990	21.4%
Lib Dem	4,952	11.8%
Majority	7,311	
Swing	11.6% to SNP	

DOWN NORTH 15 June 1995
Elected: Robert McCartney

UKUP	10,124	37.0%
UUP	7,232	26.4%
Alliance	6,970	25.4%
IndU	2,170	7.9%
Con	583	2.1%
Majority	2,892	

LITTLEBORO & SADDLEWORTH 27 July 1995
Elected: Chris Davies

Lib Dem	16,231	38.5%
Lab	14,238	34.0%
Con	9,934	24.0%
Majority	1,993	
Swing	11.6% to Lib Dem	

HEMSWORTH 1 Feb 1996
Elected: Jon Trickett

Lab	15,817	71.9%
Con	1,942	6.8%
Lib Dem	1,516	8.8%
Majority	13,875	
Swing	5.4% to Lab	

STAFFORDSHIRE SOUTH EAST 12 Apr 1996
Elected: Brian Jenkins

Lab	26,155	60.2%
Con	12,393	28.5%
Lib Dem	2,042	4.7%
Majority	13,762	
Swing	22.1% to Lab	

BARNSLEY EAST 12 Dec 1996
Elected: Jeff Ennis

Lab	13,683	76.3%
Lib Dem	1,502	8.4%
Con	1,299	7.2%
Majority	12,181	
Swing	0.2% to Lib Dem	

Share of the Vote in General, Local and Euro Elections

as %	Con	Lab	Lib Dem	Other	Lead
1986 Local elections	34	37	27	2	Lab 3
1987 Local elections	40	31	27	2	Con 9
1987 GENERAL ELECTION	43	32	23	2	Con 11
1988 Local elections	40	40	18	2	0
1989 Local elections	37	40	21	1	Lab 3
1989 EURO elections	35	40	7	19	Lab 5
1990 Local elections	32	40	18	10	Lab 8
1991 Local elections	35	36	21	8	Lab 1
1992 GENERAL ELECTION	43	35	18	4	Con 8
1992 Local elections	45	30	19	6	Con 15
1993 Local elections	31	41	24	4	Lab 10
1994 Local elections	27	42	27	4	Lab 15
1994 EURO elections	27	44	16	6	Lab 17
1995 Local elections	25	46	24	5	Lab 21
1996 Local elections	27	43	26	4	Lab 16

Figures for local elections are equivalent popular votes which estimate how the country would have voted if all local authority areas were entitled to vote.

European Elections

	1979	%	seats	1984	%	seats	1989	%	seats	1994	%	seats
Conservative	6,508,493	51	60	5,426,866	41	45	5,331,077	35	32	4,248,531	28	18
Labour	4,253,207	33	17	4,865,224	37	32	6,153,640	40	45	6,753,863	44	62
Lib Dem	1,690,599	13	0	2,591,659	20	0	986,292	6	0	2,552,730	17	2
SNP	247,836	2	1	230,594	2	1	406,686	3	1	487,239	3	2
Plaid Cymru	83,399	1	0	95,524	1	0	115,062	1	0	162,478	1	0
Green	ngs	ngs	0	ngs	ngs	0	2,292,705	15	0	ngs	ngs	0
Others	90,318	1	0	95,524	1	0	117,181	1	0	568,151	4	0
Total GB	**12,873,852**	**32**	**78**	**13,312,898**	**32**	**78**	**15,353,154**	**36**	**78**	**15,267,550**	**36**	**84**
Unionist	140,622	25	1	151,399	22	1	118,785	22	1	133,459	24	1
DUP	170,688	30	1	230,251	34	1	160,110	30	1	163,246	29	1
SDLP	140,622	25	1	151,399	22	1	136,335	25	1	161,992	29	1
Sinn Fein	0	0	0	91,476	13	0	48,914	9	0	21,273	10*	0
Alliance	39,026	7	0	34,046	5	0	27,905	5	0	23,157	4	0
Total N. Ireland	586,060	57	3	696,971	65	3	540,254	49	3	559,867	49	3

*Three Sinn Fein candidates won 9.86 per cent between them

ngs = not given separately

Polls by Newspapers

Readers of different newspapers vote in very different ways. The graphs on the next two pages show the Conservative lead over Labour among readers of different national newspapers. They are based on polls by ICM and MORI, which collect data on newspaper readership as well as voting intention. Readers of the *Daily Telegraph* are the most Conservative. In 1990 the Conservatives had a lead of 50 points among *Telegraph* readers; this rose to more than 60 points in the 1992 election, and had gradually declined to just over 20 points at the end of 1995. *Times* readers are more volatile, swinging sharply to the Conservatives at the time of the last election but now showing a lead for Tony Blair's Labour party. *Independent* readers incline more towards Labour. *Guardian* readers are the most strongly Labour among readers of the quality press, with the Liberal Democrats second and the Tories in third place.

In the tabloid market readers of the *Daily Express* are traditionally the most Conservative. Readers of the *Sun* are generally more Labour than Tory, as one would expect from their strongly working-class background, but they swung strongly to the Conservatives in the 1992 election (by enough to ensure John Major's re-election, as the paper proudly boasted in its post-election headline, 'It's the *Sun* Wot Won It'). Since the election they have swung strongly to the left, especially since the paper ditched John Major under the headline 'What Fools We Were' in January 1994. Readers of the *Daily Star* also swung strongly to the right in the 1992 election, but *Mirror* readers were much more consistently pro-Labour, recording Labour leads of 55 to 70 points.

For further information: *Was It the Sun Wot Won It?* Seventh Guardian Lecture, Martin Linton, 1995. Available from Nuffield College, Oxford.

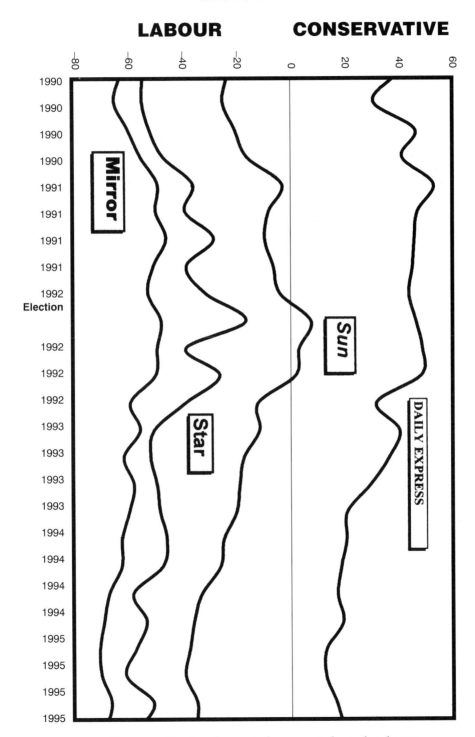

LABOUR   CONSERVATIVE

*Conservative lead over Labour or Labour lead over
Conservative (−) among readers of national newspapers*

LABOUR   CONSERVATIVE

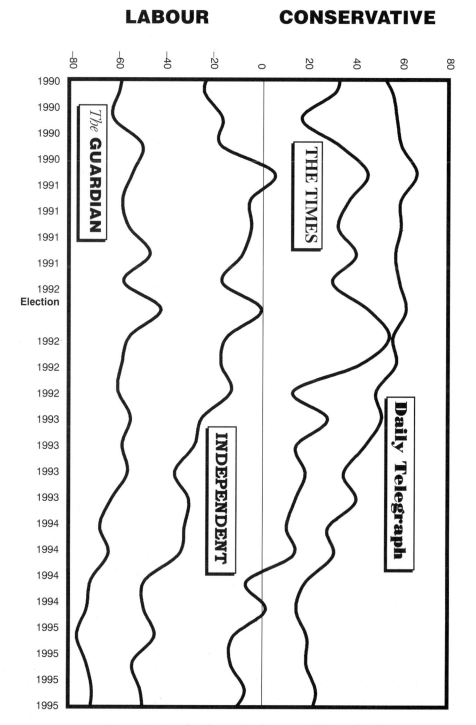

*Conservative lead over Labour or Labour lead over
Conservative (–) among readers of national newspapers*

VOTES INTO SEATS

It's no good just knowing how many votes each party is going to get. What matters is how many seats they get. And the process of translating votes into seats is fraught with difficulties. But the table on the next four pages should act as a rough guide for estimating the number of seats each party will have for any given percentage of the vote (column 1). Just read the Conservative vote from the left and the Labour vote from the top. The Liberal Democrat (Ldm) vote is not shown round the sides of the table, but it is shown in each block. The vote figures are for Great Britain only, as is the custom with opinion polls, but the seat projections cover all the seats in the UK Parliament, including the Northern Ireland seats.

For instance, the figures in the bottom left hand corner of the next page show the situation if the Conservatives win 50 per cent of the vote, Labour 30 per cent and the Liberal Democrats 16 per cent. In this case the Conservatives would win 428 seats, Labour 200 and the Liberal Democrats ten. In the top right-hand corner of the page opposite, Labour wins 41 per cent of the vote, the Conservatives 29 per cent and the Lib Dems 26 per cent. In this case Labour wins 375 seats, the Conservatives 175 and the Lib Dems 82. A fuller explanation is given on pages 19-21.

The table makes certain assumptions. First of all, it assumes that the minor parties will win 3.7 per cent of the vote (rounded up to 4 in the table) in Great Britain and that the Nationalist parties will win the same vote in each constituency as they did (notionally) in the last election. Second, it assumes that the Northern Ireland parties will share out their 18 seats according to the notional results of the last election – nine for the Ulster Unionists, four for the SDLP, four for the Democratic Unionists and one for the independent Unionist in North Down. Third, and most importantly, the table assumes a uniform swing in every constituency.

In the last election the swing was anything but uniform. Labour performed significantly better in its marginal seats and the Liberal Democrats performed much better in theirs, as the electors engaged in a complex game of tactical voting. If that happens again in this election, it means that the number of seats going to Labour and the Liberal Democrats may be significantly higher than the table implies for a given percentage of the national vote. Taking the result closest to the last election (Con 42, Lab 35, LDm 19), one would expect the Conservatives to win 334 seats, Labour 278 and the Lib Dems 22. But if there is an increase in anti-Conservative tactical voting, one should expect a seat distribution that one would get from a block further up diagonally to the right. For instance one might get Con 42, Lab 35, LDm 19 in percentages of the vote, but Con 309, Lab 301, LDm 24 in seats. With the House of Commons enlarged in this election from 651 seats to 659, the magic number that a party must win to have a majority over all the other parties is 330. A party with 330 seats will have a majority of one, with 331 seats a majority of three, with 332 seats a majority of five. In the great majority of possible results covered in this chart, the Labour Party or the Conservatives will have an outright majority. But there is a central band (shaded on the table) where no party will have 330 seats and there will be a hung parliament.

There are four main kinds of hung parliament. In the first kind, the Conservatives fall just short of 330 but they might be able to build a majority with their traditional allies in the Northern Ireland Unionist parties. To do this, they must win between 316 and 329 seats. In the second kind, the Liberal Democrats have enough seats to form a majority with either the Conservatives or Labour – in other words, they hold the balance of power. In the third kind, Labour is the largest party and could form a majority with the support of the Liberal Democrats. In the fourth kind, the Conservatives are the largest party and could form a majority with the Liberal Democrats.

❑ *The figures in the chart are taken from the* Media Guide to the New Parliamentary Constituencies *compiled and edited by Colin Rallings and Michael Thrasher and published by the BBC, ITN, PA News and Sky.*

Hung parliament

Liberal Democrats hold balance of power

Conservative-Unionist majority

Conservative outright majority

CON	LAB 30	LAB 31	LAB 32	LAB 33	LAB 34
CON 25					
CON 26					
CON 27					
CON 28					
CON 29					
CON 30					
CON 31					
CON 32					
CON 33					
CON 34					
CON 35					
CON 36					Con 36 Con Lab 34 Lab Ldm 26 Ldm
CON 37				Con 37 Con 294 Lab 33 Lab 291 Ldm 26 Ldm 49	Con 37 Con Lab 34 Lab Ldm 25 Ldm
CON 38			Con 38 Con 304 Lab 32 Lab 283 Ldm 26 Ldm 48	Con 38 Con 304 Lab 33 Lab 288 Ldm 25 Ldm 43	Con 38 Con Lab 34 Lab Ldm 24 Ldm
CON 39		Con 39 Con 323 Lab 31 Lab 265 Ldm 26 Ldm 47	Con 39 Con 317 Lab 32 Lab 275 Ldm 25 Ldm 43	Con 39 Con 314 Lab 33 Lab 269 Ldm 24 Ldm 37	Con 39 Con Lab 34 Lab Ldm 23 Ldm
CON 40	Con 40 Con 334 Lab 30 Lab 255 Ldm 26 Ldm 46	Con 40 Con 332 Lab 31 Lab 269 Ldm 25 Ldm 38	Con 40 Con 331 Lab 32 Lab 276 Ldm 24 Ldm 35	Con 40 Con 325 Lab 33 Lab 276 Ldm 23 Ldm 34	Con 40 Con Lab 34 Lab Ldm 22 Ldm
CON 41	Con 41 Con 347 Lab 30 Lab 249 Ldm 25 Ldm 39	Con 41 Con 342 Lab 31 Lab 258 Ldm 24 Ldm 35	Con 41 Con 336 Lab 32 Lab 266 Ldm 23 Ldm 33	Con 41 Con 333 Lab 33 Lab 270 Ldm 22 Ldm 31	Con 41 Con Lab 34 Lab Ldm 21 Ldm
CON 42	Con 42 Con 356 Lab 30 Lab 253 Ldm 24 Ldm 33	Con 42 Con 349 Lab 31 Lab 253 Ldm 23 Ldm 33	Con 42 Con 348 Lab 32 Lab 259 Ldm 22 Ldm 27	Con 42 Con 342 Lab 33 Lab 267 Ldm 21 Ldm 25	Con 42 Con Lab 34 Lab Ldm 20 Ldm
CON 43	Con 43 Con 366 Lab 30 Lab 240 Ldm 23 Ldm 29	Con 43 Con 362 Lab 31 Lab 246 Ldm 22 Ldm 26	Con 43 Con 356 Lab 32 Lab 254 Ldm 21 Ldm 24	Con 43 Con 352 Lab 33 Lab 260 Ldm 20 Ldm 22	Con 43 Con Lab 34 Lab Ldm 19 Ldm
CON 44	Con 44 Con 374 Lab 30 Lab 241 Ldm 22 Ldm 25	Con 44 Con 371 Lab 31 Lab 241 Ldm 21 Ldm 23	Con 44 Con 368 Lab 32 Lab 247 Ldm 20 Ldm 20	Con 44 Con 363 Lab 33 Lab 254 Ldm 19 Ldm 18	Con 44 Con Lab 34 Lab Ldm 18 Ldm
CON 45	Con 45 Con 390 Lab 30 Lab 224 Ldm 21 Ldm 25	Con 45 Con 380 Lab 31 Lab 237 Ldm 20 Ldm 18	Con 45 Con 375 Lab 32 Lab 242 Ldm 19 Ldm 18	Con 45 Con 371 Lab 33 Lab 247 Ldm 18 Ldm 17	Con 45 Con Lab 34 Lab Ldm 17 Ldm
CON 46	Con 46 Con 400 Lab 30 Lab 217 Ldm 20 Ldm 19	Con 46 Con 394 Lab 31 Lab 225 Ldm 19 Ldm 17	Con 46 Con 383 Lab 32 Lab 237 Ldm 18 Ldm 16	Con 46 Con 381 Lab 33 Lab 242 Ldm 17 Ldm 13	Con 46 Con Lab 34 Lab Ldm 16 Ldm
CON 47	Con 47 Con 408 Lab 30 Lab 212 Ldm 19 Ldm 16	Con 47 Con 405 Lab 31 Lab 218 Ldm 18 Ldm 13	Con 47 Con 399 Lab 32 Lab 225 Ldm 17 Ldm 12	Con 47 Con 387 Lab 33 Lab 237 Ldm 16 Ldm 12	Con 47 Con Lab 34 Lab Ldm 15 Ldm
CON 48	Con 48 Con 417 Lab 30 Lab 207 Ldm 18 Ldm 12	Con 48 Con 412 Lab 31 Lab 212 Ldm 17 Ldm 12	Con 48 Con 407 Lab 32 Lab 218 Ldm 16 Ldm 11	Con 48 Con 401 Lab 33 Lab 226 Ldm 15 Ldm 9	Con 48 Con Lab 34 Lab Ldm 14 Ldm
CON 49	Con 49 Con 424 Lab 30 Lab 201 Ldm 17 Ldm 11	Con 49 Con 419 Lab 31 Lab 207 Ldm 16 Ldm 10	Con 49 Con 414 Lab 32 Lab 212 Ldm 15 Ldm 10	Con 49 Con 408 Lab 33 Lab 219 Ldm 14 Ldm 9	Con 49 Con Lab 34 Lab Ldm 13 Ldm
CON 50	Con 50 Con 428 Lab 30 Lab 200 Ldm 16 Ldm 10	Con 50 Con 427 Lab 31 Lab 201 Ldm 15 Ldm 10	Con 50 Con 421 Lab 32 Lab 208 Ldm 14 Ldm 9	Con 50 Con 417 Lab 33 Lab 213 Ldm 13 Ldm 19	Con 50 Con Lab 34 Lab Ldm 12 Ldm

Labour outright majority

LAB 35	LAB 36	LAB 37	LAB 38	LAB 39	LAB 40	LAB 41	
							CON 25
							CON 26
							CON 27
							CON 28
						Con 29 Con 175 Lab 41 Lab 375 Ldm 26 Ldm 82	**CON 29**
					Con 30 Con 192 Lab 40 Lab 362 Ldm 26 Ldm 78	Con 30 Con 188 Lab 41 Lab 370 Ldm 25 Ldm 74	**CON 30**
				Con 31 Con 202 Lab 39 Lab 354 Ldm 26 Ldm 76	Con 31 Con 204 Lab 40 Lab 361 Ldm 25 Ldm 67	Con 31 Con 207 Lab 41 Lab 364 Ldm 24 Ldm 61	**CON 31**
			Con 32 Con 217 Lab 38 Lab 345 Ldm 26 Ldm 70	Con 32 Con 219 Lab 39 Lab 350 Ldm 25 Ldm 63	Con 32 Con 220 Lab 40 Lab 356 Ldm 24 Ldm 56	Con 32 Con 217 Lab 41 Lab 363 Ldm 23 Ldm 52	**CON 32**
		Con 33 Con 229 Lab 37 Lab 339 Ldm 26 Ldm 64	Con 33 Con 232 Lab 38 Lab 343 Ldm 25 Ldm 57	Con 33 Con 231 Lab 39 Lab 347 Ldm 24 Ldm 54	Con 33 Con 229 Lab 40 Lab 352 Ldm 23 Ldm 51	Con 33 Con 230 Lab 41 Lab 357 Ldm 22 Ldm 44	**CON 33**
	Con 34 Con 240 Lab 36 Lab 333 Ldm 26 Ldm 59	Con 34 Con 238 Lab 37 Lab 338 Ldm 25 Ldm 56	Con 34 Con 241 Lab 38 Lab 340 Ldm 24 Ldm 51	Con 34 Con 242 Lab 39 Lab 344 Ldm 23 Ldm 46	Con 34 Con 240 Lab 40 Lab 348 Ldm 22 Ldm 43	Con 34 Con 239 Lab 41 Lab 355 Ldm 21 Ldm 37	**CON 34**
35 Con 257 35 Lab 318 26 Ldm 57	Con 35 Con 255 Lab 36 Lab 325 Ldm 25 Ldm 52	Con 35 Con 251 Lab 37 Lab 335 Ldm 24 Ldm 46	Con 35 Con 248 Lab 38 Lab 339 Ldm 23 Ldm 45	Con 35 Con 251 Lab 39 Lab 340 Ldm 22 Ldm 27	Con 35 Con 248 Lab 40 Lab 345 Ldm 21 Ldm 45	Con 35 Con 249 Lab 41 Lab 351 Ldm 20 Ldm 31	**CON 35**
36 Con 273 35 Lab 312 25 Ldm 48	Con 36 Con 268 Lab 36 Lab 319 Ldm 24 Ldm 46	Con 36 Con 266 Lab 37 Lab 326 Ldm 23 Ldm 41	Con 36 Con 258 Lab 38 Lab 335 Ldm 22 Ldm 39	Con 36 Con 259 Lab 39 Lab 340 Ldm 21 Ldm 33	Con 36 Con 260 Lab 40 Lab 342 Ldm 20 Ldm 30	Con 36 Con 257 Lab 41 Lab 348 Ldm 19 Ldm 27	**CON 36**
37 Con 283 35 Lab 309 24 Ldm 42	Con 37 Con 280 Lab 36 Lab 314 Ldm 23 Ldm 40	Con 37 Con 279 Lab 37 Lab 320 Ldm 22 Ldm 34	Con 37 Con 275 Lab 38 Lab 326 Ldm 21 Ldm 32	Con 37 Con 267 Lab 39 Lab 336 Ldm 20 Ldm 30	Con 37 Con 264 Lab 40 Lab 342 Ldm 19 Ldm 27	Con 37 Con 263 Lab 41 Lab 345 Ldm 18 Ldm 25	**CON 37**
38 Con 300 35 Lab 299 23 Ldm 36	Con 38 Con 292 Lab 36 Lab 310 Ldm 22 Ldm 32	Con 38 Con 289 Lab 37 Lab 314 Ldm 21 Ldm 31	Con 38 Con 284 Lab 38 Lab 321 Ldm 20 Ldm 29	Con 38 Con 278 Lab 39 Lab 328 Ldm 19 Ldm 28	Con 38 Con 273 Lab 40 Lab 339 Ldm 18 Ldm 22	Con 38 Con 269 Lab 41 Lab 345 Ldm 17 Ldm 20	**CON 38**
39 Con 309 35 Lab 294 22 Ldm 31	Con 39 Con 304 Lab 36 Lab 300 Ldm 21 Ldm 30	Con 39 Con 294 Lab 37 Lab 310 Ldm 20 Ldm 30	Con 39 Con 295 Lab 38 Lab 315 Ldm 19 Ldm 24	Con 39 Con 289 Lab 39 Lab 323 Ldm 18 Ldm 20	Con 39 Con 263 Lab 40 Lab 331 Ldm 17 Ldm 20	Con 39 Con 275 Lab 41 Lab 340 Ldm 16 Ldm 19	**CON 39**
40 Con 314 35 Lab 290 21 Ldm 30	Con 40 Con 315 Lab 36 Lab 310 Ldm 20 Ldm 25	Con 40 Con 309 Lab 37 Lab 301 Ldm 19 Ldm 24	Con 40 Con 300 Lab 38 Lab 311 Ldm 18 Ldm 23	Con 40 Con 296 Lab 39 Lab 317 Ldm 17 Ldm 19	Con 40 Con 293 Lab 40 Lab 317 Ldm 16 Ldm 18	Con 40 Con 267 Lab 41 Lab 331 Ldm 15 Ldm 16	**CON 40**
41 Con 323 35 Lab 286 20 Ldm 25	Con 41 Con 320 Lab 36 Lab 290 Ldm 19 Ldm 24	Con 41 Con 318 Lab 37 Lab 295 Ldm 18 Ldm 21	Con 41 Con 314 Lab 38 Lab 302 Ldm 17 Ldm 18	Con 41 Con 305 Lab 39 Lab 313 Ldm 16 Ldm 16	Con 41 Con 301 Lab 40 Lab 317 Ldm 15 Ldm 16	Con 41 Con 296 Lab 41 Lab 323 Ldm 14 Ldm 15	**CON 41**
42 Con 334 35 Lab 278 19 Ldm 22	Con 42 Con 328 Lab 36 Lab 287 Ldm 18 Ldm 19	Con 42 Con 326 Lab 37 Lab 291 Ldm 17 Ldm 17	Con 42 Con 322 Lab 38 Lab 296 Ldm 16 Ldm 16	Con 42 Con 317 Lab 39 Lab 302 Ldm 15 Ldm 15	Con 42 Con 307 Lab 40 Lab 313 Ldm 14 Ldm 14	Con 42 Con 305 Lab 41 Lab 317 Ldm 13 Ldm 12	**CON 42**
43 Con 346 35 Lab 270 18 Ldm 18	Con 43 Con 338 Lab 36 Lab 279 Ldm 17 Ldm 17	Con 43 Con 331 Lab 37 Lab 287 Ldm 16 Ldm 15	Con 43 Con 328 Lab 38 Lab 292 Ldm 15 Ldm 13	Con 43 Con 328 Lab 39 Lab 296 Ldm 13 Ldm 12	Con 43 Con 321 Lab 40 Lab 302 Ldm 13 Ldm 11	Con 43 Con 307 Lab 41 Lab 317 Ldm 12 Ldm 10	**CON 43**
44 Con 351 35 Lab 268 17 Ldm 16	Con 44 Con 349 Lab 36 Lab 271 Ldm 16 Ldm 14	Con 44 Con 343 Lab 37 Lab 279 Ldm 15 Ldm 12	Con 44 Con 336 Lab 38 Lab 288 Ldm 14 Ldm 11	Con 44 Con 332 Lab 39 Lab 292 Ldm 13 Ldm 11	Con 44 Con 329 Lab 40 Lab 296 Ldm 12 Ldm 10	Con 44 Con 324 Lab 41 Lab 302 Ldm 11 Ldm 9	**CON 44**
45 Con 362 35 Lab 261 16 Ldm 12	Con 45 Con 356 Lab 36 Lab 268 Ldm 15 Ldm 11	Con 45 Con 353 Lab 37 Lab 271 Ldm 14 Ldm 11	Con 45 Con 345 Lab 38 Lab 280 Ldm 13 Ldm 10	Con 45 Con 338 Lab 39 Lab 288 Ldm 12 Ldm 9	Con 45 Con 334 Lab 40 Lab 292 Ldm 11 Ldm 9	Con 45 Con 330 Lab 41 Lab 296 Ldm 10 Ldm 9	**CON 45**
46 Con 370 35 Lab 255 15 Ldm 11	Con 46 Con 365 Lab 36 Lab 261 Ldm 14 Ldm 10	Con 46 Con 359 Lab 37 Lab 268 Ldm 13 Ldm 9	Con 46 Con 356 Lab 38 Lab 271 Ldm 12 Ldm 9	Con 46 Con 347 Lab 39 Lab 280 Ldm 11 Ldm 9	Con 46 Con 339 Lab 40 Lab 288 Ldm 10 Ldm 9	Con 46 Con 336 Lab 41 Lab 292 Ldm 9 Ldm 8	**CON 46**
47 Con 379 35 Lab 248 14 Ldm 9	Con 47 Con 372 Lab 36 Lab 255 Ldm 13 Ldm 9	Con 47 Con 366 Lab 37 Lab 261 Ldm 12 Ldm 9	Con 47 Con 359 Lab 38 Lab 268 Ldm 11 Ldm 9	Con 47 Con 357 Lab 39 Lab 271 Ldm 10 Ldm 9	Con 47 Con 350 Lab 40 Lab 280 Ldm 9 Ldm 6	Con 47 Con 342 Lab 41 Lab 288 Ldm 8 Ldm 6	**CON 47**
48 Con 384 35 Lab 243 13 Ldm 9	Con 48 Con 379 Lab 36 Lab 248 Ldm 12 Ldm 9	Con 48 Con 373 Lab 37 Lab 255 Ldm 11 Ldm 8	Con 48 Con 369 Lab 38 Lab 261 Ldm 10 Ldm 6	Con 48 Con 362 Lab 39 Lab 268 Ldm 9 Ldm 6	Con 48 Con 360 Lab 40 Lab 271 Ldm 8 Ldm 5	Con 48 Con 352 Lab 41 Lab 280 Ldm 7 Ldm 4	**CON 48**
49 Con 390 35 Lab 238 12 Ldm 8	Con 49 Con 387 Lab 36 Lab 243 Ldm 11 Ldm 6	Con 49 Con 382 Lab 37 Lab 248 Ldm 10 Ldm 6	Con 49 Con 376 Lab 38 Lab 255 Ldm 9 Ldm 5	Con 49 Con 371 Lab 39 Lab 261 Ldm 8 Ldm 4	Con 49 Con 365 Lab 40 Lab 268 Ldm 7 Ldm 3		**CON 49**
50 Con 406 35 Lab 226 11 Ldm 6	Con 50 Con 395 Lab 36 Lab 238 Ldm 10 Ldm 5	Con 50 Con 391 Lab 37 Lab 243 Ldm 9 Ldm 4	Con 50 Con 387 Lab 38 Lab 248 Ldm 8 Ldm 3	Con 50 Con 380 Lab 39 Lab 255 Ldm 7 Ldm 3			**CON 50**

	LAB 42	LAB 43	LAB 44	LAB 45	LAB 46	LAB 47	LAB
CON 25				Con 25 Con 123 / Lab 45 Lab 414 / Ldm 26 Ldm 95	Con 25 Con 124 / Lab 46 Lab 428 / Ldm 25 Ldm 80	Con 25 Con 126 / Lab 47 Lab 433 / Ldm 24 Ldm 73	Con 25 Con / Lab 48 Lab / Ldm 23 Ldm
CON 26			Con 26 Con 137 / Lab 44 Lab 408 / Ldm 26 Ldm 87	Con 26 Con 141 / Lab 45 Lab 412 / Ldm 25 Ldm 79	Con 26 Con 137 / Lab 46 Lab 421 / Ldm 24 Ldm 74	Con 26 Con 130 / Lab 47 Lab 432 / Ldm 23 Ldm 70	Con 26 Con / Lab 48 Labi / Ldm 22 Ldm
CON 27		Con 27 Con 152 / Lab 43 Lab 395 / Ldm 26 Ldm 85	Con 27 Con 144 / Lab 44 Lab 407 / Ldm 25 Ldm 81	Con 27 Con 143 / Lab 45 Lab 415 / Ldm 24 Ldm 74	Con 27 Con 148 / Lab 46 Lab 418 / Ldm 23 Ldm 66	Con 27 Con 146 / Lab 47 Lab 423 / Ldm 22 Ldm 62	Con 27 Con / Lab 48 Labi / Ldm 21 Ldm
CON 28	Con 28 Con 161 / Lab 42 Lab 386 / Ldm 26 Ldm 85	Con 28 Con 159 / Lab 43 Lab 393 / Ldm 25 Ldm 80	Con 28 Con 161 / Lab 44 Lab 401 / Ldm 24 Ldm 70	Con 28 Con 155 / Lab 45 Lab 412 / Ldm 23 Ldm 65	Con 28 Con 155 / Lab 46 Lab 418 / Ldm 22 Ldm 57	Con 28 Con 161 / Lab 47 Lab 421 / Ldm 21 Ldm 49	Con 28 Con / Lab 48 Labi / Ldm 20 Ldm
CON 29	Con 29 Con 172 / Lab 42 Lab 384 / Ldm 25 Ldm 76	Con 29 Con 172 / Lab 43 Lab 390 / Ldm 24 Ldm 70	Con 29 Con 172 / Lab 44 Lab 399 / Ldm 23 Ldm 61	Con 29 Con 174 / Lab 45 Lab 405 / Ldm 22 Ldm 52	Con 29 Con 170 / Lab 46 Lab 414 / Ldm 21 Ldm 47	Con 29 Con 165 / Lab 47 Lab 422 / Ldm 20 Ldm 44	Con 29 Con / Lab 48 Labi / Ldm 19 Ldm
CON 30	Con 30 Con 190 / Lab 42 Lab 377 / Ldm 24 Ldm 65	Con 30 Con 185 / Lab 43 Lab 390 / Ldm 23 Ldm 57	Con 30 Con 187 / Lab 44 Lab 395 / Ldm 22 Ldm 49	Con 30 Con 183 / Lab 45 Lab 402 / Ldm 21 Ldm 46	Con 30 Con 181 / Lab 46 Lab 407 / Ldm 20 Ldm 43	Con 30 Con 178 / Lab 47 Lab 416 / Ldm 19 Ldm 37	Con 30 Con / Lab 48 Lab / Ldm 18 Ldm
CON 31	Con 31 Con 206 / Lab 42 Lab 372 / Ldm 23 Ldm 54	Con 31 Con 203 / Lab 43 Lab 380 / Ldm 22 Ldm 48	Con 31 Con 194 / Lab 44 Lab 393 / Ldm 21 Ldm 44	Con 31 Con 196 / Lab 45 Lab 396 / Ldm 20 Ldm 39	Con 31 Con 191 / Lab 46 Lab 404 / Ldm 19 Ldm 36	Con 31 Con 191 / Lab 47 Lab 408 / Ldm 18 Ldm 32	Con 31 Con / Lab 48 Lab / Ldm 17 Ldm
CON 32	Con 32 Con 216 / Lab 42 Lab 368 / Ldm 22 Ldm 47	Con 32 Con 215 / Lab 43 Lab 376 / Ldm 21 Ldm 40	Con 32 Con 211 / Lab 44 Lab 382 / Ldm 20 Ldm 38	Con 32 Con 204 / Lab 45 Lab 394 / Ldm 19 Ldm 33	Con 32 Con 202 / Lab 46 Lab 398 / Ldm 18 Ldm 31	Con 32 Con 200 / Lab 47 Lab 405 / Ldm 17 Ldm 26	Con 32 Con / Lab 48 Lab / Ldm 16 Ldm
CON 33	Con 33 Con 225 / Lab 42 Lab 366 / Ldm 21 Ldm 40	Con 33 Con 226 / Lab 43 Lab 371 / Ldm 20 Ldm 34	Con 33 Con 221 / Lab 44 Lab 377 / Ldm 19 Ldm 33	Con 33 Con 220 / Lab 45 Lab 384 / Ldm 18 Ldm 27	Con 33 Con 210 / Lab 46 Lab 395 / Ldm 17 Ldm 26	Con 33 Con 207 / Lab 47 Lab 399 / Ldm 16 Ldm 25	Con 33 Con / Lab 48 Lab / Ldm 15 Ldm
CON 34	Con 34 Con 234 / Lab 42 Lab 361 / Ldm 20 Ldm 34	Con 34 Con 234 / Lab 43 Lab 368 / Ldm 19 Ldm 29	Con 34 Con 233 / Lab 44 Lab 371 / Ldm 18 Ldm 37	Con 34 Con 227 / Lab 45 Lab 379 / Ldm 17 Ldm 25	Con 34 Con 223 / Lab 46 Lab 384 / Ldm 16 Ldm 24	Con 34 Con 212 / Lab 47 Lab 395 / Ldm 15 Ldm 24	Con 34 Con / Lab 48 Lab / Ldm 14 Ldm
CON 35	Con 35 Con 246 / Lab 42 Lab 358 / Ldm 19 Ldm 27	Con 35 Con 243 / Lab 43 Lab 362 / Ldm 18 Ldm 26	Con 35 Con 238 / Lab 44 Lab 369 / Ldm 17 Ldm 24	Con 35 Con 235 / Lab 45 Lab 372 / Ldm 16 Ldm 24	Con 35 Con 232 / Lab 46 Lab 379 / Ldm 15 Ldm 20	Con 35 Con 227 / Lab 47 Lab 384 / Ldm 14 Ldm 20	Con 35 Con / Lab 48 Lab / Ldm 13 Ldm
CON 36	Con 36 Con 254 / Lab 42 Lab 353 / Ldm 18 Ldm 25	Con 36 Con 249 / Lab 43 Lab 358 / Ldm 17 Ldm 25	Con 36 Con 249 / Lab 44 Lab 363 / Ldm 16 Ldm 20	Con 36 Con 243 / Lab 45 Lab 369 / Ldm 15 Ldm 20	Con 36 Con 241 / Lab 46 Lab 372 / Ldm 14 Ldm 19	Con 36 Con 235 / Lab 47 Lab 379 / Ldm 13 Ldm 18	Con 36 Con / Lab 48 Lab / Ldm 12 Ldm
CON 37	Con 37 Con 263 / Lab 42 Lab 349 / Ldm 17 Ldm 21	Con 37 Con 259 / Lab 43 Lab 354 / Ldm 16 Ldm 20	Con 37 Con 255 / Lab 44 Lab 359 / Ldm 15 Ldm 19	Con 37 Con 252 / Lab 45 Lab 363 / Ldm 14 Ldm 18	Con 37 Con 247 / Lab 46 Lab 369 / Ldm 13 Ldm 17	Con 37 Con 245 / Lab 47 Lab 373 / Ldm 12 Ldm 15	Con 37 Con / Lab 48 Lab / Ldm 11 Ldm
CON 38	Con 38 Con 266 / Lab 42 Lab 350 / Ldm 16 Ldm 18	Con 38 Con 263 / Lab 43 Lab 354 / Ldm 15 Ldm 17	Con 38 Con 259 / Lab 44 Lab 359 / Ldm 14 Ldm 16	Con 38 Con 255 / Lab 45 Lab 363 / Ldm 13 Ldm 16	Con 38 Con 250 / Lab 46 Lab 371 / Ldm 12 Ldm 13	Con 38 Con 250 / Lab 47 Lab 371 / Ldm 11 Ldm 13	Con 38 Con / Lab 48 Lab / Ldm 10 Ldm
CON 39	Con 39 Con 272 / Lab 42 Lab 345 / Ldm 15 Ldm 17	Con 39 Con 272 / Lab 43 Lab 346 / Ldm 14 Ldm 16	Con 39 Con 268 / Lab 44 Lab 350 / Ldm 13 Ldm 16	Con 39 Con 265 / Lab 45 Lab 354 / Ldm 12 Ldm 15	Con 39 Con 261 / Lab 46 Lab 360 / Ldm 11 Ldm 13	Con 39 Con 259 / Lab 47 Lab 365 / Ldm 10 Ldm 10	Con 39 Con / Lab 48 Lab / Ldm 9 Ldm
CON 40	Con 40 Con 278 / Lab 42 Lab 340 / Ldm 14 Ldm 16	Con 40 Con 274 / Lab 43 Lab 345 / Ldm 13 Ldm 15	Con 40 Con 274 / Lab 44 Lab 346 / Ldm 12 Ldm 14	Con 40 Con 272 / Lab 45 Lab 350 / Ldm 11 Ldm 12	Con 40 Con 269 / Lab 46 Lab 355 / Ldm 10 Ldm 10	Con 40 Con 263 / Lab 47 Lab 362 / Ldm 9 Ldm 9	Con 40 Con / Lab 48 Lab / Ldm 8 Ldm
CON 41	Con 41 Con 289 / Lab 42 Lab 331 / Ldm 13 Ldm 14	Con 41 Con 282 / Lab 43 Lab 340 / Ldm 12 Ldm 12	Con 41 Con 278 / Lab 44 Lab 346 / Ldm 11 Ldm 11	Con 41 Con 277 / Lab 45 Lab 347 / Ldm 10 Ldm 10	Con 41 Con 274 / Lab 46 Lab 351 / Ldm 9 Ldm 9	Con 41 Con 271 / Lab 47 Lab 257 / Ldm 8 Ldm 6	Con 41 Con / Lab 48 Lab / Ldm 7 Ldm
CON 42	Con 42 Con 300 / Lab 42 Lab 323 / Ldm 12 Ldm 11	Con 42 Con 292 / Lab 43 Lab 331 / Ldm 11 Ldm 11	Con 42 Con 284 / Lab 44 Lab 340 / Ldm 10 Ldm 10	Con 42 Con 280 / Lab 45 Lab 346 / Ldm 9 Ldm 8	Con 42 Con 279 / Lab 46 Lab 348 / Ldm 8 Ldm 7	Con 42 Con 275 / Lab 47 Lab 353 / Ldm 7 Ldm 6	
CON 43	Con 43 Con 302 / Lab 42 Lab 331 / Ldm 11 Ldm 11	Con 43 Con 294 / Lab 43 Lab 332 / Ldm 10 Ldm 8	Con 43 Con 285 / Lab 44 Lab 341 / Ldm 9 Ldm 8	Con 43 Con 285 / Lab 45 Lab 341 / Ldm 8 Ldm 8	Con 43 Con 280 / Lab 46 Lab 353 / Ldm 7 Ldm 6		
CON 44	Con 44 Con 313 / Lab 42 Lab 313 / Ldm 10 Ldm 9	Con 44 Con 309 / Lab 43 Lab 317 / Ldm 9 Ldm 8	Con 44 Con 303 / Lab 44 Lab 324 / Ldm 8 Ldm 8	Con 44 Con 296 / Lab 45 Lab 333 / Ldm 7 Ldm 6			
CON 45	Con 45 Con 324 / Lab 42 Lab 302 / Ldm 9 Ldm 9	Con 45 Con 314 / Lab 43 Lab 314 / Ldm 8 Ldm 7	Con 45 Con 312 / Lab 44 Lab 318 / Ldm 7 Ldm 5				
CON 46	Con 46 Con 334 / Lab 42 Lab 296 / Ldm 8 Ldm 6	Con 46 Con 328 / Lab 43 Lab 303 / Ldm 7 Ldm 5					
CON 47	Con 47 Con 339 / Lab 42 Lab 293 / Ldm 7 Ldm 4						
CON 48							
CON 49							
CON 50							

AB 49   **LAB 50**   **LAB 51**   **LAB 52**   **LAB 53**   **LAB 54**   **LAB 55**

LAB 49

```
25 Con 11/
49 Lab 450
22 Ldm 66

26 Con 127
49 Lab 447
21 Ldm 59

27 Con 146
49 Lab 439
20 Ldm 48

28 Con 152
49 Lab 438
19 Ldm 43

29 Con 168
49 Lab 429
18 Ldm 36

30 Con 177
49 Lab 425
17 Ldm 31

31 Con 182
49 Lab 425
16 Ldm 26

32 Con 189
49 Lab 419
15 Ldm 25

33 Con 198
49 Lab 412
14 Ldm 23

34 Con 206
49 Lab 409
13 Ldm 18

35 Con 214
49 Lab 403
12 Ldm 16

36 Con 221
49 Lab 400
11 Ldm 14

37 Con 234
49 Lab 391
10 Ldm 10

38 Con 243
49 Lab 386
9 Ldm 7

39 Con 250
49 Lab 379
8 Ldm 7

40 Con 254
49 Lab 376
7 Ldm 6
```

LAB 50

```
Con 25 Con 116
Lab 50 Lab 456
Ldm 21 Ldm 61

Con 26 Con 127
Lab 50 Lab 460
Ldm 20 Ldm 52

Con 27 Con 141
Lab 50 Lab 454
Ldm 19 Ldm 43

Con 28 Con 151
Lab 50 Lab 441
Ldm 18 Ldm 41

Con 29 Con 160
Lab 50 Lab 438
Ldm 17 Ldm 35

Con 30 Con 174
Lab 50 Lab 429
Ldm 16 Ldm 30

Con 31 Con 183
Lab 50 Lab 426
Ldm 15 Ldm 24

Con 32 Con 184
Lab 50 Lab 427
Ldm 14 Ldm 22

Con 33 Con 194
Lab 50 Lab 421
Ldm 13 Ldm 18

Con 34 Con 203
Lab 50 Lab 424
Ldm 12 Ldm 16

Con 35 Con 209
Lab 50 Lab 412
Ldm 11 Ldm 12

Con 36 Con 217
Lab 50 Lab 406
Ldm 10 Ldm 13

Con 37 Con 224
Lab 50 Lab 402
Ldm 9 Ldm 9

Con 38 Con 238
Lab 50 Lab 391
Ldm 8 Ldm 7

Con 39 Con 243
Lab 50 Lab 386
Ldm 7 Ldm 7
```

LAB 51

```
Con 25 Con 111
Lab 51 Lab 467
Ldm 20 Ldm 55

Con 26 Con 127
Lab 51 Lab 460
Ldm 19 Ldm 46

Con 27 Con 136
Lab 51 Lab 454
Ldm 18 Ldm 43

Con 28 Con 148
Lab 51 Lab 449
Ldm 17 Ldm 36

Con 29 Con 161
Lab 51 Lab 442
Ldm 16 Ldm 30

Con 30 Con 169
Lab 51 Lab 440
Ldm 15 Ldm 24

Con 31 Con 179
Lab 51 Lab 431
Ldm 14 Ldm 23

Con 32 Con 184
Lab 51 Lab 428
Ldm 13 Ldm 21

Con 33 Con 188
Lab 51 Lab 430
Ldm 12 Ldm 15

Con 34 Con 196
Lab 51 Lab 424
Ldm 11 Ldm 13

Con 35 Con 206
Lab 51 Lab 416
Ldm 10 Ldm 11

Con 36 Con 212
Lab 51 Lab 412
Ldm 9 Ldm 11

Con 37 Con 222
Lab 51 Lab 406
Ldm 8 Ldm 7

Con 38 Con 227
Lab 51 Lab 403
Ldm 7 Ldm 6
```

LAB 52

```
Con 25 Con 109
Lab 52 Lab 479
Ldm 19 Ldm 52

Con 26 Con 123
Lab 52 Lab 467
Ldm 18 Ldm 43

Con 27 Con 132
Lab 52 Lab 461
Ldm 17 Ldm 40

Con 28 Con 144
Lab 52 Lab 458
Ldm 16 Ldm 33

Con 29 Con 154
Lab 52 Lab 452
Ldm 15 Ldm 27

Con 30 Con 167
Lab 52 Lab 444
Ldm 14 Ldm 22

Con 31 Con 171
Lab 52 Lab 443
Ldm 13 Ldm 19

Con 32 Con 184
Lab 52 Lab 434
Ldm 12 Ldm 15

Con 33 Con 189
Lab 52 Lab 430
Ldm 11 Ldm 14

Con 34 Con 191
Lab 52 Lab 430
Ldm 10 Ldm 12

Con 35 Con 198
Lab 52 Lab 424
Ldm 9 Ldm 11

Con 36 Con 209
Lab 52 Lab 417
Ldm 8 Ldm 10

Con 37 Con 216
Lab 52 Lab 413
Ldm 7 Ldm 6
```

LAB 53

```
Con 25 Con 109
Lab 53 Lab 479
Ldm 18 Ldm 45

Con 26 Con 118
Lab 53 Lab 474
Ldm 17 Ldm 41

Con 27 Con 130
Lab 53 Lab 471
Ldm 16 Ldm 32

Con 28 Con 141
Lab 53 Lab 465
Ldm 15 Ldm 27

Con 29 Con 152
Lab 53 Lab 460
Ldm 14 Ldm 21

Con 30 Con 158
Lab 53 Lab 455
Ldm 13 Ldm 20

Con 31 Con 168
Lab 53 Lab 446
Ldm 12 Ldm 19

Con 32 Con 175
Lab 53 Lab 444
Ldm 11 Ldm 14

Con 33 Con 185
Lab 53 Lab 435
Ldm 10 Ldm 13

Con 34 Con 192
Lab 53 Lab 431
Ldm 9 Ldm 10

Con 35 Con 193
Lab 53 Lab 431
Ldm 8 Ldm 9

Con 36 Con 203
Lab 53 Lab 426
Ldm 7 Ldm 5
```

LAB 54

```
Con 25 Con 107
Lab 54 Lab 487
Ldm 17 Ldm 39

Con 26 Con 114
Lab 54 Lab 483
Ldm 16 Ldm 36

Con 27 Con 126
Lab 54 Lab 479
Ldm 15 Ldm 28

Con 28 Con 135
Lab 54 Lab 474
Ldm 14 Ldm 24

Con 29 Con 146
Lab 54 Lab 467
Ldm 13 Ldm 20

Con 30 Con 154
Lab 54 Lab 461
Ldm 12 Ldm 18

Con 31 Con 163
Lab 54 Lab 456
Ldm 11 Ldm 14

Con 32 Con 172
Lab 54 Lab 448
Ldm 10 Ldm 13

Con 33 Con 177
Lab 54 Lab 446
Ldm 9 Ldm 10

Con 34 Con 187
Lab 54 Lab 437
Ldm 8 Ldm 9

Con 35 Con 194
Lab 54 Lab 432
Ldm 7 Ldm 7
```

LAB 55

```
Con 25 Con 105
Lab 55 Lab 492
Ldm 16 Ldm 36

Con 26 Con 114
Lab 55 Lab 490
Ldm 15 Ldm 29

Con 27 Con 123
Lab 55 Lab 485
Ldm 14 Ldm 25

Con 28 Con 133
Lab 55 Lab 480
Ldm 13 Ldm 20

Con 29 Con 139
Lab 55 Lab 475
Ldm 12 Ldm 19

Con 30 Con 147
Lab 55 Lab 469
Ldm 11 Ldm 17

Con 31 Con 158
Lab 55 Lab 463
Ldm 10 Ldm 12

Con 32 Con 164
Lab 55 Lab 459
Ldm 9 Ldm 10

Con 33 Con 174
Lab 55 Lab 450
Ldm 8 Ldm 9

Con 34 Con 178
Lab 55 Lab 447
Ldm 7 Ldm 8
```

abour outright majority

CON 25
CON 26
CON 27
CON 28
CON 29
CON 30
CON 31
CON 32
CON 33
CON 34
CON 35
CON 36
CON 37
CON 38
CON 39
CON 40
CON 41
CON 42
CON 43
CON 44
CON 45
CON 46
CON 47
CON 48
CON 49
CON 50

NOTES

NOTES

NOTES

NOTES

NOTES

NOTES

NOTES